D1545148

Pass the 6™

A Training Guide for the FINRA Series 6 Exam

6th Edition

DISCARD

by

Robert Walker

FIRST BOOKS ®

PORTLAND • OREGON

FIRSTBOOKS.COM

Contents at a Glance

Detailed Table of Contents

Introduction

FINRA has once again changed the content outline for the Series 6 exam. Similar to the Series 7, the Series 6 exam outline is now organized along the critical job functions performed by a securities representative with a Series 6 registration. I have laid out the book in four chapters to match these four critical job functions indicated by the new FINRA exam outline. I've made an alteration only to the order in which the four sections appear so that it moves like this: opening a customer account, determining suitable recommendations, processing orders, and then knowing the important industry rules and regulations. FINRA starts out with all the rules and regulations, which isn't surprising, since they write and enforce most of them. You, on the other hand, are trying to learn an awful lot of information in a short space of time, so I didn't want to introduce you to rules and regulations before I first explained who and what is being ruled and regulated.

Either way, I encourage you to download the new FINRA exam outline yourself at: http://www.finra.org/web/groups/industry/@ip/@comp/@regis/documents/industry/p376641.pdf.

Before sitting for your exam, you should be able to go through this detailed list of items and know something about each item.

While the organization of the material has changed on the outline, I don't see a lot of new items and—best of all—there has been no increase to the required passing score. You can still miss 30 of the 100 questions and pass the Series 6 exam. Unlike the other license exams, 70% is all you need to put this challenge behind you and start helping customers save for retirement, education, what have you.

This is very serious stuff, of course, but just because it's serious stuff doesn't mean we have to be all serious. You can have some fun as you learn the Series 6 material, and, if you think about it, what's more fun than learning how to help people invest? Sure, some of the material can be exhausting, but if you really like the world of financial services, you should be able to enjoy yourself, even though you're studying for a test that seems big and scary right now.

What should you do at this point? Start reading this book, one chapter at a time. If you have practice questions from either www.passthe6.com or www.solomonexamprep.com, work on the questions covering the section that you just read in the book. Then go back through the textbook chapter once again to review before moving onto the next chapter. I cover topics from many angles, so that chances are, I've explained them in a way that will help you get a possible exam question right. But this is more art than science, and anybody who tells you they know exactly what's on the exam is just trying to sell you a bill of goods.

If they don't know, they're lying to you. And, if they do know, they're violating FINRA rules and could get sued for copyright infringement—not to mention any names or anything. In any case, if you put in the work, it's likely you will pass the Series 6 in one attempt.

But, please, don't put unnecessary pressure on yourself. This is a test; this is only a test. Just give yourself enough time to complete the process.

Ready?

Let's get started, anyway.

CHAPTER 1

Job Function: Opens, Maintains, Transfers and Closes Accounts and Retains Appropriate Account Records

(Represents 21 of 100 Questions on the Series 6 Exam)

Bank deposits are backed up by the federal government's **FDIC insurance**, so the money one puts in a savings or checking account with a bank is not at risk. The money one places with a **broker-dealer,** on the other hand, is not backed up by any arm of the federal government. Broker-dealers help their clients invest in **securities** including stocks, bonds, and mutual funds. Unlike "money in the bank," money in the securities markets is always at risk. No matter how "suitable" a particular stock, bond, or mutual fund investment might be, investors can and do lose money by investing in securities, unlike when they put money into certificates of deposit at a bank.

So, it's not surprising that the process of opening an investment account for a customer of a broker-dealer is highly regulated.

OPENING AN ACCOUNT

Every business has "books," showing their financial transactions and results of those transactions. Not long ago, a company's "books" would have been on paper, but these days most "books and records" are kept electronically. My own company uses accounting software, so our books are also electronic, allowing us to easily back things up, as well as generate all kinds of reports for our CPA and various tax collection agencies. Luckily, our books and records are very simple, like our textbooks.

On the other hand, broker-dealers have some of the most complicated "books" of any business, as reflected in their balance sheet, trial balance sheet, income statement, etc. The "records" required are detailed and numerous. Imagine all the correspondence and other communications happening between the broker-dealer and their customers, all the buy and sell orders executed through the firm, and all the deposits and withdrawals of cash and securities happening through that office.

These transactions all require records to be kept, as stipulated by the Securities Exchange Act of 1934, the rules under that Act, and various FINRA rules. Most records are required to be retained by FINRA member firms for a period of three years, and when no time is specified, the records are to be kept for a period of six years.

Now, chances are you just highlighted the "three years" and the "six years." That is fine; just don't expect test questions to focus on such easily memorized trivia. Both could be testable points, but your test is not based on memorized numbers. Your test forces you to think through unfamiliar situations quickly and knowledgably, which is why I'm taking my time explaining what things mean and how they fit together.

Regardless of how long they are to be kept, the records are to be maintained and made available upon request by FINRA staff members examining the firm for compliance. Records may be produced or reproduced on "micrographic media" or "electronic storage media." Micrographic media includes the stuff old folks like me once used at the university library when researching old newspaper or magazine articles that had been converted to some of the most bizarre storage-and-retrieval media I've yet encountered. I'm thinking most firms would be using a CD-ROM, DVD, magnetic tape, or USB storage device these days, which would fall, of course, under "electronic storage media." The main thing here is that whichever electronic storage media the firm uses itself or through a third-party vendor, the system or device must:

- Preserve the records in a non-erasable, non-rewritable format
- Verify automatically the quality and accuracy of the storage media recording process
- Serialize the original and, if applicable, duplicate units of storage media, and time-date the information for the required period of retention
- Have the capacity to readily download indexes and records on the electronic storage media to other media as required by the Commission or the self-regulatory organizations of which the firm is a member

For firms using the micrographic media (microfiche/microfilm) there must be devices for viewing/projecting the media available to visiting regulators, and if the regulators request an enlargement/print-out of specific sections, these will have to be made available as well.

So, basically, FINRA has some very common-sense rules regarding either type of electronic storage and reproduction of records—make sure the records are accurate and easily accessible to the SEC or FINRA staff members.

One of the most important areas of record keeping for broker-dealers involves customer account records. FINRA requires broker-dealers to obtain and maintain the following on file concerning a customer account:

- Customer name and residence
- Determination of legal age
- Name of the registered representative responsible for the account
- Signature of the principal (supervisor) approving the account

- If customer is business entity, names of those with authority to transact business
- For discretionary accounts, record of dated manual signature of each individual with authority to exercise discretion

Broker-dealers must also make a reasonable effort to determine and maintain the following information:

- TIN (taxpayer identification number), meaning SS # or business tax ID #
- Customer occupation and employer name and address
- Whether customer is associated with a FINRA member
- Information to determine suitability: objectives, financial info, etc.

If a customer refuses to supply any of the last four bullet points, you should document that an effort was made and that the customer refused to provide it. The four bullet points immediately preceding those are required for all accounts except institutional accounts and retail accounts that are limited to open-end funds not recommended by the broker-dealer. We'll talk a lot more about open-end funds in Chapter 2. For now, let's just call them "mutual funds" and keep moving.

For purposes of this rule an "institutional account" is an account for a bank, savings and loan association, insurance company, registered investment company, an investment adviser, and any other person (individual or entity) with assets of at least $50 million. As usual, the regulators provide more protection for the average-Joe investor than for large financial institutions or even individuals with $50 million to invest. The SEC provides investor protection, but—as we said—also wants to foster capital formation and market efficiency.

Once all this customer information has been obtained, the customer has to be sent a copy of it and must provide verification that the information is accurate. The firm also asks the customer if she would like interest and dividend checks distributed to her or credited to her account. Customers often choose to have all mutual fund distributions reinvested into more shares of the fund. There are also many issuers of common stock now who will let you reinvest dividends into fractional shares of common stocks, especially the blue-chip companies that pay regular dividends. One of my buddy's IRAs is chock full of positions of 103.62 shares of this or 67.589 shares of that. I prefer to let the cash build up before making my next big purchase, and that's exactly why the account form asks what the firm is supposed to do with dividends and interest payments.

Customer information must be verified and/or updated regularly by the customer so the firm can see if the investment profile has changed due to an increase or decrease of income, educational funding needs, reaching a higher tax rate, or getting married or divorced, etc. The name on a customer's account, or the type of account, cannot be changed without a principal/supervisor approving of that action. So, suitability information can be handled by the registered representative and the customer, but to change the name or the type of account, always get a principal's approval. As you might expect, customer information is confidential, meaning you only provide information on your customers to others if the customer gives permission or if a legal action, such as a subpoena from FINRA, the courts, or a state securities regulator, requires it.

Also, broker-dealers and agents make recommendations to customers, but they don't get to spend the customer's money without the customer's permission. That's why FINRA has a rule on negotiable instruments drawn from a customer's account—to protect customers from honest and not-so-honest mistakes over a few hundred thousand dollars. Member firms "may not obtain from a customer or submit for payment a check, draft, or other negotiable paper drawn on a customer's checking, savings or similar account without that person's express written authorization." To document that express written authorization, the firm can either have the customer sign the negotiable instrument itself or sign a separate authorization form, of which they would need to maintain a copy. If the customer signs the check, draft, etc., there is no need for the firm to keep a copy of that.

Your firm is not allowed to carry an account for a customer under any sort of bogus name, but, surprisingly, the account could be identified by a number or symbol (numbered account), as long as your firm obtained and maintained evidence in writing signed by the customer attesting that the customer owns that particular account identified by only a number or a symbol. Perhaps the client is a movie star who doesn't want everyone at the firm looking into her financial affairs, let alone selling stories to the tabloids based on her trading activity.

Customers frequently transfer assets held at one broker-dealer to another, and FINRA requires that both firms expedite this process by using the system known as **ACATS** (Automated Customer Account Transfer Service). The customer may want to transfer all of the cash and securities from her account to another account, or, perhaps, just perform a partial transfer of assets. Either way, these are FINRA's concerns and requirements:

- When the member receives a customer transfer instruction form (TIF) to receive securities account assets from the carrying member firm, the receiving member must immediately submit the instructions to the carrying member in the ACATS system.
- Carrying member within one business day must validate or take exception to the transfer instructions (sent by the other firm, or the customer directly) and attach a list of customer account assets.
- Carrying and receiving members must promptly resolve any exceptions taken to the transfer instructions.

There are, unfortunately, some assets that are not ready to be transferred—for these situations, the firms need to promptly notify the customer and explain the situation. For example, stocks or bonds in a bankrupt company, or limited partnership interests that have no real secondary market are not assets that can be easily transferred. On the other hand, customers can easily transfer their cash, their stocks, and their bonds from one firm to the other without having to liquidate everything, paying commissions and maybe capital gains taxes, and then paying more commissions to turn the cash back into securities within the new account at the new firm. So, ACATS is a good thing for customers and a good thing for broker-dealers who use it correctly.

FINRA requires that [most] member firms provide "education and protection" to customers by complying with the following requirement:

Each member shall once every calendar year provide in writing (which may be electronic) to each customer the following items of information:

(1) FINRA BrokerCheck Hotline Number;

(2) FINRA Web site address; and

(3) A statement as to the availability to the customer of an investor brochure that includes information describing FINRA BrokerCheck.

As we'll explore elsewhere, FINRA's "BrokerCheck" provides registration and disclosure information on broker-dealers, principals, and agents. Whenever an agent is suspended for churning accounts or updates his information to disclose a short sale he just did on his house, such information goes into BrokerCheck. So, be on your best behavior, everybody, since you will all be searchable by name and/or CRD (**Central Registration Depository**) number indefinitely after you associate with your employing broker-dealer.

Remember that all customer written complaints must be acted upon, with the correspondence kept on file by the broker-dealer. As FINRA rules indicate:

Each member shall keep and preserve in each office of supervisory jurisdiction either a separate file of all written customer complaints that relate to that office (including complaints that relate to activities supervised from that office) and action taken by the member, if any, or a separate record of such complaints and a clear reference to the files in that office containing the correspondence connected with such complaints. Rather than keep and preserve the customer complaint records required under this Rule at the office of supervisory jurisdiction, the member may choose to make them promptly available at that office, upon request of FINRA. Customer complaint records shall be preserved for a period of at least four years.

How does FINRA define a "customer complaint"? Like this:

any grievance by a customer or any person authorized to act on behalf of the customer involving the activities of the member or a person associated with the member in connection with the solicitation or execution of any transaction or the disposition of securities or funds of that customer.

FINRA is the SRO (Self-Regulatory Organization) that regulates your firm, your principals, and you. FINRA, in turn, is registered and overseen by the SEC or **Securities and Exchange Commission** under the **Securities Exchange Act of 1934**. I've noticed that many tutoring clients seem to be skimming if not skipping over any reference to any federal securities act when studying, and I'm here to tell you—cut it out. You don't need a deep understanding of the federal securities acts, but you also don't need to miss a handful of rather easy questions, either. So, remember that the Securities Exchange Act of 1934 is the one that empowered the SEC to oversee broad aspects of the securities markets, including the authority to register the exchanges and national securities associations, e.g., NYSE, and NASD (now FINRA). Here is how the SEC—the federal government—explains themselves at www.sec.gov:

> The mission of the U.S. Securities and Exchange Commission is to protect investors, maintain fair, orderly, and efficient markets, and facilitate capital formation.
>
> As more and more first-time investors turn to the markets to help secure their futures, pay for homes, and send children to college, our investor protection mission is more compelling than ever.
>
> As our nation's securities exchanges mature into global for-profit competitors, there is even greater need for sound market regulation.
>
> And the common interest of all Americans in a growing economy that produces jobs, improves our standard of living, and protects the value of our savings means that all of the SEC's actions must be taken with an eye toward promoting the capital formation that is necessary to sustain economic growth.

That's the SEC's mission statement.

This is what they say about the Securities Exchange Act of 1934, the one that made them who they are today:

> With this Act, Congress created the Securities and Exchange Commission. The Act empowers the SEC with broad authority over all aspects of the securities industry. This includes the power to register, regulate, and oversee brokerage firms, transfer agents, and clearing agencies as well as the nation's securities self-regulatory organizations (SROs). The various stock exchanges, such as the New York Stock Exchange, and American Stock Exchange are SROs. The Financial Industry Regulatory Authority, which operates the NASDAQ system, is also an SRO.
>
> The Act also identifies and prohibits certain types of conduct in the markets and provides the Commission with disciplinary powers over regulated entities and persons associated with them.

> The Act also empowers the SEC to require periodic reporting
> of information by companies with publicly traded securities.

Sections of this Act and the Rules that the SEC writes or "promulgates thereunder" guide the brokerage industry that you are now entering. Even a quick reading of SEC rules or the federal acts that gave them their authority shows us what is considered essential to this group of rather hard-nosed attorneys:

- Full and fair disclosure of all important information
- Meticulous record keeping
- A fair and level marketplace for all investors

So, if any activity explained on the exam shows someone trying to deceive or mislead investors by making misstatements of material facts about an investment, you know there's no way that's okay. Not every single thing has to be written down in triplicate at a broker-dealer, but you also have to assume that correspondence with customers regarding recommendations or complaints with the handling of their accounts would be something for which the regulators would require records. Then again, assumptions can only take you so far on this exam, so let's see what the SEC requires in terms of record keeping for the brokerage industry under the Securities Exchange Act of 1934. Heads up—this is one detailed list:

1. Blotters (or other records of original entry) containing an itemized daily record of all purchases and sales of securities, all receipts and deliveries of securities (including certificate numbers), all receipts and disbursements of cash and all other debits and credits. Such records shall show the account for which each such transaction was effected, the name and amount of securities, the unit and aggregate purchase or sale price (if any), the trade date, and the name or other designation of the person from whom purchased or received or to whom sold or delivered.
2. Ledgers (or other records) reflecting all assets and liabilities, income and expense and capital accounts.
3. Ledger accounts (or other records) itemizing separately as to each cash and margin account of every customer and of such member, broker or dealer and partners thereof, all purchases, sales, receipts and deliveries of securities and commodities for such account and all other debits and credits to such account.
4. Ledgers reflecting: securities in transfer, dividends and interest received, securities loaned and borrowed, moneys loaned and borrowed, securities failed to receive and failed to deliver
5. Ledger or securities record showing each security held "long" or "short" for the firm or any customer account
6. Memorandum of each brokerage order. "The memorandum shall show the terms and conditions of the order or instructions and of any modification or cancellation thereof; the account for which entered; the time the order was received; the time of entry; the price at which executed; the identity of each associated person, if any, responsible for the account; the identity of any other person who entered or accepted the order on behalf of the customer or, if a customer entered the order on

an electronic system, a notation of that entry; and, to the extent feasible, the time of execution or cancellation."

7. Memorandum of each order for the member itself showing price and time of execution. And, if the transaction is with a person other than a broker or dealer (retail customer) more details are required.

8. Copies of confirmations of all purchases and sales of securities, including all repurchase and reverse repurchase agreements, and copies of notices of all other debits and credits for securities, cash and other items for the account of customers and partners of such member, broker or dealer.

9. A record in respect of each cash and margin account with such member, broker or dealer indicating a record in respect of each cash and margin account with such member, broker or dealer indicating and whether or not the beneficial owner of securities registered in the name of such members, brokers or dealers, or a registered clearing agency or its nominee objects to disclosure of his or her identity, address and securities positions to issuers, and for margin accounts the signature of each owner.

10. A record of all puts, calls, spreads, straddles and other options in which such member, broker or dealer has any direct or indirect interest or which such members, broker or dealer has granted or guaranteed, containing, at least, an identification of the security and the number of units involved.

11. A record of the proof of money balances of all ledger accounts in the form of trial balances, and a record of the computation of aggregate indebtedness and net capital, as of the trial balance date.

12. A questionnaire or application for employment executed by each "associated person" (as defined in paragraph (h)(4) of this section) of the member, broker or dealer, which questionnaire or application shall be approved in writing by an authorized representative of the member, broker or dealer

13. For each account for a natural person: An account record including the customer's or owner's name, tax identification number, address, telephone number, date of birth, employment status (including occupation and whether the customer is an associated person of a member, broker or dealer), annual income, net worth (excluding value of primary residence), and the account's investment objectives. In the case of a joint account, the account record must include personal information for each joint owner who is a natural person; however, financial information for the individual joint owners may be combined. The account record shall indicate whether it has been signed by the associated person responsible for the account, if any, and approved or accepted by a principal of the member, broker or dealer. The record or alternative document sent to the customer should prominently alert the customer to mark any corrections and return the document and to notify the firm of any changes/updates in the future.

14. For the records above: the firm must keep a record showing it has furnished the information to the customer within 30 days of opening the account and no less frequently than every 36 months thereafter. And, for each change of name or address, the firm has furnished the customer and associated person over the account of notification within 30 days—to the customer's old address, and, if applicable, to the address of each owner of a joint account.

15. For changes in investment objectives the firm must confirm the changes within 30 days or with the next account statement.

16. All guarantees of accounts and all powers of attorney and other evidence of the granting of any discretionary authority given in respect of any account, and copies of resolutions empowering an agent to act on behalf of a corporation.

A "sales blotter." Huh?

Sure, just like down at the police station, there is a "blotter" at a broker-dealer showing everything incoming and outgoing at that office over that day. The police station processes suspects and offenders, while a broker-dealer processes securities and cash—either way, there is a record of these moments called a "blotter."

A "sales blotter" is a record of "original entry" showing "an itemized daily record of all purchases and sales of securities, all receipts and deliveries of securities (including certificate numbers), all receipts and disbursements of cash and all other debits and credits." Again, the "blotter" shows all movements of cash and securities that the broker-dealer is responsible for during the business day. It's a pretty important record to keep, and, of course, if FINRA were investigating a member firm and found that one of the principals had been trying to alter such records…well, we could read about that in FINRA "BrokerCheck" if we had more time.

In any case, I notice that the accounting software I struggle to use for my own business provides many types of reports that I can customize and present to various state and federal officials. Some offices want a record of sales subject to state sales tax, others want to see all the compensation paid to employees over the quarter or over the year. If we were a broker-dealer supervised by FINRA and the SEC, there would be more reports to generate and records to produce than I care to think about.

Even though few of us who aren't CPAs use the word "ledger" on a daily basis, it's just a more precise term used for "record." The SEC requires that broker-dealers keep detailed "ledgers" or "records" of everything you would expect—assets vs. liabilities of the firm, and their income vs. expenses. Records of all movements of cash and securities within each customer account carried by the member firm must be meticulously kept—makes sense, right? We don't discuss margin accounts a lot on this exam, but you'll need to know that they are watched more closely than cash accounts because the customer is basically investing borrowed money in a margin account and can end up losing more than he puts down initially. Therefore, the SEC would likely require the signature of any margin customer just so your firm can show some evidence that the customer knows she's actually in such an account. If you had more time to read regulatory actions against the bad boys (and occasionally girls) in your business, you'd see countless incidents involving customers being put into margin accounts and not realizing it until they receive a demand for payment on trades they didn't realize they'd even made.

That sort of thing really irks the SEC. Violations of SEC rules are frequently handled by FINRA, but the SEC also has administrative hearings, and neither process would be particularly good for a financial services career, of course. Also, whenever an agent gets in trouble under FINRA disciplinary procedures, his state securities Administrator can take action as well. For those who have no hope of hanging onto their career, the state securities administrative action is often not such a big deal, since after, say, creating ATM cards connected to various elderly customer accounts but sent to the registered representative, well…that individual was done, anyway. Many of those individuals, in fact, refuse to cooperate with FINRA, which is at least two violations in one—it violates a specific FINRA rule that says oh-yes-you-do-have-to-cooperate, and the general provision that all members must "maintain high standards of commercial honor." Refusing to cooperate with FINRA might not be the worst thing an agent can do, but it is one of the surest ways of getting kicked out of the securities industry.

On the other hand, for the agents who are merely being suspended by FINRA for a few weeks or months there is plenty of incentive to deal with the state Administrator as well as FINRA to keep the job and career going. The downside here is that a state-level administrative hearing would likely add nasty legal bills to whatever the disciplined agent already spent during the FINRA hearing process.

In other words, knowing the rules that we discuss in this textbook is not just important for your exam; it's important for your career survival as well. Agents often start cutting corners and get into trouble because they're in financial dire straits, so right when FINRA and the state securities regulators start taking disciplinary action, the agent needs but doesn't have, say, $25,000 to pay for adequate legal counsel. If the test asks, yes, you can represent yourself **pro se,** though that seems about as bright as doing so in civil or criminal court from any lawyer's perspective. Then again, I have attended one hearing at a state administrator's office where the former agent did exactly this, and, frankly, things turned out just fine. But, I still don't like facing regulators without an attorney speaking for me and—maybe more importantly—telling me when *not* to speak. Always a tough one for writers and instructors, don't you know.

TYPES OF ACCOUNT OWNERSHIP

INDIVIDUAL ACCOUNTS

If an individual opens an account, the firm must only accept purchase and sell orders or instructions to move moneys from that individual. Not his wife, or his secretary, or his "investment guy"…only that individual. Surprisingly enough, we call these **individual accounts**.

A relatively new type of individual account is called a **Transfer on Death** (TOD) account. Upon death of the account holder, the assets pass directly to the **beneficiary** or beneficiaries, bypassing **probate** court. Only the assets that are in the account pass to the beneficiary, of course, and this account has no effect whatsoever on estate taxes. It just makes the transfer faster and simpler. To establish an individual account as a TOD account, the account owner signs a Transfer on Death Beneficiary Agreement with the broker-dealer. In this agreement the customer can indicate primary and contingent beneficiaries, and can indicate more than one of either type, indicating a % that each one is to receive. A "contingent beneficiary" is named in case the primary beneficiary dies or disclaims the inheritance. But, an individual might want to name his two children as primary beneficiaries, each receiving 50%, with maybe a niece and nephew named as contingent beneficiaries, with the stated percentage each is to receive in case the primary beneficiaries don't end up inheriting the assets.

Now, since nothing is ever simple in this business, there is a way that you could accept orders from someone other than the customer. Your customer would need to grant the other person **trading authorization**. Limited trading authorization means the other person can give buy and sell orders but can't withdraw cash or securities. Full trading authorization means he can do all of the above. And, just to make sure everything has at least two names, trading authorization can also be referred to as "power of attorney." When you grant **power of attorney** to someone, you give them the power to make important decisions on your behalf—the power to represent you the way an attorney represents you in a court of law. Sort of.

JOINT ACCOUNTS

Two or more people can open a **joint account**. If two (or more) individuals want to share an account, they will open it either as JTWROS or JTIC.

JTWROS stands for **joint tenants with rights of survivorship**. The phrase "rights of survivorship" means that the survivor gets the assets if the other party dies. They go straight to the surviving owner(s), again, bypassing probate if it's spouse-to-spouse.

A JTIC (**Joint Tenants in Common**) account is a little different. In these accounts, the assets do not transfer to the other account owner upon death. Instead, they pass to the deceased individual's **estate**. The account owners would list the percentage each party owns in the account on the joint account agreement, and that percentage would pass to the deceased's estate upon death.

We've used the phrase "upon death" a few times already. As we'll mention elsewhere, remember that your job as a registered representative involves verifying things rather than blindly following instructions. For example, before taking anybody's word for it, your firm would have to verify that the account owner is actually dead. No, not like with an autopsy or anything. But, a valid death certificate has to be presented, and any executor or trustee has to present the legal papers authorizing their ability to tell you what's what suddenly, before you and your firm do anything. More on this later.

If it's a joint account, remember that orders will be accepted from any party listed on the account. Account statements and related documents can be sent to either party. But if you're talking about cutting a check, the check has to be made out to all names on the account, exactly as the account is titled. In other words, you don't cut a check to Barbara and tell her to settle up with Sheila and Suzanne next time the three have lunch. If the account is titled Barbara Benson, Sheila Stevens, and Suzanne Somerville, as Joint Tenants in Common, then that is how the check will be drawn up. Why do three friends choose to jointly own an account? Maybe it's a tiny little investment club that keeps all the members accountable for their stock picks—they shop and work out together; why not invest together? Main point is—they want to open an account with you.

FIDUCIARY ACCOUNTS

UGMA/UTMA

Believe it or not, minor children are not legal persons, which means they can't open investment accounts no matter how smart they are. An adult would have to open an investment account on behalf of a minor, called a **custodial account**, if the kid is going to beneficially own securities. That makes the adult the "nominal owner" and the child the "beneficial owner" of the account.

When the child becomes an adult, the assets will be re-registered in his name, but until then we'll have a custodian, who simply has to be an adult, handle the account. If a donor wants to donate money for the benefit of a minor, all she has to do is set the account up as either an **UGMA** (Uniform Gifts to Minors Act) or **UTMA** (Uniform Transfers to Minors Act) account, which doesn't require any supporting documentation. The registered representative just opens it as either UGMA or UTMA, depending on the state of residence, making sure there's just one adult custodian and one minor child per account. If you see "Jim and Judy Smith as custodians for…" stop right there. You can't have two adults as custodians. And you can't have more than one minor child per account. Watch out, though—the Series 6 exam knows you know that, and might try to confuse you into thinking that one adult can't be the custodian for more than one minor. Nobody said that—we said that per account there can be only one adult and one minor child. If Uncle Jeffrey is a whizbang investor, he can be the custodian for all the nieces, nephews, and pizza delivery guys he wants—he just has to use a separate account for each kid.

Also, the gifts cannot be taken back once given, even if the child turns out to be a slacker. In other words, the gifts are all "irrevocable and indefeasible." We haven't discussed "margin accounts" yet, but for now know that a custodial account can only be opened as a "cash account," not a margin account.

Remember that we put the minor child's social security number on the account because these accounts are taxable if a certain amount is earned per year; however, most of these accounts will likely earn less than the amount that would force anyone to pay taxes. Still, because of the special tax treatment, a custodian could get himself into all kinds of trouble if he started using a child's UTMA account as sort of a revolving line of credit to keep various businesses afloat until the kid grows up and actually needs the money. Any use of the assets must be only for the benefit of the minor child. The account is registered in the name of the custodian (nominal owner) for the benefit of the minor child (beneficial owner). Using funds to send the child to music camp would be just fine; borrowing money that the custodian fully intends to repay someday…not so much.

I am actually the custodian for a small UTMA account with my good friend's son as the beneficiary. Right now, the kid is 4, and while the account may never generate a lot of income, it should be nice to surprise him on his 21st birthday with an investment account that he can either add to or liquidate. At age 21, I'm betting on the latter—you?

Trust Accounts

As we saw, with an UGMA/UTMA account a 21-year-old could suddenly have full ownership of a big, fat investment account. I don't know about you, but if I had had full access to a large investment account at age 21, it would have been fully depleted by age 22. For most "kids" at that age, a **trust** account would be more prudent. In a trust account, the **grantor**—the one funding the trust with a grant of assets—can specify in the **trust agreement** all kinds of things, such as how much money can be withdrawn in a given year, what types of investments are considered appropriate/allowed, etc. If you open a trust account for a customer, you'll need a copy of the trust agreement so that you can verify that the trustee has the authority to manage the account on behalf of the beneficiary and you can see what is and is not allowed. Maybe the person who established the trust, the grantor, got burned in the stock market and wrote a provision that no stocks shall be purchased unless the company is earning a profit or maybe no more than 10% of trust assets shall be invested in equities, what have you. A trust document can be written to guide the actions and inclinations of the trust long after the grantor is dead and gone. We said that an UTMA/UGMA account requires no supporting documentation. A trust account would be supported by the trust agreement, at least.

Estate Accounts

Not to bring up a sore subject, but let's say that this summer your grandmother passes away. You discover that her **will** named you as the **executor**. Had Grandma died without a will, a **probate court** would have to appoint an "administrator" of the estate. In either case, an executor or administrator of an estate can open an investment account in the name of the estate. Estate accounts require all kinds of supporting documentation—you would need the estate's **tax ID number** as issued by the federal government, a death certificate (to prove the individual is actually, you know), and court documents showing that this person is, in fact, empowered to act as the executor/administrator of the estate. The exam could call these documents a "court appointment" or "letters of office," and these documents need to be no more than 60 days old, though I doubt the exam expects you to remember the exact number of days. Why tell you the number of days then? Because! It could be on your exam. Anyway, an estate is just a legal entity that holds the assets of a deceased person—house, stocks, bonds, checking, savings, CDs, etc. The estate typically closes out in six months, sometimes in two years. Either way, your recommendations would be based on a very short time horizon.

Discretionary Accounts

As a registered representative, you typically only recommend investments to your customers. But, believe it or not, if a customer really, really trusted you, she could let you make investment decisions for her—while also paying yourself a commission. That means if you want to buy 1,000 shares of MSFT for her account, you can do so without even bothering to call her. You can, literally, use your **discretion.** Of course, the purchase would have to be suitable for the account, but if you think today is a good day to buy her some MSFT or SBUX common stock, go ahead and buy it with the money in her account.

Before the first trade pursuant to your discretion happened she would have to sign a **discretionary authorization** form, and the account would be reviewed more frequently. But, from then on, you could choose which securities to buy or sell and how many shares/ units to buy or sell. You could, for example, buy 100 shares of MSFT or put $5,000 of her un-invested cash into a mutual fund without even bothering to call her first. On the other hand, without discretionary authority a registered representative can never determine which securities are bought or sold or how many shares/units. Unless the account is a **discretionary account**, the only thing a representative can determine is the time or price at which to execute a transaction. So, if a client calls and says, "Buy some consumer staple stocks today," do you need discretionary authority before you buy 100 shares of Procter & Gamble?

Yes. If you choose the asset, that constitutes discretion.

If a client says, "Buy as much Procter & Gamble as you think I should buy today," you would also not be able to take that order as-is, not until the client okays the number of shares you're going to purchase.

But, if a client tells you to "Buy 1,000 shares of Procter & Gamble for me today," do you need discretionary authorization over the account?

No, your client has chosen the asset (PG) and the amount (1,000 shares). Only thing left for you to decide is the best time and price to do it, and time/price decisions do not require written discretionary authorization Note, however, that the order to buy 1,000 shares of PG does have to be entered that day; if not, it goes away. And, even though you wouldn't need anything signed by the customer, as a registered representative, you would indicate that you have "time and price discretion" on the order ticket.

Easy, right?

Now, if I gave you discretion over my account and was clearly an income investor with a low risk tolerance and a short time horizon, the exam might say that if you use your discretion to purchase aggressive growth funds, you have made an **unauthorized transaction**. Even though Series 6 licensees don't execute orders for individual shares of stock, you might run into the same situation if a client just wants to cut a check for, say, $25,000 to the investment company and let you and your supervisor decide how to allocate it. Without discretion over the account, you would not be able to take it from there. Rather, you would need to help the customer determine specifically how much of her money should go into which of the mutual funds you sell.

FINRA rules require that firms review any discretionary accounts very carefully, as we see here:

> The member or the person duly designated shall approve promptly
> in writing each discretionary order entered and shall review
> all discretionary accounts at frequent intervals in order to
> detect and prevent transactions which are excessive in size
> or frequency in view of the financial resources and character
> of the account.

Guardian Accounts

A **guardian account** is established for a minor when the parents are ruled mentally incompetent or the child is orphaned—or even when an adult is determined to be mentally incompetent. In other words, somebody needs to look out for the financial affairs of another person, acting as that person's guardian. As with an estate account, you would need to see the court order appointing the guardian, and it would need to be no more than 60 days old. A "receiver" is a party placed in charge of the assets of a company in bankruptcy. You would, of course, need to see the court papers putting this party in charge of the assets of a struggling company.

BUSINESS ACCOUNTS

A corporation or partnership can open an investment account, too. If your client is a corporation or partnership, you'll need to look at the documents that govern these entities. You'll need a copy of the corporate resolution for a corporation. For a partnership, you'll need a copy of the partnership agreement. These documents tell you who has authority to trade on behalf of the corporation or partnership. Even though mutual funds cannot be purchased "on margin," the term "margin" might show up on the Series 6. Buying "on margin" means to use money borrowed through your broker-dealer, backed up by the stock's current market value as collateral.

Huh? But, Cisco traded between, say, $80 and $15 in the same year—wouldn't that cause a sort of collateral crunch?

Big time, which is why margin accounts are not often appropriate. If a corporation wants to trade on margin, the registered rep needs a copy of the corporate charter to make sure those documents say it's okay. If a partnership wants to trade on margin, the rep needs to make sure the partnership agreement says it's okay.

An investment adviser, as we saw in an earlier chapter, is a firm that provides investment advice for compensation. They often have discretion over their clients' accounts and place trades through your broker-dealer. Therefore, you would need to see documentation that the adviser does have authority to place trades on behalf of its customers.

So, we've looked at various types of customer accounts. Now, let's look at all kinds of important procedures and regulations connected to opening, maintaining, and closing customer accounts.

ANTI–MONEY LAUNDERING

Broker-dealers are businesses that like to make as much profit as possible. Any effort they have to spend that doesn't lead to profit surely annoys the heck out of them. Sometimes it's their SRO (Self-Regulatory Organization) called FINRA that is sweating them, sometimes the SEC, and sometimes other parts of the U.S. Government, including the Department of the U.S. Treasury. Perhaps you recall writing that name out on a personal check when filing your income taxes—sorry, didn't mean to bring up another sore subject.

In any case, broker-dealers don't make any money by helping the federal government clamp down on money laundering and financial fraud. Fact is, however, they sort of have no choice. **Anti–Money Laundering (AML)** programs are simply a requirement at broker-dealers, along with all the other compliance requirements we look at in this textbook. As FINRA rules make clear to member firms:

> Each member shall develop and implement a written anti-money laundering program reasonably designed to achieve and monitor the member's compliance with the requirements of the Bank Secrecy Act and the…regulations thereunder by the Department of the Treasury.

The **Bank Secrecy Act** (BSA) authorizes the U.S. Treasury Department to require financial institutions such as banks and broker-dealers to maintain records of personal financial transactions that "have a high degree of usefulness in criminal, tax and regulatory investigations and proceedings." It also authorizes the Treasury Department to require any financial institution to report any "suspicious transaction relevant to a possible violation of law or regulation." These reports, called **Suspicious Activity Reports**, are filed with the Treasury Department's Financial Crimes Enforcement Network ("FinCEN").

FINRA rules state that at a minimum member broker-dealers must implement an AML program that:

- Establishes and implements policies and procedures that can be reasonably expected to detect and cause the reporting of transactions required under [the BSA].
- Provides for an annual (calendar-based) independent testing for compliance to be conducted by member personnel or by a qualified outside party.
- Designates and identifies to FINRA an individual or individuals responsible for implementing and monitoring the day-to-day operations and internal controls of the program. And promptly notify FINRA of any changes.
- Provides ongoing training.

The U.S. Treasury Department under the Bank Secrecy Act (BSA) requires that for wire transmittals of funds of $3,000 or more, broker-dealers are required to obtain and keep certain specified information concerning the parties sending and receiving those funds. In addition, broker-dealers must include this information on the actual transmittal order. Also, any <u>cash</u> transactions over $10,000 require the same type of uptight record keeping. For these, broker-dealers must file a **Currency Transaction Report** with FinCEN.

Why? Because terrorist and other criminal organizations thrive through **money laundering**. Since broker-dealers are financial institutions, they're lumped in with banks and required to do all kinds of record keeping to help the government prevent these operations. What is money laundering? It's the process of turning "dirty" money "clean." Without it, organized crime and terrorist organizations could not function. The goal of money laundering is to hide proceeds derived from illegal sources and to make them appear legitimate. For example, if a mobster can take profits made from loan sharking and turn them into shares of stock, pretty soon it appears he has a legitimate source of income.

I would expect the exam to bring up the three stages of money laundering. **Placement** is the stage when funds are moved into the system. **Layering** is the stage when a confusing set of transactions is conducted to make it unclear where these funds originated. **Integration** is the stage when the funds are invested in legitimate enterprises or investment vehicles. With the passage of the **USA Patriot Act**, broker-dealers and other financial institutions have to help the government monitor suspicious activity that could be tied to money laundering. Broker-dealers now have to report any transaction that involves at least $5,000 if the broker-dealer knows, suspects, or has reason to suspect that it doesn't pass the smell test. FINRA spells out four specific characteristics that would make a broker-dealer file a suspicious activity report (SAR-SF). An SAR-SF report would be filed if the transaction falls within one of four classes:

- the transaction involves funds derived from illegal activity or is intended or conducted to hide or disguise funds or assets derived from illegal activity;
- the transaction is designed to evade the requirements of the Bank Secrecy Act;
- the transaction appears to serve no business or apparent lawful purpose or is not the sort of transaction in which the particular customer would be expected to engage and for which the broker/dealer knows of no reasonable explanation after examining the available facts; or
- the transaction involves the use of the broker/dealer to facilitate criminal activity.

Notice that broker-dealers have to look not just at individual transactions but at patterns of transactions that, taken together, appear suspicious.

Confidentiality when complying with all of this is required by federal law—as FINRA explains:

> The rule also requires that the filing of a Form SAR-SF report must remain confidential. The person involved in the transaction that is subject of the report must not be notified of the Form SAR-SF. In other words, if subpoenaed, the broker/dealer must refuse to provide the information and notify FinCEN of the request, unless the disclosure is required by FinCEN, the SEC, an SRO or other law enforcement authority. Where two or more broker/dealers are filing one Form SAR-SF, the confidentiality provisions apply equally to each broker/dealer participating in a transaction, and not only the broker/dealer that filed the Form SAR-SF.

An exam question might ask what the agent or firm should do after filing an SAR-SF form—does that relieve them of their reporting obligations? Not necessarily. If the activity involves terrorist financing, for example, or ongoing money laundering schemes, the member firm needs to notify the appropriate law enforcement agency and/or call FinCEN's hotline if the activity appears to be related to terrorism. As with everything else, broker-dealers have to keep records connected to any SAR-SF reports, which they maintain for 5 years, making them available to FINRA staff upon request.

Broker-dealers now have to have a **customer identification program (CIP)** whereby they require more information to open an account. If the customer is not a U.S. citizen, the firm will need:

- taxpayer ID number
- passport number and country of issuance
- alien ID card
- other current (not expired) government-issued photo ID card

Even the U.S. citizen may need to show a photo ID, just as you do when you go take your Series 6 exam. The CIP program requires agents and their firms to take reasonable steps to verify the identity of anyone opening an account, to maintain the records used to verify the person's identity, and to consult a list of known and suspected terrorists to prevent opening an account for anyone on *that* list.

The federal government now maintains an **Office of Foreign Asset Control** (OFAC) designed to protect against the threat of terrorism. This office maintains a list of individuals and organizations viewed as a threat to the U.S. These suspected threats are called "Specially Designated Nationals" or SDNs. Broker-dealers and other financial institutions now need to make sure they aren't setting up accounts for these folks, or—if they are—they need to block/freeze the assets. A compliance officer needs to be designated to handle this responsibility.

REGULATION S-P

Sharing customer information with law enforcement officials is one thing. Providing it to telemarketers and identity thieves is quite another. To fight identity theft and to protect customers from having too much of their information shared with people they've never met, the SEC enacted **Regulation S-P** to put into place a requirement from the Gramm-Leach-Bliley Act. Basically, "a financial institution must provide its *customers* with a notice of its privacy policies and practices, and must not disclose nonpublic personal information about a **consumer** to nonaffiliated third parties unless the institution provides certain information to the consumer and the consumer has not elected to opt out of the disclosure." A "consumer" is basically a prospect, someone interested in establishing some type of account. A **customer** is someone who has now opened a financial relationship with the firm. Broker-dealers now

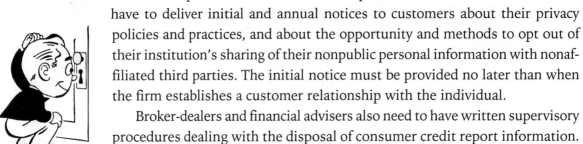

have to deliver initial and annual notices to customers about their privacy policies and practices, and about the opportunity and methods to opt out of their institution's sharing of their nonpublic personal information with nonaffiliated third parties. The initial notice must be provided no later than when the firm establishes a customer relationship with the individual.

Broker-dealers and financial advisers also need to have written supervisory procedures dealing with the disposal of consumer credit report information. Since firms typically look at a consumer's credit history before opening accounts—especially margin accounts—selling annuities, or providing financial planning services, the firms need to safely dispose of the information rather than just setting it all in a big box out back.

WORKING WITH CUSTOMERS

The first thing an agent needs to do is get to know the customer. FINRA calls their rule on this topic the "Know Your Customer Rule," FINRA Rule 2090. Under this rule FINRA requires that agents and their firms "use reasonable diligence, in regard to the opening and maintenance of every account, to know (and retain) the essential facts concerning every customer and concerning the authority of each person acting on behalf of such customer." FINRA says that the *essential facts* involved with *knowing the customer* "are those required to (a) effectively service the customer's account, (b) act in accordance with any special handling instructions for the account, (c) understand the authority of each person acting on behalf of the customer, and (d) comply with applicable laws, regulations, and rules."

A FINRA Notice to Members explains that requesting the information from the customer is usually considered using reasonable diligence. But—as always—there are buts. FINRA follows up that statement with this one: when customer information is unavailable despite a firm's reasonable diligence, however, the firm must carefully consider whether it has a sufficient understanding of the customer to properly evaluate the suitability of the recommendation.

So, as usual, FINRA tells its members and their associated persons (you and your supervisors) what their obligations are and gives them some guidance. But, ultimately, it's up to the member firms, their principals, and their agents to either get it right or get a hearing date scheduled. Similarly, we'll see that in order to follow suitability rules, you'll need to obtain the customer's investment profile, but not all of that information will be relevant in all cases. Therefore, firms have to use their judgment as to whether a particular document or response from a customer is necessary to really know the customer well enough to recommend securities or strategies. And, as always, they must obtain and retain the records connected to gathering all of this required information.

FINRA Rules require broker-dealers to forward certain communications from securities issuers to their stock- or bondholders if the firm is holding the customer's securities on their behalf. In other words, some investors are now directly registered as the owners of shares of stock, but most title them in the name of the broker-dealer for the beneficial ownership of themselves. This very common practice of letting your broker-dealer hold title of your securities on your behalf is called registering the securities in **street name,** by the way. Annual and special shareholder meetings involve routine and/or critical shareholder votes on matters affecting the company. In connection with these shareholder votes a **proxy statement** is sent to shareholders by the issuer, and since broker-dealers usually hold the shares on behalf of the customer, they need to be sure their customer—the shareholder— receives them promptly. Issuers also send out quarterly and annual reports (10-Q and 10-K reports) that broker-dealers forward to their customers, and issuers of corporate bonds also send out communications to their bondholders, which would also need to be promptly forwarded to the firm's customers. Later, we'll see that your particular customers will hold shares of mutual funds as opposed to holding shares of, say, Starbucks or McDonald's. If you get your Series 7 license in the future, many of your customers will hold shares of stock or individual bond issues, and they will be receiving communications directly from those issuing corporations.

In addition to communications from issuers, broker-dealers send customers **trade confirmations** for every purchase or sale of securities and **account statements** to verify the positions of securities and cash currently in the account. What if a customer wants you to hold such mail for a while? FINRA, as always, has already thought of it and has a rule:

Holding of Customer Mail

Upon the written instructions of a customer, a member may hold mail for a customer who will not be at his or her usual address for the period of his or her absence, but (A) not to exceed two months if the member is advised that such customer will be on vacation or traveling or (B) not to exceed three months if the customer is going abroad.

Chapter 1 Review Quiz

(21 questions)

1. **Which of the following accounts can be opened without supporting documentation?**

   A. UTMA

   B. Guardian

   C. Trust

   D. Estate

2. **A registered representative (RR) must obtain all of the following information when opening a customer account except for one item, for which he must make a reasonable inquiry only. For which item is a "reasonable attempt" sufficient when opening a new customer account?**

   A. A determination that the customer is of legal age

   B. Customer name

   C. Customer residence

   D. Customer tax identification number

3. **Broker-dealer member firms must obtain and maintain all of the following signatures connected to a customer account EXCEPT:**

   A. Dated manual signature of each party authorized to exercise discretion over any discretionary account

   B. Signature of the registered representative with responsibility over the account

   C. Signature of the principal approving the account

   D. Signature of the branch manager of the customer's provided bank reference

4. **What is true concerning changes to the name or designation of a customer account?**

   A. Only registered representatives managing discretionary accounts may sign off on such changes without principal approval

   B. All such changes must be approved by a principal

   C. Once opened, basic account information may not be altered; accounts must be closed and re-titled to accommodate such changes

   D. In order to change the name or designation of a customer account, the customer must present him or herself at the premises of the member's place of business

5.   Which statement below is accurate concerning an UTMA/UGMA account?

   A.   Upon death of the minor, the assets pass to the minor's estate

   B.   Earnings grow tax-deferred until the beneficiary reaches the state's age of majority

   C.   The custodian must be related to the beneficiary as an "immediate family" member

   D.   All of these statements are accurate

6.   Identify the one accurate statement below regarding individual accounts opened for a customer at a member firm.

   A.   Such accounts may be opened only with the signature of an impartial witness

   B.   Such accounts are for tax-advantaged accounts only

   C.   Only orders from the account owner may be accepted

   D.   Only orders from the account owner or a duly authorized third party may be accepted

7.   Which of the following types of account ownership allow(s) assets to transfer outside the probate court process?

   A.   Transfer on Death (TOD)

   B.   Joint Tenants in Common (TIC)

   C.   Both choices

   D.   Neither choice

8.   What should a registered representative do if she receives a call from the executor for the estate of an elderly customer, and the executor informs her that his grandmother has died, with detailed instructions as to which securities to liquidate immediately?

   A.   Ignore the instructions and inform a principal of the call upon receipt of proper court documents

   B.   Inform the executor that your firm will require a death certificate, letters of office, and various other documents before executing any transactions upon his instructions

   C.   Upon receipt of a photo ID verifying the executor's identity, follow his instructions

   D.   Upon receipt of a photo ID verifying the executor's identity and principal approval, follow the executor's instructions

9.   All of the following statements of custodial accounts (UGMA/UTMA) are accurate EXCEPT:

   A.   The original gift to the account is typically treated as a loan to the beneficiary

   B.   At the age of adulthood, the former minor controls all assets in the account

   C.   The gifts are irrevocable and indefeasible

   D.   If the parents object to the opening of the account, it may still be opened by an adult

10. **One of your customers is the custodian for an UTMA (Uniform Transfers to Minors Act) account. The custodian tells you to liquidate 100 shares of ABC preferred stock so that he can fund the purchase of some landscaping equipment for his business, a business which frequently provides financial benefit to the minor named as beneficiary on the account. What should you do at this point?**

    A.   Execute the unsolicited order without adding any commentary

    B.   Inform the custodian that withdrawals are to be used only for the benefit of the minor on the account

    C.   Hang up, and immediately contact the parents of the beneficiary named on the account

    D.   Execute the transaction, but inform the custodian that your firm will be forced to represent the child in family court if any funds are used to benefit his business

11. **If a registered representative lacks written discretionary authorization over the account, which of the following customer orders could be accepted?**

    A.   Allocate this $20,000 among three different mutual funds

    B.   Allocate this $20,000 among three different large cap growth funds

    C.   Buy 1,000 shares of ABC sometime this week when you think the price is right

    D.   Buy 1,000 shares of ABC this afternoon

12. **Fiduciary accounts include all of the following EXCEPT**

    A.   UTMA

    B.   IRA

    C.   Guardian

    D.   Investment advisory

13. **A true statement regarding a Currency Transaction Report (CTR) is that it would be filed**

    A.   For any wire transfer exceeding $3,000

    B.   For any incoming wire transfer exceeding $5,000

    C.   For any cash transaction or series of transactions exceeding $10,000 in a single day

    D.   For any cash transaction or series of transactions under $10,000 in a single day

14. **Which of the following is an accurate statement of brokerage procedures in connection to the Bank Secrecy Act (BSA)?**

    A.   Special forms and recordkeeping are required for all wire transmittals of $3,000+

    B.   Broker-dealers are exempt from all requirements unless affiliated with a retail bank

    C.   FinCEN, a subdivision of the Securities and Exchange Commission (SEC), must be alerted of all wire transmittals by or for non-U.S. citizens regardless of the amount involved

    D.   Because of Dodd-Frank, broker-dealers may opt-in or opt-out of compliance with requirements under the Bank Secrecy Act

15. Which of the following is NOT one of the stages of money laundering?

    A.   Placement

    B.   Layering

    C.   Integration

    D.   Subordination

16. The stage in the money laundering process in which a series of complex transactions is used in order to obscure the origin of the illicit funds is known as

    A.   Layering

    B.   Placement

    C.   Integration

    D.   Obfuscation

17. A brokerage customer would request that her previous broker-dealer move her account assets to your firm through which of the following?

    A.   ACT

    B.   ACAT

    C.   SIPC

    D.   SARS

18. FINRA member broker-dealers routinely forward all of the following mail to their customers EXCEPT:

    A.   Account statements

    B.   Proxy statements

    C.   IRS Form 1040

    D.   10-K Reports

19. Which of the following statements accurately addresses the process of updating personal information associated with a customer account?

    A.   Only the customer may make such a change, and not more often than annually

    B.   Only the customer may make such a change, and not more often than quarterly

    C.   Personal information is updated no more frequently than annually when the customer responds to a request from a registered broker-dealer

    D.   Personal information should be updated whenever the customer informs the registered representative of relevant changes

20. Which of the following requires that a principal sign off on the information being changed or recorded?

    A.   A customer calls to inform the firm that her husband has lost his job

    B.   A customer calls to inform the firm that she and her husband are switching to a JTIC (Joint Tenants in Common) account designation

    C.   A customer calls to inform the firm that she has lost her job

    D.   A customer calls to request information about a tax-exempt bond fund not sponsored by the firm

21. Which of the following is an accurate statement of individual accounts?

    A.   Orders may only be accepted from the individual listed as the account owner

    B.   Orders may only be accepted from the individual listed as the account owner and anyone granted power of attorney orally by the customer

    C.   Orders may only be accepted from the individual listed as the account owner and anyone granted power of attorney in writing by the customer

    D.   Orders may be accepted from immediate family members of the customer only

Chapter 1 Review Quiz Answers

1. **ANSWER:** A

    WHY: As long as the person is an adult and has the child's social security number, an UTMA/UGMA account can be opened, without any legal documents to support it.

2. **ANSWER:** D

    WHY: if the customer does not supply a tax ID #, the account can be opened, but a "backup withholding" will result.

3. **ANSWER:** D

    WHY: the customer does provide a bank reference, but you don't need the signature of the branch manager.

4. **ANSWER:** B

    WHY: imagine the uproar a registered representative could cause if he took the husband off an account just before the wife liquidated all the assets and filed for divorce? Or, if the registered representative changed a corporate account to an individual account in the name of just one of the owners—the one with the gambling problem? For these reasons and more, the principal has to approve such changes.

5. **ANSWER:** A

    WHY: the assets would not pass to the parents or the custodian, should the test question bring that up. The account is not tax-deferred; rather, some of the income generated is exempt from taxation.

6. **ANSWER:** D

    WHY: only take orders from the individual and/or anyone granted trading authorization/power of attorney by the customer.

7. **ANSWER:** C

    WHY: there are no tax advantages, but the assets do pass directly to the named beneficiary for a TOD account or to the other account owner(s) in a TIC account.

8. **ANSWER:** B

    WHY: try not to fall for the old "my grandmother is dead" ruse if you can help it. Your firm needs all kinds of documentation before retitling the account and executing any buy or sell orders from the executor of the estate.

9. **ANSWER:** A

    WHY: the gifts are not to be revoked or treated as loans (irrevocable and indefeasible).

10. **ANSWER:** B

    WHY: the custodian might not know any better, so the registered rep should inform him that the account is only to be used for the benefit of the minor. But, you're not the police or an officer of the court, or anything like that. Nor are the parents to be contacted about this account unless one of them is the custodian.

11. **ANSWER:** D

    WHY: an order to buy a certain number of shares on that same day can be accepted without having written discretionary authority over the account. But, the order is only good for that day. If the rep has to determine the investment the client is making—that requires written discretionary authority over the account.

12. **ANSWER:** B

    WHY: an IRA is an individual account—an Individual Retirement Account.

13. **ANSWER:** C

    WHY: this rule is not just for the brokerage industry—cash transactions > $10,000 get the federal government interested enough to require a form.

14. **ANSWER:** A

    WHY: a special form is required for such wire transmittals—don't confuse this with suspicious activity, which is reported on an SAR-SF (Suspicious Activity Report).

15. **ANSWER:** D

    WHY: the term "subordination" is fictitious in this question. The other three phases should be remembered for the exam.

16. **ANSWER:** A

    WHY: know the three stages of money laundering—placement, layering, and integration.

17. **ANSWER:** B

    WHY: brokerage customer assets are transferred between firms through ACAT transfers.

18. **ANSWER:** C

    WHY: your tax forms would come from the IRS or your CPA, not your broker-dealer. Proxy statements and 10-K reports are sent by the issuer of the common stock held by the broker-dealer for the benefit of the customer.

19. **ANSWER:** D

    WHY: whenever the customer needs to update her contact or suitability information, the change should be noted by the registered representative.

20. **ANSWER:** B

    WHY: changes to the name or designation of the account must be approved by a principal.

21. **ANSWER:** C

    WHY: only accept orders from the account owner and anyone authorized by the customer's signature to trade the account. Do not assume "immediate family members" have any authority whatsoever.

CHAPTER 2

Evaluates Customers' Financial Information, Identifies Investment Objectives, Provides Information on Investment Products, and Makes Suitable Recommendations

(Represents 47 of 100 Questions on the Series 6 Exam)

Notice that this chapter of the book and section of the outline covers just under *half* the material. So, please, don't try to rush through it.

And don't try to rush through the process of landing customers and selling them investment products, either. When you open a customer account with your broker-dealer, you need to gather important facts in order to understand the customer's **investment profile**. It's important to know your customer because all of your investment recommendations to him have to make sense given his needs, goals, time frame, risk tolerance, etc. Your recommendations of mutual funds and variable annuity **subaccounts** will not always turn out to be profitable, but they all have to be **suitable**. The only way to make a suitable recommendation to a customer is to first get to know the essential facts about that customer as well as possible.

SUITABILITY

FINRA is the **Self-Regulatory Organization (SRO)** formed when the NASD and NYSE regulators merged several years ago. As we saw in Chapter 1, SROs (Self-Regulatory Organizations) including FINRA register with the SEC under the Securities Exchange Act of 1934. The NYSE had a "know your customer" rule, while the NASD had a "suitability" rule. FINRA has taken elements of each while also adding some new requirements in order to assure that registered representatives and their firms do their due diligence when getting to know the customer and when making recommendations to buy, sell, or hold securities.

FINRA's "know your customer rule" requires firms to use "reasonable diligence" in regard to opening and maintaining customer accounts. It requires firms to know the "essential facts" on every customer, as well. Essential facts are defined as:

> those required to (a) effectively service the customer's account, (b) act in accordance with any special handling instructions for the account, (c) understand the authority of each person acting on behalf of the customer, and (d) comply with applicable laws, regulations, and rules.

The "know your customer" obligation starts at the beginning of the broker-dealer and customer relationship, even before any investment recommendations have been made to that customer. FINRA's new suitability rule requires that agents/registered representatives have:

> a reasonable basis to believe that a recommended transaction or investment strategy involving a security or securities is suitable for the customer, based on the information obtained through the reasonable diligence of the member or associated person to ascertain the customer's investment profile.

This is how FINRA defines an *investment profile*:

> a customer's investment profile includes, but is not limited to, the customer's age, other investments, financial situation and needs, tax status, investment objectives, investment experience, investment time horizon, liquidity needs, risk tolerance, and any other information the customer may disclose to the member or associated person in connection with such recommendation.

Suitability requirements for the agent and his broker-dealer are triggered only when there is an investment **recommendation** made to the client. As usual, defining the term "recommendation" is more complicated than one would like. FINRA is pretty straightforward in one of their regulatory notices concerning the new suitability rules, so let's allow them to tell us:

For instance, a communication's content, context and presentation are important aspects of the inquiry. The determination of whether a "recommendation" has been made, moreover, is an objective rather than subjective inquiry. An important factor in this regard is whether—given its content, context and manner of presentation—a particular communication from a firm or associated person to a customer reasonably would be viewed as a suggestion that the customer take action or refrain from taking action regarding a security or investment strategy. In addition, the more individually tailored the communication is to a particular customer or customers about a specific security or investment strategy, the more likely the communication will be viewed as a recommendation. Furthermore, a series of actions that may not constitute recommendations when viewed individually may amount to a recommendation when considered in the aggregate. It also makes no difference whether the communication was initiated by a person or a computer software program. These guiding principles, together with numerous litigated decisions and the facts and circumstances of any particular case, inform the determination of whether the communication is a recommendation for purposes of FINRA's suitability rule.

Okay, so the new suitability rule mentions securities and strategies. As soon as an agent recommends that a customer do—or not do—something in relation to a security or investment strategy, he has made a recommendation for purposes of the suitability rule. And, he will be much better off if he knows what he's talking about. On the other hand, if the agent or broker-dealer put out purely educational material that explains investment strategies without actually recommending any particular security or strategy, then those materials are exempt from the suitability rule. However, if the agent/firm is recommending that customers consider using margin or liquefied home equity to purchase securities, that is covered by the suitability rule. Even if it doesn't mention particular securities, and even if it doesn't lead to a transaction, a recommended strategy has to be suitable. And, guess what, margin accounts and liquefied home equity are not suitable for most investors.

So, the margin handbook or margin disclosure brochure simply explains how margin works—that is educational material and has to be provided to customers before they open margin accounts. On the other hand, any brochure that recommends or implies that a customer ought to actually open a margin account and buy securities on credit would be considered a recommended strategy. If you, therefore, send it to my 87-year-old Aunt Bessie, living on social security and the kindness of fellow church members, well...that wouldn't be suitable.

By the way, an explicit recommendation to *hold* a security is just as much a recommendation as a recommendation to buy or sell a security. As FINRA states:

> The rule recognizes that customers may rely on firms' and asso-
> ciated persons' investment expertise and knowledge, and it is
> thus appropriate to hold firms and associated persons respon-
> sible for the recommendations that they make to customers,
> regardless of whether those recommendations result in trans-
> actions or generate transaction-based compensation.

However, an agent has to specifically tell a client not to sell a security—or not to sell securities in general—before he has made an explicit recommendation to hold. The fact that the agent did not tell the customer to sell is not a recommendation to hold. Right? FINRA adds:

That is true regardless of whether the associated person previously recommended the purchase of the securities, the customer purchased them without a recommendation, or the customer transferred them into the account from another firm where the same or a different associated person had handled the account.

See? The regulators are not out to get you guys—they are reasonable. Just a bit wordy at times. In any case, the new rule tries to clarify an agent's responsibility when it comes to making recommendations to customers. There are now three explicit suitability obligations spelled out in the rule:

1. Reasonable-basis suitability: the agent must use reasonable diligence to understand the potential risks and rewards associated with the recommended security or strategy and have a reasonable basis to believe the recommendation is suitable for at least some investors.

2. Customer-specific suitability: the agent must have a reasonable basis to believe that a recommendation is suitable for a particular customer based on his/her profile. The profile now adds new items to the existing list (age, investment experience, time horizon, liquidity needs and risk tolerance).

3. Quantitative suitability: an agent with control over an account must make sure that a series of transactions that might make sense in isolation are not unsuitable based on an excessive number of transactions given the customer's investment profile. This would not apply to unsolicited transactions initiated by the customer.

For the three requirements above, understand that Number 1 and Number 3 apply equally to retail and **institutional investors**. However, Number 2 is applied differently for the two types of customer. Above, we see how **retail investors** are to be handled. But, if the investor is an "institutional account," the firm can meet their "customer-specific suit-ability" requirement by having a reasonable basis to believe the customer is able to evaluate investment risks independently and by having the institutional customer acknowledge in writing that it is exercising independent judgment—unlike the typical retail investor, who relies on what her stockbroker tells her in most cases.

So, if an agent/firm tries to provide evidence that they had a reasonable basis to believe that a particular recommendation is suitable to at least some investors, one would think that having documentation would be important. Actually, that depends. As FINRA states in one of several member notices, the suitability rule:

> does not include any explicit documentation requirements. The suitability rule allows firms to take a risk-based approach with respect to documenting suitability determinations. For example, the recommendation of a large-cap, value-oriented equity security generally would not require written documentation as to the recommendation. In all cases, the suitability rule applies to recommendations, but the extent to which a firm needs to evidence suitability generally depends on the complexity of the security or strategy in structure and performance and/or the risks involved. Compliance with suitability obligations does not necessarily turn on documentation of the basis for the recommendation. However, firms should understand that, to the degree that the basis for suitability is not evident from the recommendation itself, FINRA examination and enforcement concerns will rise with the lack of documentary evidence for the recommendation. In addition, documentation by itself does not cure an otherwise unsuitable recommendation.

Did you enjoy that? In English, they're saying that a recommendation that an equity investor purchase shares of Walmart or a blue chip equity mutual fund would not require a bunch of documentation that such an investment might be suitable for at least some investors. However, some of the mortgage-based derivatives that preceded the meltdown in September 2008? Maybe *nobody* should have been pitched those things, regardless of the "documentation" one might try to provide backing up the madness.

If the agent uses reasonable diligence to obtain all the necessary information from a customer, what happens if the customer does not supply all the information requested? In that case the agent and firm have to use their best judgment to determine whether they have enough information to make suitable recommendations to that customer. Perhaps the investor refuses to supply her age—what if all other information makes it pretty clear that she should be in short-term bonds and money market mutual funds? Could the agent make those recommendations? Probably. Just keep good case notes. Also, firms can decide that for certain categories of customers the information FINRA requires is not relevant—for example, a broker-dealer can decide to not ask for the age of customers that are not human beings but merely legal persons/entities (trusts, estates, corporations, etc.) or not ask about liquidity needs *if* the firm is only going to recommend liquid securities in the first place. As FINRA explains:

> The significance of specific types of customer information
> generally will depend on the facts and circumstances of the
> particular case, including the nature and characteristics of
> the product or strategy at issue.

Some firms use product committees of really smart people to review whether a particular investment product or strategy is suitable for at least some customers. Can you, as an agent, simply rely solely on the committee's findings?

No. FINRA clarifies that as an agent you have a responsibility to assure that you understand the risks and rewards of a particular product or strategy before recommending it to any investor.

FINRA and the SEC have determined that agents must not just make recommendations that make sense. Agents must be sure to "act in their customer's best interests." That means that the agent must never place his own interests ahead of the customer's. Examples of agents violating that rule include an agent recommending one product over another based on the higher commissions he can earn, or an agent asking customers to make loans to him so he can start a business, backed up with "promissory notes."

Now, an agent does not have to recommend the least expensive investment to a customer, as long as it is suitable, and as long as the higher expenses are not related to higher commissions to the agent. In other words, if your broker-dealer only sells three families of mutual funds, then you simply recommend the ones that are suitable from these mutual fund families. The fact that there may be other, less-expensive mutual fund families out there? Not your problem. Where an agent will be disciplined and, perhaps, barred from the business is when he pushes customers to do things that benefit the agent while potentially harming the customer. A margin account, for example, allows a customer to buy roughly twice as much stock as he otherwise could. That might lead to higher commissions to the agent, but if he puts someone in a margin account for that reason, he's in big trouble. And probably should be, right? I mean, if you discovered that a securities agent had put your mother into a margin account, something she doesn't seem to be fully aware of, how might you react?

In any case, don't try to put customers into four different large cap growth funds offered by four different front-end-loaded mutual fund families. If you had determined that it was suitable for the customer to pay a front-end load, you should have put all her money into one large cap growth fund to minimize the sales charges. It would be pretty clear that this move was designed to maximize the sales charges you and/or your broker-dealer earn on the transaction. And, again, that is not a good reason to use to justify a transaction to a securities regulator.

INVESTMENT OBJECTIVES, TIME HORIZON, RISK TOLERANCE

So, getting to "know your customer" involves digging into his situation enough to determine or help determine his investment profile. What are the investor's **investment objectives?** Investment objectives include: capital preservation, income, growth & income, growth, and speculation. If the individual is in his 30s and is setting up a retirement account, he probably needs growth to build up his net worth before reaching retirement age. If he's already in retirement, he probably needs income since by definition he's no longer working or not working as much as he used to. He might need income almost exclusively, or, to protect his purchasing power, he might also need growth. And, as you might expect, this is where growth & income funds come in very handy. But, any blue chip stock that pays regular dividends would fit that bill, also. Or, even a bond that is convertible—that would be income plus potential growth. This test—you'll see—likes to make you think outside the box.

Some firms separate growth from **aggressive growth.** Aggressive growth investments include international funds, sector funds (healthcare, telecommunications, financial services, etc.) and emerging market funds (China, India, Brazil, etc.). For **speculation**, there are options and futures, and most investors should limit their exposure to these derivatives to maybe 5–15% of their portfolio. I, myself, currently allocate zero percent to speculation and plan to continue this allocation indefinitely.

If you're "saving up for retirement," that generally means you need capital appreciation, right? On the other hand, some folks are already rich, and they just want to preserve their capital (**capital preservation**). We won't tell them about buying U.S. Treasury securities all on their own, without commissions. Instead, we'll put them into a U.S. Treasury mutual fund. Even though the fund is not guaranteed, the securities the fund owns are.

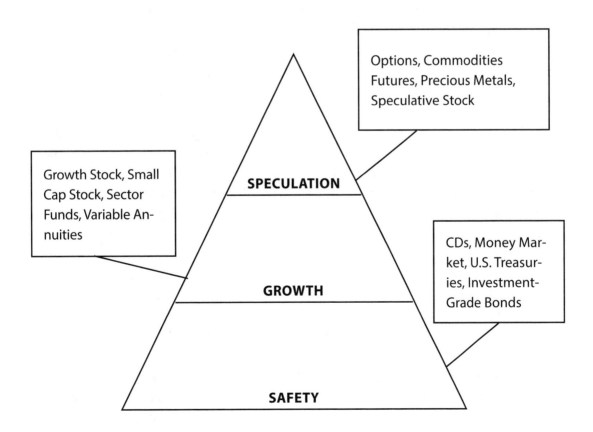

INVESTOR'S OBJECTIVE	RECOMMENDATIONS
Capital Preservation, Safety of Principal	U.S. Government/Treasury, Ginnie Maes
Liquidity	Money market funds
Income	Bonds (other than zero coupons)
Tax-Exempt	Municipal bonds/bond funds
High-Yield	Low-rated corporate or municipal bonds/ funds
From Stock	Preferred stock, large cap value funds, equity income funds
Growth	Common stock, stock funds
Portfolio Diversification	Add bonds, stock, and money market as needed to diversify investments among different instruments, industries, maturities, etc.
Speculation	Options, high-yield bonds, precious metals funds

Knowing the investor's objective is important, but it has to be tempered by the **time horizon** before you start recommending investments. In general the longer the time horizon the more volatility the investor can withstand. If you have a three-year time horizon, you need to stay almost completely out of the stock market and invest instead in high-quality bonds with short terms to maturity. If you're in for the long haul, on the other hand, who cares what happens this year? It's what happens over a 20- or 30-year period that matters. With dividends reinvested, the S&P 500 has historically gained about 9% annually on average, which means your money would double approximately every 8 years. Sure, the index can drop 30% one year and 20% the next, but we're not keeping score every year—it's where we go over the long haul that counts. A good way to see the real-world application of risk as it relates to time horizon would be to pull out the prospectus for a growth fund and see if you can spot any two- or three-year periods where the bar charts are pointing the wrong way—then compare those horrible short-term periods to the 10-year return, which is probably decent no matter which growth fund you're looking at. That's why the prospectus will remind folks that they "may lose money by investing in the fund" and that "the likelihood of loss is greater the shorter the holding period." See how important "time horizon" is?

Younger investors saving for retirement have a long time horizon, so they can withstand more ups and downs along the road. On the other hand, when you're 69 years old, you probably need some income and maybe not so much volatility in your investing life. So the farther from retirement she is, the more likely she'll be buying stock. The closer she gets to retirement, the less stock she needs and the more bonds/income investments she should be buying. In fact, you may have noticed that many mutual fund companies are taking *all* of the work out of retirement planning for investors, and offering **target funds**. Here, the investor picks a mutual fund with a target date close to her own retirement date. If she's currently in her mid 40s, maybe she picks the Target 2040 Fund. If she's in her mid 50s, maybe it's the Target 2030 Fund. For the Target 2040, we'd see that the fund is invested more in the stock market and less in the bond market than the Target 2030 fund. In other words, the fund automatically changes the allocation from mostly stock to mostly bonds as we get closer and closer to the target date. The same happens with the age-based portfolios in the educational 529 plans—as the child gets closer to college age, the portfolio allocation shifts away from stocks and into short-term bonds and money market securities.

Understand that an investor might have the primary objective of growth/capital appreciation. He might also have a time horizon of 10+ years. However, if he doesn't have the **risk tolerance** required for the stock market, we have to keep him out of stocks. Remember that risk tolerance has to do with not only the financial resources, but also the psychological ability to sustain wide fluctuations in market value, as well as the occasional loss of principal that really annoys some people. The terms "risk-averse," "conservative," and "low risk tolerance" all mean the same thing—these investors will not tolerate big market drops. They invest in safe, boring things like fixed annuities, U.S. Treasuries, and investment-grade bonds. In order to invest in sector funds or emerging market funds, the investor needs a high risk tolerance. Moderate risk tolerance would likely match up with balanced funds, equity income funds, and conservative bond funds.

Let's put the three factors together: investment objective, time horizon, and risk tolerance. If we know that the investor in the suitability question seeks growth, we then have to know his time horizon and risk tolerance. If he's a 32-year-old in an IRA account, his time horizon is long-term. Unless he can't sleep at night knowing the account balance fluctuates, you would almost *have* to recommend growth funds. His risk tolerance would tell us whether to use small cap, mid-cap, or large cap growth funds—the higher the risk tolerance the smaller the "cap." If the investor is 60 years old and living on a pension income, she might need to invest in common stock to protect her purchasing power over the next several years. If so, her time horizon is long, but her risk tolerance is probably only moderate or moderate-low. So, we'd probably find a conservative stock fund—maybe a growth & income, equity income, or large cap value fund.

If another investor seeks income primarily, we need to know her time horizon and risk tolerance. We don't buy bonds that mature beyond her anticipated holding period. If she has a 10-year time horizon, we need bonds that mature in 10 years or sooner. Her risk tolerance will tell us if we can maximize her income with high-yield bonds, or if we should be smart and buy investment-grade bond funds. If she needs tax-exempt income, we put some of her money into municipal bond funds. For capital preservation nothing beats U.S. Treasury securities. GNMA securities are also very safe. Money market mutual funds are safe—though not guaranteed by the U.S. government or anyone else—but they pay low yields. Money market mutual funds are for people who want to not only preserve capital but also make frequent withdrawals from the account. See, even though your money is safer in a 30-year Treasury bond than in a money market mutual fund, the big difference is that the market price of your T-bond fluctuates (rates up, price down), while the money market mutual fund stays at $1 per share.

Seriously. So if **liquidity** is a major concern, the money market mutual fund is actually better than T-bonds, T-notes, and even T-bills, all of which have to be sold at whatever price. With the money market mutual fund you can write checks, and the fund company will redeem the right number of shares to cover it.

Total liquidity.

The questionnaire that the client fills out when opening an account with your firm will try to gauge what is more important—going for large returns or maintaining a stable principal? Earning a return *on* his money, or getting the return *of* his money? Does he need to withdraw a large portion of his portfolio at a moment's notice? If so, put that portion in money market securities and short-term bonds. Here is an over-simplified chart that will help you at least begin sorting out the major investment options according to risk tolerance.

AGGRESSIVE	Emerging Markets
	International/Global
	Small-cap (growth or value)
	Sector funds
MODERATE – HIGH	Mid-, Large-cap Growth
	Growth & Income
MODERATE – LOW	Balanced, Equity Income
	Large-cap Value
LOW	Investment-Grade Bonds
VERY LOW	Treasuries, Money Market

AGGRESSIVE VS. DEFENSIVE STRATEGIES

So, if investing is a game, do you prefer playing offense or defense? Do you like to risk it all in an attempt to put some serious points up on the board (offense), or do you prefer to prevent a bunch of bad stuff (defense) from advancing against you?

If you're an aggressive investor, you need to have several things going for you:

- good job
- long time horizon
- good cash flow
- high risk tolerance

The first thing to remember is that investing in stocks is inherently more "risky" than investing in bonds. I was reading my *Business Week* on the El yesterday and saw an advertisement for a mutual fund. You can see how accepted this stock-is-riskier notion is in the industry from the following line in the advertisement:

Investors should note that the higher a fund's allocation to stocks, the greater the risk.

So, in the world of equity/stock, you are by definition more aggressive than a bond investor. Of course, a bond investor who consistently buys long-term bonds and/or bonds with low credit scores is much more aggressive than an investment-grade municipal or a U.S. Treasury bond investor. But, usually, we associate the word "aggressive" with "stock." Not all stocks are equally aggressive, of course. Small cap stocks tend to be more "aggressive" as investments than large cap stocks, and "blue chip" stocks are so called because of their relative "stability" and ability to pay dividends.

A more defensive investment strategy would not focus so hard on the potentially bright future but would concentrate more on all the bad news that this company could survive. Companies like Walmart, GE, or Microsoft offer a strong defense against economic downturns that might take out smaller competitors. There are companies that still sell their products/services during a recession. Supermarkets and discount retailers will keep selling food, underwear, and razor blades. On the other hand, companies that sell big-ticket items like automobiles or home appliances could take a hit. So, a defensive investor would buy stock in established companies that will likely sell the following products/services even during a recession:

- Food
- Basic clothing
- Healthcare/pharmaceuticals
- Alcohol
- Tobacco

An aggressive investor is willing to take on more risk. He'll buy stock in companies involved with unproven technologies working in an undeveloped industry. As soon as he reads an article on fuel cells, he wants to buy stock in *any* company involved with fuel cells. Trouble is, these companies aren't profitable, and nobody knows how long it will take for fuel cells to really take off, assuming they ever do. Not to mention, we have no clue which three of the current fifty companies will survive, let alone become profitable. An aggressive investor would be interested in the following:

- Aggressive Growth funds
- Emerging Market funds
- Small Cap funds
- Sector funds
- Growth stocks

CLIENT PROFILES

No matter who your client is, you must gather some information so that you can make suitable recommendations. You must determine the financial status of the client, gathering key information such as:

- Income sources
- Current expenditures (bills, obligations)
- Discretionary income (what's left after paying bills)
- Assets (cash, real estate pension/retirement accounts, life insurance)
- Tax bracket

Probably the most important figure to obtain from a client is known as "discretionary income" or "excess cash flow." This is the money left over after covering all essentials. A personal income statement might look like this:

<u>Monthly Income</u>
- Salary $7,000
- Investment Income $1,000
- Other Income $500

Total Monthly Income $8,500

<u>Monthly Expenditures</u>
- Taxes $2,000
- Mortgage Payment $2,000
- Living Expenses $2,000
- Insurance Premiums $300
- Loan Payments $200
- Travel/Entertainment $300
- Other Expenses $200

Total Monthly Expenses $7,000
Monthly Capital for Investing $1,500

So, a client with the above income statement has excess cash flow or discretionary income of $1,500. If you start talking him into investing $3,000 a month in speculative investments…well, you'd never do a thing like that, right? Instead, you'd make recommendations that make sense given the fact that he has $1,500 available for investing in a typical month. Notice how the client above had income from a job and income from investments. That's the way to become affluent or wealthy—let your money make money as you go out and earn a living. Pretty soon, they tell me, you can stop going out to earn a living and just manage your investments from the captain's quarters of your 80-foot yacht.

Of course, taxes always play a part in an investment strategy. If your client is in a high **marginal tax bracket**, you may want to recommend municipal bonds, which, generally, pay interest that is tax-free at the federal level. This same client probably doesn't want to do a lot of short-term trading, either, since any gain taken within the space of a year will be taxed at the short-term capital gains rate (which equals the ordinary income rate). He also might want to buy stocks that pay qualified dividends rather than REITs or royalty trusts, which will force him to pay his ordinary income rate on the dividends. Of course, one of the best answers you can give a client is, "Please consult with a qualified tax professional."

A business has both an income (earnings) statement and a balance sheet (statement of financial condition). So do your clients. Remember that assets represent what somebody owns, while liabilities represent what he owes. The difference would be his net worth. A client's assets would include the value of his home(s), automobiles, personal possessions (furniture, jewelry, Armani suits), investments, savings, and checking accounts. Liabilities would include mortgages and other loans, credit card balances, and, perhaps, debit balances in margin accounts.

A personal balance sheet might look like this:

<u>Assets</u>

Tangible Property
- House $400,000
- Automobiles $30,000
- Personal possessions $15,000

Investments
- Stocks and Bonds $100,000
- Keogh Plan $80,000
- IRA $20,000

Savings
- Checking $5,000
- Savings Account $5,000
- Money Market $5,000

<u>Liabilities</u>
- Mortgage $250,000
- Auto Loans $10,000
- Credit Card Balances $15,000

Net Worth = $385,000
Note: net worth is just all assets minus all liabilities.

This represents **total net worth**. Since some assets are difficult to liquidate, we could exclude those items (house, limited partnerships, rental property) to calculate **liquid net worth**. If a client has high total net worth but low liquid net worth, you might try to steer the client toward more liquid investments, like the money market, or at least heavily traded stocks and bonds, as opposed to hedge funds, principal protected funds, or thinly traded securities.

INVESTMENT VEHICLES

Now that we've looked at opening an account and determining both a client's investment profile and suitable recommendations for the account, let's dig into the various securities investment vehicles available to the customer. Let's start with the higher-risk category, **equity securities,** because I sense some readers may be starting to lose that fire in their bellies and in need of a little excitement.

EQUITY SECURITIES

Pretend you own a car wash. You're convinced you could turn it into a regional chain of car washes if you only had $500,000 to use for expansion. Trouble is, you don't seem to have an extra half-million dollars lying around. However, you do have a friend with some extra money. You ask if you can borrow the $500,000, but your friend has a better idea. Rather than borrow money from him, why not let him buy into your company as an owner? This way you print up a stock certificate and sell this piece of paper to him for $500,000, which you will use to grow your business. He'll use the paper as evidence that he has equity or ownership in your company, and now if the company does well, so do you and so does he. If his equity stake represents 20% of your company's profits, as your profits grow, so does the value of his 20% ownership. Maybe someday you'll have such a large profit that you'll start cutting him a check every three months and call it a "dividend."

That's basically the deal with equity securities. The folks who buy equity securities don't get interest payments, because they aren't lenders. They're just investors who like the company's chances of making a profit. Do you own your own home? Chances are you own a percentage of it, known as your equity. In the same way, you can own a percentage of a public company such as Home Depot or Starbucks by purchasing their equity securities. The most basic form of "equity" is called common stock.

Common Stock

Why would you start your own business? To make a profit. Why would you buy shares of somebody else's business? To take a share of their profits. A share of common stock gives the investor a share of the company's profits. That's why it's so much fun to own a percentage of a really profitable company. As the company's profit rises, either the share price rises or they pay you a dividend. Or both. We just saw that investors interested in stocks whose share prices rise are called "growth investors." Those who buy stocks primarily for their dividends are called "income investors." And, those who seek a little of both are cleverly called "growth and income investors."

See, the Series 6 is a tough test, but we also aren't exactly discussing quantum mechanics here, either, so let's not get too discouraged, people. I mean, think of some of the folks walking around your office today who managed to pass. Right? Anyway, common stock is nothing but a share of any profits the company might make now or in the future.

Advantages

Owners of common stock enjoy several important advantages the exam may bring up. The first advantage is called **limited liability**, and it means exactly what you'd expect: your liability as an investor is limited to the amount you invest. In other words, the creditors of the corporation can't come after you if the company goes into bankruptcy, and you're also shielded from any lawsuits brought against the corporation. So, the bad news is that you can lose all the money you invest in the company's stock. The good news is you can lose only the money you invest in the company's stock.

Shareholders also have the right to transfer their shares to others, by selling them, giving them away, or leaving them to others through a will. A bank or other company keeps a list of all the shareholders and deals with all the transfers of ownership, and we call this entity the **transfer agent**, for obvious reasons. If somebody loses a certificate, or if the certificate is destroyed, the transfer agent can issue new certificates—for a fee, of course. Another entity, usually a bank, audits/oversees the transfer agent to make sure the numbers all add up right. We call this entity the **registrar**. If you're reading closely and have a good memory, you might remember that these entities are also registered by the SEC under the Securities Exchange Act of 1934.

Shareholders have the right to inspect certain books and records of the company, such as the list of shareholders and the minutes of shareholder meetings. Again, because of the Securities Exchange Act of 1934, public companies have to file quarterly and annual reports with the SEC; therefore, shareholders can view these reports to see how their money is being spent by the corporation. That's how I know that Starbucks made a profit of about $400 million recently—I looked it up in their annual report. See, they're a *public* company, which means they have to disclose more information to me than I would dream of disclosing to my own wife. Oh well. That's the price they pay for "going public." Public investors finance these public companies by purchasing stock with their hard-earned money, so the companies have to disclose things to the public they'd probably rather keep private. There is no law that forces companies to go public, remember. The deal is if you want to raise money from public investors, you have to disclose all the good and bad news to the public from then on. If you don't think you can handle that level of scrutiny, keep your little company and its affairs private. Use bank loans, lines of credit, and contributions from a few limited partners or members of an LLC. But once your company taps the public markets with an IPO or bond offering, you'll have to start telling everybody your business no matter how embarrassing and humiliating. If you try to conceal the bad news from investors, you can end up in prison. More on that later.

Unlike owners of the company's preferred stock or bonds, owners of common stock have the right to vote for any major issue that could affect their status as a proportional owner of the corporation. Stock splits, mergers & acquisitions, board of directors elections, the authorization of more shares, and changes in business objectives all require shareholder approval. Remember that shareholders do not get to vote for dividends. If they did, why wouldn't we vote to have the corporation pay out every last penny of profits right now, dump our shares, and move on to destroy the next company?

Dividends

Some stocks pay **dividends**, but only if the board of directors decides to declare them. That's right, if a corporation's board of directors doesn't declare a dividend, the dividend doesn't get paid.

End of story. But, if it does declare a dividend, common stockholders have a "claim" on those dividends, as the exam may say. Remember, the Series 6 may want you to say that owners of common stock have a claim on, or a right to, earnings and dividends. The board of directors gets to decide three dates. FINRA decides the fourth one through their "uniform practice codes." Here's how it works. The day that the Board declares the dividend is known as the **declaration date**. The board wonders who should receive this dividend—how about investors who actually own the stock as of a certain date? We call that the **record date** because an investor has to be the owner "of record" on or before that date if he wants to receive the dividend. The board decides when it will pay the dividend, too, and we call that the **payable date**.

Now, since an investor has to be the owner of record on or before the record date to receive the dividend, there will come a day when it's too late for investors to buy the stock and also get the dividend.

Why? Because stock transactions don't "settle" until the third business day following the trade date. Settlement means that payment has been made to the seller and stock has been transferred to the buyer officially on the books. So, if a stock is sold on a Tuesday, the trade doesn't actually settle until Friday, the third business day after the trade. This is known as **regular way settlement**, or "**T + 3**." The "T" stands for "Trade Date," so just count forward three business days to find the settlement date.

So, if an investor has to be the owner of record on the record date, and it takes three business days for the trade to settle, wouldn't she have to buy the stock at least three business days prior to the record date?

This means that if she buys it just two business days before the record date, her trade won't settle in time. We call that day the **ex-date** or **ex-dividend date**, because starting on that day investors who buy the stock will not receive the dividend. On the ex-date, it's too late. Why? Because the trades won't settle in time, and the purchasers won't be the owners of record (with the transfer agent) on or before the record date.

FINRA sets the ex-date, as a function of "regular way" or "T + 3" settlement.

The ex-date is two business days before the record date.

So, remember DERP. Declaration, Ex-Date, Record Date, Payable Date. The board sets all of them except the Ex-Date, which is set by FINRA. If the test question gives you the record date, go back two *business* days to find the ex-date. Don't count weekends or holidays, either. If the record date is Tuesday, go back Monday and then…*Friday* for the ex-dividend date.

In the real world, it looks like this:

```
Equity Office declares first quarter common dividend

Mar 16, 2005— Equity Office Properties Trust (EOP), a publicly
held office building owner and manager, has announced today
that its Board has declared a first quarter cash dividend in
the amount of $.50 per common share. The dividend will be paid
on Friday 15 April 2005, to common shareholders of record at
the close of business on Thursday 31 March 2005.
```

So, March 16 is the Declaration Date. The Payable Date is April 15. The Record Date is Thursday, March 31. The article doesn't mention the Ex-Date (because that's not established by the company), but we can figure that it must be…right, Tuesday, March 29. If you bought the stock on Tuesday, your trade wouldn't settle until Friday, April 1, which means the seller's name would be on the list of shareholders at the close of business on Thursday, March 31. Remember that when stock is purchased on the ex-date, the seller is entitled to the dividend, not the buyer. Also note that the year "2005" does not make this book "dated." I've been using this historical example for years now to avoid having to update it every year. EOP is no longer a public company, but the press release serves our purposes just fine.

Companies can pay dividends in the form of cash, stock, shares of a subsidiary, and even the product they make. No, I don't have an actual example of a company sending out product as a dividend, and all stories about Procter & Gamble doing so are urban legends according to the folks in shareholder relations in Cincinnati.

Rights and Warrants

Another right common stockholders enjoy is the right to maintain their proportionate ownership in the corporation, known as a **pre-emptive right**. The corporation can sell more shares to the public, but it has to give the existing shareholders the right to buy their proportion of the new shares before others get to buy theirs. If they didn't do that, current shareholders would have their equity "diluted" or diminished. If you own 5% of a company now, it has to give you the right to maintain your 5% ownership, so for every share owned, investors receive what's known as a **subscription right**. It works like a coupon that lets the current shareholders purchase the new stock below the market price over the course of a few weeks. If a stock is trading at $20, maybe the existing shareholders can take one right plus $18 to buy a new share. Those rights act as coupons that give the current shareholders two dollars off the market price. So, the investors can use the **subscription rights**, sell them, or let them expire in a drawer somewhere, like most coupons.

A **warrant** is a long-term equity security that lets you purchase a company's stock at a predetermined price. If you have a warrant that lets you buy XYZ for $30 per share, then you can buy a certain number of shares at that price whenever you feel it makes sense to do so, like when XYZ is trading for a lot more than $30. When issued, the price stated on the warrant is above the current market price of the stock. It usually takes a long time for a stock's price to go above the price stated on the warrant—if it ever makes it, that is. But, they're good for a long time, typically somewhere between 2 and 10 years.

Warrants are often attached to a bond offering. Corporations pay interest to borrow money through bonds. If they attach warrants, they can "sweeten" the deal a little and maybe offer investors a lower interest payment in exchange for the potential upside on the common stock.

ADR

"ADR" stands for **American Depository Receipt**, and like many of the acronyms you'll need to know for the exam, this one means exactly what it says. It's a <u>receipt</u> issued to somebody in <u>America</u> against shares of foreign stock held on <u>deposit</u> in a bank. If you want to buy stock in Toyota, for example, you'll buy the Toyota ADR, which trades on the NYSE under the symbol "TM." This way, you don't have to buy a stock trading at 1,176.568 yen, and you don't have to wake up in the middle of the night to trade your stock while the exchange is open in Japan.

The exam might say that ADRs make it convenient for Americans to buy stock in foreign corporations such as Toyota, Nokia, etc. They are just shares of stock that might receive dividends, but they have a special risk the exam might talk about, called foreign currency or **currency exchange risk**. See, when Toyota declares a dividend, they declare it in the yen. That is then converted to dollars. Therefore, if, say 1,000 yen are being converted to American dollars for you, would you want the American dollar to be strong or weak versus the yen?

If the dollar were strong, those 1,000 yen wouldn't work out to very many dollars. If the dollar were weak, those 1,000 yen would convert to *more* dollars, so the owner of an ADR would be better off with a weak dollar, in case the exam feels like playing hardball.

ADR holders have the ability to exchange their ADRs for the actual foreign share certificates, should the exam ask such a question.

Preferred Stock

Preferred stock is a little peculiar. It's a fixed-income security, but it's also an equity security. See, usually when you hear "fixed income," you think about debt securities, which we'll look at in a few pages. But, preferred stock, which also pays a fixed income, is actually an equity security. The exam might point out that "equity" securities are held by "owners," while most "fixed-income investments" are held by "creditors." Well, preferred stock is, as I said, a little different. It pays a fixed income stream, but it's an equity or ownership/stock position. See, there are two basic types of ownership in a public company—common stock and preferred stock. Common stock might pay dividends or not, but its value can rise infinitely with the profits of the company. Preferred stock, on the other hand, simply pays a fixed income stream and does not rise in market value if and when the company's profits increase. As an owner of the company, the question is whether you're more interested in a stated rate of income paid out to you on a regular schedule or an unlimited potential gain.

Why do we call it "preferred" stock, by the way? Because preferred stock owners get preferred treatment over common stock owners if the company has to be liquidated to pay their creditors/lenders, and they always get their dividend before the company even thinks about paying common stockholders a dime. Remember that common stock simply gives the investor an ownership stake in the company—not a stated rate of return. If you buy 1,000 shares of MSFT, you don't get a piece of paper telling you you'll earn, say, 3% every year in dividends or interest. You just get a piece of paper congratulating you on owning a really tiny piece of a really big public corporation. Preferred stock, unlike common stock, does pay a stated rate of return, which just means that the dividend is printed right on the stock certificate and on the trade confirmations and account statements you get from your broker-dealer.

The par value for a preferred stock can be any amount the issuer wants, but for a test question it is assumed to be $100. Actually, I would fall out of my chair if the Series 6 threw me a question expecting me to assume what the par value for preferred stock is. If they bring it up at all, I'm willing to bet big money the question would go ahead and tell you what the par value is. I mean, the only preferred stock your customers will ever be exposed to would come through a mutual fund or similar investment company product, which is a large, well-diversified portfolio selected or managed by professional investors. But, let's use $100 as the par value for preferred stock because it works well for a test question. The stated dividend to the investor is a percentage of that par value. Six percent preferred stock would pay 6% of $100, or $6 per share per year. What if the company's profits increased? Six percent preferred stock would still pay $6 per share per year.

We hope.

See, dividends still have to be declared by the Board of Directors. Preferred stockholders aren't lenders, remember. They're owners, owners who like to receive dependable dividends. But, if the board doesn't declare a dividend, do you know how much an owner of a 6% straight preferred stock would receive?

Not a darned thing. However, if the investor owned cumulative preferred stock, that might be different. He wouldn't necessarily get the dividend now, but the company would have to make up the missed dividend in future years before it could pay dividends to any other preferred or common stockholders. If the company missed the six bucks this year and wanted to pay the full six bucks next year, cumulative preferred stockholders would have to get their $12 before anybody else saw a dime.

By the way, this 6% works more like a maximum than a minimum. If an investor wants the chance to earn more than the stated 6%, he'd have to buy participating preferred stock. Now, if the company raises the dividend for common stock, they raise the dividend on this participating preferred stock, too. A correct answer on participating preferred stock might be something like "a type of preferred stock whose dividend rate is fixed as to the minimum, but not as to the maximum."

Huh? Yes, that's the type of language used in many of the questions on the Series 6 exam. Most of the questions seem confusing at first; hopefully, you have studied enough to figure out what you're supposed to do with them.

In any case, the two biggest concerns for a preferred stock investor are interest rates and credit quality. If you receive a fixed income stream, the market will re-price your investment whenever interest rates in general move around. Your interest rate risk is that when interest rates rise, the market price of your fixed-income security will drop. If interest rates rise, the market price of preferred stock drops. The par value never changes, but the amount someone would pay for your preferred stock will drop if interest rates rise. On the other hand, when interest rates drop, the market price of your preferred stock will rise. That, however, is not a risk. That is known in the financial services industry as "a good thing." Credit quality means that the issuer has to be able to make steady profits and manage those profits wisely if they're going to be able to pay the promised dividend. So, most preferred stockholders look for companies with financial strength before buying their preferred stock. Remember, it's not about growth of profits with preferred stock—it's about the company's ability to pay the promised dividend.

Except when it isn't. As I said, common stock represents the opportunity to make an unknown amount of money should the corporation become the next Microsoft, Coca-Cola, Apple Computer, etc. Preferred stock, on the other hand, is a fixed-income security, which means the income it pays is fixed. So, you might feel pretty smart getting a very likely 6% return every year on your 6% preferred stock, but what if the company pulls a Google on you? The common stock goes from $85 to $750 a share. What would that do for you, as a preferred stockholder?

Probably annoy the heck out of you, since you wouldn't enjoy any of that upside. If you want the chance to ride the upside on common stock, you have to buy a funky type of preferred stock known as convertible preferred stock. This stuff lets an investor exchange one share of preferred stock for a certain number of common shares whenever the investor wants to make the switch. If the convertible preferred stock is convertible into 10 shares of common stock, the convertible preferred stock is usually worth at least whatever 10 shares of common stock are worth. If so, they trade at parity, which means "equal." Just multiply the price of the common stock by the number of shares the investor could convert the preferred into. That gives you the preferred stock's parity price.

So, if the convertible preferred stock were convertible into 10 shares of common stock and the common stock went up to $15 a share, how much would the convertible preferred be worth at parity?

10 X $15, or $150.

Imagine if you could have bought convertible preferred stock in Google. It went public at $85, so maybe each share of preferred was convertible at $100, or into just one share of common stock. Sounds pretty chintzy, but how much was a share of common stock soon worth? Maybe $475. Imagine paying $100 for a preferred stock that is suddenly worth about $475 a share.

That's known technically as a really good thing. So, other types of preferred stock are income investments, while convertible preferred stock is actually growth-and-income. While other types of preferred stock are interest-rate sensitive, convertible preferred stock is not as dependent on interest rates, since its value has that other factor—the market price of the company's common stock.

Finally, while the par value of preferred stock and bonds is meaningful, if you get a test question about the par value of common stock, remember that to an investor the par value of common stock is meaningless. It's just an arbitrary value (1 penny, 1 dollar, no par value) that the lawyers assign in the articles of incorporation. I just pulled out the articles of incorporation for Pass the Test, Inc., and saw that the par value of the 1,000 shares we're authorized to issue to investors is exactly zero. Who came up with that value? The attorney who handled the process of incorporation.

	COMMON	PREFERRED
Ownership stake	X	X
More likely to receive dividends		X
Priority in bankruptcy		X
Growth potential	X	
Voting rights	X	
Stated rate of return		X

Yield, Total Returns

Measuring the return on equity securities really comes down to two concerns: **growth** and **income**. The exam might call growth **capital appreciation** and refer to the income as "dividends" because everything needs to have at least two or three names in this industry. But, whatever we call it, this stuff is simple. If you buy a stock at $10, and a year later it's worth $12, that's capital appreciation or "growth" of 20%. If the stock pays $2 in dividend income after you paid $10, that's a **yield** of 20%. Notice how capital appreciation refers to the stock price rising, while yield just refers to the income you receive compared to what you paid for the stock. So, what if you wanted to factor in the growth in share price plus the dividend? Now, you're talking about **total return**. So, this stock that went up by $2 and also distributed $2 in dividends showed a total return of 40%. Put down $10, receive $2 in dividends and $2 in growth for a "total return" of $4. Compared to the $10, you got back a 40% total return, right?

Remember that dividends are paid quarterly or four times a year. So if the test question says it's a 25-cent quarterly dividend, you may need to annualize it (multiply by 4) to get a $1 annual dividend first.

Annual Dividend divided by the Market Price = YIELD

I would generally expect the exam to test this concept like this:

If the dividend paid on XYZ common stock remains stable while the market price falls, current dividend yield will

A. increase

B. decrease

C. remain stable

D. take a fall

If you were getting $1 for paying $10, that's a yield of 10%. If you get a dollar for paying just $5, that's a much higher yield of 20%. So, the yield would increase as the market price drops, right? As always, if the question says that price goes one way, tell it that yield goes the other way. That's known as an inverse relationship, by the way, like the relationship between your velocity and the time it takes to get where you're going. When one goes up, the other goes down, and vice versa.

Options

Those warrants we talked about gave an investor the right to buy stock at a set price. They were sold to the investor by the issuer/issuing corporation. Maybe Microsoft wants to sell you the ability to buy their stock at $30 a share. You pay maybe $3 a share now for that privilege, and if the stock goes above your purchase price, you'd probably be tickled to death. That's a warrant.

Options, on the other hand, are just little contracts (bets) between two parties not related to the issuing corporation that let the owner buy 100 shares of stock for a set price or sell 100 shares of stock for a set price. The options that give investors the right to buy stock at the strike price are called calls. The options that give investors the right to sell stock at the strike price are called puts, since anything else would have sounded weird. So, if you hold a MSFT Mar 30 call, you have the right to buy 100 shares of Microsoft common stock for $30, no matter how high the stock actually goes. What if it gets stuck at $30, or falls to $20? You bought the wrong call. Maybe you're so ticked about being burned on the calls that, next month, you decide to buy the right to sell Microsoft for $25, figuring it's going to drop to, like $7, and wouldn't it be fun to sell it to some sucker for $25, after buying it for $7? Well, that's what you think when you pay your premium of, say, $250, only the stock doesn't fall that far. It only falls to $26, so, once again, your option expires worthless. I guess I could have come up with an example of somebody making money by purchasing options, but I chose to be realistic instead.

In any case, if you think a stock price is about to rise, you are bullish on the stock. Bulls buy calls. If you think a stock price is about to drop, you are bearish on the stock. Bears buy puts. What if you want to sell an option? That just means you're willing to give somebody the right to buy stock from (call) or the right to sell stock to (put) you because you want that $200, $300, whatever the premium is, and you figure they'll lose the bet and never be able to force you to do anything beyond laugh your way to the bank. What if they win the bet?

That could be very painful. If you gave somebody the right to buy Google at $150 a share, and they paid you $800 for that call option, you probably felt pretty smart taking their bet. See, you'd get $800 per contract, and maybe you sold 100 contracts for $80,000 in premiums. Which would have been great except that Google went up to, say, $350, and the call buyer has the right to buy stock at the strike price. You now have to go buy 10,000 shares of Google for $3.5 million and then turn around and sell them for just $1.5 million. Which explains why many former options traders would now like to know if you'd like fries with your order this evening.

So, if you sold somebody a call, you figured they were wrong. They're a bull—you're a bear. If you sold somebody a put, you figured they were wrong. They're a bear—you're a bull.

Bulls are in a position to buy stock.

Bears are in a position to sell stock.

In a few years, maybe I'll see you for the Series 7, where you'll get maybe 20 questions on options. At that point, I'll slow down and really explain options to you. But, since this is the Series 6, we've probably covered enough on options. Expect somewhere between zero and two questions on the exam.

DEBT SECURITIES

Back to your successful car wash chain. What if you and your buddy need another round of financing but want to keep the profits to yourselves for now? As I mentioned, you could look for investors willing to be loaners rather than owners. How much interest will you have to pay them? Depends on the current interest-rate climate seen through mortgage rates, bank CDs, etc., and, of course, your credit rating. And, the term of the loan—are you borrowing for 90 days, 2 years, 10 years, 30 years, what?

While it might get a little scary owing these investors interest payments every six months, at least you don't have to share profits with them or let them vote. All you have to do is pay the interest on time, return the principal at maturity, and they disappear. If you go this route, you will be using **leverage**, and, frankly, this is the only type of financing I've ever used myself. I figure if I'm really worried about the interest payments, I don't borrow the money. But the last thing I want is a bunch of shareholders telling me what's what and demanding a share of profits. Most mature public companies have issued common stock, various types of preferred stock, and also **debt securities**. The amounts raised by each type of security would be called the company's **capital structure**, by the way. Unlike the preferred and common stockholders, the investors who buy the debt/fixed-income securities are not owners of the company. They're just lenders interested in earning a stream of income and then getting their money back at the end. The most common name for debt securities is **bonds**, which represent loans from investors to the corporation. Investors buy the bonds, and the corporation then pays them interest on the loan and promises to return the principal amount of $1,000 at the end of the term. But, the company takes all the money upfront, paying only the interest payments going forward, until the very last payment comes due—only then would a purchaser of $1 million worth of bonds see the $1 million again.

A bond has a specific value known as either the "par" or the "principal" amount printed right on the face of the certificate. In Series Sixland, bonds have a **par value** of $1,000.

This is the amount an investor will receive along with the very last interest payment from the issuer, on what is known as the **maturity date**. A mortgage will eventually be paid off and so will a bond. We call the day that the last interest and principal payments are made "maturity." At maturity, the bond is all paid up.

So the bond certificate has "$1,000" printed on the face, along with the interest rate the issuer will pay the investor every year. This interest rate could be referred to as the **coupon rate** or **nominal yield**. Don't let the word "nominal" intimidate you. It means "name." Just like "nom de plume" means "pen name," as in "Mark Twain." Or, if you cut your neighbor's grass for a "nominal fee," you might accept payment in the form of a cold beverage—a fee "in name only." Anyway, the nominal yield is named right there on the certificate. If you saved your closing documents on your mortgage, you'll find that you, too, likely have a "nominal rate of interest" fixed on your loan, and then a slightly different actual rate of interest that factors in the closing costs you paid. That also happens with bonds—if the investor pays more than the par value, his yield/interest rate will actually be lower than the nominal rate printed on the bond. We'll get to that in just a second—promise.

So, if a bond pays 8% of the par value, that's $80 in interest income each year. And when it's all over, you get your $1,000 back. Not terribly exciting, but it's kind of fun to watch your money earning money. Common stock might grow more than 8%, but it also might drop 50–100%, and it might take 10 years to realize that you've lost your money and made no return on the stock whatsoever in the meantime. At least a bond keeps spitting out interest payments every six months and always pays you back your principal, except when it doesn't. The 8% is just an example, of course.

Also note that the term **leverage** or "leveraged capital structure" simply means that the corporation has raised money by selling bonds. These companies are more susceptible to rises in interest rates and probably more prone to bankruptcy, too.

Now, many of us are used to being on the borrowing end of a debt. We owe the mortgage company, the automobile financing company, the credit card company, etc. So, we understand what it's like to be a borrower—we always want to pay the lowest rates of interest possible. Well, when a corporation issues bonds, it is simply borrowing money, which is why it likes to pay the lowest rates of interest possible, also. When you apply for a mortgage, the rate you pay is determined by your credit history, your budget, your earnings, and the length of time you want to borrow the money for. Same thing for a corporation—if it has a solid credit history and high income, it gets to borrow at a lower rate. Time is also a factor, as it pays more to borrow for 10 years than to borrow for 3 months, just like you'd pay more for a 30-year mortgage than a 15-year. If it puts up collateral, that can knock the rate down, too, just like your mortgage is offered at a much lower rate than the unsecured borrowing you do through a credit card.

So, it's easy to relate to a borrower. Borrowers want to pay low rates of interest.

The corporations that issue bonds are borrowers trying to borrow at the lowest possible interest rate.

Who's lending them the money? Bond investors. If you buy their bonds, you are loaning the corporation money. Now, what type of interest rate are you hoping to see? The highest one possible, right? Suddenly, you're like the mortgage or credit card company. Somebody owes you money, and the higher the rate of interest, the more money you make. So, there's a natural tension between bond investors and bond issuers. The issuers want to pay, say, zero percent interest. The bond investors want to receive, say, 100% interest. Since both demands are equally absurd, they meet somewhere in the middle, based on how solid the company's credit rating is and where interest rates are in general. If rates are high, bond issuers will pay high rates. Heck, bond rates *are* interest rates, so that's sort of redundant. If you issue a bond, you borrow money. The rate of interest you pay will be in line with other interest rates in the economy.

Interest Rates and Bond Yields

So, interest rates represent what new bonds would have to pay in order to attract new investors. If a bond pays a fixed 8% interest, whenever interest rates change, they will change the bond's market price. When rates go up above 8%, the bond's price will go down, since new bonds would be issued with coupon rates higher than 8%. Investors like high coupon rates. They won't pay as much for an 8% coupon as they will for a 10% coupon. Wouldn't you put your money into the bank CD paying 10% over the one offering 8%?

On the other hand, when rates go down below 8%, the bond's price will go up, since new bonds would be issued with coupon rates lower than 8%. And suddenly this 8% coupon looks excellent. Remember, it's all relative. What is 8% worth? Depends on interest rates. When new debt pays more than 8%, an 8% bond looks bad. But, when new debt pays only 6%, suddenly that same old 8% bond looks terrific. It's all relative—relative to interest rates. You'll need to be able to explain this concept to the investors who buy bond mutual funds from you. "How the heck could my account be down 15% that fast—they're all Government bonds!" someone might politely scream at you one morning.

Interest rates, Charlie. Just like we talked about. Rates up, price down, buddy.

Remember, even though a bond has a par value of $1,000, we don't necessarily expect the bond to trade at $1,000 in the open market. As with a stock, a bond's price fluctuates. Why?

Interest rates.

If a bondholder has a bond that pays a nominal yield or "coupon rate" of 8%, what is the bond worth when interest rates in general climb to 10%? Not as much, right? If you had something that paid you 8%, when you knew you could be receiving more like 10%, how would you feel about the bond?

Not too good.

But, when interest rates fall to 6%, suddenly that 8% bond looks pretty good, right? When we take a bond's price into consideration, we're looking at a concept known as **current yield** (CY). Current yield just takes the annual interest paid by the bond to an investor and divides it by what an investor would have to pay for the bond. If the bond will pay you $80 a year, would you rather put down $1,000 or $800? You'd probably rather only have to put down $800, leaving you with $200 to invest elsewhere.

Current Yield = Annual Interest divided by the Bond Price

It's just how much you get compared to what you put down to get it. In fact, it's the same formula we use for dividend yield, only bonds make interest payments while stocks pay dividends. I would expect the exam to expect you to associate rising interest rates with inflation and falling interest rates with deflation. If a test question asks what happens to bonds during an inflationary period, tell it that yields rise and prices of outstanding bonds drop. During a deflationary period, where consumer prices are dropping, bond yields drop and bond prices rise. Notice that you can memorize what I just told you, or you can go one step further and say, "Oh—of course. Bonds pay a fixed income stream. If consumer prices (CPI) are rising, bonds aren't worth as much, so their market price drops. If consumer prices are falling (deflation), the fixed income stream a bond pays is worth more, meaning it has more purchasing power. Therefore, its market price rises." Be prepared to think creatively and analytically at the testing center. No matter how well prepared you are, the test will still stretch your mind in many painful and unanticipated directions. If you're looking to spit back a bunch of memorized facts, you could be in for a very long and painful 2 hours, 15 minutes.

So, why are interest rates rising in our example above? Must be an inflationary period. As interest rates rise, bond prices drop. The nominal yield of 8% means that investors keep receiving $80 per year in income. But if the bond price drops on the secondary market to $800, the current yield rises to 10%. $80/$800 gives us a current yield of 10%, right? So when interest rates on new bonds are rising, the yields on existing bonds have to rise, too. How can that happen? They begin trading at lower prices. Rates up—price down. A bond trading below the par value is called a **discount bond.**

Of course, whatever can go up can also go down. What happens when interest rates fall? Bond prices rise. If you owned this 8% bond and saw that interest rates have just fallen to 6%, how would you feel about your bond?

Pretty good, right? After all, it pays 2% more than new debt is paying.

Do you want to sell it? Not really. But you might sell it to me if I paid you a premium. If I paid you $1,200 for the $1,000 par value bond, you might be willing to sell it. From my perspective, I see that new debt is only going to pay 6%, which is too low for my needs. Even though I have to pay more than par for your 8% bond, it will all work out if I can get all those interest payments at a higher-than-prevailing rate.

So, we've just pushed the price of the bond up as interest rates went down. Dividing our $80 of annual interest by the $1,200 I put down for the bond gives me a current yield of only 6.7%. That's lower than the coupon rate, and whenever you see a current yield that is lower than the nominal/coupon rate, you know you're looking at a **premium bond**. Remember, the coupon rate doesn't change. Therefore, the only way to get the yield lower than the coupon is for somebody to pay more than par for the bond. Just like the only way to get the yield higher than the coupon is to pay less than par for the bond on the secondary market.

So, if the exam says the coupon or nominal yield is 5%, and the current yield is higher than that—it's a discount bond. Rates went up, knocking the price of this bond down in order to make the yield go up. If the exam says the coupon or nominal yield is 5% and the current yield is less than that—it's a premium bond. Rates dropped, pushing the price of this bond up on the secondary market in order to make the yield go down in line with the current low-interest rate-environment.

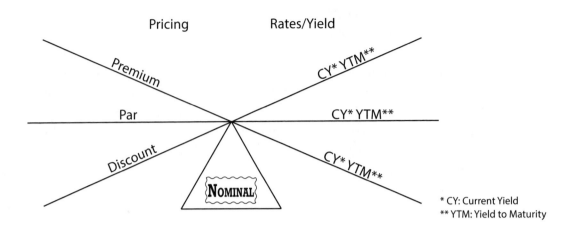

Choosing a bond investment really comes down to this question for the investor—how much of a yield do you want, and how much risk are you willing to take in order to get it? Your customers would generally prefer no-risk, high-yield bonds. They'd probably also prefer a free Lexus and a case of Dom Perignon. Sorry, doesn't work that way. If you buy a safe bond, you get a lower return. If you go for a higher return, you have to buy a bond from an issuer with a shaky credit score. Maybe you compromise by purchasing bonds rated right at the cutoff between **investment grade** and **high yield**. If the exam asks about these credit ratings from **S&P** and **Moody's**, remember that for S&P, the highest rating is AAA, and the lowest investment-grade rating is BBB. Anything below that is attached to a high-yield or "junk" bond. For Moody's, the highest rating is Aaa, with the cut-off called Baa. Anything below either "BBB" from S&P, then, or "Baa" from Moody's, would be issued by a company or municipality with shaky finances. You want to go for a high yield by purchasing a bond on the cheap? Okay, but also ask yourself why that guy was so willing to sell you a bond with "$1,000 par value" printed on it for just $300.

To help with the bond rating, and to make sure the principal can actually be returned at maturity, corporations and municipalities often establish a **sinking fund**, which is an escrow account earning safe little rates of interest. A sinking fund would be invested in guaranteed U.S. Treasury securities primarily, since putting it in the stock market would be really stupid.

When we talk about suitability and clients in more detail we'll mention that many mutual funds would put, say, 80% of their assets into investment-grade bonds and limit their high-yield forays to 20%. That would be conservative, actually. If it were a "High Yield" or "High Income" bond fund, they would focus primarily on bonds rated below BBB/Baa, and they would warn you of the inherent risks there, on top of the interest rate, reinvestment, and other risks we already discussed.

The best way to delve into the risks of holding bonds is to read through several mutual fund prospectuses for bond funds. The risk/return summary is laid out on the first page and is usually just a few paragraphs long. You'll be explaining this stuff to investors in a few weeks or months. Might as well start learning it for yourself.

CREDIT RISK	
STANDARD & POOR'S	**MOODY'S**
AAA	Aaa
AA	Aa
A	A
BBB	Baa
NON-INVESTMENT GRADE, HIGH-YIELD, JUNK	
BB	Ba
etc.	etc.

Types of Corporate Bonds

Which interest rate would be lower: the rate you pay for your home equity line of credit, or the rate you pay for a cash advance on your credit card? Obviously, the home equity loan will charge you a lower rate of interest. Why? Because if you don't pay it back, they'll take your house. What's backing up your cash advance from the credit card company? Nothing but your good name and your credit score. Since there is no collateral on that loan, the interest rate you pay is much higher.

In the world of corporate bonds, we have **secured bonds** that are backed up by specific assets, collateral. This way, if the borrowing corporation can't pay the interest and principal, the bondholders can make a claim on the assets. An equipment trust certificate is backed up by airplanes or railroad cars. A mortgage bond is backed up by real estate. A collateral trust certificate is backed up by a portfolio of securities. In all cases, these bonds would offer a lower interest rate compared to the issuer's same bonds that have no specific assets backing them up.

If we buy a bond backed simply by the full faith and credit of an issuer, we are buying a **debenture**. Debenture holders are general creditors. If the company is forced into liquidation, debenture holders have a claim that is lower than that of secured bondholders. Therefore, debentures pay a higher coupon/nominal yield than secured bonds, since they carry more risk.

"Sub-" means "below," as in "submarine" for "below the water," or "subterranean" for "below the ground." **Subordinated debentures** have a claim on corporate assets that is below that of regular ol' debentures when it comes to liquidating a company and paying out money to the bondholders. Since these bonds are riskier, they pay a higher coupon than debentures or secured bonds. Perhaps you've heard of an "80/20" mortgage? The lender uses 80% of the appraised value of your house to get you a decent interest rate, but when they make the second loan using the final 20% of market value, the rate jumps up considerably. If you're maxing out your borrowing, you pay a higher interest rate on that second loan that really stretches your budget. Since the lender is taking on more risk, they demand a higher yield.

By the way, what about stockholders? Well, if the company goes into bankruptcy and has to be liquidated, stockholders are below all three types of bondholders. Preferred is ahead of common, but that's about the extent of their bragging rights.

So, if a company goes belly up, interested parties would see that their claims on assets rank in the following order of priority:

1. Secured creditors
2. Debentures/general creditors
3. Subordinated debentures
4. Preferred stock
5. Common stock

Then, there are **convertible bonds**, which can be converted into a certain number of shares of the issuer's common stock. Bonds have a par value of $1,000, so the investor applies the $1,000 of par value toward purchasing the company's stock at a pre-set price. When a convertible bond is issued, it is given a conversion price. If the conversion price is $40, that means that the bond is convertible into common stock at $40. In other words, the investor can use the par value of her bond towards the purchase of the company's common stock at a set price of $40.

Bonds have a par value of $1,000, so if she applies that $1,000 toward the purchase of stock at $40 per share, how many shares would she be able to buy? 25 shares, right? $1,000 of par value divided by $40 per share of stock tells us that each bond can be converted into 25 shares of common stock. In other words, the two securities trade at a 25:1 relationship, since the big one (bond) can be turned into 25 of the little ones (stock). The company sets the conversion price; they have no control over where their common stock trades on the open market, right? If the price goes up, the value of the convertible bonds goes up. Just like if the price goes down, that drags down the market value of the bonds.

So how much is this particular bond worth at any given moment? Whatever 25 shares of the common stock are worth. Just take par and divide it by the conversion price to find out how many shares of common stock the bond could be converted into. In this case it's 25 shares, since $1,000 would go exactly that far when purchasing stock priced at $40 a share.

Par *divided by* Conversion price = # of common shares

So how much is the bond worth?

Depends. How much are 25 shares of the common stock worth? Since the bond could always be converted into 25 shares, it generally has to be worth whatever 25 shares of the common stock are worth. If the common stock price goes up, so does the price of the bond. If the common stock falls, so does the price of the bond. We call this relationship "parity," which is just a fancy word for "same" or "equal." Since one's price depends on the other, the two should have a price that is at "parity."

So, if a bond is convertible into 25 shares of IXR common stock, and IXR is trading @50, what is the bond's price at parity?

25 X $50 = $1,250.

And if the common stock went up to $60 a share, the bond should be worth 25 times that number, right?

25 X $60 = $1,500.

If the exam feels like playing hardball, it might expect you to know that tying the value of the bond to the company's stock makes its price less sensitive to interest rates. I mean, I don't care how high rates are going; if I can turn my bond into 10 shares of Google, with Google common stock trading at $450 a share, I'm as happy as a frog in milk.

U.S. Treasury Securities

By far, the safest debt on earth is the stuff issued by the U.S. Government's Treasury Department. So, if you buy a bill, note, or bond from Uncle Sam, you do not have to worry about credit/default risk. You're going to get your interest checks on time, and you're going to get your money back at maturity. You just aren't going to get rich in the process. In fact, you usually need to be rich already to get excited about U.S. Government debt, but that's another matter.

For the test, just remember that U.S. Government/Treasury debt is the safest debt known to humankind. Safe and boring. Basically, there are **T-bills**, **T-notes**, **T-bonds**, and **Treasury STRIPS**, depending on your time horizon. If you have a short time horizon, you buy the T-bills, which mature in one year or less. Currently, the three- and the six-month T-bills are what most investors purchase, but that could change whenever the Treasury Department decides to change it, just as they stopped issuing 30-year T-bonds a while back and then started up again. T-bills pay the face amount, and investors try to buy them for the steepest discount possible. If the T-bill pays out $1,000, you'd rather get it for $950 than $965, right? In the first case you make $50 interest; in the second case you make only $35. So, as always, as interest rates rise, the price of T-bills falls, and vice versa. In a low-interest rate-environment, the price you'd have to pay for a T-bill would be annoyingly close to the face amount you'll be getting back in three or six months. The minimum denomination for a T-bill, T-note, or T-bond is $100, by the way. If the exam says your investor is primarily concerned with interest rate risk, remember that Treasuries all have no default risk, but do carry various levels of interest rate risk. T-bills, being extremely short-term, are the best place for this investor.

If the investor has a longer time horizon, say two to ten years, there are T-notes available with 2- to 10-year maturities. Unlike the T-bill which simply puts back more money into your bank account than it took out three or six months earlier, T-notes actually pay interest every six months (semi-annually), returning the principal with the last interest check. T-bonds have maturities as long as 30 years. If you want a higher yield, you buy the longer-term T-bond, but you take on more interest rate risk, as we discussed. T-bonds are just like T-notes, only longer.

Treasury STRIPS don't make interest payments to investors. Instead, the investor buys the thing for, say, $650. Eleven years later the STRIP pays out $1,000. The difference of $350 is treated as interest income, but you don't touch a dime of it until maturity. Since it makes zero coupon payments, the creative types named this category of bonds "zero-coupon bonds." Zero coupons are a little funky. The investor doesn't receive any interest income until the thing matures, but the IRS—who is here to help—goes ahead and taxes the interest the investor hasn't received every year, anyway. If you were making $350 over an 11-year period, the tax collectors figure you're "earning" $31.81 each year, so they tax you on that amount each year. Some call that "phantom tax exposure," which is a pretty good name for it.

So, why would somebody buy a zero coupon such as a STRIP? Well, if these things pay no interest every six months, the investor would have nothing to reinvest every six months at varying rates. Remember "reinvestment risk"? Sure you do, we just talked about it. Okay, well zero coupons allow investors to avoid "reinvestment risk," should the exam feel like asking. They also require a smaller investment as opposed to paying the full $1,000 for a bond that will then pay interest to the investor.

The interest income received on T-bills, T-notes, T-bonds, and STRIPS is taxed as ordinary income, but only at the federal level—states and local governments can't touch the interest you receive from the U.S. Treasury, which is probably why residents of Maryland, New York, and other high-tax states love to buy them. What's not to love about securities that are safer than taking a shower, are only taxed at the federal level, and can be purchased online (www.treasurydirect.gov) with *no commissions or fees, period?* I mean, I'm not trying to create my whole retirement nest egg with these ridiculously safe things, but I'm definitely using them for part of the nest. Investors who want "capital preservation" generally buy Treasuries, since the chance of default is so low it's not even worth thinking about. These investors might not make huge returns on their T-notes or T-bonds, but they'll also know their money will be there when they need it, which is a lot more than you can say for the stock market, right?

NON-MARKETABLE GOVERNMENT SECURITIES

EE and HH Savings Bonds, I-bonds

Series EE bonds are purchased at a discount and redeemed at their much higher face value at maturity. The denominations are as low as $50 and as high as $10,000. The tax on the accrued interest can be paid annually or deferred until maturity. For those who really like to avoid tax, the EE bonds can be turned into HH bonds at maturity, allowing the tax to be deferred a little longer.

Series HH bonds can be "purchased" only by trading in Series EE bonds at maturity. These things pay semi-annual interest rather than being issued at a deep discount. The maturity is 10 years, but the investor can redeem them at face value at any time. Remember that when things are no longer issued, they are not removed from the face of the earth. So, the exam may want you to know a little bit about savings bonds, since people may have questions about them when they meet with you.

An **I-bond** is issued by the U.S. Treasury, which means it's absolutely safe and also exempt from state and local income taxes. An I-bond pays a guaranteed rate that is fixed but also pays more interest income when inflation rises. The semiannual inflation rate announced in May is the change between the CPI (inflation) figures from the preceding September and March; the inflation rate announced in November is the change between the CPI figures from the preceding March and September. So, since they adjust the interest income to levels of inflation, there's no default risk and no real purchasing power risk, either. There are also tax advantages. First, the interest isn't paid out; it's added to the value of the bond. You can, therefore, defer the taxes until you cash in the bond. And, if you use the proceeds for qualified education costs in the same calendar year that you redeem the bonds, the interest is tax-*free*. The investor does not even have to declare that the I-bonds will be used for educational purposes when she buys them. As long as she uses the proceeds in the same year she redeems the bonds—and meets the other requirements of the Education Savings Bond Program—the interest is tax-free.

Remember that EE, HH, and I-bonds are "non-marketable," which means they cannot be traded. They are *savings* bonds. T-bills, T-notes, T-bonds, and Treasury STRIPS are all negotiable, which means they have a liquid secondary market.

Municipal Bonds

A "municipality" is any state or local government, including school districts, water and sewer districts, park districts, sports authorities, what have you. States and local governments borrow money to build roads, schools, and convention centers. Remember that borrowing money is accomplished by issuing bonds to investors. Since these bonds are issued by municipal authorities, the creative types long ago named them **municipal bonds**. Municipal bonds pay interest that is tax-free to investors. Since the interest income you receive on your municipal bond is tax-free, the city or state issuer can pay you less interest than a corporation would have to offer— and you can still come out ahead. Yes, a 5% yield on a municipal bond would be much *higher* than a 7% corporate yield for someone in the 30% tax bracket. You get taxed at your ordinary income rate on corporate bond interest. For municipal securities, the federal government generally does not tax the interest paid to the investor.

What about the states and local governments—can they tax me?

Great question, and, yes, they can. It depends on where you live. If you live in Kansas but buy a bond issued by some out-of-state government, Kansas can tax you. If you bought a municipal security issued by the state of Kansas or any local government within the state, the test wants you to assume the state of Kansas won't tax that interest. Same for the local government—if you live in Topeka and buy a bond issued by Wichita, the federal government won't tax the municipal security interest, the state of Kansas won't tax the interest since both cities are in that state, but the city of Topeka could tax the bond interest since you didn't do them any favors. So, in order to receive interest checks exempt from federal, state, and local government taxation, a resident of Topeka, Kansas, could buy a municipal bond issued by Topeka, Kansas.

SITUATION	FEDERAL	STATE	LOCAL
Resident of Topeka, KS, buys a Toledo, Ohio, municipal bond	EXEMPT	TAXABLE	TAXABLE
Resident of Topeka, KS, buys a Wichita, KS, municipal bond	EXEMPT	EXEMPT	TAXABLE
Resident of Topeka, KS, buys a Topeka, KS, municipal bond	EXEMPT	EXEMPT	EXEMPT

Municipal Yields vs. Corporate Yields

If there are two triple-A rated bonds, both with 10-year maturities, should the investor buy the municipal bond paying 5% or the corporate bond paying a 7% nominal yield? All depends on the investor's tax bracket. For high-tax-bracket investors, put them in the municipal security more often than not. For the low-bracket investor, corporate bonds will end up paying more, since these investors are only coughing up a small percentage of the bond interest to Uncle Sam. Those are general statements. To calculate precisely which bond actually yields more, we would need some quick math. Sorry about that. To compare a corporate yield to a municipal yield, take the corporate bond yield and multiply it by the percentage the investor keeps after tax (100% minus tax bracket). If you're in the 30% bracket, you keep 70% of the bond interest paid to you. If the corporate bond pays 10%, you keep 70% of that, or 7% as your **after-tax yield**. Bond pays you $100, Uncle Sam takes $30 and lets you keep 70% after-tax. That's your "after-tax yield" or your "tax-free equivalent" yield, meaning that the 10% corporate (taxable) yield is equivalent to a hypothetical 7% municipal security yield.

If they give you the municipal security yield and want you to figure the **tax-equivalent yield**, just DIVIDE by the same 100% minus the investor's tax bracket. Take an 8% municipal security yield and divide it by 100% minus the investor's tax bracket. If she's in a 25% bracket, divide .08 by .75 and you'll see that the corporate bond would only be equivalent to this 8% municipal security yield if the corporate bond were yielding 10.67%. That's the municipal security's "tax-equivalent yield," meaning it's equal to a corporate bond yielding 10.67%.

If the customer is thinking about a corporate bond that's similar in quality to this municipal security, the corporate bond has to pay at least 10.67%; otherwise, recommend the municipal security.

Municipal securities backed by the issuer's "full faith and credit" are called **general obligation bonds**. They require voter approval before getting issued, because they are backed by taxes that voters pay to the municipal government/taxing authority. The bonds that are just backed up by the revenues generated from the toll road or convention center being built with the proceeds...guess what we call them? **Revenue bonds**. The test might call the revenue used to pay bondholders **user fees** or **user charges.** Either way, these are not backed by the full faith and credit of the issuer and sometimes there's, like, no revenue to pay you back.

Oops. That's why revenue bonds usually yield more than general obligation bonds. Both, however, are municipal bonds that pay tax-exempt interest at the federal level. Notice how we said nothing about capital gains? If you sell a municipal bond for more than you bought it, first, congratulations, and, second, don't forget your pals and mine at the IRS. The interest income may be tax-exempt, but capital gains are still taxable as—get this—capital gains. That's why a municipal bond mutual fund usually pays dividends that are tax-exempt at the federal level but capital gains distributions that are taxable at capital gains rates.

Don't worry, we'll go over the taxation again before this book is over. Oh yeah, for whatever reason, the exam outline has always placed **industrial revenue bonds** or "IDRs" on it. These bonds build facilities that are then leased long-term to a corporation. Remember that the interest and principal are only as dependable as the corporation leasing the facility from the municipality, so it's their credit rating that S&P/Moody's focus on. Also, these bonds might not get the favorable tax-exempt treatment most municipal bonds offer, just to keep things nice and simple.

Mortgage-Backed Securities

The more you learn about debt securities, the more you suspect that just about any time somebody owes money to someone, a debt security could probably be structured on the future payment of that loan. In the sophisticated world of Wall Street and international finance, the smart people in the room routinely create debt securities backed up by assets a regular guy like me would have never thought of all by himself. For example, the way my Uncle Stash—God rest his soul—would buy up bad debts at a discount around the old neighborhood is quite similar to an asset-backed debt security backed by a company's accounts receivable. If a company has, say, $100 million in accounts receivable owed by customers and would rather get most of that money right now in cash, maybe they'll sell those receivables for $85 million and let somebody like Uncle Stash go around collecting the full $100 million, keeping the difference for their trouble. Debt securities can be backed up by accounts receivable, inventory, student loans, etc. And, they can be backed up by mortgages.

To create a **mortgage-backed security**, mortgages are pooled together, packaged, and sold to investors, who then receive interest and principal payments from that pool of mortgages. Interest comes in regularly, since every month mortgage holders pay their mortgage. Principal is returned gradually until, all of a sudden, it's paid off in full. When interest rates drop, homeowners refinance and suddenly return the principal all at once. This is not great for the investor, who usually reinvests at a lower interest rate. The exam may call this risk **prepayment risk**.

If the investor buys a GNMA (**Government National Mortgage Association**) **pass-through certificate**, she buys a mortgage-backed security with mortgages all guaranteed by the United States Treasury. If she buys an **FNMA** or **FHLMC mortgage-backed security**, she has to remember that the U.S. Treasury probably would—but does not have to—bail out those two quasi-agencies if necessary.

GNMAs would typically yield more than Treasuries, and are considered safe, income-producing securities. We used to say pretty much the same about FNMA and FHLMC, but, well, things change.

CMOs

A CMO, or **collateralized mortgage obligation**, is a very complicated "derivative" that gets its value from underlying mortgages or mortgage-backed securities. The key word for a CMO is "**tranche**." Investors purchase certain tranches, which receive interest regularly as mortgage payments are made from homeowners. Principal is returned to just one tranche at a time, so the earliest maturing tranches are up for receiving all of their principal first. The exam could say that the early tranches have the most "prepayment risk." That's the risk that interest rates will drop and homeowners will refinance, returning the principal suddenly and without warning. It would seem way over-the-top for the Series 6 to drill down on CMOs, but these FINRA exams have a habit of going over the top. Since they're on the exam outline, we had to bring them up. But we're not going to discuss them in great detail. We'll simply throw out some bullet points and hope that A) they don't show up on the test or B) if they do, you'll be able to recall them and get the question right:

- PAC stands for "planned amortization class"
- PACs are protected from prepayment risk and extension risk
- TAC stands for "targeted amortization class"
- TACs present more extension risk (the risk that principal will be paid back too slowly)
- TACs generally yield more than PACs

REMIC

The abbreviation "REMIC" stands for "Real Estate Mortgage Investment Conduit." A **REMIC** is another type of mortgage-backed pass-through vehicle. What separates it from a CMO is that REMICs offer mortgage pools separated into different risk classes, not just different maturity classes.

Money Market Securities

The money market just refers to debt securities (no stock) set to mature in one year or less. Safe, liquid instruments. If the investor has a short time horizon because she's about to buy a house in the next 6–9 months, put her money in the money market. She'll get back what she put in, plus a little interest income along the way. Money market funds simply pay whatever the short-term interest rates happen to be. Whatever the rates are on T-bills and bank CDs, that's about what you'll get in the money market, since T-bills and CDs are both **money market instruments**.

Municipal securities pay tax-exempt interest, so a tax-exempt money market fund would be buying short-term debt securities issued by municipalities. When cities and school districts borrow long-term, we call those things "bonds." When they borrow short-term, we call the instruments "anticipation notes." There are **TAN**s, BANs, RANs, and TRANs (**tax anticipation notes**, bond anticipation notes, revenue anticipation notes, tax *and* revenue anticipation notes). If the city is about to collect taxes in a few months, why wait? Why not issue a Tax Anticipation Note and get their hands on the money right now?

When corporations borrow short-term, we call what they issue **commercial paper**. Commercial paper is probably the main ingredient of most money market mutual funds. It's just a short-term corporate IOU. Spot us $99 million today, and we'll give you back $100 million in 270 days. Seriously.

The CDs that you buy at the bank are just longer-term deposits that pay a higher rate than your savings account. You can't sell your CD deposit to somebody else, and if you take the money out early, you'll wish you hadn't. Well, **negotiable CDs** or "Jumbos" are purchased in denominations from $100,000 to several million. These things are negotiable, meaning you can sell them to somebody else. But, they're not fully insured by the FDIC. Why would you want a CD not fully insured by the FDIC—wouldn't that be riskier?

Exactly—which is why it would pay a higher yield.

As opposed to just walking into a local bank and accepting the yields they're currently offering on their certificates of deposit, investors who purchase **brokered CDs** open their portfolio up to yields offered by banks all across the country. A brokered CD account would also provide liquidity for the investor since he could ask the broker/registered representative to sell the CD on the secondary market as opposed to taking an early withdrawal penalty from a bank. Assuming the CDs are all FDIC insured (up to $250,000), investors can put a substantial amount of money into brokered CD accounts and receive FDIC insurance on each individual certificate of deposit in the portfolio. All without opening up accounts at dozens of different banks to avoid exceeding the $250,000 FDIC coverage. Of course, there are fees, and these work pretty much like brokered mortgages—the interest rate you receive is a little bit less favorable after the broker takes his cut. Although most CDs are short-term, there are also long-term certificates of deposit with maturities as long as perhaps 20 years. Although brokered CDs can be a great option for many investors, some investors have been shafted by brokers who put them into 20-year CDs which then led to large losses when the investors needed their cash. As one might imagine, these long-term CDs may have limited or even no liquidity and investors can actually lose money by selling these things on the secondary market. Also, the interest payments on long-term CDs are often complex and explained in fine print few investors understand. Broker-dealers and registered representatives selling these long-term CDs need to be sure that investors understand how these products differ from traditional bank CDs and must disclose all potential risks. Higher yields on the one hand, but the secondary market for the products might not be as liquid as one would hope—suddenly, rather than sacrificing the interest on a bank CD, the individual could actually lose principal. I don't know about you, but "losing money" and "CDs" really don't go together in my mind. The regulators tend to have similar difficulty squaring the two in their own.

Finally, a **banker's acceptance** (BA) facilitates foreign trade. Somebody imported $50 million worth of rice but didn't feel like paying for it upfront, so their bank issued a letter of credit to let the other side letting them know that payment is guaranteed by the bank. Now, the loan becomes a security that you buy at a discount, receiving the higher face amount, usually in no more than 270 days.

MUTUAL FUNDS

So, when issuers borrow long-term, we call that the "capital market." When they borrow for one year or less, we just call it what it is—the *money* market.

Imagine what it's like to let a perfect stranger come into your home and ask you a bunch of awkward personal questions about your finances, health problems, credit card debt, you name it. As if trusting this person weren't hard enough, he is also asking you to understand all the different investment options available and all of their implications. How do you decide how much risk to take? How do you do an accurate comparison of all the sales charges and operating expenses for a mutual fund or annuity, knowing that the sales representative helping you with your decision will only get paid if you invest through him, and will get paid more if you're willing to spend more?

That's pretty much what it's like to be your customer, so let's take a look at things from their perspective. They meet with you, maybe at the kitchen table, and you all share a cup of coffee or maybe a cold drink depending on the time of year and their willingness to be nice to a salesperson. You ask them to bare their soul concerning how much money they make, how much credit card debt they've amassed at this point, how far they've stretched the equity in their home in a vain attempt to cover that foolish credit card debt, and how miserably they've failed to save over the years. Then, you pull out a slick, colorful catalog of various mutual funds they can choose from. First, they don't know a mutual fund from a hole in the ground. Second, they're even less curious about mutual funds than the average Series 6 candidate, which is frightening. And, third, they don't understand half of what you're saying about 12b-1 fees, expense ratios, Morningstar ratings, and contingent deferred sales charges. Even before they settle on a particular fund from a particular family, they have to decide on the following *categories* of mutual funds:

Domestic Equity Funds
- Small Cap Growth
- Small Cap Value
- Small Cap Blend
- Mid-Cap Growth
- Mid-Cap Value
- Mid-Cap Blend
- Large Cap Growth
- Large Cap Value
- Large Cap Blend
- Specialty—natural resources
- Specialty—real estate
- Specialty—communications
- Specialty—technology
- Specialty—financial services
- Specialty—utilities
- Specialty—healthcare

Balanced Funds
- Target-Date
- World Allocation

- Convertibles
- Moderate Allocation
- Conservative Allocation

International Stock Funds
- Specialty—Precious Metals
- Latin America Stock
- Diversified Emerging Markets
- Foreign Small/Mid Growth
- Foreign Small/Mid Value
- Foreign Small/Mid Blend
- Foreign Large Cap Growth
- Foreign Large Cap Value
- Foreign Large Cap Blend

Fixed-Income Funds
- High-Yield Bond
- Emerging Markets Bond
- Short-Term Bond
- Short-Term Government
- Intermediate-Term Bond
- Intermediate-Term Government
- Long-Term Bond
- Long-Term Government
- Inflation-Protected Bond

Municipal Bond Funds
- High-Yield Muni
- Short-Term Muni
- Intermediate-Term Muni
- Long-Term Muni

Money Market
- Taxable
- Tax-Exempt

We haven't even begun to show the investor all the different names of funds from different fund families—the above represent just *categories* under which most funds could be placed. Do they want the Fidelity Intermediate-Term Municipal Bond Fund or the Intermediate Tax-Exempt Bond Fund from T. Rowe Price? Which of the 29 domestic stock funds that you sell would they like to choose this evening?

Since mutual fund investing can be extremely baffling to an investor, FINRA insists that you be able to help your clients sort it out.

The Mutual Fund Concept

First of all, what is a mutual fund? Think of a mutual fund as a big investment portfolio that can serve up as many slices as investors care to buy. Investors send in money to buy slices of the big portfolio; the fund uses the money to buy ingredients, like KKD, MSFT, and SBUX. When an investor sends in, say, $10,000, the portfolio gets bigger, but it also gets cut up into more slices—however many she is buying with her $10,000. That way each slice stays the same size. The only way for the slices to get bigger and become more valuable is when the securities in the portfolio pay income, go up in market value, or both. And, nobody is guaranteeing that your shares/slices of the mutual fund portfolio will become more valuable. Even though the portfolio is diversified and run by a professional, it is not uncommon to see mutual funds lose 1/3 or 1/2 of their value very quickly. It probably happens more often to investors buying two or three stocks in their "trading accounts," but, still, with so many thousands of mutual funds out there, please, understand that your job of recommending the products is a very big one. Some of these things can turn out to be disastrous for your customers, and some of your customers are friends and family. Not that you would find it any easier running into a customer you didn't much like after helping him lose half his 401(k).

Right?

Now, couldn't an investor bypass the mutual fund and just buy stocks and bonds in whatever companies or governments he chooses? Sure, but most people refuse to change the oil in their car—why would they suddenly become do-it-yourselfers with six- and seven-figure retirement nest eggs? Takes a lot of work to decide which stocks or bonds to purchase. If you only have $400 to invest, you can't take a meaningful position in any company's stock, and even if you tried, you'd end up owning just *one* company's stock. Remember that "non-systematic risk" we discussed, the risk of owning just a few stocks? We said that diversification would protect against that risk, and mutual funds own stocks and bonds from many different issuers. Also, the portfolio is run by professionals who know when it's time to rebalance the portfolio as sure as the crew at JiffyLube knows when it's time to rotate the tires and replace the filters.

ADVANTAGES OF MUTUAL FUND INVESTING

The exam may bring up the many advantages of mutual fund investing over picking stocks and bonds individually, so let's take a look:

- Investment decisions made by a professional portfolio manager
- Ease of diversification
- Ability to liquidate a portion of the investment without losing diversification
- Simplified tax information (Form 1099-DIVs make tax prep easier)
- Simplified record keeping (rather than getting 50 annual reports from 50 companies, you get two reports per year from one mutual fund)
- Ease of purchase and redemption of securities
- Automatic reinvestments of capital gains and income distributions at NAV
- Safekeeping of portfolio securities

Most of the above bullet points are self-explanatory, but let's add some clarification, anyway. The first point is probably the main reason people buy mutual funds—no way are they willing to try this stuff at home. They have no knowledge of stocks, bonds, taxation, etc., and they have even less interest in learning. Let a professional portfolio manager—often an entire *team* of portfolio managers—decide what to buy and when to buy and sell it. As we mentioned, it's tough to have your own diversified portfolio in individual stocks and bonds because a few hundred or thousand dollars will only buy a few shares of stock or a few bonds issued by just a few companies. Any one company could go belly up, and most investors don't have the emotional capacity to withstand a $10,000 investment that drops to zero when the company declares bankruptcy. On the other hand, a mutual fund would usually hold stock in, say, 50 or more companies, and their bond portfolios are also diversified. Therefore, even with the smallest amount of money accepted by the fund, the investor is immediately diversified. The exam calls this the "undivided interest concept." That just means that your $50 owns a piece of all the ingredients in the portfolio, just as the rich guy's $1 million does. Yes, you own a much smaller piece, but you're also just as diversified as the rich guy is—you both own your percentage of everything inside the portfolio. You both have an undivided interest in all securities owned by the fund. Notice that another bullet point said, "Ability to liquidate a portion of the investment without losing diversification." See, if you own 100 shares of IBM, MSFT, and GE, what are you going to do when you need $5,000 to cover an emergency? If you sell a few shares of each, you'll pay three separate commissions. If you sell 100 shares of any one stock, your diversification is seriously reduced. With a mutual fund, you redeem a certain number of shares and remain just as diversified as you were before the sale. And, you can usually redeem/sell your shares without getting hit up for any fees.

What exactly do we mean by "diversification"? As the FINRA exam outline indicates, mutual funds can diversify their holdings by:

- Industries
- Types of investment instruments
- Variety of securities issuers
- Geographic areas

If it's a stock fund, it is basically a growth fund, a value fund, an income fund, or some combination thereof. No matter what the objective, the fund will usually purchase stocks from issuers across many different industries. In a mutual fund prospectus you'll often find a pie chart that shows what percentage of assets is tied up in a particular industry. Maybe it's 3% in telecommunications, 10% retail, 1.7% healthcare, etc. That way if it's a lousy year for telecommunications or retail, the fund won't get crushed the way a small investor who owns only one telecomm company's and one retailer's stock or bonds would. A bond fund can be diversified among investment instruments. That means they buy some debentures, some secured bonds, some convertible bonds, some zero coupons, some mortgage-backed securities, and even a few money market instruments to be on the safe side. Even if the fund did not spread their investments across many different industries (telecomm, pharmaceutical, retail, etc.) and chose instead to focus on just a few industries, they would still purchase securities from a variety of issuers. So, if they like retail, they can still buy stock in a variety of companies—Walmart, Target, Sears, Nordstrom, Home Depot, etc. And, since any geographic area could be hit by an economic slump, a tsunami, or both, most funds will spread their holdings among different geographic areas. I mean, the Pacific Rim countries sure look promising, but I don't want all my holdings in companies from Japan, Taiwan, and Singapore.

If the exam is in an especially mean-spirited mood, it might require you to regurgitate the definition of a **diversified fund**. Let's go to the most important document on mutual funds, the Investment Company Act of 1940, which defines a diversified fund like so:

> "Diversified company" means a management company which meets the following requirements: At least 75 per centum of the value of its total assets is represented by cash and cash items (including receivables), Government securities, securities of other investment companies, and other securities for the purposes of this calculation limited in respect of any one issuer to an amount not greater in value than 5 per centum of the value of the total assets of such management company and to not more than 10 per centum of the outstanding voting securities of such issuer.

So, how does the "Act of 1940" then define a "**non-diversified company**"?

> "Non-diversified company" means any management company other than a diversified company.

Ouch. That just means that if the fund wants to promote itself as being "diversified," it has to meet the definition—on 75% of the portfolio, no more than 5% of its assets are in any one company, and they don't own more than 10% of any company's outstanding shares. What happens if the mutual fund allocates exactly 5% of its assets to XYZ common stock, and then XYZ rises so much that the investment now represents more than 5% of assets? Does the fund have to sell off some shares? No. They just don't buy any more XYZ at this point. If the fund doesn't feel like meeting the definition under the 75-5-10 test it will simply have to refer to itself as a "non-diversified fund." Also, if the board of directors wanted to change the fund from being diversified to non-diversified, or vice versa, that would require a shareholder vote.

Many students seem miffed that I don't buy a lot of mutual funds, myself. That's because I like to own something more tangible than a "proportionate share of an investment company portfolio." I like to own a percentage of particular companies of my own choosing, especially companies with locations here in Chicago, so that I can drive by an actual place called Abbott Labs, Northern Trust, Boeing, Allstate, or Walmart and know that I own a little piece of that company's profits. I'm also willing to do a little research myself. Unfortunately, I end up getting proxy (voting) materials and annual reports from, like, 20 different companies. And, keeping track of all the dividends I've received from the various sources is slightly annoying. With a mutual fund, I'd get one 1099-DIV that would keep track of all the dividends and capital gains distributions, and I'd also get just one semi-annual report and one annual report from the fund. But, I'd have to give up maybe 1.5% a year in operating expenses, and over 20–40 years that really adds up to a lot more than the meager commissions I pay to purchase and occasionally sell shares of stock. Just something to think about, something that might help you understand mutual funds, and their differences from individual stocks, a little better. It's not a slam against mutual funds. For most retail investors, mutual funds are going to provide the best investment vehicle.

TYPES OF MUTUAL FUNDS

We already took a look at the overwhelming array of mutual funds available. Now, let's get into the nitty-gritty.

EQUITY FUNDS

You probably won't be surprised to learn that the primary focus of **equity funds** is to invest in equity securities. Might have been simpler to just call them "stock funds," but that wouldn't sound as fancy and would, therefore, make them harder to sell. **Growth funds** invest in companies that appear likely to grow their profits faster than competitors and/or the overall stock market. These stocks usually cost a lot compared to the profits that they might or might not have at this point. In other words the market price compared to the earnings is very high. What should we call the comparison between price to earnings?

How about the "price-to-earnings" ratio? The "p/e ratio" just compares how high the stock price is to the earnings per share. A share of stock is just a slice of the company's profit pie—how much of the profits or "earnings" belong to each slice of the pie? That's the earnings per share. The question is, how many times the earnings per share are you willing to pay for the stock? If you're willing to pay high "p/e ratios," you're a growth investor. Also note that dividend income, if any, would be secondary to the fund's goal of finding growth opportunities. In other words, if your investor is seeking income, by definition, she doesn't want growth funds.

What if you prefer to buy stocks trading at low price-to-earnings ratios? You're looking for *value*, so the industry decided to call you a value investor. **Value funds** seek out companies trading for much less than the portfolio management team decides they're actually worth. GM is struggling even more than most auto manufacturers as I write this witty monologue. But, if a value fund thinks the stock is worth a lot more than folks realize, they'll snap it up now at a low price-to-earnings multiple and wait for the turnaround that inconveniently hasn't happened yet. The exam might say that value funds buy stocks in established companies that are currently out of favor. Or, a test question writer might want you to declare that value funds "seek to purchase stocks trading below their estimated intrinsic values." Right—they like stocks trading cheaper than they ought to be. Since the share price is depressed while the dividend keeps getting paid, value stocks tend to have high dividend yields. Therefore, they are considered more conservative than growth stocks. What if you just can't make up your mind between a growth fund and a value fund? Luckily, there are funds that blend both styles of investing, and the industry cleverly calls these **blend funds**. They would be a little more aggressive than "value funds" and a little less volatile than "growth funds." The test might also bring up "core" or "blend/core" funds. If the question uses the dubious phrase "middle of the road approach," it is talking about a blend/core fund. These funds are not purely growth or purely value. They may also blend blue-chip stock with more speculative small cap investments. The idea is to allow investors to get a diversified investment that can also maximize their growth potential. Investors should remember, however, that diversification is just one risk management technique—the funds are still subject to all the investment risks we looked at earlier.

If your investor's objective is to receive income from equities, the industry would be happy to sell her an **equity income fund**. Believe it or not, what these funds do is buy equities that provide dependable income. While a growth fund would not look for dividend income at all, dividend income is the main reason that an equity income fund would purchase a particular stock. You would probably see oil companies, utility companies, and drug companies in the typical equity income fund portfolio. Receiving dividends tends to reduce the volatility of an investment, so equity income funds are lower risk than equity growth funds. Also, companies that pay dividends are paying them out of actual profits, which means the stock is not completely speculative; it has a value that can be determined. I mean, if a stock is in a company with little revenue and no profits, the market price is based almost entirely on speculation, while shares of Starbucks or Walmart trade at some multiple to the company's profits. As I write this, shares of SBUX trade at a much higher multiple than Walmart, but that makes sense; the market simply expects Starbucks to open a lot more stores over the next few decades than Walmart, as both companies' business plans would probably confirm.

What if you can't decide between a mutual fund family's growth funds and its income funds? Chances are they'll be happy to sell you a **growth and income fund**. A growth and income fund buys stocks in companies expected to grow their profits and also in companies that pay dependable, respectable dividends. Or, maybe the same company offers both a steady dividend and the prospect of future growth. Either way, since they've added the income component, growth & income funds would have lower volatility than growth funds. So, from highest to lowest volatility, we would find growth, then growth & income, and then equity income funds. I have a catalog from one of the largest mutual fund families in the world which puts them in exactly that order, and even uses the color red for the highest volatility—growth—as in, "Warning! This stuff can jump up and down in a hurry."

That same catalog places **balanced funds** in a lower volatility category than growth, growth & income, and equity income funds. Why? Because a balanced fund keeps a large percentage of its assets in both the stock and the bond markets. What percentage is devoted to each? Read the prospectus, and don't expect the fund to maintain an exact mix, either. One of the prospectuses on my desk says, basically, that the balanced fund will always maintain a mix of 80% stocks–20% bonds, except when it maintains a mix of 80% bonds–20% stocks.

And you wonder why I write from both sides of my mouth.

Both **international** and **global funds** appeal to investors who want to participate in markets not confined to the U.S. The difference between the two is that an international fund invests in companies located anywhere but the U.S. A global fund would invest in companies located and doing business anywhere in the world, including the U.S. Remember that when you move away from the U.S., you take on more political/social risk as well as currency exchange risk.

What if you don't believe that portfolio managers are likely to beat an index such as the S&P 500 over the long-term? First of all, you're in good company with plenty of evidence to support the idea. Second, if you can't beat the S&P 500 index, join it. Just buy an **index fund** that contains the same 500 stocks and only trades a stock if Standard & Poor's kicks it out of the index, forcing you to sell that one and buy the one that S&P is welcoming into the club. **Passive management**, in other words, as opposed to **active management**. An index is just an artificially grouped basket of stocks. Why are there 30 stocks in the Dow Jones Industrial Average, and why are the 30 particular stocks that are in there in there?

Because the Dow Jones publishing company says so. Same for the S&P 500. S&P decided that these 500 stocks make up an index, so there you have it. I know, it's often disappointing to discover how freaking simple most of this scary-sounding jargon actually is. Anyway, investors buy index funds because there are typically no sales charges and very low expenses. Since there's virtually no trading going on inside the portfolio, the "management fees" should be—and typically are—very low. So, for a no-brainer, low-cost option, you can put your money into an index and expect to do about as well as that index, no better, no worse.

In case they're not overwhelmed enough with choices, the industry has also developed a bunch of other funds, which the exam outline calls **specialized funds**. As we saw at the beginning of the chapter, there are categories such as "specialty—healthcare." As you might assume, this type of fund specializes in companies in that sector of the economy. That means that during a slump in that industry, we can't expect the fund to do particularly well. What about when the industry is on a tear? Everything's great. Isn't it kind of risky to predict which way an industry is headed? Absolutely—that's why a sector fund (one type of specialty fund) is generally considered volatile/high-risk. Some funds specialize on a particular industry, some on geographic regions. As we said, you can buy the Latin America, the Europe, or the Pacific Rim fund. You would then hope that those regions don't go into a major economic slump or suffer a natural disaster. See, when the fund concentrates heavily in a particular industry or geographic region, it, generally, takes on more volatility. As I write this sentence, the "specialty—financials" has been battered about as badly as any sector could be, with more room to be pummeled. In other words, I am *really* glad I did not buy that sector fund specializing in banks and broker-dealers that a former student was trying to recommend to me a while back.

BOND FUNDS

Stock is not for everyone. Even if an investor wants to own some stock/equity, chances are you'll still put a percentage of her hard-earned money into bond funds just to keep her calm when the stock market tanks if nothing else. A rule-of-thumb is that whatever your age is, that's the percentage that you should put into fixed-income. Also, if you're a big wimp, you can devote, say, 85% of your assets to fixed-income even though you're only 27. Yes, you would probably be wiser to put more money in the stock market, but if you can't sleep that way, the option is not available. You can't go without sleep for 40 years just to try and get a better return in the stock market.

Which type of fixed-income (bond) funds should the investor purchase? If the investor is not in a high tax bracket or is investing in an IRA, 401(k), etc., we'll be recommending taxable **bond funds**. The investor's time horizon will determine whether we should purchase short-term, intermediate-term, or long-term bond funds. Her risk tolerance will tell us if she needs the absolute umbilical safety of U.S. **Treasury funds** or is willing to spin the roulette wheel with **high-yield corporate bond funds**. If the investor is in a taxable account and wants to earn interest exempt from federal income tax, we put her into a **tax-exempt bond fund**, which purchases municipal bonds. If the investor is in a high-tax state such as Maryland, Virginia, or California, we can sell her the "Tax-Exempt Fund of Maryland," Virginia, or California. Now, the dividends she receives will generally be exempt from both federal and state income taxes. Whether she ends up getting ahead or not, at least she'll know that Uncle Sam and her state governments will get squat from her dividend distributions (notice how we said nothing about capital gains except in this cheap little parenthetical). But, we're not done just because we put her into a tax-exempt bond fund—how much of a yield does she want and how hard is she willing to party? If she's willing to roll the dice, we can put her into a **high-yield tax-exempt fund** and pray that not too many of the cities or water and sewer districts actually stiff us on the interest and principal they're supposed to pay. If she's more conservative, we buy funds that stick to issuers with higher credit ratings from S&P, Moody's, and Fitch. Again, this is not rocket science. An agent just needs to be diligent, honest, and well-educated on the world of investments. And, he needs to pass the Series 6, so let's keep moving.

MONEY MARKET MUTUAL FUNDS

We've seen that an investor's need for liquidity tells us how much to park in safe, boring **money market mutual funds**. There are both taxable and tax-exempt money market mutual funds. The **tax-exempt money market funds** buy short-term obligations of states, counties, cities, school districts, etc. They pay *really* low rates of interest, but since it's tax-free, rich folks still come out ahead. But, you would only sell a "tax-exempt" fund to an investor in one of the top marginal tax brackets.

ASSET ALLOCATION FUNDS

Asset allocation funds—believe it or not—allocate their assets. The percentage for equity, fixed-income, and money market is fairly rigid, so if you're too lazy to buy your own equity, fixed-income, and money market mutual fund, you can buy an asset allocation fund and let them subdivide things for you. I've seen definitions that say that asset allocation funds are another name for balanced funds, and I'm not sure how I could argue with that. I mean, if a balanced fund invests a percentage in equity and a percentage in debt, how is that different from an asset allocation fund, which invests a percentage in equity and a percentage in debt securities? If we had to distinguish the two, I would say that asset allocation funds are generally more rigid in their percentages compared to a balanced fund. But I would not bring that up at a seminar unless I wanted to kill 45 minutes with spirited, pointless debate.

PRECIOUS METALS FUNDS

Could you take a guess as to what a **precious metals fund** would invest in? I thought so. In general a gold fund would hold stock of gold mining companies. I'm not sure how "real world" the test will be, but there are now funds that own actual gold, as well. Is that distinction a possible test question? Almost anything is a possible test question; our job is to hit the fundamentals really hard and make up for any surprises with extreme test-taking strategy.

Since FINRA decided to add a few new items to this exciting list of fund types, we will now devote a disproportionate amount of verbiage to "funds of hedge funds" and "principal protected funds."

FUNDS OF HEDGE FUNDS

Mutual funds are open to the average investor, not just to the big, sophisticated individuals and institutional investors that include pension funds, insurance companies, university endowments, etc. Since the mutual fund is open to the average Joe and JoAnn, they can't focus on extremely risky investment strategies. It would be sort of rude to take the average Joe and JoAnn's retirement nest egg and lose it all on a couple of ill-placed foreign currency bets or ill-timed short sales. But, when the investors are all rich folks and institutions, the regulators can relax a little bit.

This is where **hedge funds** come in. In general, hedge funds are only open to institutions and to individuals called "accredited investors." We'll look at these "accredited investors" when we discuss another fascinating topic called "Reg D private placements under the Securities Act of 1933." There, too, the well-moneyed accredited investor can do things the average Joe and JoAnn cannot, but we'll save that excitement for another section. An accredited investor has over $1 million in net worth and makes > $200,000 per year. If it's a married couple, the assets held jointly count toward that $1 million figure, and the annual income needs to be > $300,000, just to make sure you have even more numbers to learn for your exam. These numbers are subject to change, so you can check www.passthe6.com/updates to see if that's the case.

Why does the investor need to be rich? Because these hedge funds use some very high-risk strategies including short selling, currency bets, risky options plays, etc. If you're an average Joe and JoAnn, it wouldn't be cool to let you risk all of your investment capital on such high-risk investing. On the other hand, if you're a rich individual or a big institution, chances are your hedge fund investment is just a percentage of the capital you invest. So, if you lose $1 million, chances are you have several more million where that came from.

A typical arrangement for a hedge fund is to have a limited number of investors form a private investment partnership. The fund typically charges 1–2% of assets as a management fee and extracts the first 20% of all capital gains. Then, they start thinking about their investors (we hope). Once you buy, there's a good chance you will not be able to sell your investment for at least one year, even if it stinks. Rather than trying to beat an index such as the DJIA, hedge funds generally go for "absolute positive investment performance"—usually 8% or so—regardless of what the overall market is doing.

Now, just to keep everything nice and simple, although a non-accredited investor cannot invest directly in a hedge fund, there are mutual funds called **funds of hedge funds**, which she *can* invest in. As the name implies, these mutual funds would have investments in several different hedge funds. In most cases, the investor would not be able to redeem her investment, since hedge funds are illiquid (they don't trade among investors). Also, these investments would involve high expenses, since there would be the usual expenses of the mutual fund, on top of the high expenses of the hedge funds the mutual fund invests in.

So, they're expensive, risky, and illiquid. Other than that, they're a great investment. The main testable points on hedge funds would seem to be:

- Open to sophisticated, accredited investors with high net worth
- Illiquid—usually can't be sold for at least 1 year
- Employ riskier, more diverse strategies
- Charge high management fees and usually 20% of all gains
- Non-accredited investors can buy mutual funds that invest in hedge funds

FUNDS OF FUNDS

I can't see spending a lot of time on this one. I mean, the name pretty well tells you what a **fund of funds** is, right? Just to be sure, a "fund of funds" is a mutual fund that holds shares in a bunch of other mutual funds. If the question asked about expense ratios, I would say that these funds of funds would tend to be expensive. But, it would be impossible to say much about the risk-reward characteristics, since that would depend entirely on the mix of funds that the fund chooses. Maybe an investor prefers to get statements and other communications from just one mutual fund as opposed to receiving communications from all the funds inside the fund of funds. I don't know, I guess some people are actually that lazy. My only concern is this—what if I pick a fund of funds that underperforms its peers in the fund-of-funds category? To avoid forcing investors to pick just one fund of funds, perhaps the mutual fund industry needs to take the innovation one step further and roll out a fund-of-funds-of-funds investment vehicle. Something tells me the sales charges and operating expenses could be pretty high on that one. Speaking of which...

PRINCIPAL-PROTECTED FUNDS

Would you believe that **principal-protected funds** focus on protecting investors' principal? Why these people can't just buy Treasuries and hold them to maturity, I do not know. Perhaps they prefer paying expenses to getting the principal guarantee for free. These funds take a lot of steps to keep the principal invested stable, but those steps usually cost something—buying puts on indexes or individual stocks, for example, carries a cost. So, these funds can be rather expensive. In exchange for the guaranteed principal, the fund also might limit the upside that the investor can make. Reminds me of an "indexed annuity," but let's not get into that right now. Principal-protected funds would be suitable for a very conservative investor who needs a lump sum at a fixed point in the future. These are not for income investors, as there will be no income for a long while. Generally, the investor has to deal with a lock-up period of 5 to 10 years, during which no redemptions can be taken and all dividends/capital gains must be reinvested. The guaranteed principal begins after this lock-up period. And, whenever the industry rolls out a sophisticated product like this, assume that the sales charges and operating expenses are high. Which pretty well explains why it's being rolled out—hello, somebody.

COMPARISONS OF MUTUAL FUNDS

Once we decide which types of funds an investor should purchase, how do we go about comparing one fund to another? The mutual fund prospectus would be a darned good place to go. In this handy document we will find the fund's investment objectives and style. Do they focus on companies with outstanding stock valued at $5 billion and above? $1 billion and below? Do they use fundamental analysis, poring over income statements and balance sheets, possibly meeting with senior management of the companies whose stock they hold? Or, do they rely more on technical analysis—charts, patterns, trends, etc.? Is this a small cap, mid-cap, or large cap fund, and how is the fund defining "small, mid-, and large cap," anyway? There are also investment policies disclosed in the prospectus and the statement of additional information. Maybe the fund is telling you that it may invest up to 10% of its assets in securities of issuers outside the United States and Canada and not included in the S&P 500. Or, that they allow themselves to invest 10% of their assets in lower-quality debt securities rated below BB/Ba by S&P and Moody's, or even in debt securities no one has *ever* actually rated. If that stuff all sounds too risky for the investor, well, that's why we're disclosing it here in the prospectus.

The prospectus provides information on the party managing the portfolio. We call that party the investment adviser or the portfolio manager. Often, it's a team approach, so we can see the names of the individual portfolio counselors and how much experience they have doing this sort of thing. The prospectus I happen to be looking at now has a team of eight advisers, and their experience in the industry ranges from 18 to 40 years.

One of the most misunderstood aspects of mutual fund investing has to do with the **fees and expenses.** You'll often hear people say, "No, there are no expenses on any of my mutual funds—they're all no-*load.*" As we'll see in more detail later, whether the fund is "no load" or not, all funds charge operating expenses. You might not get a bill for your share of the expenses, but the fund takes out enough money from the portfolio to cover their expenses, whether this happens to be a "no load" fund or one that charges either front- or back-end sales charges. **Sales charges** are one thing; **expenses** are another. Not all funds have sales charges, but all funds have expenses. Even the lowest of the low-cost ETFs charge management fees and other operating expenses.

In the prospectus the investor can see how much of her check is going toward the sales charge, and how much of the dollars she then invests will be eaten up by ongoing operating expenses. The section that details the fees and expenses of the fund has been entitled "Fees and expenses of the fund" in the prospectus sitting on my desk at the moment. If two growth funds have similar 10-year track records but one has expenses of 1.5% while the other charges just .90%, that could certainly be the tiebreaker the investor is looking for. **Expense ratios,** in other words, are important factors when determining your investment into a particular fund. A large fund family that starts with "V" has been playing up the significance of expense ratios on long-term returns quite successfully lately. Perhaps you've seen the print ads or heard the radio commercials. An index fund would have very low management fees (or should), since there is no active trading going on. A fund with a high turnover rate is actively trading the portfolio and would, therefore, typically charge higher management fees. Basically, if a fund is charging high operating expenses, there needs to be a good explanation for those charges; otherwise, look for another fund. If the fund has a stellar track record of actively trading its portfolio and/or provides all kinds of wonderful services then *maybe* it's worth it to investors. If not, keep looking. The exam, by the way, might say that the expense ratio "indicates the administrative efficiency/effectiveness of the fund."

So, what are these sales charges all about? Well, if you and your friends wanted to launch a new mutual fund, how would you go about doing that? Forget the nightmare of SEC registration, I mean just from a business standpoint—how would you go about launching this mutual fund? You would need investors, right? Okay, how do you find investors? You have to advertise the fund and give people a number to call or a website to visit for more information. You'd have to print up a bunch of colorful prospectuses and mail them out whenever somebody requests one. And, most of these customers are going through a sales representative, and—believe it or not—sales representatives like you do not generally work for free. So those distribution costs are going to have to be covered somehow. You can cover them with a sales charge. If the net asset value (NAV) of our aggressive growth fund is $9.50, we might actually charge people $10.00 for a stock worth $9.50 and call the difference of 50 cents a sales charge. What's more, we will get away with it. Yes, mutual fund investing is somewhat unique in this way. It's a little bit like going into a high-end retail store and hearing the sales clerk say, "That will be $274 for the ridiculously overpriced sandals, plus $12.50 to cover the cost of the ad we had to put out to bring you into the store."

What? They're charging the customer an additional fee to cover the expense of bringing the customer into the mutual fund? Absolutely. If the mutual fund is sponsored/under-written/distributed by a member firm, there will be a sales charge on purchases or redemptions of the fund. This sales charge covers the **distribution expenses** of printing, selling, mailing, and advertising the fund, and also leaves a really nice profit for the underwriter/sponsor/distributor of the fund. How much of a sales charge will the investor pay?

Depends on the fund. 5.5% is not uncommon for small investments. The maximum allowed sales charge is 8.5%, but anything over 5.75% is generally considered rude. So, if a mutual fund charges a maximum sales charge of 5.5%, that means that when the investor cuts her check, 5.5% of it goes to the distributors. Only the other 94.5% goes into the mutual fund for investment purposes.

Please keep two categories entirely separate in your mind: shareholder fees vs. expenses, as explained in the following table. Both sales charges and redemption fees can be avoided or reduced, as we'll see. And, many funds do not have sales charges or redemption fees. But all funds have expenses.

SHAREHOLDER FEES	EXPENSES
Sales charge (one-time charge, added to purchase price of mutual fund share)	Deducted from fund's assets on ongoing basis; examples include:
Added to investor's check when he buys	Management fee

SHAREHOLDER FEES	EXPENSES
Redemption fee (designed to discourage investors from redeeming shares soon after they buy them)	12b-1 fee
Subtracted from investor's proceeds when he sells	Custodial fee
	Transfer agent fee
	Consulting and legal work
	Board of director salaries

So, that stuff has to do with how much the fund costs to buy and hold. How well does the fund perform for investors? The prospectus will show you total return, usually as a bar chart and a table of numbers. Since I'm looking at a growth fund prospectus, the red bars are often very long and pointing in both upward and downward directions. Over the past 10 years, the fund has gone up as high as 45% and down as much as 22% over a calendar year. As we said, investing in growth stocks requires a high risk tolerance, a long time horizon, and a healthy supply of antacid. There was a 3-year period here where the fund averaged returns of negative 9%. Gee, sure hope you didn't need any of this money during that little blip. Oopsie.

What is "total return"? As usual, it's much simpler than you might assume. The point of buying a mutual fund share is that it might go, you know, up. We call that "capital appreciation" since "going up" wouldn't make us sound smart enough. The mutual fund will usually also pay out dividends from all those stocks and bonds they're sitting on. And, at the end of the year, if they took more profits than losses while trading their stocks and bonds, they will distribute a capital gains check to shareholders. Total return takes all three of those things and compares it to where the fund started. If the fund started out with a **net asset value** or **NAV** of $10 and finished the year at $11 per share, that's $1 of "capital appreciation." If the fund also paid a dividend of 50 cents per share and a $1 capital gains distribution, we would add that $1.50 to the capital appreciation of $1 for a total of $2.50 of good stuff. Comparing that $2.50 to where we started—$10—gives us a total return of 25%. How likely is it that a fund could have a total return of 25%? The prospectus I happen to be looking at did 26%, 31%, and 45% during 1997, 1998, and 1999. So, naturally, it had a similar return the next three years, right? No, after that, it was anybody's guess: 7% in 2000, *negative* 12% in 2001, *negative* 22% in 2002. Which means the following year was probably even worse, right? No. In 2003 the fund had a total return of nearly 33% in a positive direction. Now we see why the prospectus says that "past results are not predictive of future results." Yeah. I guess not.

As you can see from the completely unpredictable returns on a growth fund, mutual funds, especially equity funds, are not short-term investments. You need a long time horizon, as this prospectus tells you on the very first page. Nobody knows what will happen this year or next. We can show you the returns over 1, 5, and 10 years and let you be the judge. If we've only been in existence four years, we'll show you the figures for one year and also "life of fund" or "since inception." But no one can tell you which funds will go up this year, let alone which funds will go up the most. If they could do that, why the heck wouldn't they just buy the funds that will go up the most each year and quit their day job?

As we've seen, taxation always plays a part on an investor's returns, so the prospectus will also show results after taxes have been figured in. Of course, this is a little tricky, as we see from the caveat in the prospectus on my desk:

> Your actual after-tax returns depend on your individual tax situation and likely will differ from the results shown below. In addition, after-tax returns may not be relevant if you hold your fund shares through a tax-deferred arrangement, such as a 401(k) plan, IRA, or 529 Savings Plan.

Remember that funky stuff about the "duration" of a bond or the "beta" of a stock? Those are what the exam may refer to as "quantitative risk measurements." A mutual fund could be compared to another based on how much interest rate risk they take on (duration) or how aggressive they are in their stock selections (beta).

A-, B-, AND C-SHARES

A mutual fund that levies sales charges can get the sales charge from investors either when they buy or when they sell. **A-shares** charge a front-end load when the investor acquires them. *A = acquire*. **B-shares** charge a back-end load when the investor sells them. *B = back end*. For a B-share, the investor pays the NAV when she buys the shares, but she will leave a percentage behind when she sells. The percentage usually starts to decline in the second year, and after several years (6 to 8), the back-end load goes away completely—effectively, the B-shares are converted to A-shares at that point, in order to keep things nice and simple. B-shares are associated with **contingent deferred sales charges**. Break down those words. The sales charge is deferred until the investor sells, and the amount of the load is contingent upon when the investor sells. For a test question on the proceeds of a B-share redemption, just take the NAV and deduct the appropriate percentage from the investor's proceeds. If the NAV is $10, the investor receives the $10, minus the percentage the fund keeps on the back end. So, if she sells 100 shares and there is a 2% back-end sales charge, she gets $1,000 minus $20, or $980 out the door.

So, since the back-end or deferred sales charge eventually goes away, as long as the investor isn't going to sell her shares for, say, seven years, she should purchase B-shares, right? Wouldn't it be great if things were *ever* that simple in the world of investing? See, we've been acting as if distribution expenses are covered only by sales charges, either on the front-end (A-shares) or back-end (B-shares). Turns out, distribution expenses are covered only by the sales charge, unless the fund has a **12b-1 fee**.

What?

Yes, a "12b-1" fee *also* covers distribution costs, and if you're annoyed at these things right now, you'll eventually learn to love them, as they will put money in your pocket once you begin to sell. 12b-1 fees, like sales charges, go to salespersons like yourself. No doubt you've heard about so-called **"no-load funds."** Well, you may not have gotten the whole story. A no-load fund can still charge a 12b-1 fee, as long as it doesn't exceed .25% of the fund's assets. Every quarter, when they take money out to cover expenses, these so-called "no-load funds" can also take an amount not to exceed 25 basis points. Money market mutual funds are "no load," but that also means they can charge 12b-1 fees up to .25%.

Hmm. So, again, should the investor buy the A-share or the B-share? The choice has to do with this 12b-1 fee I'm currently babbling about. See, the A-shares for our aggressive growth fund might be as high as 5.5%, but the 12b-1 fee will often be .25% going forward, while the B-shares will pay an ongoing 12b-1 fee of, say, 1.00%. That complicates things, doesn't it? While the person who bought the B-shares is waiting for that contingent deferred sales charge schedule to hit zero, he's paying an extra .75% every year in expenses. .75% times seven years is an extra 5.25%. Yeah, but still, the A-shares start out with a maximum of 5.5% upfront sales charge, so the B-shares are still better.

Oh, if things were only that simple. See, this 12b-1 fee is a percentage. As your assets are growing over time, that .75% is also taking more *money* from you, even if it's a flat percentage—almost like the reverse of compounded interest. We're probably going beyond the depth of the exam, but I just can't stop myself. See, if you invest $10,000 into a fund, the first year's 12b-1 fee would be $75.00. If your investment grew to be $11,000 (as it should, since it's sort of the whole "growth" part of the so-called "growth fund"), the 12b-1 fee is going to be $82.50. If the assets are eventually $13,000, the extra .75% in 12b-1 fees equals $97.50.

And, as we'll soon see, 5.5% would probably be the *maximum* sales charge on the A-shares. If the investor puts in more money, she can maybe knock down the sales charge to 3% or even 2%, which is why long-term investors with a decent amount of money should almost always buy the A-shares.

Just to make the decision harder, there are also **C-shares**, which usually don't charge an upfront load but do carry a high 12b-1 fee. The level 12b-1 fee (which is so much higher than the .25% allowed for a "no load" fund) is where we got the clever "level load" nickname, by the way. Some C-shares also charge a contingent deferred sales charge if the investor sells in less than 1 year or 1½ years.

So, which type of share should an investor buy? Although I think this concept is a little too subjective (like what makes something "small cap" versus "mid-cap"), I'd recommend the following answers.

- Long-term investor with $50,000+ to invest – A-shares
- Intermediate or Long-term investor with small amount to invest – B-shares
- Short-term investor with < $500,000 to invest – C-shares

The difference in expenses between A-shares on one hand, and B- and C-shares on the other, has to do with the 12b-1 fee. The fund also charges a management fee to cover the cost of hiring a portfolio manager. That would be the same for everybody and would have to be a separate line item—remember that. A mutual fund can't bury their management fees under the 12b-1 fees or sales charges. Sales charges and 12b-1 fees cover distribution costs. The management fee covers portfolio management—the fund has to keep the two separate. The next item in the expenses table of the prospectus would be "other expenses." When you add the management fee, the 12b-1 fee and the "other expenses" fee, you have the expense ratio for the fund. For the A-shares, maybe the expense ratio is .70%. But, the expense ratio for the B- and C-shares could be 1.45%, due to that extra .75% 12b-1 fee. Please don't assume that the difference would always be .75%, though. I'm just using that as a typical, credible number. The fact that I'm too lazy to get up and look at a different prospectus has nothing to do with it.

If the investor purchases a B-share, she pays the NAV or net asset value. Only if/when she sells would the fund take a sales charge from her. If the investor purchases the A-shares, she pays more than the NAV. That extra that she pays is the sales charge, as we said. When you add the sales charge to the NAV, you get the public offering price (POP).

So, a formula the exam could throw at you is:

POP *minus* NAV **equals the** Sales Charge

If the POP is $10 and the NAV is $9.45, the sales charge is the difference of $.55 (55 cents). If you're asked to calculate the sales charge as a percentage, use this formula:

POP minus NAV divided by POP

If we took $10 minus $9.45, we'd get a sales charge of 55 cents. Divide that 55 cents by the POP of $10, and you see that the sales charge percentage is 5.5%. Remember that the sales charge is expressed as a percentage of the POP, not the NAV.

How and when is this net asset value (NAV) figured? The exam wants you to know that mutual funds use **forward pricing**. That means that if you take my check for $10,000 at 11 a.m., you won't know how many shares I'll end up buying. The fund will re-figure the NAV when trading closes that day, and then put my $10,000 into the fund at the NAV they come up with then. Same thing for a seller. A seller "redeems" her shares to the fund. When she turns in a redemption order at 1 p.m. she won't know the exact dollar amount of her check because the NAV won't be determined until after the markets close at 4 p.m. Eastern. The "net asset value" or NAV is nothing more than the value of one slice of the portfolio pie. The assets of the portfolio would be the value of the securities plus any cash they've generated minus any liabilities. Where did the liabilities come from? The fund might borrow money from time to time to handle redemptions—they don't always want to sell off stocks and bonds to pay investors ready to sell their shares, so they borrow some money. If the fund has $10,000,000 in assets and $550,000 in liabilities, the net assets of the fund would be $9,450,000. If there are 1 million shares, the NAV per share is $9.45. Sellers will receive $9.45 per share when they redeem their A-shares today, but they'll pay a POP higher than that if they're buying. Buyers of the B-shares will pay $9.45, but those redeeming/selling their shares will receive $9.45 per share minus whatever percentage they leave behind to the contingent deferred sales charge.

To figure the POP (public offering price) that a particular investor pays, use the following formula:

NAV *divided by* (100% – sales charge) = POP

So, if the NAV is calculated at $9.45 today, an investor paying a 3% sales charge would pay a public offering price of $9.74. To calculate that, divide $9.45 by .97. If the investor were paying just a 1% sales charge, the POP would be $9.55. To calculate that, divide $9.45 by .99.

REDUCING THE SALES CHARGE

Although A-shares do charge the front-end sales charge, you can also reduce that sales charge by employing various methods laid out in the prospectus.

Breakpoints

Perhaps you've noticed that in general the more you want to buy of something, the better the deal. Doesn't a small box of Lucky Charms™ at the convenience store cost a lot more per ounce than a shrink-wrapped pack of 10 boxes from Sam's Club? Same with mutual funds. If you want to invest $1,000, you're going to pay a higher sales charge than if you want to invest, say, $100,000. For mutual funds, investors are rewarded with **breakpoints**. Let's say that the L & H Fund had the following sales charge schedule:

INVESTMENT	SALES CHARGE
< $25,000	5.5%
$25,000 – $49,999	5.0%
$50,000 – $99,999	4.0%
$100,000 – $199,999	3.0%

That means that an investor who buys $100,000 worth of the fund will pay a much lower sales charge than an investor who invests $20,000. In other words, less of her money (as a percentage) will be deducted from her check when she invests. A breakpoint means that at this <u>point</u> the fund will give you this <u>break</u>. A lower sales charge means that an investor's money ends up buying more shares. For mutual funds, we don't pick the number of shares we want; we send in a certain amount of money and see how many shares our money buys us. With a lower sales charge, our money will buy us more shares. Keep in mind that fractional shares are common. For example, $1,000 would buy 12.5 shares if the POP were $80.

Letter of Intent

So, what if we didn't have the $100,000 needed to qualify for that breakpoint? We could write a **letter of intent** explaining to the mutual fund our intention to invest $100,000 in the fund over the next 13 months. Now, as we send in our money, say, $5,000 at a time, the fund applies the lower 3% sales charge, as if we'd already invested the full amount. The lower sales charge means we end up buying more shares, right? So, guess what the fund does? It holds those extra shares in a safe place, just in case we fail to invest that $100,000 we intended to. If we don't live up to our letter of intention, no big deal. We just don't get those extra shares. In other words, the higher sales charge applies to the money actually invested.

Also, that letter of intent could be backdated up to 90 calendar days in order to cover a previous purchase. If an investor bought $3,000 of the L & H fund on March 10, he might decide in early June that he should write a letter of intent to invest $50,000 over 13 months. He could backdate the letter to March 10 to include the previous investment and would then have 13 months from that date to invest the remaining $47,000.

Breakpoints are available to individuals, husbands & wives, parents & minor child in a custodial account, corporations, partnerships, etc. So, if the mom puts in $30,000 and also puts in $20,000 for her minor child's UGMA account, that's a $50,000 investment in terms of achieving a breakpoint. The child cannot be an adult; he must be a minor. Corporations and other businesses qualify for breakpoints. About the only folks who don't qualify for breakpoints are investment clubs.

Another important consideration for breakpoints is that a sales rep can never encourage an investor to invest a lower amount of money in order to keep him from obtaining a lower sales charge offered at the next breakpoint. That's called breakpoint selling and is a violation punishable by death or dismemberment. Likewise, if a rep fails to point out to an investor that a few more dollars invested would qualify for a breakpoint, that's just as bad as actively encouraging him to stay below the next breakpoint. Remember, sales reps (broker-dealers) get part of the sales charge. It would definitely be to their advantage to get the higher sales charge. Unfortunately, they have to keep their clients' interests in mind, too.

Yes, unfortunately, they take all the fun out of this business.

Rights of Accumulation

If an investor's fund shares appreciate up to a breakpoint, the investor will receive a lower sales charge on additional purchases. In other words, when an investor is trying to reach a breakpoint, new money and account accumulation are counted the same way. So, if an investor's shares have appreciated to, say, $42,000 and the investor wanted to invest another $9,000, the entire purchase would qualify for the breakpoint that starts at $50,000. In other words, the $42,000 of value plus an additional $9,000 would take the investor past the $50,000 needed to qualify for the 4% sales charge.

This is known as rights of accumulation.

Please note that this has *nothing* to do with a letter of intent. If you write a letter of intent to invest $100,000, you'll need to invest $100,000 of new dollars into the fund to get the breakpoint you're intending to get. Rights of accumulation means that you could save money on future purchases, based on the value of your account.

Combination Privilege

Most "funds" are part of a "family" of funds. Many of these fund families will let you combine your purchase in their Income Fund with, say, their Index or Growth Fund in order to figure a breakpoint. They call this, very cleverly, a **combination privilege**. So, if the individual invests $20,000 in the Income Fund and $30,000 in the Growth Fund, that's considered a $50,000 investment in the family of funds, and that's the number they'd use to figure the breakpoint.

Just trying to keep everybody in our happy family.

Conversion/Exchange Privilege

The fund might also offer a **conversion/exchange privilege**. This privilege allows investors to sell shares of, say, the L & H Growth Fund, in order to buy shares of the L & H Income Fund at the NAV, rather than the higher POP. If we didn't do that, the investor might get mad enough to leave our happy family, since there would be no immediate benefit to his staying with us. I mean, if he's going to be charged the POP, why not look for a new family with a growth fund that might actually, you know, grow?

But remember that buying the new shares at the NAV is nice for the investor, but the IRS still considers the sale a taxable event. So if you get a test question on the tax treatment, tell the exam that all gains or losses are recognized on the date of the sale.

And then move on with your life.

BUYING AND SELLING YOUR MUTUAL FUND SHARES

We already looked at the detailed and slightly perplexing options for purchasing mutual fund shares. A no-load fund is purchased at the NAV, but every quarter 12b-1 fees are deducted from the fund's assets to cover the cost of distribution. If the fund has a "load," you can pay it upfront by buying an A-share and then save money on expenses going forward. You can also knock down your front-end sales charge by purchasing in quantity either all at once or through a Letter of Intent (LOI). If you buy the B-shares, you avoid the front-end sales charge, but you have two other concerns to keep in mind: 1) you'll leave a percentage on the table if you sell for the first several years and 2) the fund will take a much higher 12b-1 fee on your behalf every quarter, driving up your expenses. If you were only going to hold a fund for, say, two or three years, the C-shares would probably make sense. You would pay no front-end or back-end sales charge, and even though the 12b-1 fee of 1% is a bit annoying, it's only being charged for two or three years.

PURCHASING SHARES

Who do you buy your mutual fund shares from? Or, for you English majors, from whom do you buy your mutual fund shares? Usually, through a well-dressed, overly caffeinated financial sales representative such as yourself. However, an investor could also just set up an account with the fund company and buy shares directly from them. Usually, the fund company will strongly encourage you to go through a financial adviser/registered representative, though, who is licensed to discuss investments with clients and maybe even get paid for it. If you go directly through the fund, the folks on the phone are just taking whatever order you'd like to place—don't ask 'em nothin'. They haven't even taken a Series 6 or gotten a license. Would you save money by bypassing the registered representative? No. The distributor of the fund would just keep all of the sales charge, rather than sharing it with the registered rep's broker-dealer and the registered rep. Believe it or not, most people do not wake up thinking, "Gee, I think I need to buy some shares of a well-diversified growth & income mutual fund today," so a registered representative such as yourself will be the one getting the ball rolling 99% of the time. Even if somebody calls the fund company, the person on the other end will probably recommend that he/she consult with a financial representative such as yourself (once you pass your exams and get licensed). Once they've set up an account through the registered representative, they can purchase additional shares in any of the following ways:

- Contacting your registered representative
- Mailing in your payment to the fund's customer service department (transfer agent)
- Telephoning the fund company

- Purchasing online
- Wiring the money from a bank account

Many people choose to set up an automatic investment program whereby, say, $300 per month is drawn from their bank account and sent to the fund company. This puts them on a disciplined schedule of investing and also makes sure they don't purchase all their shares at just one price. With their luck, some investors will put in $50,000 at the absolute highest price of all time. The automatic plan uses "dollar cost averaging," which will be explored later in exciting detail.

When the investor opens her account, the fund needs to know if she wants to receive dividends and capital gains in the form of a check, or in the form of more shares. If she decides to automatically reinvest, there will be no tax advantages, but there is a big advantage to her in that she gets to reinvest at the net asset value, avoiding sales charges. Her money will grow faster this way, since every dollar she reinvests goes back into the fund and not a dime goes to the distributors. If she's in a retirement plan, she will automatically reinvest, since there are penalties for early withdrawals from retirement plans.

Mutual funds have minimum initial investments that are usually lower for IRA accounts than taxable accounts. Some funds will let you in the door for as little as $25 or $50. Others are upscale clubs who won't talk to you for less than $3,000. The minimum initial investment would be found in the prospectus, along with all the other vital information.

SELLING SHARES

Open-end mutual fund shares are not traded with other investors. When you want to sell your L&H Aggressive Growth Fund, you don't sell it to me; you sell it back to the L&H Aggressive Growth Fund. This is called a **redemption** or "redeeming your shares." When you **redeem** your shares, you receive the NAV per share if it's an A-share and the NAV minus the back-end sales charge if it's a B-share.

How do you go about putting in your redemption order?

- By contacting your registered representative
- By writing to the fund company
- By telephoning or faxing the fund company
- By going through the fund company's website

The fund company reserves the right to require what's known as a "signature guarantee" on any redemptions. A signature guarantee is an official stamp that officers of a bank can put on the required paperwork. When I inherited shares from a family member a few years back, I had to go to my bank for a signature guarantee in order to transfer ownership from the individual to the individual's estate, of which I am the executor. A "signature guarantee" is just a very common requirement when stock is being transferred or sold. They are usually obtained from a bank officer, or a member of a stock exchange.

The prospectus I've been using to write most of this chapter tells me that the fund reserves the right to require the pain-in-the-neck signature guarantee on any redemptions. The fund *will* require a signature guarantee if the redemption is:

- Over $75,000
- Made payable to someone other than the registered shareholder(s); or
- Sent to an address other than the address of record, or an address of record that has been changed within the last 10 days

Of course, if the Series 6 expects you to memorize even that bullet point list, God help us all. Also note that some mutual fund shares are actually issued (or were) as paper certificates. If that's the case, the investor will have to send in the certificates after signing them and also getting the signature guarantee.

Mutual funds are not exactly in love with redemptions. In fact, many will charge a redemption fee during the first year or so just to encourage you to sit tight. If you sell too soon, you might leave 1% of your investment behind. Note that this is not a back-end sales charge going to the distributors. This is just a little penalty that compensates the fund for the hassle of having to pay out redemptions.

But, whether mutual funds enjoy redeeming shares or not, the fact is that they have to redeem your shares promptly. The answer to the test question is "within 7 days." That requirement could only be suspended if an emergency shut down the exchanges and there was no way to value the fund's portfolio. So, be very skeptical of any answer that's trying to convince you that the fund can "halt redemptions." They'd *like* to do that, the same way you'd like to start selling mutual funds without having to sit for your Series 6.

SYSTEMATIC WITHDRAWAL PLANS

Many investors choose to invest into the fund systematically through an automatic deduction from their bank account. This way they actually invest rather than procrastinating, and they also use "dollar cost averaging," which avoids buying all the shares at an inconveniently high price. Well, when you go to sell/redeem your shares, it sure would stink to sell them all at the *lowest* price of all-time, right?

Therefore, some investors set up **systematic withdrawal plans**. You might think of this as "dollar cost average on the way in, dollar cost average on the way out," in case you don't have enough to think about at this point. In order to set up a systematic withdrawal plan, the investor must have a minimum account value, often $5,000 or so. Payments are made first from dividends and then capital gains. If the dividends and capital gains don't cover the amount the investor wants to withdraw, the fund then starts redeeming shares. It's also a good idea to stop putting money into the fund once you begin the withdrawal plan. If you recall the wash sale rule, buying shares of a fund that were just sold at a loss a few days ago is going to make tax season even more annoying than it already is.

There are several payout or withdrawal options that might pop up on the exam.

Fixed-Dollar Period Payments (Fixed-Dollar Plan)

As the name implies, if the investor wants to receive a fixed-dollar payment periodically, we can offer her the cleverly named "fixed-dollar periodic payment." If she wants $300 per month, the fund will send her $300 a month. How long will her investment last? Until it's all gone. She's not fixing the time period—she's fixing the monthly payment, which will keep coming until all the money has been withdrawn.

Fixed-Percentage Periodic Payments (Fixed-Percentage Plan)

The investor might prefer to receive 2% of her account value each month, or maybe 5% each quarter. How much will the investor receive with each withdrawal? Who knows? Whatever 2% or 5% of the current account value happens to be.

Fixed-Shares Periodic Payments (Fixed-Share Plan)

The investor can also have the fund redeem/liquidate, say, 10 shares per month and send a check. How large will that check be? Whatever 10 shares are worth that month. As we'll soon see, that's pretty much how a variable annuity works during the annuitization phase, except that in a mutual fund, the account value is eventually exhausted.

Fixed Time

Finally, if the investor wants her account liquidated/withdrawn over, say, three years, she'll give the fund an exact date, and they'll figure out how much to redeem each month (or other period) in order to exhaust the account by that date.

STRUCTURE AND OPERATION OF THE MUTUAL FUND COMPANY

So far we've been looking at mutual funds in terms of what they are, who buys which ones, and how investors go about buying and selling them. Now, let's take a look at a mutual fund as a company—who performs which functions at, say, Fidelity, American Funds, AIG, etc.?

BOARD OF DIRECTORS

A mutual fund has a **board of directors** that oversees operations of the fund or family of funds. The board's responsibilities include:

- establish investment policy
- select and oversee the investment adviser, transfer agent, custodian
- establish dividends and capital gains policy
- review and approve 12b-1 plans

Remember, the board of directors does not manage the portfolio; it manages the company. The shareholders of the fund elect and re-elect the board members. Shareholders also vote their shares to approve the investment adviser's contract and 12b-1 fees.

INVESTMENT ADVISER

Each fund has an **investment adviser**, whose job is to manage the fund's investments according to its stated objectives. Shareholders and the board vote to hire/retain investment advisers who are paid a percentage of the fund's net assets. That's why they try so hard. The more valuable the fund, the more they get paid. Their fee is typically the largest expense to a mutual fund. Investment advisers have to advise the fund (select the investments) in keeping with federal securities and tax law. They must also base their investment decisions on careful research of economic/financial trends rather than on hot stock tips from their bartender. Since everything needs at least two names, the investment adviser is also called the "portfolio manager."

CUSTODIAN

The fund also keeps its assets in a safe place at the **custodian**. The custodian is basically a bank that has legal responsibility for all the cash and securities owned by the mutual fund. The test will likely try to trick you into thinking that the custodian holds *customer* securities, but, no, it's the transfer agent who holds the customer securities. The custodian holds the portfolio securities and cash in custody. What an amazing pain in the neck it must be to keep track of all the purchases and sales of maybe 100 different portfolio stocks or bonds, all the dividends and interest received, all the stock splits or mergers with other companies! Of course, somebody's got to do it, and that somebody is called the "custodian." I would give an example of a real-world custodian, but given the volatile nature of the banking industry these days, I'm afraid the name would change due to a merger or a bankruptcy before the book goes to print. In any case, the custodian is the keeper of the assets, so to speak, so the custodian receives the dividends and interest payments made by the stocks and bonds in the fund's portfolio. The custodian is also responsible for the payable/receivable functions involved when the portfolio buys and sells securities. That means that they release the funds to cover purchases by the investment adviser and receive those securities that were purchased. And, they receive funds after the adviser sells securities and deliver those securities to the buy side. Think of the custodian as the record keeper for the mutual fund portfolio. The next entity keeps records of shareholders and often acts as a customer service provider to the shareholders.

TRANSFER AGENT

The **transfer agent** is incredibly busy. This is the party that issues new shares to buyers and cancels the shares that sellers redeem. Most of these "shares" are simply electronic files (book entry), but it still takes a lot of work to "issue" and "redeem" them. While the custodian receives dividends and interest payments from the portfolio securities, it is the transfer agent that distributes income to the investors. The transfer agent acts as a customer service rep for the fund and often sends out those semi-annual and annual reports that investors have to receive. As we just saw, investors can purchase and redeem shares directly with the transfer agent, should their registered representative develop an attitude or an unhealthy love of golf.

UNDERWRITERS/DISTRIBUTORS/WHOLESALERS

Some funds are sponsored by **underwriters**, who bear the costs of distributing the fund up front and then get compensated by the sales charge that they either earn themselves or split with the broker-dealers who make the sales. Underwriters (a.k.a. "wholesalers," "distributors," or "sponsors") also prepare sales literature for the fund, since they're the ones who will be selling the shares, either directly to the public or through a network of broker-dealers. If a fund distributes itself, it usually covers the distribution costs through a 12b-1 fee, as we mentioned. The fund can call itself "no load" as long as the 12b-1 fee does not exceed .25% of net assets. There is also a very famous mutual fund family that sells "100% no-load funds." That means there is no sales charge and no 12b-1 fee. How are they able to stay in business?

Through the management fees. The "100% no load" label helps them pull in more assets. The management fee is simply a % of those assets, so .50% of $1 million is nice, but .50% of $1 *billion* is even nicer.

Don't worry—mutual funds have figured out how to make a profit. That's why you're sitting for the Series 6, as a matter of fact.

These are the methods of distribution for mutual fund shares:

- Fund/to underwriter/to dealer/to investor (assume sales charge here, a nice big one, probably)
- Fund/to underwriter/to investor (underwriter cuts out the other middleman but still gets a sales charge)
- Fund/to investor (no-load funds, which can charge 12b-1 fees no larger than .25% of assets, deducted quarterly)

SHAREHOLDER VOTING

In class, I usually see some very confused faces when I tell students that mutual fund shareholders get to vote. Perhaps my students have been too busy to notice, or perhaps they file all their proxy materials with the junk mail. In any case, mutual fund shareholders are, obviously, shareholders, so they get to vote their shares in matters of major importance. If you get a test question about voting rights, tell the test that mutual fund shareholders vote on:

- Changes in investment policies and objectives
- Approval of investment adviser contract
- Approval of changes in fees
- Approval of and discontinuation of 12b-1 fees
- Election of board members
- Ratification of independent auditors

Remember that a mutual fund that distributes its own shares directly to the public does so under Rule 12b-1 and covers distribution costs with this ongoing, asset-based "12b-1" sales fee. To approve and renew (at least annually) a 12b-1 fee, there must be a majority vote of outstanding shares and the board of directors, including a majority of the non-interested board members. But, to discontinue the 12b-1 fee, it would take only a majority of the outstanding shares and a majority of the non-interested board members.

Also know that investment companies may not do any of the following without getting a majority vote of outstanding shares:

- Change from an open-end to a closed-end fund and vice versa
- Change from a diversified to non-diversified fund and vice versa
- Borrow money, lend money, purchase real estate or commodities
- Cease functioning as an investment company

CLOSED-END FUNDS

The third type of investment company defined by the Investment Company Act of 1940 is the **management company**. Within this category, we find both **open-end funds** and **closed-end funds**. So far, we've been talking about the open-end funds. Let's say a few words on the closed-end variety at this point. The main difference between the two is that open-end fund companies continually issue and redeem shares. When you find an investor for the L&H Aggressive Growth Fund, the fund will issue brand-new shares to the investor, which is why you had to sell them with a prospectus. Open-end funds don't do an IPO and then force shareholders to trade the fixed number of shares back and forth. Rather, they issue new shares every time somebody wants to buy them, and they let the shareholders sell back/redeem the shares when they get tired of holding them.

On the other hand, closed-end funds do an IPO at which point there is a fixed number of shares. What if you want to sell your closed-end fund? You trade it the same way you trade any other share of stock. How much will you receive? Whatever a buyer is willing to pay. These things can trade at a discount to their NAV, or at a premium. It just depends on the supply and demand for these shares. So, if the test question says that the NAV is $9.45 with the POP at $9.00, something's up, right? You can't buy an open-end fund at a discount. As we saw, the cheapest you can buy it is at the NAV. B-shares are sold at the NAV and so are no-load funds. But, no way can an investor buy open-end shares at a discount. So, if the fund shares are selling below NAV, they have to be closed-end fund shares. Doesn't mean that closed-end funds *always* trade at a discount. If people really want your shares, they might pay a premium. So, we're not saying that closed-end funds always trade at a discount to their NAV; we're saying that *only* the closed-end fund *could* do that. Since closed-end shares trade the same way that GE or MSFT shares trade, investors can both purchase them on margin and sell them short. To "sell short" involves borrowing shares from a broker-dealer and selling them, with the obligation to buy them back and replace them later. If the price falls, you buy low after you already sold high. If the price goes way up, you're screwed.

Another difference between open and closed-end funds is that you would purchase, say, 100 shares of the closed-end fund and pay whatever that costs. For an open-end fund, you would just cut a check for, say, $1,000, and see how many shares you end up with. In almost all cases, you'll get "full and fractional shares" with an open-end fund, which is just a way of saying that $100 would turn into 12.5 shares if the POP were $8.00. That little "point-5" of a share is the "fractional share." For a closed-end fund, you would either buy 12 shares or 13 shares, not 12.5. In fact, you would usually buy at least a "round lot" of 100 shares, but that's neither here nor there.

The exam might also bring up the fact that open-end funds only issue common stock to investors. That's right—even if it's a bond fund, the investor isn't buying bonds in the mutual fund company. The investor is buying a percentage of the bond portfolio. How do you evidence ownership? Common stock. Another way to say it is that the open-end fund does not issue "senior securities." A closed-end fund can use leverage by issuing bonds to investors—I mean, borrowing their money and paying them back a rate of interest. They can also issue preferred stock and even common stock with greater/lesser voting rights, should the exam care to be that difficult the day you sit down to take it. So, remember that open-end funds do not use a lot of leverage and do not issue "senior securities." Just the opposite is true for closed-end funds.

The investment objectives between an open-end and a closed-end fund could be exactly the same—there are closed-end corporate bond funds, tax-exempt bond funds, aggressive growth funds, etc. Nuveen Investments is a major issuer of closed-end municipal bond funds (www.nuveen.com offers a nice primer on open-end and closed-end funds). Why would you want those versus the open-end variety? Well, what happens to your yield when the price of the bond drops—it goes up, right? So, if you can buy somebody's closed-end bond fund at a discount, you just pumped up your yield a little bit. What about when you want to sell your shares? Well, let's hope they're trading at a premium by then. If not, welcome to the NFL.

OPEN-END	CLOSED-END
Continuous offering of unlimited # of shares and shareholders	Fixed offering of shares
Issues only one class of stock	Can issue different classes of common stock, preferred stock, and bonds
Shares are purchased and redeemed with issuer/primary market only	Shares are not redeemable; must be traded on secondary market
Ex-Date established by Board of Directors	Ex-Date established by exchanges

FACE AMOUNT CERTIFICATE COMPANIES, UNIT INVESTMENT TRUSTS

Okay, so that's a compare/contrast between open-end and closed-end investment companies. They both represent the type of investment company called the "management company." These two types of "management companies" make up the lion's share of questions on investment companies, but we can't forget the other two types: face amount certificate company and unit investment trust. When purchasing a face amount certificate, the investor either pays installments or a lump sum into the program, and later receives the higher *face amount* on the certificate on a future date. The exam might ask if these carry sales charges and/or management fees. The answer to both questions is yes. Sales charges cover the cost of marketing and selling the shares; management fees cover the cost of managing the investments in order to pay out more than they took in.

Then, there is the unit investment trust or UIT. These pooled investments are not actively managed/traded portfolios, so they don't charge a management fee. If it's a portfolio of bonds, they just let the bonds mature. So, like any trust, it just kind of sits there holding title to vast quantities of assets, and smiles all the way to the bank every time a big, fat dividend or interest check comes in the mail. Investors buy units of this investment trust, which is why the creative types just couldn't stop themselves from dubbing these things unit investment trusts. The units are redeemable, meaning they can be sort of "cashed in" for their current value.

ETFs

Perhaps you have heard of "ETFs" or seen advertisements for the well-known varieties called "Spiders," "Diamonds" and "Cubes." An **ETF** is an **exchange-traded fund**. Why did they name it that? Because it is a fund that trades on an exchange and this is not an industry brimming with creative types. An ETF is organized as a Unit Investment Trust (UIT) and it trades among investors throughout the day, unlike a mutual fund, which shareholders redeem for the same NAV next calculated by the fund.

TRADE LIKE SHARES OF STOCK

An ETF is typically an index fund. That means that if an investor wants to do as well as a particular index, she can track that index with an exchange traded fund (ETF). To track the S&P 500, she can buy the "Spider," which is so named because it is an "SPDR" or "Standard & Poor's Depository Receipt." Of course, she could already have been doing that with an S&P 500 open-end index fund. But, that is a boring old open-end fund, and how does an investor buy or sell those shares? Directly from the open-end fund. No matter what time of day, if we put in a redemption order, we all receive the same NAV at the next calculated price—forward pricing. So, if the S&P 500 drops 80 points in the morning and rises 150 points by mid-afternoon, there is no way for us to buy low and then sell high with an open-end fund.

But with the ETF version investors can buy and sell their shares as often as they want to. They can try to buy when the index drops and sell when it rises. Unlike the open-end versions, these ETFs can be bought on margin and can be sold short for those who enjoy high-risk investment strategies. The test might say that ETFs facilitate "intra-day trading," which just means that you can buy and sell these things as many times as you want throughout the day. I also mentioned them under "systematic risk," because investors can bet against the overall market by selling ETFs short. Of course, there is only so much one mind can keep track of, so let's keep moving.

COST COMPARISONS

So, are ETFs cheaper than the open-end index fund versions?

Depends how you do it. If you were only going to invest $500, the open-end fund would probably be cheaper. You wouldn't pay a sales charge and the expenses are only about .18% (18 basis points) at the time of this writing. The ETF has an expense ratio of only .11% (11 basis points). But, since the ETF version (Spider) is a stock, you would pay a commission to buy it, just as you would pay to buy shares of GE, Walmart, etc. So, if you invested $500 into the ETF and paid a $10 commission, that commission would work out to be 2% (200 basis points), which is much higher, and that's before we factor in the expenses. On the other hand, if you're investing a larger amount, such as $100,000, the same $10 commission is now 1 basis point (.0001) versus the 18 basis points (.0018) for the open-end index fund's operating expenses. So, I think it's safe to say that for a small amount of money—as usual—the open-end mutual fund is a great option. For larger amounts of money, though, the ETF might be cheaper, assuming the investor is paying low commissions.

DIVERSIFICATION

As with the open-end index funds, ETFs offer **diversification**. For a rather small amount of money, an investor can own a little piece of, say, 500 different stocks with the SPDR, or 30 different stocks for a Dow-based ETF. It is also easy to implement asset allocation strategies with ETFs. An investor can find ETFs that track all kinds of different indexes (small cap, value, growth, blue chip, long-term bonds, etc.). If an investor wanted to be 80% long-term bonds and 20% small cap stock, that goal could be achieved with just two low-cost ETFs. This point is not necessarily a comparison to the open-end index funds, which would offer the same advantage. Rather, it is a comparison to purchasing individual bonds or small cap stocks. In order to spread the risk among many bonds and small cap stocks, an investor would have to spend large sums of money. With an ETF (as with the open-end index funds) diversification can be achieved immediately with a much smaller investment.

SUMMARY

The main testable points concerning ETFs would seem to be:

- Trade like shares of stock, intra-day
- Investors pay a commission rather than a sales charge
- Shares can be bought on margin, sold short
- ETFs have low expense ratios
- ETFs are convenient for investors seeking diversification/asset allocation
- ETFs are very low-cost when purchased in larger quantities
- Indexes include small cap, mid-cap, large cap, growth, value, S&P 500, Dow Jones, NASDAQ, even fixed income
- Series 6 holders can't sell ETFs (or closed-end funds) trading on secondary market

ANNUITIES

CONCEPT AND TYPES OF ANNUITIES

An **annuity** is an investment sold by an insurance company that either promises a minimum rate of return to the investor or allows the investor to allocate payments to various mutual funds that invest in the stock and bond markets. These products offer regular payments for the rest of the annuitant's life, but owners of annuities can instead take money out as lump sums or random withdrawals on the back end. Annuities are part of the retirement plans of many individuals, and they can either be part of the "safe-money" piece or can provide plenty of exposure to the stock and bond markets.

The three main types of annuities are fixed, indexed, and variable. That's actually only two types, since an indexed annuity *is* a fixed annuity, but it has many features that make it completely different from a plain-old fixed annuity. A **fixed annuity** promises a minimum rate of return to the investor in exchange for one big payment into the contract or several periodic payments. The **purchase payments** are allocated to the insurance company's own **general account,** so the rate of return is "guaranteed." But, that just means it's backed by the claims-paying ability of the insurance company's general account—so before turning over your hard-earned money to an insurance company, expecting them to pay it back to you slowly, you really might want to check their **AM Best** rating and their history of paying claims.

With so many of my clients working as annuity salespeople, it's always dangerous for me to explain annuities in terms of suitability. In fact, just using the word "annuity" makes me a little nervous. Please know that I have no interest in bashing annuities. As always, I'm just trying to help you deal with potential test questions. What folks actually invest in—not my concern.

In any case, a fixed annuity would be suitable for someone who wants a "safe money" investment that is more dependable than anything in the stock or bond markets, something that promises to make dependable payments for the rest of his life, no matter how long he ends up living. The fixed annuity offers peace of mind if not a high rate of return. What does the investor want—peace of mind or high rate of return? Sorry, this is an either-or thing.

At the risk of receiving a hundred hostile emails from the safe-money crowd, I have to say that to me the rate of return seems *so minimal* that the whole deal looks like a proposition in which I agree to turn over, say, $100,000 to an insurance/annuity company, and they agree to pay it back to me in the future when I throw the switch to receive payments, with the most meager rate of interest tacked on for good measure. Uhm, but I already *have* the $100,000! I could invest that $100,000 in the stock market and easily turn it into $175,000 over a decade—or sooner.

Then again, while I could afford a BMW, Lexus, or Mercedes-Benz, I choose instead to drive a 1996 Toyota Camry with 188,000 miles on the odometer and various interior parts held together with Gorilla Glue™. Unlike me, most investors would spend $100,000 so dang fast it'd make your head spin, and they have no confidence in their ability to turn $100,000 into $175,000 *ever*, while I have had far better investment returns over similar periods. So, for many people, a fixed annuity from a good insurance company is not just a good idea; it may be their only hope. On a related note, while I definitely "buy term and invest the difference," that is horrible advice for most people. First, I have no kids or wife to protect as beneficiaries, so I don't need to lock in some massive income protection with a whole life insurance policy. All I do is make sure nobody gets stuck with my funeral bill by renting a term life insurance policy. But, I also know I will probably one day let the policy lapse. I mean, if I'm 72 years old with $1,000,000 in the bank, I don't need to worry about funeral expenses. Second, I actually do the second step—invest the difference. I maximize my SIMPLE IRA and often fund a regular old taxable account. I'm afraid that most people who hear the advice to "buy term and invest the difference" end up buying term and then buying an SUV. By the time the reality of the Cadillac Escalade payments set in, they probably let the term insurance lapse, too, and now they're left with no savings, no death benefit, and an automobile they neither need nor can afford.

So, there are no blanket statements for all investors. Some investors can get by with purchasing term insurance and investing the difference, just as some can live with the variable returns of the stock and bond market. Your job is to make sure you know your investor and make suitable recommendations. For many investors, you might even recommend that they do not purchase an annuity. Of course, you have to know the product inside out before you can make a determination like that. Also, none of that little spiel is intended to be investment advice. It's intended to lay a foundation for some topics that we'll discuss up ahead. If you're an investor looking for investment advice—stop investing immediately, as you just paid 7 times more than you had to in order to buy an *actual* book on investing from an *actual* professional investor.

There. Now my attorneys can sleep a little better. Anyway, an interesting type of fixed annuity is the **equity-indexed annuity.** With this product, the investor receives a guaranteed minimum rate of return. But, he/she receives a higher rate of return when an index—usually the S&P 500—has a good year. Do they receive the full upside, as if they owned an S&P 500 index fund? No, and that should be made clear by the sales representative. Equity indexed annuities have a **participation rate.** A participation rate of 70% means that the contract only gets credited with 70% of the increase in the S&P 500. If the index goes up 10%, the contract makes only 7%. Except when it doesn't. The contracts also have a **cap** placed on the maximum increase for any year, regardless of what the stock market does. So with a participation rate of 70% and a cap of 12%, what happens if the S&P goes up 30%? Well, 70% of that would be 21%; however, if you're capped at 12%, then 12% is all the contract value will rise that year. As you can see, indexed annuities are really all about the downside protection, which is why a securities license is not required to sell fixed annuities, equity-indexed or otherwise.

If the individual buys a **deferred annuity**—whether it's fixed or variable—that means his money is sort of tied up, for maybe 10 years. During this **surrender period,** he would lose money to the annuity company if he took his money back out. In other words, this is not for investors who have high liquidity needs—it's for the money they don't plan to touch any time soon. Not only is there a **surrender charge** on a deferred annuity, but the investor will have tax problems if he is under age 59½. So, the following should be disclosed to the investor buying any deferred annuity:

- Surrender periods cause investors who sell early to pay surrender penalties
- Early withdrawals subject to 10% penalty tax

And if he's buying an indexed annuity, also disclose that:

- There is usually a cap (participation rate) placed on how much upside the investor earns when the stock market index rises
- There is often a cap on how much the account value can increase annually

A fixed annuity (including the indexed annuity) is an insurance contract where somebody puts money into the contract, and the insurance company promises to pay the money back plus a certain rate of return and keep making monthly payments for as long as the annuitant is alive. A **variable annuity** doesn't promise a particular rate of return, which is where they got the "variable" part. Since investors are investing in little mutual fund–type accounts of their choosing, maybe they'll end up doing much better than the modest rate that the fixed annuity guarantees. In other words, in a variable annuity, the annuitant bears the investment risk rather than having the insurance company promise a certain rate of return. In exchange for bearing the risks we've looked at in the stock and bond markets, the variable annuitant gets the opportunity to do much better than he would have in a fixed annuity.

Could he do worse? Sure, but what does he want? If he wants a guarantee, he buys a fixed annuity where the insurance company guarantees a certain rate of return. Now he lives with "purchasing power risk," because if the annuity promises 2%, that's not going to be sufficient with inflation rising at 4%. If he wants to protect his purchasing power by investing in the stock market, he buys a variable annuity, but now he takes on all the investment risks we've discussed.

Life is full of tough choices. Your job is to help investors make the one that's right for them.

Variable annuities use mutual fund accounts as their investment options, but we don't call variable annuities "mutual funds." We call the investment options that would otherwise be called "mutual funds" **subaccounts.** Salespeople must go out of their way to avoid confusing customers into thinking an annuity *is* a mutual fund. It is not a mutual fund. Mutual funds aren't subject to early withdrawal penalties from the issuer or the IRS. Mutual funds don't offer a death benefit or add expenses to cover it. On the other hand, mutual funds are not tax-deferred accounts. A mutual fund held in a regular old taxable account will subject investors to taxation every year. The dividend and capital gains distributions are taxable, and if the investor redeems some shares for a gain, that's also taxable for the year it occurs. This tax burden reduces the principal in the account each year, which is a major drag on long-term returns. A variable annuity, however, is really a retirement plan where you get to keep all the dividends and capital gains in the account, adding to your principal, and compounding your returns forever and ever and ever.

Whoa, sorry. Not forever. You get to defer taxation until you take the money out, which is usually at retirement. Your money grows much faster when it's not being taxed for 10, 20, maybe 30 years, but every dance reaches the point where you have to pay the fiddler. It's been a fun dance, for sure, but the reality is that you will pay ordinary income tax rates on the earnings you've been shielding from the hungry hands of the IRS all these years—if and when you decide to get your own hands on the money. Ordinary income rates, remember. If you're in the 35% tax bracket, the gains coming out of your variable annuity are taxed at that rate.

FEATURES OF ANNUITIES

So, tax deferral is a big advantage, and there are other advantages to the complex packaged product known as an "annuity." I'm looking at a handy brochure that compares mutual funds and variable annuities. The company, which sells both, is pointing out that no matter how diligently you save for retirement, you could end up outliving your nest egg. Unless you buy an annuity, that is. An annuity comes with a **mortality guarantee**, which means that once you go into the pay-out phase, you will receive monthly payments as long as you are alive (a mortal). Of course, the fixed annuity tells you what the check will be worth at a minimum, while the variable annuity—well, it varies, people. In the variable annuity, the annuitant will get a check each month, but it could be mighty meager if the markets aren't doing particularly well.

A fixed annuity is really just an insurance product providing peace of mind and tax deferral. A variable annuity functions like a mutual fund investment that grows tax-deferred and offers some peace of mind. See, whether it's fixed or variable, the insurance company offers a **death benefit** that promises to pay a beneficiary at least the amount of money invested by the annuitant during his life—period. The same annuity salespeople who occasionally misinterpret something I've written about annuities as a slam r-e-a-l-l-y don't like a certain financial planner/TV personality who frequently bashes annuities. They would probably like to point out to her that in a regular old mutual fund investment, you could put in $80,000 and when you die the investment could be worth $30,000, which is all your family would inherit. In a variable annuity (not just a *fixed* annuity), the death benefit would pay out the $80,000. In fact, if the value of your investments was worth more than the $80,000 you had put in, your family would receive the $90,000 or whatever the account was worth. Note that in the variable annuity, this death benefit is only in effect while the annuitant is deferring any payments from the contract. As we'll see, once you flip the switch to receive payments in a variable annuity, well, anything can happen.

Insurance companies sell peace of mind. Both the mortality guarantee and the death benefit help a lot of investors sleep better. Pretty tough to put a price tag on that. For maximum peace of mind, individuals should buy a fixed or indexed annuity. For some peace of mind and the chance to invest in the stock and bond markets, individuals should consider a variable annuity. A variable annuity offers the investment choices that you'd get from a family of mutual funds (growth, value, high-yield bonds, etc.), the tax deferral you'd get from an IRA or 401(k) plan, plus a death benefit similar to what you'd get from a life insurance policy. A fixed annuity—or indexed annuity—offers the tax deferral, the death benefit, and a dependable stream of minimum payments, even if you live to 115.

Interestingly, an annuity gives the insurance company a different kind of "mortality risk." In a life insurance policy, their risk is that somebody will put in $10,000 and die the next year, forcing the company to pay out hundreds of thousands, maybe a million. In an annuity, their mortality risk is that the annuitant will end up living to 115. The insurance company makes a mortality guarantee, which promises to pay the annuitant each month for the rest of her life. But, they cover their risk with a fee, called a mortality risk fee. An insurance company has the risk that their expenses will rise. They promise to keep expenses level, but they charge an expense risk fee to cover their risk. In fact, usually the two are combined and referred to as a "mortality and expense risk fee," or "M & E" for those in the real world who love to abbreviate. Variable annuities use mutual fund–type accounts as investment vehicles, but they add charges in excess of what those mutual funds charge investors—all the guarantees offered in the annuity contract can easily add an extra 1% to annual expenses, which can really add up over 20 or 30 years.

While holding a deferred annuity, the individual can **surrender** the contract for its "surrender value." But, watch out here. The first several years typically comprise your **surrender period**. During that time if you decide to cash in the annuity, you will get hit with a **surrender charge**, which is often called a "contingent deferred sales charge" just as we discuss elsewhere in connection with mutual fund B-shares. Yes, many annuities allow people to withdraw 10% of the contract value per year, but anything beyond that is subject to some nasty surrender charges. These surrender charges start out pretty high—say 8% or higher—which is one reason that deferred annuities are long-term investments. Don't be pitching a deferred annuity to a senior citizen, who might need to access a big chunk of her money for an emergency. You need to be pretty sure the individual can leave the money alone for at least as long as the surrender period.

When the individual purchases the annuity, the following are deducted from the check:

- Sales charge (if they have a front-end load)
- Administrative fee
- State premium tax

Most annuities use the contingent deferred sales charge called the "surrender period," but some are still sold with front-end sales charges. Either way, there is a premium tax and administrative fees are taken out of the check.

In a variable annuity the individual then allocates what's left of his **purchase payment** to the various subaccounts, the little mutual fund portfolios. Maybe 20% goes into the conservative income subaccount, 20% into the growth subaccount and 60% to the high-yield long-term bond subaccount. From the money invested there are plenty of fees that will be deducted. We have all the operating expenses we saw for mutual funds: management fee, 12b-1 fee, other expenses. And, we also have the "mortality and expense risk fee" charged for the annuity features.

What is the maximum that an insurance company can charge for sales charges and expenses? The current regulations just say that the charges and expenses have to be "reasonable."

Seriously.

BONUS ANNUITIES

As if annuities weren't complicated enough already, the exam may expect you to know something about **bonus annuities**. With a bonus annuity the annuity company may offer to enhance the buyer's premium by contributing an additional 1 to 5% of what he/she puts in. Of course, this comes with a price. First, there are fees attached and, second, the surrender period is longer. Third, if the investor surrenders the contract early, the bonus disappears. Remember that an investor will get penalized by the annuity company with a "surrender charge" if they pull all their money out early. For "bonus annuities" that period where the investor could get penalized is longer.

Bonus annuities are not suitable for everyone. Variable annuities in general are not good for short-term investment goals, since the surrender charge will be applied during the first 7 years or so. Should you switch a customer into a bonus annuity? Maybe. But, remember, even though the annuitant can avoid taxes through a 1035 exchange, when she exchanges the annuity, her surrender period starts all over again. And, yes, FINRA will bust you if it looks like you did the switch just to make a nice commission, forcing the investor to start the surrender period all over again. In general, investors should maximize their 401(k) and other retirement plans before considering annuities. Annuities are ideal for those who have maxed out those plans, since the annuity allows investors to contribute as much as they would like.

PURCHASING ANNUITIES

The categories of fixed, indexed, and variable annuities refer to the way payments will be calculated on the way out. In terms of buying annuities, the two major types are "immediate" and "deferred." These terms refer to how soon the contract holder wants to begin receiving payments—now, or later? These are retirement plans, remember, so you do need to be 59½ to avoid penalties. Therefore, some customers might want or need to wait 20 or 30 years before receiving payments. If so, they purchase a **deferred annuity**, because "deferred" means "I'll do it later," the way some readers may have "deferred" their study process a few weeks—or months—before buckling down.

The tax deferral is nice, but if the individual is already, say, 68, she may want to retire now and start receiving payments immediately. As you can probably guess, we call that an **immediate annuity**. While there are immediate *variable* annuities, it just makes more sense somehow to buy the fixed *immediate* annuity. Why? Well, the whole point of buying an immediate annuity is to know that—no matter what happens to social security and your 401(k) account—there is a solid insurance company contractually obligated to make a payment of at least X amount for as long as you live. An immediate *variable* annuity would work out well only if the investments did—while there would be some minimal payment guaranteed, it would be meager. An immediate fixed annuity does not offer a high rate of return, but it does provide peace of mind to investors in retirement. Many financial planners would suggest that at least some of their clients' retirement money be sitting in a fixed immediate annuity—maybe just enough to provide a monthly payment covering all monthly expenses. Figuring withdrawal rates from retirement accounts is very tricky, so having a payment of X amount from a solid insurance company could really smooth out the bumps.

Customers can buy annuities either with one big payment or several smaller payments. The first method is called "single premium" or "single payment." The second method is called "periodic payment." If an investor has a large chunk of money, she can put it in an annuity, where it can grow tax-deferred. If she's putting in a big single premium, she can choose either to wait (defer) or to begin receiving annuity payments immediately. She has to be 59½ years old to annuitize, but if she's old enough, she can begin the pay-out phase immediately. That's called a **single-payment immediate annuity**. Maybe she's only 42, though, and wants to let the money grow another 20 years before taking it out. That's called a **single-payment deferred annuity** (SPDA).

Many investors put money into the annuity during the accumulation phase (pay-in) gradually, over time. That's called "periodic payment," and if they aren't done paying in yet, you can bet the insurance company isn't going to start paying out. So, if you're talking about a "periodic payment" plan, the only way to do it is through a **periodic *deferred* annuity**. There is no such thing as a "Periodic Immediate Annuity" since no insurance company I'm aware of would let me start sending in $100 a month while they go ahead and start sending me $110.

To review, then, there are three methods of purchasing annuities:

- Single-Payment Deferred Annuity
- Periodic-Payment Deferred Annuity
- Single-Payment Immediate Annuity

Again, understand that variable annuities use mutual funds (called subaccounts) as the investment vehicles in the plan. But, annuities add both features and extra expenses for the investor on top of all the investment-related expenses. Tax deferral is nice. So are the death benefit and the annuity payment that goes on as long as the individual lives. But, that stuff also adds maybe 1.0–1.5% per year in expenses to the investor. You can either slide that fact past your investor or fully disclose it. Depends on whether you want your name up on FINRA's website or not.

RECEIVING PAYMENTS (SETTLEMENT OPTIONS)

So, some investors make periodic payments into the contract while others make just one big payment. Either way, when the individual gets ready to annuitize the contract, he tells the insurance company which payout option he's choosing. And, he is not able to change this decision—he makes the decision and lives with it. Or, maybe more accurately, dies with it. Essentially, what's going on at this point in the contract is that the individual is about to make a bet with the insurance company as to how long he will end up living.

Seriously. And, as in Las Vegas, the house has a major advantage here. The actuaries can estimate how long any individual is likely to live plus or minus X number of years. They can then calculate a rate of payout on the fixed and indexed annuities that all but guarantees the insurance company will come out way ahead—ever visited the Allstate or State Farm campuses? Larger than most universities. Anyway, in case we haven't made this clear, even though the fixed annuity promises a certain minimum payment for the rest of your life, if you die in a couple years, they keep the balance of your account.

Seriously. Same thing for a variable annuity, but it's probably not as surprising on the variable side. But, either way, if the individual throws the switch to receive payments and chooses **life only** or **straight life** he'll typically receive the largest monthly payout. Why? Because the insurance company sets those payments and the insurance company knows better than he does when he's going to die. Not the exact day or the exact method, of course, but they can estimate it with amazing precision. Since the insurance/annuity company only has to make payments for as long as he lives, the payments are typically the largest for a "life only" or "straight life" annuity settlement option. How does the individual win the "bet"? By living a lot longer than the actuarial tables would predict. Not a bad motivation for exercising and eating right, huh? If this option seems too risky, the individual can choose a "unit refund life annuity." This way he is guaranteed a certain number of payments even if he does get hit by the proverbial bus. If he dies before receiving them, his beneficiary receives the balance of payments.

So, does the annuitant have family or a charity she wants to be sure receives the balance of her payments? If not, why not go with the life only/straight life option—tell the insurance company to pay her as much as possible for as long as she lives. If she dies—well, what does she care if State Farm or Northwestern Mutual comes out ahead? If she does have family, friends, or a charity that she'd like to name as a beneficiary, she can choose a **period certain** settlement option. In that case, the insurance company has to do what the name implies—make payments for a certain period of time. To either her or the named beneficiaries. For older investors, this option typically leads to a lower monthly payment, since the insurance company will now be on the hook for several years even if the annuitant conveniently expires early. If it's a 20-year period certain payout, the payments have to be made to the beneficiary for the rest of that period, even if the annuitant dies after the first month or two. The annuitant could also choose **life with period certain**, and now we'd have a complicated either-or scenario with the insurance company. With this option the company will make payments for the greater of his life *or* a certain period of time, such as 20 years. If he dies after 2 years, the company makes payments to his beneficiary for the rest of the term. And if he lives longer than 20 years, they just keep on making payments until he finally expires. Please read that sentence again, because it seems that no one ever believes me when I say that if the annuitant chooses a 20-year life-with-period-certain settlement option and inconveniently lives 23 years, the insurance company makes payments for 23 years. When he dies, no more payments.

Finally, the **joint with last survivor** option would typically provide the smallest monthly check because the company is obligated to make payments as long as either the annuitant or the survivors are still alive. The contract can be set up to pay the annuitant while he's alive and then pay the beneficiaries until the last beneficiary expires. Or, it can start paying the annuitant *and* the beneficiary until both have finally, you know. Covering two persons' mortality risks (the risk that they'll live an inconveniently long time) is an expensive proposition to the insurance company, so these monthly checks are typically smaller than either period certain or life-only settlement options.

VOTING RIGHTS

Just like owners of mutual fund shares, owners of variable annuities get to vote their units on important decisions such as:

- Electing the Board of Managers
- Changing the Investment Objectives, Policies
- Ratifying the Independent Auditor/Accounting Firm

ACCUMULATION AND ANNUITY UNITS

There are only two phases of an annuity—the **accumulation period** and the **annuity period**. If insurance companies talked like actual humans, they would call it the "pay-in" and the "pay-out" phase. An individual making periodic payments into the contract, or one who made one big payment and is now just deferring the payout phase, is in the accumulation phase, holding **accumulation units**. When he throws the switch to start receiving payments, the insurance company will convert those accumulation units to **annuity units**. Remember that in a fixed annuity, the annuitant knows the minimum monthly payment he can expect. A variable annuity, on the other hand, will pay out the fluctuating value of those annuity units. And, although the value of annuity units fluctuates in a variable annuity during the payout phase, the *number* of those annuity units is fixed. To calculate the first payment for a variable annuity, the insurance company uses the following:

- Age of the annuitant
- Account value
- Gender
- Settlement option

Remember that health is not a factor—you don't receive money based on a health exam here. This is also why an annuity cannot suddenly be turned into a life insurance policy, even though it can definitely work in the other direction, as we'll discuss elsewhere.

AIR and Annuity Units

As we said, once the number of annuity units has been determined, we say that the number of annuity units is fixed. So, for example, maybe every month he'll be paid the value of 100 annuity units.

Trouble is, he has no idea how big that monthly check is going to be, since nobody knows what 100 annuity units will be worth month-to-month, just like nobody knows what mutual fund shares will be worth month-to-month. Remember the "fixed-shares systematic withdrawal plan" from a mutual fund? We said that the fund will redeem a fixed number of shares and pay you whatever they happened to be worth. Again, the units really are mutual fund shares; we just can't call them that. During the pay-in phase, we call the shares **accumulation units**. During the pay-out phase, we call them **annuity units**, just to keep things nice and simple.

So, how much is an annuity unit worth every month? All depends on the investment performance of the separate account compared to the expectations of its performance.

Seriously.

AIR

If the separate account returns are better than the assumed rate, the units increase in value. If the account returns are exactly as expected, the unit value stays the same. And if the account returns are lower than expected, the unit value drops from the month before. It's all based on the **Assumed Interest Rate (AIR)** that the annuitant and annuity company agree to use. If the **AIR** is 5%, that just means the separate account investments are expected to grow each month at an annualized rate of 5%. If the account actually gets a 6% annualized rate of return one month, the individual's check gets bigger. (Remember, during the payout phase, the investor is paid the value of his fixed number of annuity units, so to say that the annuity units have increased in value is the same as saying the individual's check gets bigger.) If the account gets the anticipated 5% return next month, that's the same as AIR and the check will stay the same. And if the account gets only a 4% return the following month, the check will go down.

Don't let the exam trick you on this concept. If the AIR is 5%, here is how it would work:

Actual Return:	5%	7%	6%	5%	4%
Check:	$1,020	$1,035	$1,045	$1,045	$1,030

When the account gets a 7% return, the account gets much bigger. So when it gets only a 6% return the following month, that's 6% of a bigger account, and is 1% more than we expected to get. So, just compare the actual return with the AIR. If the actual return is bigger, so is the monthly check. If it's smaller, so is the monthly check. If the actual return is the same as the AIR, the check stays the same.

THE SEPARATE ACCOUNT

Let's get excessively detailed for a moment to discuss the important difference between guaranteed insurance products and variable products. An insurance company is one of the finest business models ever constructed. See, no one person can take the risk of dying at age 32 and leaving the family with an unpaid mortgage, a bunch of other bills, and a sudden loss of income, not to mention the maybe $15,000 it takes just for a funeral these days. But, an insurance company can take the risk that a certain number of individuals will die prematurely by insuring a huge number of individuals and then using the very precise laws of probability over large numbers that tell them how many individuals will die each year with only a small margin of error. Once they've taken the insurance premiums that individuals pay, they then invest what's left after covering expenses and invest it very wisely in the real estate, fixed-income, and stock markets. They have just as much data on these markets, so they can use the laws of probability again to figure out that if they take this much risk here, they can count on earning this much return over here within only a small margin of error.

And, of course, insurance companies are very conservative investors. That's what allows them to crunch a bunch of numbers and know with reasonable certainty that they will never have to pay so many death benefits in one year that their investments are totally wiped out. This conservative investment account that guarantees the payout on whole life, term life, and fixed annuities is called the **general account**. In other words, the general account is for the insurance company's investments.

They then created an account that is separate from the general account and, believe it or not, decided to name it the **separate account**. It's really a mutual fund family that offers tax deferral, but we don't call it a mutual fund, even though it's also covered by and registered under the same Investment Company Act of 1940. The Investment Company Act of 1940 defines a separate account like so:

> "Separate account" means an account established and maintained by an insurance company pursuant to the laws of any State or territory of the United States, or of Canada or any province thereof, under which income, gains and losses, whether or not realized, from assets allocated to such account, are, in accordance with the applicable contract, credited to or charged against such account without regard to other income, gains, or losses of the insurance company.

Well, that certainly clears things up, doesn't it? Anyway, you might get a few questions talking about the "general account" versus the "separate account," so please keep the two separate. When your purchase payments are invested into the general account, you are guaranteed a certain rate of return—whole life, fixed annuity. When your purchase payments are invested into the separate account, welcome to the stock and bond markets, where anything can happen.

From the perspective of the nice couple sitting across from you at the table, it all looks pretty much the same. You were talking about the Platinum Equity Income Fund a few minutes ago—now that you've switched to your variable annuity spiel, we're still seeing the same Platinum Equity Income Fund. What's up with that? It's the same darned fund, but if you buy it within a variable annuity contract, we call it a **subaccount**, just to keep everything nice and simple. Actually, there's a good reason to avoid calling subaccounts "mutual funds." If the investor thinks he's in a "mutual fund," he might think he can take out his money whenever he wants. He also might not realize that he's paying an extra 1.0–1.5% a year to place the annuity wrapper around the "mutual fund" investments. So, be careful with the language out there once you get licensed, people.

LIFE INSURANCE

I've always felt that it would be awfully rude of me to die without insurance and leave family and friends footing the bill for my funeral. That's why I basically "rent" insurance coverage through something called **term life insurance**. It's very cheap, but it's only good for a certain term—maybe it's a 5-, 10-, or 20-year term. The individual pays premiums in exchange for a guaranteed **death benefit** payable to a **beneficiary** if **the insured** dies during that period. If the insured does not die during that period, the policy expires. If the **policyholder** wants to renew, he can, but he's older now and more costly to insure. In other words, his premiums will go up, even though the death benefit will stay the same, because he's older and more likely to have some medical condition that raises his rates, too, or even that prevents him from being offered the insurance at all. So, as with all products, there are pluses and minuses. Term insurance is cheap and offers nice protection, but it does not build any cash value and has to be renewed at higher and higher rates, just like renting an apartment.

Now would be a good time to note the language used in insurance:

- **Policyholder**: the owner of the policy, responsible for paying premiums
- **Insured**: the person whose life is insured by the policy, usually the policyholder
- **Beneficiary**: the party that receives the death benefit upon death of the insured
- **Death benefit**: the amount payable to the beneficiary upon death of the insured, minus any unpaid premiums or loan balances
- **Cash value**: a value in the policy account that can be partially withdrawn or borrowed against

So, let's say that Joe Smith buys an insurance policy with a $100,000 death benefit payable to his wife. He's the policyholder and the insured. If he dies, the death benefit of $100,000 is paid to the beneficiary, his wife. As we'll see, most insurance also builds up cash value, which can be withdrawn or borrowed while Joe is still alive (note that term insurance does not build up this cash value, which is also why it's relatively cheap insurance).

PERMANENT VS. TEMPORARY INSURANCE

As with housing, some people prefer to rent insurance for a term, and some prefer to buy it. Some feel that if you're going to be putting money aside, you might as well end up with something to show for it, so they purchase permanent insurance. The most common type of permanent insurance is called **whole life insurance**. The premiums are much higher than on the term insurance you sort of "rent," but insurance companies will guarantee a minimum **cash value**, and you can also pretty well plan for an even better cash value than that. This way it works to protect your beneficiaries if you die unexpectedly and also acts as a savings vehicle where the cash value grows tax-deferred. Maybe at age 55 you decide to borrow $50,000 of the cash value for *whatever* reason. Could come in really handy, yes?

One other thing to remember: to renew a term policy means you pay a higher premium. Premiums are "level" in a whole life policy, meaning they don't go up. You lock in your rate for your whole life.

So, term is "cheap," but after a few years you have no cash value. And, to keep it going, you'd have to pay more for the same benefit. Reminds me of how I spent five years paying "cheap" rent to a landlord. It was definitely lower than a mortgage payment would have been on a similar-sized house. But at the end of this 5-year term, I had forked over 40 g's to the landlord and was left with nothing but the opportunity to renew my lease at a higher rate. I covered myself with a roof for five years, and at the end of the five years I owned absolutely no part of that roof—not even one cracked, loose shingle.

Whole life insurance is more like buying the house, which is exactly what I did after five years of renting. I had to come up with a down payment, and my monthly mortgage is now $200 more per month than my rent was. The upside is that at the end of five years, I'll have some equity in the house that I can tap into for a loan maybe (kind of like cash value in an insurance policy that I can borrow against some day). Just like with a whole life policy, I'll be getting at least something back for all those payments I've made over the years. And the time will come when the full value is all paid up and mine.

So, whole life insurance involves premiums that are higher than those for term life insurance, but you end up with something even if you stop paying into the policy. There is a guaranteed cash value, whereas term leaves you with nothing. The death benefit is guaranteed (as it is on a term policy), too, so whole life insurance is a very popular product for people who want to protect their families and also use the policy as a savings vehicle, where all that increase in cash value grows tax-deferred.

If the exam asks which type of client should purchase term insurance, I would look for a young, single parent, maybe, or someone who absolutely has to protect the kids from a sudden loss of income and wants to do it as cheaply as possible.

Nothing is simple in either the securities or insurance industry. Since some clients crave flexibility, the industry bent over backwards to come up with a flexible form of permanent insurance called **universal life insurance**. Think "flexibility" when you see the words "universal life insurance." The death benefit and, therefore, the premiums can be adjusted by the client. They can be increased to buy more coverage or decreased to back off on the coverage and save some money. If the cash value is sufficient, premiums can actually stop being paid by the client and start being covered by the cash value. The cash value grows at a minimum, guaranteed rate, just like on traditional whole life policies, and if the general account does particularly well, the cash value goes up from there. As mentioned, at some point the policyholder may decide to withdraw part of the cash value, or may usually borrow up to 90% of it.

Variable Policies

So, whether it's term, traditional whole life, or universal life insurance, we're talking strictly about insurance products. Death benefits and cash values (term has no cash value) are guaranteed by the insurance company, who invests the net premiums (what's left after deducting expenses, taxes, etc.) into their general account. Once you start attaching cash value and death benefits to the ups and downs of a separate account, however, you have created a new product that is both an insurance policy and a security. Opens a whole new market for the company, but it also means that those who sell them need both an insurance and a securities license.

Whole life and term life insurance policies tell clients exactly how much they will pay out upon death. So, in term and whole life policies, the investment risk is borne totally by the insurance company through their "general account," which is, more or less, a pile of cash and securities as tall as Mount Everest.

Well, with **variable insurance products**, the death benefit—as well as the cash value—fluctuates just like it does in a variable annuity. That's what they mean by "variable." It all varies, based on the investment performance of the separate account. The separate account, as we discussed under variable annuities, is made up of subaccounts. The investor chooses from these little quasi-mutual funds that are trying to meet different investment objectives: growth, long-term bonds, short-term Treasuries, etc. He can even choose to invest some of the premiums into a fixed account, just to play it safe, and he can switch between the subaccounts as his investment needs change without a tax problem. This stuff all grows tax-deferred, remember.

The cash value is tied to account performance, period. So if the test question says that the separate account grew, it doesn't matter by how much. The cash value increases when the separate account increases. But death benefit is tied to actual performance versus AIR, just like an annuity unit in a variable annuity. So if the AIR is 6% and the account gets a 4% return, the cash value will increase due to the positive return, but the death benefit will decrease since the account returned less than AIR.

Variable Life Insurance (VLI) policies will pay out the cash value/surrender value whenever the policyholder decides to cash in the policy. Now, there's no way to know what the value might be at the time of surrender. If the little subaccounts have performed well, the cash value might be better than expected. But if the market has been brutal, the cash value could go all the way down to zero. Probably not gonna happen, but it could.

A minimum or fixed death benefit is guaranteed, however. Some refer to it as the "floor." No matter what the market does, the insurance company guarantees a minimum death benefit that could only be reduced or depleted by failure to pay premiums or taking out loans against the policy. Remember that any guaranteed payments are covered by the insurance company's general account. So, the minimum death benefit is guaranteed, and the policyholder also has the chance of enjoying an increased death benefit, depending on how well the little subaccounts (inside the separate account) do.

As we said, that's tied to AIR, so if the market is kind, the death benefit increases, but if the market is unkind, it could, theoretically, drag the death benefit all the way down to the floor.

As with variable annuities, after the money's been allocated to the little subaccounts of the separate account, the insurance company charges regular fees, just like they do in variable annuities:

- mortality risk fee
- expense risk fee
- investment management fees

The value of the subaccounts and, therefore, the cash value are calculated daily. The death benefit is calculated annually. If the separate account has several below-AIR months, it will take several above-AIR months after that before the customer's death benefit starts to increase.

Remember that flexibility we discussed that separates traditional whole life from universal life? Well, it probably isn't too surprising that somebody eventually married that benefit to variable life to get **Variable Universal Life Insurance**. With VUL we have the death benefit and cash value tied to the separate account (variable), plus we have the flexible premium thing (universal) going on. Regular old variable life is called "scheduled premium." That means the insurance company puts your premium payments on a schedule, and you better stick to it. Variable Universal or Universal Variable Life policies are funded as "flexible premium." That means the client may or may not have to send in a check. With a VUL policy, the customer has to maintain enough cash value and death benefit to keep the policy in force. If the separate account rocks, no money has to roll in from the customer. If the separate account rolls over and dies, look out. Since that's a little scary, some VULs come with minimum guaranteed death benefits.

Variable Universal Life can get to be a sort of complicated product, and as with anything you sell, before you do so, make darn sure you understand all the ins and outs. And talking to a firm specialist or old-timer might not hurt, either, on this or any other product that's new to you. A good question is always, "Worst-case scenario, what could go wrong?"

The advantages of variable life over whole life insurance include the ability to invest some of the premiums into the stock market, which has historically enjoyed relatively high average returns and done very well at beating inflation. A robust investment market can increase the cash value and death benefit, often faster than the rate of inflation. A traditional whole life policy, on the other hand, that promised to pay $50,000 when it was purchased in 1964 represented a lot of money then. But if it pays that $50,000 out in 2014, the $50,000 doesn't go very far, due to inflation.

Policy Loans

Variable policies make 75% of the cash value available to the customer as a loan after three years. Guess what, though?—they charge interest on that loan, just as they do on a whole life policy. If the loan is not repaid, that reduces both the cash value and the death benefit of the policy. And, if the customer takes out a big loan and then the separate account tanks, he'll have to put some money back in to bring the cash value back to a sufficient level, or risk having the policy lapse. Don't worry, though. Some people take out a loan with absolutely no intention of repaying it. They simply don't need as much death benefit at this point, so why not have some fun with the money right now? The test might point out that whole life insurance policies allow the policyholder to borrow a higher percentage of cash value, while VLI, on the other hand, being backed up by the subaccounts only lets the policyholder borrow up to 75% of cash value.

Settlement Options for Insurance Policies

The policyholder can choose from many options concerning the method of payment to the beneficiary. These are called "settlement options." The "lump-sum" method is self-explanatory. "Fixed-period" means that the insurance company will invest the proceeds of the policy into an interest-bearing account and then make equal payments at regular intervals for a fixed period. The payments include principal and interest. How much are the payments? That depends on the size of the principal, the interest rate earned by the insurance company, and the length of time involved in this fixed period.

The "fixed-amount" settlement option has the insurance company invest the proceeds from the policy and pay the beneficiary a fixed amount of money at regular intervals until both the principal and interest are gone. The amount received is fixed, but the period over which the beneficiary receives payments varies.

So, for "fixed-period" versus "fixed-amount," the decision comes down to this: do you want to receive an uncertain amount of money for a fixed period of time, or do you want to receive a fixed amount of money for an uncertain period of time? In other words, do you want to be paid something like $25,000 for exactly three years (fixed-period)? Or, would you prefer being paid exactly $25,000 for about three years (fixed-amount)?

In a "life-income" settlement option, the proceeds are annuitized. That means the insurance company provides the beneficiary with a guaranteed income for the rest of his/her life. Just like with annuities, the beneficiary's age expectancy is taken into account to determine the monthly payout, along with the size of the death benefit and the type of payout selected.

There is also an "interest-only" settlement option, whereby the insurance company keeps the proceeds from the policy and invests them, promising the beneficiary a guaranteed minimum rate of interest. The beneficiary might get more than the minimum, or not, and may receive the payments annually, semiannually, quarterly, or monthly. He/she also has the right to withdraw all the principal if he/she gets antsy, or to change settlement options.

Exchanges

Since these variable policies are a little confusing to some, the company has to give the policyholder at least two years (24 months) to switch back to traditional whole life without having to provide proof of insurability. The new whole life policy will have the same issue date as the original variable policy.

If you buy a variable life policy, you have the opportunity to exchange it for a different policy *even if issued by a different company*. You don't have to pay taxes since you aren't taking the cash value and, like, going on a fly-fishing trip to Alaska. You just cash in one policy and exchange it, tax-free, for another insurance policy. Or, believe it or not, you can even exchange a life policy for an annuity. You can't turn an annuity into a life policy, though.

This tax-free exchange is called a **1035 exchange**.

When selling variable insurance policies, the rep needs to remember that these are insurance policies first and foremost. You can discuss the benefits of investing in the subaccounts, but you can't present these insurance policies primarily as investment vehicles. Primarily, they're to be sold for the death benefit. They also offer the opportunity to invest in the separate account's little subaccounts, but they're not to be pitched primarily as investment vehicles.

Four federal acts are involved with variable life insurance and variable annuities. The Securities Act of 1933 covers variable life insurance (and annuities). These products must be registered with the SEC and sold with a prospectus. Even though the company that issues these contracts is an insurance company, the subdivision that sells the securities products has to be a broker-dealer registered under the Securities Exchange Act of 1934. The separate account is defined as an investment company under the Investment Company Act of 1940 and is either registered as a UIT or an Open-End Fund as defined under that act. The "money manager" or "investment adviser" has to register under the Investment Advisers Act of 1940.

And, at the state level, both securities and insurance regulators are watching these products and those who sell them, too.

TYPES OF INVESTMENT RISKS

So, we've looked at many types of investment vehicles that customers can buy either individually or as part of a mutual fund investment. All of the securities investment vehicles we looked at present one or more types of risk to an investor. The most basic type of risk is **capital risk,** and it represents the risk that an investor can lose some or all of his investment capital. Obviously, U.S. Treasury Securities provide almost none of this risk, but all common stock and all corporate bonds do present capital risk to one degree or another. Mutual funds are more diversified than individual investors are, but as any prospectus warns, investors can and do lose money by investing in mutual funds. Losing money—that's capital risk.

One of the best ways to understand investment risks is to read through the first few pages of a mutual fund prospectus. I'm looking at the prospectus for a growth fund myself at the moment, and it declares that its investment goal is "growth of capital," and then goes on to say that "dividend income, if any, will be incidental to this goal." In other words, the fund invests in growth stocks, but some of those companies will also pay dividends, and this fund does not mind cashing their checks. It's just that the dividends have nothing to do with the fund's reasons for investing in the stock—it's the growth or capital appreciation that they're after. The "principal strategy" tells me that the fund focuses on companies with $10 billion or more of market value (market cap) and uses fundamental analysis to determine which companies show strength in terms of earnings, revenue, profit margins, etc.

SYSTEMATIC RISKS

The next section of the prospectus is called "important risks," and it lists investment risks such as:

> Stock market risk, or the risk that the price of securities held by the Fund will fall due to various conditions or circumstances which may be unpredictable.

Market Risk

The exam might refer to the above "stock market risk" as "market risk." **Market risk** is a type of **systematic risk,** which means it affects the overall market across the board, as opposed to an **unsystematic risk**, which affects only particular stocks or bonds. Market risk is the risk that an investment will lose its value due to an overall market decline. As the prospectus says, the circumstances may be unpredictable. For example, no one can predict the next war or where the next tsunami, hurricane, or nuclear disaster will hit, but when events like that take place, they can have a devastating effect on the overall market. Whether they panic because of war, weather, or whatever, the fact is that when investors panic, stock prices plummet. We might think of stock market risk as the fact that even though the company might be doing just fine, your stock investment in that company could plummet just because the overall stock market plummets due to a market panic. Human behavior is what ultimately determines stock prices, and if you've read your history, you know that human behavior can get a little volatile from time to time.

The S&P 500 index is generally used to represent the "overall market," so what can an investor do to combat overall market risk? He can make a little side bet against the overall market by purchasing put options on a **broad-based index** such as the **S&P 500**. Or, he can sell the **ETFs (exchange traded funds)** that track a broad-based index short. Now, if the market rises, his stocks make money. If the market drops, his little side bet against the overall market makes money. To bet the other way is called **hedging**. So, if you own a broad spectrum of the overall market, you can buy puts or sell calls on the S&P 500 index, or you can sell Spiders™ short. That way, you can make a little money whether the overall market goes up or down, and—best of all—you can sleep at night. Also, remember that **diversification** will NOT help reduce overall market risk—if the overall market is going down, it doesn't matter how many different stocks you own; they're all going down. That's why you'd have to bet against the overall market to protect yourself.

Natural Event Risk

Natural event risk is fairly self-explanatory, as it refers to the fact that a tsunami, earthquake, hurricane, etc., could have a devastating effect on a country's economy, and possibly the economy of an entire area such as Europe or Southeast Asia. A recent annual report from Starbucks mentions a "global pandemic" as a major risk to the price of the stock, something I would not have thought of. In other words, if disease sweeps the globe or any part of it, public gathering places (like coffee shops) are going to be shut down, people will be too sick to pick coffee beans, and transportation routes may be closed to prevent the spread of illness. None of that would have anything to do with the taste of Starbucks coffee or the management skills of the company. It's all just part of that unpredictable thing called market risk.

Interest Rate Risk

Investing in bonds is inherently less volatile than investing in stocks, but there are still several risks involved with bond investing, starting with **interest rate risk**. Interest rate risk is the risk that interest rates overall will rise, knocking down the market price of your bond. Remember that the longer the term on the bond, the more volatile its price. Note that we don't care who issued the bond at all—U.S. Treasury securities are just as subject to this risk as high-yield corporate bonds. When rates go up, all bond prices fall, but the long-term bonds (Treasury, municipal, or corporate) suffer the most. And, when rates go down, all bond prices rise, but the long-term bonds go up the most. So, a 30-year government bond has no default risk, but carries more interest rate risk than a 10-year corporate bond. The reason we see short-term and intermediate-term bond funds is because many investors want to reduce interest rate risk. Maybe they have a shorter time horizon and will need this money in just a few years—they can't risk a huge drop in market value due to a sudden rise in interest rates. They will probably sacrifice the higher yield offered by a long-term bond fund, but they will sleep better knowing that rising rates won't be quite as devastating to short-term bonds.

The prospectus I'm looking at covers several of the family's funds, which means I won't have to get up and find another one after all—yes! In the bond fund prospectus, we see that the important risks include:

```
Risk that the value of the securities the Fund holds will
fall as a result of changes in interest rates.
```

Interest rate risk. Rates up, price down—and it's more severe the longer the term to maturity. Frankly, I can't imagine anyone taking the Series 6 and not being asked to prove he knows this important fact in at least one or two questions.

Purchasing Power Risk

Purchasing power risk is sometimes called **inflation risk** and even **constant dollar risk** to make sure it has three names. If inflation erodes the value of money, an investor's fixed return simply can't buy what it used to. Fixed-income investments carry purchasing power or inflation risk, which is why investors often try to beat inflation by investing in common stock. The ride might be a wild one in the stock market, but the reward is that we should be able to grow faster than the rate of inflation, whereas a fixed-income payment is, you know, *fixed*. Retirees living solely on fixed incomes are more susceptible to inflation or purchasing power risk than people still in the workforce, since salaries tend to rise with inflation. The longer the retiree has to live on a fixed income, the more susceptible she is to inflation risk. Unfortunately, common stock is often too volatile for investors with shorter time horizons and high needs for liquidity. The solution is often to put the majority of a retiree's money into short-term bonds and money market instruments, with a small percentage in large cap stock, equity income, or growth & income funds. That way, the dependable income stream from the short-term debt securities will cover the living expenses, while the smaller piece devoted to conservative stock investments will likely provide some protection of purchasing power. Not to mention that blue chip stocks almost by definition pay dividends, and dividends tend to increase over time. So, putting a reasonable percentage of a retiree's money into blue chip stocks is not necessarily "risky," as might have been thought in the past. In fact, Modern Portfolio Theory suggests that by adding some conservative stocks to a bond portfolio, one may actually reduce overall volatility. Volatility and risk are synonymous these days, so try not to write off any of the major asset classes if you can help it. Blue chip stocks can balance out a primarily fixed-income portfolio, just like fixed-income securities balance out a stock portfolio.

Call Risk

The bond fund prospectus on my desk also warns of **call risk**, or "the risk that a bond might be called during a period of declining interest rates." Most municipal and corporate bonds are **callable**, meaning that when interest rates drop, corporate and municipal bond issuers will borrow new money at today's lower rate and use it to pay off the current bondholders much sooner than they expected. The problems for the current bondholders are that, first, the bond price stops rising in the secondary market once everyone knows the exact call price that will be received. And, second, what do they do with the money they just received from the issuer? Reinvest it, right? And, where are interest rates now? Down—so they probably take the proceeds from a 9% bond and turn it into a 6% payment going forward. Hmm—you used to get $90 per year; now you can look forward to $60. Couldn't you protect yourself by buying non-callable bonds? Sure—and they'll offer you lower rates than what they pay on callable bonds. As they say, there is no free lunch.

Reinvestment Risk

Remember that bonds paying regular interest checks force investors—if they don't just spend the money—to reinvest into new bonds every few months or so. What kind of rates/yields will debt securities be offering when they go to reinvest the coupon payments? Nobody knows, which is why it's a risk, called **reinvestment risk**. It's very annoying to take a 9% interest payment and reinvest it at 3%, but it does happen. To avoid reinvestment risk, buy a debt security that gives you nothing to reinvest along the way: zero coupons, i.e., Treasury STRIPS. We'll look at the features of various securities in depth later in this chapter, in the section entitled "Issuing Securities," by the way.

So, even though bond investing is less risky than stock investing, notice how bondholders can get hit coming and going. If it's a corporate bond—and plenty of municipal securities—you could end up getting stiffed (credit risk). If rates go up, the price of your bond gets knocked down (interest rate risk). If rates go down, callable bonds are called (call risk), and the party's over, and with non-callable bonds you still have to reinvest the interest checks every six months at a lower rate going forward (reinvestment risk). And, even if none of the above happens, inflation could inch its way up, making those coupon payments less and less valuable (purchasing power risk).

Oh, well. If you want fixed income, you take on these risks to varying degrees, depending on which bond you buy and when you buy it. So, am I saying that nobody ever wins by purchasing bonds?

No. Can you think of a situation where buying bonds could turn out to be profitable? What if you purchased a bunch of 30-year, non-callable bonds right when interest rates were sky-high and getting ready to drop? Wouldn't that make your purchase price extremely cheap (rates high/price low) and, then, suddenly the market price would shoot to the moon as interest rates started to fall, the faster the better?

How are you going to know when rates have peaked? No idea, but if you figure it out, please text me at your earliest convenience.

Prepayment Risk

Prepayment risk is really just call risk that comes with owning a mortgage-backed security. A homeowner with a mortgage will typically take advantage of a sudden drop in interest rates by refinancing. Therefore, if an investor holds **mortgage-backed securities** like those issued by GNMA, FNMA, or FHLMC (Ginnie, Fannie, Freddie), that investor will take a hit if interest rates drop suddenly and all the principal is returned sooner than expected. This is called **prepayment risk.** When the investor receives the principal sooner than expected, she typically ends up reinvesting it into similar mortgage-backed securities and receiving a lower rate of interest going forward, while the homeowners in the pool of mortgages, on the other hand, are enjoying *paying* lower interest rates going forward. Since GNMA (Ginnie Mae) securities are guaranteed by the U.S. Treasury, their main risk is this prepayment risk. Also, notice that call risk is essentially the same thing as prepayment risk; it's just that prepayment risk is related specifically to mortgage-backed securities while call risk refers to bonds and preferred stock.

NON- OR UN-SYSTEMATIC RISK

Non-systematic risk means that any particular stock or bond could take a huge hit all by itself for all kinds of reasons. Diversifying a portfolio reduces these risks by spreading them out among diverse holdings. In fact, Modern Portfolio Theory states that this type of risk is "diversifiable" and that investors should not expect to be compensated for taking on non- or un-systematic risks. They should only expect to be compensated for taking on systematic risk.

Business Risk

Buying stocks or bonds in any company presents **business risk**. Business risk includes the risk of competition, poor management of the company, and **obsolescence risk,** which is the risk that a company's products/services suddenly become obsolete, no longer relevant. In the past, shareholders in 8-track player and electric typewriter manufacturing companies experienced this type of investment risk. These days, I could almost picture movie theaters becoming a thing of the past, so investing in a movie theater chain carries more "risk of obsolescence" than investing in a company that makes underwear or shoes. The risk of poor business decisions by the officers and directors, of better competitors, or of products/services becoming obsolete are all part of business risk. In other words, the stock you own is only as solid as the businesses who issued it. So, you need to diversify your portfolio so that it's not all subject to the same type of business risk. Airlines, retailers, and financial services companies, for example, would all face different business risks. If you look at the prospectus or SAI for a mutual fund, you'll see that most stock funds hold stocks across many different industries for the sake of diversification.

Political Risk

The American business climate and financial markets are pretty darned dependable, especially when compared to, say, Syria. Of course, we might occasionally want to raise the bar a little bit, but you get the point. Remember that **political risk** is part of the package if you want to invest in **emerging markets**. An emerging market is a country or region where the financial markets are immature and unpredictable. They're not fully developed, a little awkward, a bit volatile, basically like teenagers—bright future, but some days you really aren't sure if they're going to make it. If you own stocks and bonds in companies operating and trading in undeveloped economies, lots of fits and starts can make the ride a wild one—what happens if the Chinese government gets tired of capitalism and nationalizes/seizes the companies whose shares you used to own? Total loss. Or maybe the transition from communism to "capitalism" doesn't go so well, and suddenly the whole country is shut down with riots in the streets and government tanks rolling in. When this type of thing happens, emerging market investments naturally are affected, and not in a good way.

Currency Exchange Risk

Also, since most countries use a different currency from the American dollar, **currency exchange risk** is also part of the package when investing in foreign markets, emerging or otherwise. The value of the American dollar relative to foreign currencies, then, is a risk to both international and emerging markets investors. So, even if it's a **developed market**, such as Japan, if you're investing internationally into Japanese stocks, the value of the yen versus the dollar presents foreign exchange or currency risk. If you're investing in China, you have that risk, plus the political risk of investing in companies operating in an immature capitalist system likely to suffer many fits and starts before all the kinks are worked out.

Legislative or "Regulatory" Risk

Legislative or **regulatory risk** means that if laws change, certain securities could be negatively affected. Suddenly, car makers have to get 35 mpg for all light pick-up trucks or pay stiff fines to the federal government—that would probably knock down the value of certain stocks and bonds. Or, what if an investor bought a portfolio of tax-exempt municipal bonds, and then Congress decided to dump the exemption for municipal bond interest—investors would dump their municipal bonds en masse, forcing the market prices of municipal bonds down suddenly.

Different industries are subject to different regulatory risks, so perhaps if I diversify my stocks and bonds among many different industries, I will protect myself from legislative risk somewhat. Also, watch out—the exam might try to trick you into thinking that this risk is called "political risk." No, political risk, remember, is linked with emerging markets, where the political, social and economic systems are immature and unpredictable. The risk that legislators in a stable, first-world country will mess up the stock and bond markets with their bad ideas is called legislative or regulatory risk.

Credit/Default Risk

Credit risk is the risk that the issuer of a bond will be unable to pay interest and/or return principal to the bondholders. U.S. Treasury securities have little or no default/credit risk, but some municipal securities and most corporate bonds carry default/credit risk to some degree. Even if the issuer never misses a payment, if S&P and Moody's downgrade their credit score, the market value of the bonds could plummet. So, either an actual or perceived loss of credit quality can send the market price of a bond down in a hurry. If interest rates are also rising at the time—ouch.

Duration

Duration measures the interest rate risk of a particular bond, predicting how a change in interest rates would affect the bond's market price. The longer/higher a bond's duration, the more sensitive it is to a change in interest rates. So, when interest rates go up, they smack the prices of bonds with long/high durations down much harder than those with lower durations.

Another way of talking about duration is to say that at some point all the coupon payments received by an investor will represent what the investor paid for the bond. If you pay par for a 30-year bond paying $50 a year, it would take you 20 years to receive $1,000 in the form of interest/coupon payments, right? So the duration could be expressed as 20 years. Since a coupon payment of 5% is pretty low and a 30-year maturity pretty long, the bond's duration is high. A bond with a high duration is more susceptible to a rise in interest rates. To express that mathematically, we could see how much the bond's price would decline if rates rose 1%. Just multiply the 20 (duration) by 1% to get an expected 20% decline in the bond's price should rates rise by just 1 point. And if rates shot up 2%, the price decline would be 40%. That's pretty volatile. If the bond paid a higher coupon, you'd get your original investment back sooner, knocking down the duration and making the bond's price less sensitive to interest rates.

Remember: the lower the coupon and the longer the maturity, the higher/greater the duration. And the greater the duration, the more susceptible the bond's price is to interest rate spikes.

For interest-paying bonds, the duration is always less than the years to maturity, thankfully. I'd sure hate to be planning to get my original money back several years after they would have already given me my original money back.

But, for zero-coupon bonds, the duration IS the maturity. Surprisingly, the mathematical formula for duration is very helpful in understanding the concept, but it's just so intense that I decided not to include it in the book. If you really want to spend 15 minutes crunching the numbers, do a Google search and have at it. You'll quickly see why the longer you have to wait for your money, the riskier it is for you, although some of you may not actually need a complex math formula to convince you of that. You may have already had the pleasure of lending too much money to the wrong "friend." In case the question on the exam is only asking for a definition, tell it that duration "equals the weighted average of a bond's cash flows."

Liquidity Risk

Marketability or liquidity has to do with the ability to quickly turn an investment into cash and at a fair price. Money market securities are easy to buy and sell at a fair price; municipal bonds, DPPs (limited partnerships), closed-end funds, and thinly traded stocks are not. How much money could you make on your house if you absolutely had to sell it by tomorrow? Might have to drop your asking price pretty severely, unless there were, like, 10 buyers pounding on your door for an opportunity to put in a bid, right? So, thinly traded securities have **liquidity/marketability risk** compared to securities with more active secondary markets. When a stock gets kicked off NASDAQ and lands in that purgatory known as the OTC Bulletin Board, it starts to trade in a less liquid market. That means you don't get nearly as good a price when you sell or when you buy.

Timing Risk

Investors take a big risk if they buy all the shares of a mutual fund that they were ever going to buy all in one transaction. To avoid the **timing risk** of purchasing shares at too high of a price compared to their historical average, many investors instead put the same dollar amount into an investment regardless of its price. That technique is known as **dollar cost averaging** and it is used to avoid timing risk. By definition, investors utilizing dollar cost averaging will purchase fewer shares when they're expensive and more shares when they happen to be cheap. Investing $400 a month into a varying number of shares = dollar cost averaging. Purchasing 100 shares at whatever price each month is not.

Opportunity Cost

Opportunity cost is the shoulda/coulda principle. If you pass up an investment opportunity to make 5%, your opportunity cost is 5%, and you need to do better than 5% with the opportunity you choose instead. If you coulda made 5% and you end up making 7% with another investment, you made 2% better than your opportunity cost.

INVESTMENT RISK	SIGNIFICANCE	NOTES	
Systematic	Affect the overall market	"Non-diversifiable"	Diversification won't help; investor must "hedge"
Unsystematic	Affect particular stocks only	Diversifiable	Buy many stocks in many industries
Market	Markets panic due to war, weather events, etc.	Measured by Beta	Hedge with options, futures, ETFs, etc.
Business	How strong is the issuer?	Competition, obsolescence	Diversify your holdings
Political	Emerging markets, e.g., China, Vietnam	Unstable political-economic systems	Don't confuse with "legislative risk"
Legislative Regulatory	Changes to laws regulations	Tax code changes EPA requirements, OSHA mandates	Could have negative effect on stock or bond price
Currency	Value of dollar	ADRs, international and global investing	Weak dollar makes ADR more valuable
Interest Rate	Rates up/Market price down	Long-term bonds most susceptible, measured by "duration"	Preferred stock is rate-sensitive, too
Credit, Default	Issuer could fail	Downgrade in credit rating lowers value of bond	Low bond values = high-yield
Purchasing Power	Inflation erodes buying power	Fixed-income presents purchasing power risk	Live and die by the CPI
Reinvestment Risk	Investing at varying rates of interest	If rates down, investor goes forward at lower rate	Zero-coupons avoid this risk
Liquidity Risk	Trying to sell when there are few or no buyers	Esoteric securities, partnerships, hedge fund investments are illiquid	Thinly traded stocks less liquid
Opportunity Cost	What you give up to invest elsewhere	If you give up a 5% T-bond investment, 5% is your opportunity cost	Try to do better than 5%

INVESTMENT RISK	SIGNIFICANCE	NOTES	
Capital Risk	Risk of losing your money	Avoided with U.S. Treasuries and GNMA securities	
Timing Risk	Risk of buying investment near all-time high	Avoided through dollar cost averaging	

SUITABLE INVESTMENT RECOMMENDATIONS

Let's take a look at suitability from a more "real world" standpoint. We'll look at some fairly typical clients and try to figure out what you should recommend to them and—just as important—what you should *not* recommend.

```
Investor: Heather Sams

Age: 42

Occupation: real estate agent

Profile: Heather earned $50,000 last year as a full-commission
real estate agent. She made 2/3 of her income in May,
June, and July, closing on just one property from August
through December. Heather has two children, ages 3 and
5. She is a single parent. Her monthly mortgage payment
is $1,100. She has a $100,000 term life policy. Your
firm's risk tolerance survey determines that she falls
within the "moderate risk tolerance" category.

Objective: save for retirement (in 20+ years) and the
college education of her two children.
```

What should you recommend to a client such as Heather Sams? Luckily, she does have life insurance, and there is no credit card debt, so Heather can definitely invest some money, even if it's a small amount. What are her specific needs? She wants to grow her investment dollars over the next 13 years for the eldest child, 15 years for the youngest child, and at least 20 years for herself. Those are long time horizons. However, she also has serious liquidity needs right now—she's going months without a paycheck during the seasonal slump in home sales. So, we can't just focus on capital appreciation over the long term—we have to put a percentage of her capital into safe, boring money market mutual funds. During the lean times when she's unable to sell a house, she can write checks against the money market shares to meet monthly expenses. How much should we invest there? We should probably just take her monthly expenses and figure out how much she'd have to invest in order to generate that much income for at least four or five months each year. If it turns out to be 75% or more allocated to the money market, I would not be surprised.

Okay, so we've got her doing better than a bank savings account or CD. Surely we can do more than that for her. Heather's time horizon for retirement is 20 years. There haven't been many 20-year periods where the S&P 500 was anything less than decent. She doesn't have a lot of money to waste on sales charges and operating expenses, so why don't we put half of her remaining 25% into an S&P 500 index fund? Or, if the index fund doesn't strike her fancy, I don't have a problem with just about *any* lower-risk equity fund for a small percentage of her investment capital. Maybe it's a growth & income fund, an equity income fund, a large cap value fund, or a "conservative growth fund." Maybe it has the words "blue chip" in it and a portfolio that is, truly, "blue chip," meaning dependable. If she had a higher risk tolerance, I would recommend small cap or aggressive growth funds, but the investor has to be able to tolerate wide price fluctuations financially *and* psychologically. I can't impose my own views about risk on my clients. After all, it's their money. I get a commission either way.

That leaves us with about 12.5% of Heather's investment capital for education. When you hear the word "education," you might automatically think "529 plan." Those are very effective for people with a lot of money to invest, people interested in making gifts that take things right up to the limit (currently $13,000 per year). That sounds like a pair of wealthy grandparents, not a single mom with two kids working a hit-or-miss full commission sales job. A Coverdell Savings Account will allow $2,000 per child per year to grow on a tax-deferred basis. I don't think Heather will end up maxing out either child's account this year, so we could certainly go with a Coverdell account and invest the money conservatively.

There are alternate solutions, too. Her high expenses relative to income tell me that reducing her current tax burden would be a major benefit. How can we reduce her tax burden? Instead of simply investing in mutual funds in a taxable account, we might persuade her to set up a Traditional IRA. That way when she files her 1040 in April, maybe she'll get a refund from Uncle Sam. A few hundred or even a thousand dollars would go a long way toward helping her keep her head above water. If her income increases steadily over the next few years, we can get her set up with a SIMPLE IRA, which allows for much higher annual contributions and, therefore, bigger tax benefits.

How will the Coverdell accounts help her current tax situation? They won't. But, she does need to save for her children's education, and why not get the benefit of tax deferral and tax-free withdrawals. Think about that—maybe she'll contribute $20,000 for each child over the next 13–15 years. If those investments are worth $40,000 when the kids go to college, there is no tax due on the $20,000 of growth. The money doesn't have to be tapped between here and there, so why not lock it up in a tax-deferred account meeting a long-term goal? In the Coverdell, she can invest as conservatively as she wants.

Or, forget the Coverdell. I-bonds might be the ticket. Remember that an I-bond is a savings bond issued by the U.S. Treasury, which means it's absolutely safe and also exempt from state and local income taxes. An I-bond pays a guaranteed rate that is fixed over the life of the bond, but also pays out more interest income when inflation rises. So, there's no default risk and no real purchasing power risk, either. There are also tax advantages. First, the interest isn't paid out; it's added to the value of the bond. You can, therefore, defer the taxes until you cash in/redeem the bond. And, if you use the proceeds for qualified education costs in the same calendar year that you redeem the bonds, the interest is tax-*free*. Heather would not even have to declare that the I-bonds will be used for educational purposes when she buys them. As long as she uses the proceeds in the same year she redeems the bonds—and meets the other requirements of the Education Savings Bond Program—the interest is tax-free.

Am I saying that a "mid-cap growth fund" or 10-year Treasury notes have been ruled out? Not at all. Both could easily fit into or replace our recommendation. The point is, she needs liquidity for sure. She also needs some capital appreciation without taking on extreme risk. And, she needs to take care of her children's education. Therefore, there are some things that we can rule out. Municipal bonds have no place in Heather's portfolio—she is not in a high tax bracket. Of course, we're not even going to talk about options (puts and calls), as speculation is clearly not for Heather. I don't see how we could justify a recommendation for emerging market or sector funds, not when the test question is pointing out a "moderate risk tolerance."

So, as you can see, it's tough to know for sure what the right answer is for suitability questions. Your best bet is to think through things analytically and try to eliminate recommendations until you get to something that seems to work best for the investor given the facts provided.

Let's try another one.

Investor: Linda McManus

Age: 69

Occupation: school teacher, semi-retired

Profile: Linda taught third graders for 45 years before finally retiring. Only, she didn't completely retire. As soon as she added her name to the district's substitute teaching list, she has been teaching at least twice a week since her so-called "retirement." Education is, not surprisingly, a major theme of Linda's life. Although her grandchildren have yet to show that they share her love of learning, the thought that they would not attend at least four years of college has never entered Linda's mind. Even though her children earn modest livings and are both saddled with too much credit card debt and too much of what she calls "champagne tastes on beer salaries," Linda decided long ago that her grandchildren would not miss out on college due to their parents' financial blunders. Linda's teacher's pension is decent, paying 65% of what she made during her last year as a full-time teacher. The house was paid off long ago, although the property taxes have risen beyond the comfort level. Her husband died five years ago and left an insurance policy of $110,000, most of which is now sitting in bank CDs. Linda would like to invest for her three grandchildren's educations, ages 8, 11, and 12 currently. She would like to cover her property taxes without using so much of her monthly pension check. And, she would like to protect her purchasing power against the threat of inflation. Your firm's survey determines that Linda has a low-to-moderate risk tolerance.

Objective: current income, capital appreciation.

What should you recommend to an investor like Linda McManus? Her grandchildren are not 3 and 5 years old, so the time horizon for a 12-year-old is considerably shorter than that of a 3-year-old in terms of investing for educational needs. The portfolio will probably have a higher allocation to fixed-income and a lower allocation to equity/stock than it would for younger children's education funds. If we do go mostly fixed-income for the educational needs, the maturities need to fit the time horizon. Remember that an income investor wants her bonds to mature within her time horizon. If she has a 10-year time horizon, a 30-year bond would force her to sell before maturity at who knows what price. If rates have risen, she could get taken to the cleaners. So, if Linda's granddaughter is six years away from her freshman year, we need debt securities that mature in six years or sooner. Maybe an intermediate-term, investment-grade corporate bond fund would work best. Yes, Treasury notes are safer, but investment-grade corporate bonds are not exactly high-risk, either, and they pay a higher return. She might also purchase I-bonds and use the proceeds for the grandkids' education without paying taxes on the interest that gets paid out upon redemption.

A 529 Savings Plan might be a good idea, too. She has about six figures sitting in bank CDs. When the next one matures, maybe she could put it into a 529 Savings Plan for her oldest grandchild, and do the same for the younger grandchildren when the next two CDs mature. Linda can put up to the current gift tax exclusion per year without triggering gift taxes. And, when the grandkids use the money for education later on, there will be no taxes due at the federal level. What about the state level? That's the tricky part of 529 Plans. You would typically start by looking at the plan offered by Linda's state, since she may get to deduct her contributions from state taxes. If Linda preferred to just buy tuition credits at today's prices, she could do that, too. But it's important that we know the grandkids are definitely going to be okay with attending college in a particular state. If Linda buys tuition credits from the State of Virginia, the grandkids will need to attend a state college in Virginia; otherwise, things could get ugly. So, if we aren't sure in which state the kids will be willing to attend college, the I-bonds might be looking real tempting. Those are Treasuries and, therefore, not taxed as ordinary income at the state level.

However we take care of the grandkids' education, we're still going to devote part of Linda's money for Linda. She has property taxes due twice a year, so we need a safe, dependable debt security that pays interest semi-annually. Sounds like United States Treasury Bonds to me. Or, maybe we don't want to lock into a fixed interest rate for such a long time period and choose to buy 5-year T-notes, instead. As they mature, we can buy new T-notes at, perhaps, a higher (or lower) interest rate. Either way, Linda's principal is as safe as it gets, and we can use the semi-annual interest payments to cover part or all of her semi-annual property tax bills.

Since she wants to protect her purchasing power, we'll put a percentage of her capital into the stock market, but we'll be about as conservative as a stock investor can be. Blue chip stocks are issued by dependable, mature companies. Linda can reinvest the dividends into a blue chip or conservative growth fund for now. As time goes by, she can always choose to start cashing the dividend checks instead to keep the lights on or maybe update her kitchen. And, if she has to redeem a few shares of the funds once in a while to replace an old furnace or washing machine, well, that's why we invest. Eventually, somebody's gotta spend the money. Otherwise, what's the point?

How much should we allocate to each? I would probably start with her property tax bill. Let's say she qualifies for a senior citizen exemption and pays $1,500 a year in property taxes. How much would she need to invest in order to generate $1,500 a year on a U.S. Treasury security? Treasury bonds are yielding a little more than 5% as I write this, so how much principal has to be invested to generate $1,500 per year? $30,000. Of course, before she pays her property tax, she gets taxed on the interest by the federal government. So, we should probably invest enough to leave her with $1,500 *after-tax*. If she's in the 25% bracket, she'll need to invest $40,000. And, since her property taxes will rise over time, she should consider investing a little more than that just to be on the safe side.

The amount she invests for her grandchildren's education will depend largely on her monthly expenses versus her pension check and the modest amount she earns as a substitute teacher. She currently receives a pension check of $2,000 and grosses between $800 and $1,100 per month as a substitute teacher. So, with $2,800 in employment income and about $300 in CD interest, let's say she has $3,100 per month to cover the following expenses:

- $200 heating and cooling
- $100 prescriptions, healthcare
- $350 groceries
- $100 clothing
- $250 automobile, insurance, etc.
- $150 miscellaneous

Looks like she has about $2,000 a month to invest, or $24,000 per year.

That means she can easily max out a 529 Plan for her oldest granddaughter this year and still have $12,000 to invest for herself. Or, she can max out 529 Savings Plans for her two oldest grandchildren if she chooses to be more self-sacrificial. Or, she can use the maturing bank CDs to fund the 529 plans and invest the rest for herself. Whatever you recommend here, chances are the numbers will end up getting tweaked before the signature goes on the dotted line. It's just important that you begin with an appropriate recommendation and a good understanding of the issues.

Again, I see no reason to talk about municipal securities and even less reason to talk about puts and calls (options), emerging market funds, sector funds, funds of hedge funds, or any other speculative, high-risk, aggressive investment strategy. I would also be very leery of a registered representative recommending a deferred annuity. A deferred variable annuity will promise that Linda receives an income stream for the rest of her life, but we don't know how much that income will be from month to month. There is also going to be a surrender period of about eight years during which she'd get penalized for taking out money. A 69-year-old could easily end up with a medical emergency, a busted water heater, a leaky roof, etc., and so we would assume that her need for liquidity is too high to be tying up a bunch of money into a deferred annuity. Annuities also charge "mortality and expense risk charges," "administrative fees," "management fees," etc., that might make them worthwhile for a long-term investor. But, the older the investor, the more skeptical I'd be about recommendations for variable annuities, especially on a regulatory exam, especially when both FINRA and NASAA have written explicitly of their own skepticism of senior citizens being pitched variable annuities.

What if Linda still wanted some tax deferral? Well, given her age, a Traditional IRA doesn't work, given that she'll have to start taking distributions on April 1 following her $70\frac{1}{2}$th birthday, which is just around the corner. I mean, if she already has one started, she can make a few more contributions up to the current maximum, but that's about it. However, a Roth IRA would work just fine. Since that money comes out after-tax, the IRS will let her make continued contributions to a Roth. She has ordinary income from the substitute teaching, so, she can always buy her stocks or equity mutual funds within a tax-deferred Roth IRA, putting in up to the current maximum contribution. Her grandkids aren't going to college for at least five years, so Linda can make tax-free withdrawals and send part or all of it to her grandkids once they get set up at college.

As always, there are many ways to take care of an investor's objectives. The registered representative just needs to know as much as possible about the investor's financial situation, needs, objectives, and risk tolerance.

Investor: Bryan Biesterfield

Age: 37

Occupation: sales manager

Profile: Bryan was never much of a student, but within one year of finishing college, he hit the ground running as a software sales rep. He made $110,000 his first full year in the business, followed by $250,000 and, finally, peaked at $320,000 during 2001, after which he has had to learn how to squeak by on just $120,000 a year, give or take. Mostly, Bryan's income is tied to the overrides he makes on a team of five sales representatives. Maybe it's the 15 years of marriage, the two children, or the 55-minute commute, but something has started to douse the fire that used to rage in his belly. Now, as he approaches middle age, Bryan is focused more on the end game strategy—will he have enough money to retire and how long will it

take to get there? Are his wife and kids protected should he get clipped in Philadelphia traffic on the way to and from the office? If he got pushed out of his current cushy management position, how long would it take to land a comparable job?

Objectives: capital appreciation consistent with a conservative strategy, capital preservation.

So, this guy is a little weird, actually. Given his high-risk career, generous salary, and relatively young age, you'd probably be leaning toward an aggressive growth/speculative strategy. But everything he's telling me is pointing toward a much more conservative strategy. His bright-lights-big-city days are far behind him at this point. Of course, a wife and two kids in the suburbs will do that, even to a former hell-raising bachelor from the big city. So, the first thing you would probably discuss is his need for insurance. If he's been earning six figures for many years, his family has become accustomed to buying pretty much what they want when they want it, within certain limits. I mean, no, you can't have a new Porsche this week, Sweetie, but as far as the cashmere sweater goes, well, we can probably swing it. If Bryan's wife and daughters had to someday choose between designer blue jeans and a Walmart private label brand, well, let's not even consider a fate so cruel. Let's make sure he has enough life insurance to cover their lifestyles for several years. Sounds like about a $1 million death benefit to me. Now, you might think that's a little excessive, given the fact that the mortgage balance is surely quite low given Bryan's high salary.

Au contraire. Like many high earners, this family is leveraged to the gills. They have taken so many home equity lines of credit and done so many refinancings that their mortgage balance still sits at an astonishing $485,000. So, the $1 million life policy will only leave slightly over $500,000 after paying off the house, slightly less when you cover the funeral expenses. It may take a few years for Bryan's wife to go back to school, finish her degree, and get a job that pays anything like what Bryan earned, so let's leave a nice cushion there.

Assuming Bryan has sufficient insurance, we could then move on to other objectives. Notice how he wants to make sure he can retire young enough to enjoy his retirement, which is sort of a thin line to have to walk. On the one hand, he'll need sufficient capital appreciation to get where he wants to go. On the other hand, he can't risk losing it all on speculation. Reminds me of when I'm running late for an appointment. On the one hand, I have to go fast enough to get there on time. On the other hand, if I get caught speeding, I'll be pulled over and end up not even making the darned appointment. So, we need a fairly conservative mutual fund—perhaps a growth & income fund or a balanced fund. That way, part of his investments will seek the capital appreciation/growth required to put together a nest egg big enough to retire on, and another part will seek a dependable income stream that can be reinvested for now and spent later on if needed. This could make for a tricky test question, though. Exactly how I would choose "balanced fund" over "growth & income fund" or even a "value fund" I'm not sure. They could all provide growth and some fairly dependable income, so I'm hoping the other choices can be easily ruled out because they're too risky, or they don't offer enough growth potential.

Unfortunately, I don't get to write the exam. Like you, I have to play the cards I'm dealt.

So, Bryan has played defense by purchasing enough life insurance to pay off the mortgage and give his wife and kids some breathing room should tragedy strike. We're considering an equity strategy that offers growth at a reasonable risk and also seeks income to smooth out an otherwise bumpy ride. What about his concern that he could lose his job and need a cushion to carry him to the next position? That's a need for liquidity. A sales manager will get fired if he doesn't make his numbers, and getting fired from one position doesn't exactly help land the next one, especially as he gets older and grayer. If he loses his job, would he have enough of a reserve to tap for at least a year, maybe two? Maybe go back to school, retrain for a new career, etc.? That all costs money, and with no employment income, who's going to cover that stuff, let alone all the cashmere sweaters his wife and daughter might require at a moment's notice?

I think he should try to build up a money market or Treasury portfolio with a principal of around $100,000. I don't think he has the cash flow to cut a check all at once, so I'd figure out how much of each monthly paycheck can go toward this safety net, with the excess going into a conservative equity mutual fund, maybe a balanced fund to add some exposure to the bond market, as well.

Investor: Michelle Mathers

Age: 33

Profile: Michelle is a divorced woman with no kids earning $62,000 a year in middle management for a large printing company in Sandusky, Ohio. After a messy divorce, Michelle is basically starting over financially. Since her ex-husband is a semi-professional musician earning $10,000 in a good year, Michelle has to pay $350 per month in alimony to her late-sleeping, big-talking, doobie-rolling deadbeat of a former husband.

Not that she's bitter.

Michelle lives in a modest two-bedroom townhouse with a monthly mortgage payment of $900. She drives a five-year-old Toyota Corolla and does not spend excessively on clothes. Although she likes to go out, she generally keeps the activities low-cost: coffee, window shopping, lounging at a local bookstore, maybe a museum.

Michelle's former employer in Columbus is still holding her $30,000 401(k) plan, which Michelle would like to roll over to her current company's plan. Unfortunately, her current employer is a little on the frugal side—they offer no matching contributions. Therefore, the only benefit to participating in the non-matching 401(k) would be the higher contribution limits versus a Traditional or Roth IRA. She also invested a modest sum into a deferred variable annuity a few years back. The annuity contract is currently worth $15,000, and Michelle is less than pleased with the slow growth in value and high fees.

Your firm determines that Michelle's risk tolerance is moderate.

Objective: capital preservation, primarily for retirement and possibly the purchase of income/investment property.

Well, we obviously can't help Michelle with the whole alimony-to-a-deadbeat-former husband thing. But, we can definitely help her move the 401(k) money into our more trustworthy, competent hands. Unless the test question calls it a "Roth 401(k)" we assume this account has been funded with pre-tax dollars. Therefore, it can be rolled into her own Traditional IRA without any tax implications. Not only will there be no tax hassles when we move the $30,000 from her 401(k) to a Traditional IRA, but the money won't even be counted towards her current year contribution limit. So, we'll help her fill out the paperwork for a "direct rollover," whereby the 401(k) custodian—which happens to be Fidelity—cuts a check directly to the IRA custodian, which happens to be us. Michelle can also contribute to the IRA this year, which will reduce her taxable income for the year and grow tax-deferred until retirement. Since Michelle does not have an IRA set up, we will help her set up a "Rollover IRA." This is not an investment in and of itself. An IRA is a protective shell that we wrap around the mutual funds we plan to sell her to provide for current tax deductions on the contributions and tax-deferred growth. Since she has a moderate risk tolerance and is looking to build a nest egg for retirement and possibly the purchase of investment property, I'm leaning toward a mid-cap growth fund for most of her account, possibly a more conservative fund for the remainder—large cap value, equity income, even a balanced fund.

What about the annuity? Is she stuck with what she purchased? Not necessarily. The IRS allows us to do a tax-free "1035 contract exchange." This means that we can take her current annuity and turn it into one of our superior offerings. However, nothing is simple in this business, not even the simple stuff. The 1035 exchange allows Michelle to move the value of her annuity to another annuity contract without paying ordinary income or a 10% penalty tax. However, it has nothing to do with the agreement between Michelle and the insurance/annuity company. See, the insurance company wants Michelle to leave her money alone for the first eight years. To help encourage her to play along, they charge her 7% of the contract value if she surrenders during the first year. In the second year, the surrender charge drops to 6%. In the third year it drops again, all the way down to 6%. Michelle is only in the third year of her contract, which means she would lose 6% of whatever the contract is worth, or about $900.

Hmm. While we can help with the tax-free contract exchange and would certainly enjoy spending the commissions earned on the sale of the annuity, we have to keep FINRA's suitability rules in mind. Is it suitable to do something that costs Michelle 6% of her contract value? Are we really that convinced that our own product will provide for superior performance at lower expenses?

Time to consult with your principal/supervisor. He or she will help you figure out if it is, in fact, a suitable transaction and, if so, what type of documentation will be needed to cover the firm's backside.

What about Michelle's need for supplemental income? Frankly, I don't see it. She earns $62,000 and has a $900 monthly mortgage payment. She doesn't buy $700 business suits or $500 handbags. She doesn't own a boat or collect wine at $200 a bottle. She's already been promoted to middle management, and she's confident that she'll continue to climb the ladder, either at this or another company. The $350 alimony payment to the husband is annoying but not devastating financially.

I think we should help her with the 401(k) direct rollover (the check is cut to our custodian, not in Michelle's name) to a rollover IRA. We should proceed with the 1035 annuity exchange carefully, under the guidance of our compliance principal. And, we should recommend equity funds that are neither too stodgy nor too aggressive.

Finally, it might be fun and educational to consider your own age, occupation, profile, objectives, and risk tolerance to come up with some investment recommendations for yourself. Or for your mom, sister, brother-in-law, bowling buddy, what have you. The more "real world" we can make this process, the more comfortable you'll be at the testing center when the goofy test questions start popping up. Reading several mutual fund prospectuses would be a great way to familiarize yourself with the different options out there, the pros and cons of different funds, etc.

If you can find the time, of course.

ISSUING SECURITIES

Google made headlines several years ago with their famous **initial public offering** or **"IPO,"** in which they sold stock to public investors at $85 per share and those investors then watched the stock climb to $800 or more per share! The difference between the initial $85 price and the eventual market price of, say, $850, is the difference between the primary and secondary markets. Securities are issued to investors in the **primary market**. Securities are traded among investors in the **secondary market**.

To do an initial public offering on the primary market, a formerly privately owned company sells a percentage of ownership to public investors in exchange for an infusion of cash that can be used to expand the business. In the not so distant past, formerly privately owned Groupon and Facebook "went public," or completed their IPOs. In an initial public offering of stock the company takes the money investors pay for the stock and buys factories, manufacturing equipment, computers, etc. In exchange for their money/capital the investors end up owning a percentage of the company's profits, nothing more, and nothing less. Now, nothing makes the securities regulators more nervous than to hear that a company wants to raise money from investors. Let's face it, many business owners would say just about anything investors wanted to hear in order to get their hands on a few billion dollars. That's why the state and federal securities regulators like to slow down the issuers in much the same way they're slowing you down right now. Just tying you up with a little paperwork, giving you a chance to rethink your whole decision, making sure it's something you really, *really* want to do.

The SEC requires the issuer to file a detailed **registration statement** because the regulators want to see exactly what the issuer will be telling their potential investors in the prospectus. They want the issuer to provide the whole story on the company: history, competitors, products and services, risks of investing in the company, financials, board of directors, officers, etc. And, like a fussy English composition instructor, they want it written in clear, readable language. Only if investors clearly understand the risks and rewards of an investment do they really have a fair chance of determining a good investment opportunity from something better left alone. If investors consistently get burned on the primary market, pretty soon investors will stop showing up to provide companies with capital, which means companies would have one heck of a time expanding, hiring more workers, and pushing along the local and national economies.

So, the government is very much interested in what goes on in the securities markets, which is why Congress passed the **Securities Act of 1933**. Sometimes referred to as the "Paper Act," or the "Truth in Securities Act," the Securities Act of 1933 requires issuers of securities to register the securities offering and provide full disclosure to investors before taking their hard-earned money. The SEC will make the issuer write and rewrite the registration statement, just like a hard-nosed composition instructor might make you do four rewrites of a research paper before finally agreeing to let you graduate. If this section is awkward and this paragraph is unclear, rewrite it. The SEC calls their equivalent of red pen marks "letters of deficiency" and sometimes, when they're feeling especially punchy, "deficiency letters."

Now, an issuer would know their own business and industry sector very well, but they probably know jack about issuing securities. So, they hire underwriters, also called "investment bankers." An underwriter or investment banker is simply a broker-dealer who helps issuers raise money by issuing securities to investors. All the big-name Wall Street firms such as Morgan Stanley, Goldman Sachs, and Merrill Lynch have major underwriting or investment banking departments.

Once these underwriters help the issuer file registration papers under the Securities Act of 1933 the offering goes into a cooling off period, which will last a minimum of 20 days. This process can drag on and on if the SEC is copping an attitude against the registration statement, but no matter how long it takes, the issuer and underwriters can only do certain things during this "cooling off" period. Number one, they can't sell anything. They can't even advertise. About all they can do is take **indications of interest** from investors, but those aren't sales, just names on a list of people expressing some interest in a securities offering. And those who indicate their interest have to receive a **preliminary prospectus** or "red herring." This disclosure document contains almost everything that the final prospectus will contain except for the **effective date** and the final **public offering price** or "POP." Remember that the registered representative may not send a research report (sales literature) along with the red herring and cannot highlight it or alter it in any way.

It is what it is. The issuer and the underwriters perform due diligence during the cooling off period, which just means they make sure they provided the SEC and the public with accurate and full disclosure. It's up to them to do this—the SEC is only reviewing the information for clarity. It had better be accurate.

Even though the SEC makes issuers jump through all kinds of hoops, once it's all done, the SEC pretty much washes its hands of the whole affair. They don't approve or disapprove of the security. They don't guarantee accuracy or adequacy of the information provided by the issuer and its underwriters. In other words, if this whole thing goes belly up because of inaccurate disclosure, the liability still rests squarely on the shoulders of the issuers and underwriters, not on the SEC. And there has to be a disclaimer saying basically that on the prospectus. In fact, take a look at the cover of any mutual fund prospectus. The one I'm looking at now says it this way:

The Securities and Exchange Commission has not approved or disapproved of these securities. Further, it has not determined that this prospectus is accurate or complete. Any representation to the contrary is a criminal offense.

As it turns out, every issuer has to register their securities with the Securities and Exchange Commission, except for every issuer who doesn't.

Seriously. The Securities Act of 1933 is a piece of federal legislation, so it's not surprising that the folks who passed it gave themselves an exemption from the rule. That's right, government securities are exempt from this act. They don't have to be registered.

Neither do municipal securities, e.g., a State of California General Obligation bond or a School District 207-U capital improvement bond. Charitable organization securities, such as church bonds, are exempt from the act. So are bank securities, which are already regulated by bank regulators. Debt securities that mature in 270 days or less—commercial paper, banker's acceptances—are also exempt from this arduous registration process.

So, **exempt securities** don't have to be registered under the Securities Act of 1933 because they get a special excuse from that requirement. Unfortunately, there are also transactions that qualify for an exemption to registration requirements. The regulators call these, quite cleverly, **exempt transactions**. Just means that if you issue your securities through a certain type of transaction, you can avoid the typical registration hassles. For example, if the issuer and underwriters sell the securities through a **private placement**, the SEC won't even make them register the securities.

PRIVATE PLACEMENTS

See, the federal government requires most securities to be registered in order to protect the average Joe and JoAnn. If the investors are all sophisticated and well-funded, the regulators can ease up a bit. While the Securities Act of 1933 would require a company doing a general <u>public</u> offering of stock to provide a standard registration statement and prospectus, the Act also offers companies the ability to do a much easier <u>private</u> placement. A private placement is sold to sophisticated, well-funded investors, and because these investors are so incredibly sophisticated the stock does not even have to be registered. That's right, if you purchase a private placement, that stock has not even been registered. Of course, if no one has ever called to interest you in one of these private placements, don't feel bad. You'd have to find yourself on the following list before expecting a phone call:

Accredited Investors:

- Bank, savings & loan, other similar institution
- Broker-dealer
- Insurance company
- Registered investment company, business development company, small business investment company
- Employee benefit plans with > $5,000,000 in assets (includes government, ERISA, and 501c3 plans)
- Any trust with assets > $5,000,000
- Any director, executive officer, or general partner of the issuer of the securities being offered or sold
- Any natural person whose individual net worth, or joint net worth with that person's spouse, at the time of his purchase exceeds $1,000,000 (not including primary residence)
- Any natural person who had an individual income in excess of $200,000 in each of the two most recent years or joint income with that person's spouse in excess of $300,000 in each of those years and has a reasonable expectation of reaching the same income level in the current year
- Any entity in which all of the equity owners are accredited investors

If you didn't see yourself on that list, you could still get in on one of these private placements, as they allow the issuer to sell to no more than 35 non-accredited investors. The issuer/underwriters would have to be reasonably sure that you and the other non-accredited investors are sophisticated enough to get in on a private placement.

Since the shares are unregistered, a legend needs to be printed on the certificates reminding the investor that the transfer/sale of the shares is restricted. Therefore, since everything needs at least three names in this industry, private placement securities are also referred to as "legend stock" or "restricted stock." They need to be held fully paid for a particular period of time before the investor sells them—that is the "restriction" that gives them their name.

Purchaser Representatives

Since a private placement may be sold to 35 unsophisticated, non-accredited investors, the regulators decided to provide some protection to those folks. So, a non-accredited investor who lacks sufficient knowledge of financial matters must have a **purchaser representative** to help evaluate the risks/suitability of the investment. The purchaser representative is simply someone who can help act as a mentor to the investor, explaining the merits and potential risks of the investment. The purchaser representative cannot be some guy who steps out of an office at the issuer's headquarters volunteering his time to the buyer. The purchaser representative cannot be affiliated with the issuer unless they also happen to be a relative of the buyer. So, if the guy stepping out of the office happens to be the buyer's father-in-law, that's a different story.

Finally, note that variable life insurance is sometimes sold through a private placement to sophisticated, wealthy investors who want more sophisticated investment options than those offered from conventional variable products. This is likely the reason I have to prepare you for a possible exam question on this topic.

UNDERWRITING COMMITMENTS

Issuers receive different levels of commitment from their underwriters. Under a **best efforts** commitment, the underwriters act as agents. In other words, no money at risk. They try to sell, and whatever they can't sell goes back to the issuer. Underwriters have money/capital at risk only when they give **firm commitments**. Now, they're agreeing to buy the securities outright, then turn around and sell them to the public. The difference between the value at which they buy from the issuer and sell to the public is known as the **spread**. The managing underwriter takes a manager's fee, the underwriters split up the underwriting fee, and whoever makes the sale gets the selling concession. Maybe the POP or "public offering price" is $10.00 and the issuer receives $9.20 per share. That would be a total spread of 80 cents per share. So, if the underwriters can sell 1 billion shares, they can keep $800 million, which, you know, wouldn't stink.

If your luck is running low and you get a question about a **standby offering**, tell the exam that this is a firm commitment underwriting for a rights offering. A rights offering is done in connection with an additional offer of stock. Why the exam would expect you to know this, I have no idea. It's FINRA's world; we simply try our best to live in it.

FREERIDING AND WITHHOLDING

If the underwriters have set the POP of a stock at $10, what happens if the stock is expected to shoot up to $20 on the secondary market, while they're still selling shares at $10? Wouldn't it be tempting to hold all the shares for their own account and sell them later for a huge profit? Might be tempting, but it's not allowed by FINRA, who calls the violation "freeriding and withholding." These public offerings have to be bona fide (good and true) distributions. That means that if your firm is an underwriter or a selling group member, it has to make a good faith effort to sell all the shares it is allotted to investors, no matter how tempting it might be to keep most of them for its own account and take a "free ride" by "withholding" the securities from hungry buyers. In other words, investment bankers cannot pretend to be offering stock to the public and then sort of change their minds and keep the good ones for themselves.

THE NEW ISSUE RULE

Not so long ago it seemed that the only IPOs that were readily available to investors were the lousy ones. The good ones seemed to get snatched up by people in the industry. These days, there are many investors who are not allowed to buy initial equity offerings. An investor who may not purchase a new issue of common stock is called a restricted person. Restricted persons include:

- Member firms and their owners
- Broker-dealer personnel (not restricted to registered persons)
- Finders and fiduciaries (finders, accountants, consultants, attorneys, etc.)
- Portfolio managers for institutions (banks, S&Ls, insurance companies, etc.) buying for their own account

Of course, it would be fun to help your immediate family members profit from a wildly successful IPO such as the one pulled off by Google not so long ago. Unfortunately, FINRA prohibits the offering of new issues to immediate family members, defined as:

- parents
- mother-in-law or father-in-law
- spouse, brother or sister
- brother-in-law or sister-in-law
- son-in-law or daughter-in-law
- children
- any other individual to whom the person provides material support

Notice that the above list did not mention all family members. Specifically, aunts, uncles, grandparents, and cousins are not considered to be restricted. And, the immediate family members above are only restricted if they give or receive "material support," which FINRA defines as:

"Material support" means directly or indirectly providing more than 25% of a person's income in the prior calendar year. Members of the immediate family living in the same household are deemed to be providing each other with material support.

Or, they would be restricted only if the family member working for a broker-dealer works for a firm that is actually selling the new issue (not a ban for employees of all broker-dealers), or if the employee has the ability to control the allocation of the new issue to investors. The new issue rule also requires that before selling a new issue to any account, a member firm must obtain a representation that the account is eligible to purchase new issues in compliance with this rule. The firm can obtain these "affirmative statements" either in paper form or electronic, but must not rely on oral statements from customers. And, these affirmative statements have to be re-verified every 12 months, with copies maintained at least three years. Note that an investment club could buy a new issue, but not if a registered rep is part of the club.

Finally, remember that the new issue rule only covers initial public offerings (IPOs) of common stock. The following are not subject to this rule:

- Secondary offerings
- Debt security offerings
- Preferred stock
- Investment company offerings
- Exempt securities
- REITs
- DPPs

ISSUING SECURITIES TIMELINE		
QUIET PERIOD	COOLING OFF PERIOD	EFFECTIVE DATE
• Prepare documents • No discussions with investors	• File registration statement • No sales or $ collected • Deficiency Letters SEC • Blue Sky the issue • Indications of Interest • Preliminary Prospectus • Due diligence meeting	• Sales confirmed • Final prospectus delivered

TRADING SECURITIES

Again, remember that "primary" and "secondary" are different terms altogether. The primary market refers to an issuer raising money by selling brand new securities to investors and using that "capital" to expand or improve the business. In the secondary market, investors trade *their* securities back and forth, just like my friends and I used to take the baseball cards issued through a network of discount stores that served as a primary market and then trade the cards back and forth on our own secondary market. What were the baseball cards worth? Whatever the market would bear on any given day, just like the stock and bond markets. Remember that Google was sold to investors on the primary market for $85. After giving the underwriters the spread, Google kept the proceeds and reinvested the money into the business. After that, investors became so enthusiastic over Google's common stock that the price rose to more than $800 a share on the secondary market. Why? Same reason the price of anything rises—supply and demand. High demand and a tight supply will lead to high prices on corn oil, concert tickets, and common stock.

It may also help to keep in mind that you will be selling annuities, variable life insurance, and mutual funds with your Series 6, and none of those things trade at all. An investor purchases those packaged products from the issuer and sells them back to the issuer when it's time to cash in. We don't sell our shares of the open-end ABC Aggressive Growth Fund to other investors. We redeem the shares, which means we sell them back to the issuer for what they're currently worth.

But, you're not that far removed from trading securities, because the mutual funds that you sell are being managed by portfolio managers/investment advisers. Those professional investors are buying and selling stocks and bonds for the portfolio. They purchase shares of initial public offerings on the primary market, and they also trade the portfolio securities with other investors on the secondary market. And that is why you have to know the basics here for your exam. Also, wouldn't you be embarrassed if you couldn't answer basic questions from investors about IPOs, primary offerings, NASDAQ, etc.? It would be like a baseball "expert" not knowing what ERA or RBI stand for. Next?

Within the secondary market, there are different marketplaces that people use to trade securities. Let's start with the "first" or "exchange market," which the exam will likely call an **auction market**. Imagine a clanging bell and the roar of frantic buyers and sellers in funny-looking jackets all day long until the bell rings again at four o'clock eastern standard time. That's the New York Stock Exchange, the main part of the **first market**. There are also regional exchanges in Chicago, Boston, Philadelphia, and San Francisco that are based on the NYSE. Since there are both buyers and sellers, the exam could call this a "double auction" market. Either way, associate the word "auction" with "exchanges" or "the first market." The OTC or over-the-counter market is not a physical marketplace, but it's definitely a market. It is also known as the **second market**, and the exam will refer to it as a **negotiated market**. Market makers put out a **bid** and **ask** price, and stand ready to take either side of the trade, for at least one round lot. For stocks a round lot is 100 shares. So if a dealer or market maker says their quote is 20.00–20.11, they stand ready to buy 100 shares at $20.00 or sell 100 shares at $20.11. The difference between where they buy and where they sell is called the "spread," just like the difference between what a car dealer will pay for your trade-in, and what he'll sell it for to a buyer later on. So, yes, the word "spread" is used both on the primary and secondary markets—sounds like a few flash cards may be in order. Go ahead; I'll wait.

People trade these "OTC" stocks by computer rather than gathering at a big building on Wall Street. The big names such as ORCL, MSFT, or CSCO trade on an electronic system you have no doubt heard of called "NASDAQ." That stands for the National Association of Securities Dealers Automated Quotation system, by the way. Maybe you bought some of those wild and crazy Internet stocks a few years ago and watched them get kicked off NASDAQ when the share price became embarrassingly low. When that happens, they end up in a purgatory known as the "OTC Bulletin Board," where, no matter how hard investors pray, the stocks never seem to make it back to that electronic paradise known as NASDAQ. The exam may refer to "Non-NASDAQ OTC" stocks, which is what we're talking about. Also the "pink sheets." The problem with OTC stocks that don't trade on NASDAQ is the problem of "liquidity." There isn't as much buying interest on these stocks, so when you go to sell, you take a big haircut. If your stock trades on NASDAQ, there is more activity and, therefore, usually you get a better price when you buy or sell. In other words, NASDAQ offers better liquidity, while the Bulletin Board, Pink Sheets, or any "illiquid market" would leave you with serious "liquidity risk." Similarly, a car dealer would probably give you a better trade-in price for your Camry™ and sell it for a smaller markup later on compared to the deal he'd give you and the ultimate buyer of some car no one really wants.

Anyway, the exam may also bring up the third and fourth markets. If a broker-dealer purchases a large block of stock that normally trades on the NYSE/exchange markets off the floor through a market maker, we have ourselves a negotiated or "over-the-counter" transaction of an exchange-listed stock. Sort of a hybrid between the two markets I just described where a broker-dealer buys a block of GE or IBM not on the New York Stock Exchange, but over-the-counter through a dealer. Let's just call this the third market and keep moving.

The fourth market is where big institutional investors—pension funds, insurance companies, mutual funds, etc.—trade directly through electronic communications networks (ECNs). Sort of like an eBay for institutional investors. A famous ECN is called INSTINET, which is a good one to remember. INSTItutional investors trade directly over INSTINET. They don't, in other words, call up a registered representative and ask for some hot recommendations. They know what they want to buy and sell, so they just buy and sell electronically without anybody's help, thank you very much.

SECONDARY MARKET
1st Market
• NYSE, auction market
2nd Market
• Negotiated market
• Functions through "market makers"
• NASDAQ
• OTC BB, Pink Sheets
3rd Market
• OTC transaction of an NYSE-listed security
4th Market
• Direct institutional trading, e.g., "INSTINET"

ECONOMIC FACTORS

Gross Domestic Product (**GDP**) measures the total output of the American economy. It's the total value of all goods and services, measured as the price paid by the consumer for, say, all the gallons of milk or haircuts purchased over a 3-month period. If GDP is increasing, the economy is growing. If GDP is declining, so is the economy. The American economy rides a continuous roller coaster known as the business cycle. The phases of the **business cycle** are: expansion, peak, contraction, trough, recovery. All this means is that the economy goes up (expands), hits a peak, declines, hits bottom (trough), and then comes back up again (recovery)…just like a roller coaster. Although we refer to the period following the "trough" as a "recovery," it's really just the next expansion, so I would say there are four phases to the business cycle if I got that question on the exam.

Also remember that rising prices (known as **inflation**) are factored into this GDP calculation to arrive at "real GDP." In other words, we don't want to kid ourselves that rising prices is the same thing as rising economic output. We use the CPI (consumer price index) to factor in the effects of inflation, which we'll discuss shortly. Note that the word "real" generally means to subtract the rate of inflation from something. If you got a test question that said Orville Olmeyer has an investment that grows 6% while the CPI rises 3%, Orville's "real rate of return" is 3%—the amount above inflation.

The period of contraction/decline can be referred to as either a **recession** or a **depression**. A recession is defined as 6 months (2 consecutive quarters) of GDP decline, up to 18 months.

A depression is defined as > 18 months (6 quarters) of GDP decline. Technically, a recession is when your neighbor loses his job. A depression is when you lose *your* job.

INFLATION, DEFLATION

Ever noticed how the "Fed" often seems obsessed with the price of stuff? If the economy grows/expands too fast, prices can go higher and higher until they're out of control. That's called **inflation**. Inflation is indicated/measured by the CPI, or "consumer price index." The CPI surveys the prices consumers are paying for the basic things consumers buy (movie tickets, milk, blue jeans, gasoline) and tracks the increases in those prices. They actually give more weighting to the stuff people buy more of, and sometimes they exclude certain items that are volatile (food and energy) because how many people actually buy food or gasoline in any given month? When we exclude food and energy, we're measuring "core inflation," which will not be on the exam, unless it is. The exam might say that inflation occurs when the demand for goods and services is growing faster than the supply of these items. Or, it could say something like, "too many dollars chasing too few goods." I like to think of inflation in terms of what would happen if they ran out of beer during the third inning at Wrigley Field and suddenly everyone realized they have nothing to do but watch a baseball game. Luckily, some enterprising young dude stands up and says he'd be happy to sell a cold six-pack he somehow managed to smuggle past security. How high would the price of cold beer rise on a hot August afternoon with 40,000 thirsty fans vying for six cold, sweaty cans of beer?

That's in-flation. Sometimes the "Fed" worries about the opposite scenario, **deflation**. A beach ball can be inflated or deflated, and so can the economy. If you over-inflate a beach ball it will pop; if you under-inflate it, it's just as useless. Same for the economy. While inflation can make things too expensive for consumers to buy, deflation can make things ever cheaper. "Cheaper goods" sounds good until you consider that profit margins at businesses will be ever shrinking, as they pay last month's prices for raw materials and then struggle to sell them at next month's cheaper prices. Assuming they can sell anything to anyone—would you rush out to buy something today if you knew it would be cheaper tomorrow? Wouldn't you be tempted to put off your purchases indefinitely, waiting for the price of DVD players, clothing, and automobiles to drop in your favor?

That's an economic slowdown, right? Everybody sitting around waiting to see who'll be the first one to open up his or her wallet. Which is why deflation—while rare—is just as detrimental to the economy as inflation. And that's why the Fed is forever manipulating interest rates in an attempt to find the right economic temperature—not too hot, not too cold. Like Goldilocks, they hope to find the economic porridge just right. Which is another way of saying that demand for stuff and the supply of that stuff are in the right balance. If we have strong demand and tight supply, prices will rise, just as the demand for a Dave Matthews Band concert in a 1,000-seat venue will send the ticket price into the stratosphere. If demand for stuff is weak and the supply of that stuff is high, prices will fall, like the price of a ticket to see the Spin Doctors at a college football stadium.

To review, if the economy grows too fast, we can end up with inflation. And, as we'll soon see, the **Federal Reserve Board** (or **FOMC**) will raise interest rates to let some air out of the over-expanding economy. If the economy starts to sputter and stall, we can end up with deflation. And, as we'll soon see, the Fed will have to pump some air back into the economy by lowering interest rates. A likely approach for an exam question would be to combine economics with bond prices and yields. As we saw earlier, during an inflationary period, bond prices usually drop. During a deflationary period, bond prices rise. And, yes, that means that their yields do the opposite in both cases.

FISCAL AND MONETARY POLICY

Fiscal policy is what the President and Congress do: tax and spend. To stimulate the economy, just cut taxes and increase government spending. Lower taxes leave more money for Americans to spend and invest, fueling the economy. If the government is spending more on interstate highway construction, that means a lot more folks are going to be hired for construction crews. Or maybe the federal government orders 10 million computers from Dell or Hewlett-Packard. Dell and HP would suddenly buy more equipment and raw materials and hire more workers, which is how to push the economy forward.

On the other hand, if we need to cool things down, the federal government increases taxes and cuts spending. Higher taxes leave less money for Americans to spend and invest, and decreased spending puts less government money into projects that would otherwise be hiring subcontractors, laborers, etc.

Monetarists—the Federal Reserve Board—feel that controlling the money supply (**monetary policy**) is the key to managing the economy. What is the money supply?

It's the supply of money. Money, like any commodity, has a cost. The cost of money equals its "interest rate." If there's too much demand and too little supply, the cost of money (interest rate) goes up. That slows down the economy and fights inflation. If there's too little demand and too much supply, the cost of money (interest rate) goes down. That helps to stimulate the economy and pump some air back into a deflated economy.

Wait, money has a cost? I thought I paid the cost of things *with* money. Sure, but if I want to start a business, I need money. How much do I have to pay to borrow this money? That's the interest rate—the cost of borrowing money.

So, how can the money supply be influenced? Through monetary policy, enacted by the Federal Reserve Board. Because of that embarrassing little fiasco known as the 1930s, the Fed likes to make sure that banks don't lend out and invest every last dollar they have on deposit. So, the Fed requires that banks keep a certain percentage of their customer deposits in <u>reserve</u>. This is called, surprisingly enough, the reserve requirement. If the Fed raises the reserve requirement, banks have less money to lend out to folks trying to buy homes and start businesses. So if the economy is overheating, the Fed could raise the reserve requirement in order to cool things down, and if the economy is sluggish, they could lower the requirement in order to make more money available to fuel the economy. The most often used tool is open market operations. The Fed can either buy or sell Treasury and agency securities from/ to banks. If they want to cool things down/raise interest rates, they can take money out of banks by selling them Treasuries. If they want to fuel a sluggish economy/lower interest rates, they can buy Treasuries from banks, thereby pumping money into the system.

Again, interest rates can be thought of as the price of a commodity known as money. Whenever a commodity—corn, sugar, concert tickets—is scarce, its price rises. Whenever something is widely available, its price drops. When money is tight, its cost (interest rate) rises. When money is widely available, its cost (interest rate) falls. So, if the Fed wants to drop rates, they make money more available by buying T-bills from banks. If they want to raise rates, they make money scarce by selling T-bills to banks (who pay for them with... money). Just follow the flow of money.

Then there's the tool that gets talked about the most in the news, the **discount rate**. When people talk about the Fed raising interest rates by 25 basis points, they're talking about the discount rate. The discount rate is the rate the Fed charges banks that borrow directly from the Fed, while banks lend each other money at the **fed funds rate**. Either way, if banks have to pay more to borrow, you can imagine that they will in turn charge their customers more to borrow from them. So, if the Fed wants to raise interest rates, they just raise the discount rate and let the banking system take it from there. The Fed doesn't directly set the **prime rate** or the fed funds rate. They do have influence over the rates through the discount rate, but they don't actually set the other rates. And, of course, they never, ever have anything to do with taxes.

So, think of the Fed as the driver of the economy. If the economy starts going too fast, they tap the brakes (raise interest rates) by raising the reserve requirement, raising the discount rate, and selling T-bills. If the economy starts to stall out, the Fed gives it gas by lowering the reserve requirement, lowering the discount rate, and buying T-bills.

INTEREST RATES

Let's take a look at this concept of "interest rates." Interest rates represent the cost of money. If you wanted to borrow that $100,000 to expand your business as opposed to taking on owners, you would have to pay some money on top of the money you borrow. How much you pay for that "capital" is what we call interest rates. When there's a ton of money to be loaned out, lenders will drop their rates in order to get you to borrow. When money is tight, however, borrowers have to compete with each other to get a share of the limited capital and pay higher and higher rates.

The exam may ask you to work with the following interest rates. They don't really warrant an in-depth discussion, so here's a quick list that should suffice:

- Discount rate: the rate banks have to pay when borrowing from the Federal Reserve Board
- Fed funds rate: the rate banks charge each other for overnight loans in excess of $1 million. Considered the most volatile rate, subject to daily change
- Call money rate or "broker call loan rate": the rate broker-dealers pay when borrowing on behalf of their margin customers
- Prime rate: the rate that the most creditworthy corporate customers pay when borrowing

Whether we use fiscal or monetary policy, our efforts will influence interest rates. And interest rates can make it either easier or harder for companies to do business and for consumers to consume.

VALUE OF U.S. DOLLAR VS. OTHER CURRENCIES

If you do business with foreign companies, you might have to pay for the stuff you buy in their currency, or you might receive their currency when you sell them the stuff you make. You are now subject to currency exchange risk. If you import hard drives from Japan and pay for them in yen, your risk is that the American dollar will weaken, which is the same thing as saying the yen will strengthen. How does that work? Well, you have signed on the dotted line to pay 1 million yen in 90 days. You will convert dollars to yen, in other words, so if the dollar is suddenly weak, you will lay more dollars on the table. If you export to Japan and receive 1 million yen in 90 days, what happens if the dollar has strengthened/yen has weakened? The 1 million yen you receive won't be worth very much.

Be ready to tell the exam that a weak dollar helps our exports, because our goods suddenly look cheap to the other country. A strong dollar hurts our exports, because our goods suddenly look expensive to the other country. Of course, if you've ever vacationed in Mexico when the dollar was strong vs. the peso, you know that that makes for a much better vacation. If the dollar were weak, everything would suddenly seem expensive.

The exam might want you to know what could cause our currency to strengthen or weaken relative to foreign currencies. If interest rates were rising in this country, that fact would actually attract foreign investment into American fixed-income securities, which tends to strengthen the dollar. If interest rates were falling, there would be less incentive for foreign investors to park their money in Treasuries, for example, and, therefore, we would expect the dollar to weaken.

FINRA RULES

In this chapter we have looked at the features of various investment vehicles and also looked at their risk and reward characteristics. We looked at suitability requirements when making investment recommendations to customers, as well as the tax consequences of buying, holding, and selling securities. While Chapter 4 is focused on rules and regulations, the exam outline also places several regulatory concerns within the context of the other sections. So, let's see what concerns FINRA has when recommending securities and dealing with customers.

FINRA RULE. STANDARDS OF COMMERCIAL HONOR AND PRINCIPLES OF TRADE

Really, the FINRA Conduct Rules could all be boiled down to this:

> A member, in the conduct of his business, shall observe high standards of commercial honor and just and equitable principles of trade.

Putting your investor's money in your own bank account would be inconsistent with this rule, wouldn't it? So would buying stock in your customer's account without, like, discussing the idea with the customer. If a broker-dealer is pushing a particular mutual fund just because the fund has agreed to trade through the broker-dealer and generate fat commissions, that would also be "conduct inconsistent with just and equitable principles of trade."

FINRA RULE, CUSTOMERS' SECURITIES OR FUNDS

This rule is basically telling member firms to watch what they do with the funds and securities they hold on behalf of customers. Since some of the customers might not pay close attention to their account statements, it might be tempting to, like, borrow a few grand here and there, as long as you put it back, right? Maybe even add a little bit of interest since you're such an honest broker, right?

Tempting, sure. And real stupid. The firm cannot lend out customer securities to themselves or others who might want to sell them short, unless the customer has authorized that in writing. Also, the firm has to segregate (separate) customer securities that have been fully paid from the firm's own securities. In other words, they need to keep a really tight set of books of who owns what.

I'm sure it's tempting to tell a skeptical customer, "Even if you lose money on this stock transaction—don't worry. We'll guarantee you and give you your money back." I have recently seen many real-world examples of registered reps dropping the ball on customer accounts and then trying to appease the angry investor with a personal check.

Don't do that. Firms may not offer guarantees against loss, nor would they really want to. You make a suitable recommendation and help your customer manage risk, but when he buys a stock, anything can happen.

Remember that the word "sharing" is a red-flag word. If a registered representative wants to share in the account of a customer, they will need the customer's written authorization and the firm's written authorization, and they have to share only in proportion to their investment in the account. The exception to the proportional sharing requirement is if the customer happens to be a member of the rep's immediate family (parents, mother-in-law or father-in-law, husband or wife, children, or any relative to whose support the member or person associated with a member otherwise contributes directly or indirectly).

Let's not be confused over the use of the word "guaranteed." We looked at several types of U.S. Treasury securities, all of which are guaranteed as to timely interest and principal payments. There are even corporate bonds and stocks that are guaranteed as to interest, principal, or dividends by a third-party. Notice that we're talking about what an issuer of securities has promised to do. On the other hand, agents and broker-dealers don't guarantee customers against a loss. To do so is a violation and also does not represent high standards of commercial honor, even if it seems like it when you offer to personally guarantee a nervous customer against any further losses in her account. Securities involve various risks that we looked at in detail, and your job is not to shield investors from these risks. Rather, your job is to help them plan for and manage these risks. I have seen many agents up on the FINRA website after they mess up a customer's account, then offer to meet him or her for lunch and slip a big check under the table. The customer generally cashes that check before turning the agent into the appropriate supervisor. Agents are adults, and adults have to face up to bad news. Trying to make it all go away with "personal guarantees" is a recipe for disaster, one FINRA will not let you or your firm cook up, no matter how honest or forthright it might feel to you to offer to make the pain go away. This is not the insurance industry—individuals can and do lose money investing in securities. That, in fact, is why you have to know so much before offering and selling securities to investors, most of whom are absolutely clueless and proud of it.

Note that we're only talking about investment losses. On the other hand, when a broker-dealer or agent screw up, the firm will routinely refund the customer for an over-charge, or even go back and fill a security purchase or sale order at a price the customer was due but did not receive because of a mistake. Still, an agent would never try to enact some sort of refund like this without a supervisor/principal getting on board. Right?

Again, if you put a customer into a mutual fund that goes down—that happens, and there is nothing you can do about it except discuss strategies with the customer going forward. If you started to process a purchase or redemption order on a Monday and then for some reason never followed through, your firm would likely go back to that date and execute a purchase or redemption order based on the price the customer should have paid or received, making up the difference from their own account. These are completely different situations.

FINRA RULE. BORROWING FROM OR LENDING TO CUSTOMERS

A registered representative may never borrow money from or lend money to a customer, except when he can. As this FINRA rule makes clear:

> No person associated with a member in any registered capacity may borrow money from or lend money to any customer unless the member has written procedures allowing the borrowing and lending of money between such registered persons and customers of the member and the lending or borrowing arrangement meets one of the following conditions.

Here are the conditions that would allow a registered rep to borrow from/lend to a client:

- the customer is a member of such person's immediate family
- the customer is a financial institution regularly engaged in the business of providing credit, financing, or loans, or other entity or person that regularly arranges or extends credit in the ordinary course of business
- the lending arrangement is based on a personal relationship with the customer, such that the loan would not have been solicited, offered, or given had the customer and the associated person not maintained a relationship outside of the broker/customer relationship
- the lending arrangement is based on a business relationship outside of the broker-customer relationship
- the customer and the registered person are both registered persons of the same member firm

How does FINRA define "immediate family"? Very broadly:

> parents, grandparents, mother-in-law or father-in-law, husband or wife, brother or sister, brother-in-law or sister-in-law, son-in-law or daughter-in-law, children, grandchildren, cousin, aunt or uncle, or niece or nephew, and shall also include any other person whom the registered person supports, directly or indirectly, to a material extent.

Also note that the member firm would always have to pre-approve the borrowing/lending arrangement, except when they wouldn't. If it's an arrangement with a lending institution or an immediate family member, the firm can write their policy in a way that does not require notification. But the arrangement between a fellow registered rep or somebody with whom you have a business relationship—that would have to be pre-approved.

Just to keep everything nice and simple.

But, the bottom line is this—the borrowing and lending policies are established by your firm. If you get a test question implying that a registered representative can borrow money from a client because the client is a family member or a lending institution, read carefully. The firm can allow this activity or not allow it. Whatever the written policy is, that's how things work at that broker-dealer.

FINRA RULE, VARIABLE CONTRACTS

This rule tells member firms that when they accept payment from a customer for a **variable contract**, the price at which the money is invested is the price next computed when the payment is accepted by the insurance company. The member firm has to transmit the application and payment promptly to the insurance company. No member who is a principal underwriter may sell variable contracts through another broker-dealer unless the broker-dealer is a member, and there is a sales agreement in effect between the parties. The agreement must also provide that the sales commission be returned to the insurance company if the purchaser terminates the contract within seven business days. Sorry, that rule doesn't favor you very much, but it is what it is. Also, member firms can only sell variable annuities if the annuity/insurance company promptly pays out when clients surrender their contracts.

Associated persons (you) may not accept compensation from anyone other than the member firm. The only exception here is if there is an arrangement between you and the other party that your member firm agrees to, and your firm deals with a bunch of other requirements. Associated persons (you) may not accept securities from somebody else in exchange for selling variable contracts. The only non-cash compensation that can be offered or accepted would be:

- gifts that do not exceed an annual amount per person fixed periodically by the Association, and that are not preconditioned on achievement of a sales target. The gift limit is still $100, by the way.

- an occasional meal, a ticket to a sporting event or the theater, or comparable entertainment that is neither so frequent nor so extensive as to raise any question of propriety and is not preconditioned on achievement of a sales target
- payment or reimbursement by offerors in connection with meetings held by an offeror or by a member for the purpose of training or education of associated persons of a member

For that last bullet, remember that the associated person (you) would have to get your firm's permission to attend and that your attendance and reimbursement of expenses cannot be preconditioned on your meeting a sales target. Only you—not your guest—can have your expenses reimbursed. The location of the meeting has to be appropriate, too, meaning if the offeror's office is in Minneapolis, it looks real suspicious when the meeting is held in Montego Bay, mon. And—as always—the recordkeeping requirements are tougher than we'd like. As the rule states, your "member firm shall maintain records of all compensation received by the member or its associated persons from offerors. The records shall include the names of the offerors, the names of the associated persons, the amount of cash, the nature and, if known, the value of non-cash compensation received."

Your firm can give you non-cash compensation for selling variable contracts, but they can't compensate you more for selling one variable contract than for another. This rule states that the non-cash compensation arrangement requires that the credit received for each variable contract security is equally weighted.

FINRA RULE. INVESTMENT COMPANY SECURITIES

Mutual funds and variable annuities are both investment companies covered under the Investment Company Act of 1940. Since they are so similar, it's not surprising that this FINRA rule on investment company securities is very similar to the one we just looked at on variable contracts. Like the previous rule, this one tells member firms who act as underwriters/distributors of investment companies that they need to have a written sales agreement between themselves and other dealers. If the other dealer is not a FINRA member, they would have to pay the full public offering price, which would make it real tough for them to make a profit. As before, member firms need to transmit payment from customers to the mutual fund companies promptly.

Excessive Charges

This rule also tells member firms not to offer or sell shares of investment companies if the sales charges are excessive. What makes the sales charges excessive? 8.5% of the public offering price is the maximum sales charge. Also note that if the fund does not offer breakpoints and rights of accumulation that satisfy FINRA, the fund cannot charge 8.5%. Of course, it would be a violation to describe a mutual fund as being "no load" or as having "no sales charge" if the investment company has a front-end (A shares) or deferred (B shares) sales charge, or if their 12b-1 fees exceed .25 of 1%.

Withhold Orders

Although I would have thought this truth were self-evident, this FINRA rule states that, "No member shall withhold placing customers' orders for any investment company security so as to profit himself as a result of such withholding." Another part of this rule says that member firms can only purchase investment company shares either for their own account or to fill existing customer orders—they can't just pick up a batch of shares and then see if anybody wants them, in other words.

Anti-Reciprocal Rule

This next thing seems highly testable to me. Broker-dealers cannot decide to sell particular investment company shares based on how much trading business the investment company does or would consider doing through the firm. The ol' "pay to play" method is a big no-no, in other words. Be very broad in your understanding of this rule—if it looks at all as if a member firm is tying the promotion of particular funds to the amount of trading commissions they receive when the fund places trades through them, it's not passing the smell test. This would also apply to a member firm offering to compensate their branch managers and reps more for selling the shares of those investment companies who execute transactions through the firm, generating fat commissions.

So, I just told you that a broker-dealer (member firm) cannot sell mutual fund shares if the mutual fund trades through the broker-dealer, generating commissions for the member firm, right?

No. What I'm saying is that the firm can't tie the promotion/sale of the mutual fund to the level of trading the fund does or intends to do through the firm. Similarly, firms definitely compensate their branch managers and representatives for selling mutual fund shares; they simply can't compensate them more for selling the shares of the funds willing to "pay to play."

Interestingly, as I look at FINRA's website this morning, I see that the regulators just fined a firm over $12 million for placing mutual funds on a "preferred list" in exchange for those funds doing lots of lucrative trading business through the firm. The news release calls it a "shelf-space program," which is a great name for it. See, in the supermarket, all the products you see are there because the company paid a fee for "shelf space." Well, that's okay for cookies and crackers, but not for mutual funds.

This all boils down to the fact that a broker-dealer should recommend a mutual fund because it's the best investment for a particular client, not because the broker-dealer will make money from the mutual fund when it executes its trades through the firm.

If a transaction involves the purchase of shares of an investment company that imposes a deferred sales charge when the investor redeems the shares some day, the written confirmation must also include the following legend: "On selling your shares, you may pay a sales charge. For the charge and other fees, see the prospectus." The legend must appear on the front of a confirmation and in at least 8-point type.

I am not making that up. 8-point type. What's more, I understand that the members of the rowdy 9-point-font faction of the rules committee had to be forcibly restrained several times before finally bowing to the demands of their relentless, 8-point-font-favoring colleagues. They're a wild, impassioned bunch, these regulators, let me tell you.

If a customer buys mutual fund shares but then redeems them within seven *business* days, any compensation earned by the broker-dealer and the registered rep must be returned to the underwriter. This puts a damper on registered representatives getting all their fraternity brothers to buy mutual fund shares and then dump them so that their buddy can earn sales charges, apparently.

Finally, everything I told you about the FINRA rule concerning receipt of payment from other sources, including non-cash compensation, holds true here, too. So, assuming you haven't fallen asleep or died of boredom yet, you might want to do a quick review of that section.

FINRA RULE. BREAKPOINT SALES

Open-end mutual funds with front-end loads typically offer **breakpoints,** as we saw earlier. Remember that preventing a customer from receiving a breakpoint, or failing to inform her of the breakpoints—even though they are printed in the prospectus—is a violation called **breakpoint selling**. An exception to this concern is when a broker-dealer offers a diversification/asset allocation program that spreads the customer's investments among many funds. As long as the firm discloses to the customers that this program may prevent them from receiving breakpoints and keeps records of this, there is no breakpoint selling occurring.

FINRA RULE. INFLUENCING OR REWARDING EMPLOYEES OF OTHERS

In many ways financial services sales efforts must be tamed down considerably from what might fly in other industries. For example, if I were still in the carpet cleaning business, no one would have a problem with my offering large cash payments to sorority sisters who can get my company a contract with various sorority houses. Or, if I knew someone who worked at a rival janitorial services company, there would be no law against paying him or her to flip some of the smaller accounts my way.

So, if you come from a sales career in a different industry, you might need to tone down the approach. FINRA doesn't want you or your firm rewarding or influencing other firms or their members with large cash payments or gifts worth over a certain amount. That annual limit on gifts has been at $100 for quite some time, and, of course, not much influence can be purchased with things worth $100 or less, which is exactly how the regulators want it. If your firm sponsors a mutual fund, they may not offer a $500 cash prize to the broker-dealer or agent who sells the most shares, for example. If you start a small underwriting firm, you may not buy your way into the next syndicate by sending the decision makers at Goldman Sachs Cuban cigars worth thousands of dollars.

FINRA is prohibiting payments for influence; they are not prohibiting legitimate compensation for work performed in connection to a legitimate written contract between the member and the person receiving payment. If your firm agrees to let you work for another firm on weekends structuring small bond offering, and there is a written agreement in place, that would be an exception. As long as the other member is paying you to do legitimate work and not trying to influence you or your firm, they are not violating this rule. Also note that a gift of $100 includes cash and items that could easily be resold for. So, you can't give a big player at another firm $400 cash-money or $400 worth of imported wine. You could take him out for an occasional business meal or take him out to the ballgame. How about slipping him season tickets to your company's skybox? No—slip them to me, instead. I'm not associated with any FINRA-member firm, and neither will you be if you don't appreciate all these rules we're going over.

FINRA RULE. USE OF INFORMATION OBTAINED IN FIDUCIARY CAPACITY

Broker-dealers and their various affiliated companies provide services we might not think of right off. If a member firm acts as the "paying agent" for the issuer of a bond, they have access to information on all the bondholders to whom they pay interest and, eventually, principal. Therefore, FINRA prohibits that member firm from using the information in any way without the consent of the issuer. As the rule states:

> A member who in the capacity of paying agent, transfer agent, trustee, or in any other similar capacity, has received information as to the ownership of securities, shall under no circumstances make use of such information for the purpose of soliciting purchases, sales or exchanges except at the request and on behalf of the issuer.

NASD RULE. DEALING WITH NON-MEMBERS

FINRA still uses NASD rules—many have been retired, but many are still effective. This one, which is obviously still in effect, states, "No member shall deal with any non-member broker or dealer except at the same prices, for the same commissions or fees, and on the same terms and conditions as are by such member accorded to the general public." What they're saying is that member firms can't treat broker-dealers who don't belong to FINRA or another registered securities association any differently from how they treat any other public customer. Section 15A of the Securities Exchange Act of 1934 calls for registration of securities associations, such as FINRA, NYSE, MSRB, etc. So, if the broker or dealer is not registered under that Act, the member firm can't share commissions with them, or participate in a syndicate with them, or trade securities with them at special prices not available to a schmuck like me.

The rule would allow a FINRA member firm to do business on more favorable terms with a member of a different securities association—as long as it's registered under Section 15A of the Securities Exchange Act of 1934.

And you thought this Series 6 stuff was going to be boring!

NASD RULE. CONTINUING COMMISSIONS

As long as there is a written agreement in place, a retired representative can receive continuing commissions from his former firm on business placed when he was in the industry. There can be no payment for any new business, of course, since the retired rep is no longer registered. Member firms can also have a contract to pay a widow or other beneficiary for the former rep's business pursuant to a written agreement.

INSIDER TRADING

If you had dinner last night with your sister-in-law, who told you that her company was going to be purchased by GE, that would be some pretty interesting news, right? If the announcement hadn't come out yet, you could pretty well bet that GE's stock will drop and your sister-in-law's company's stock will shoot up when that announcement is made in the *Wall Street Journal*, CNBC, Bloomberg, etc. So, it would be lots of fun to buy a bunch of calls on your sister-in-law's company's stock and maybe a few puts on GE for good measure, too.

Unfortunately, it would also be unethical, illegal, and extremely painful if you got caught. See, like the other Acts, the Securities Exchange Act of 1934 is frequently amended and updated, just like the Series 6 exam. In 1988 Congress passed the **Insider Trading and Securities Fraud Enforcement Act**, which amended the Securities Exchange Act of 1934. The Act of '34 had already prohibited insider trading, but the legislation in 1988 raised the penalties a bit. Even if the person doesn't end up in prison, the SEC can sue him in civil court and extract the following penalties:

- For the individual who passed out the inside information or was dumb enough to use it, the court can impose a civil penalty of three times the profit gained or loss avoided as a result of such unlawful purchase, sale, or communication.
- If that person happened to be "controlled" by somebody else (a boss, the broker-dealer who hired the agent, for example) that "controlling person" could receive a civil penalty of the *greater* of $1,000,000, or three times the amount of the profit gained or loss avoided as a result of the controlled person's violation.

A person caught trading on inside information can also be held liable to "contemporaneous traders." That means that if you profit big time from your little put-call play, I might have to sue you and show how your actions caused me to lose money. How much would you have to pay me for "pain and suffering"?

You wouldn't. The maximum under this statute is the profit you made or the loss you avoided by trading on inside information.

INVESTMENT COMPANY ACT OF 1940

Back in 1940, the United States Congress formed a committee and several subcommittees who after many hours of extensive effort and expense concluded that a company whose primary activity is investing shall henceforth be referred to as an "investment company."

Our tax dollars at work, I'm afraid. But, I'm not doing it justice—check out how beautifully the legislation lays it out with the following passage:

```
1. When used in this title, "investment company" means any
issuer which—

A. is or holds itself out as being engaged primarily, or
proposes to engage primarily, in the business of investing,
reinvesting, or trading in securities
```

So, if your company is primarily engaged in making investments in securities, your company is an **investment company**. The definition also states that if more than 40% of the company's total assets are tied up in securities investments, that's an investment company.

The most well-known type of investment company is commonly called a "mutual fund." Under the Investment Company Act of 1940, the so-called "mutual fund" represents the third type of investment company, properly called **management companies**. A management company is either an open-end or a closed-end fund. An open-end fund issues securities that investors redeem/sell back to the fund when they want to cash in. How much will the investor receive? Whatever the securities happen to be worth at the time. The **closed-end fund** sells their securities in an IPO, but if you want your money later, you have to trade the closed-end fund shares with other investors on the big, scary secondary market. How much will you receive? Whatever a buyer is willing to pay. As the Investment Company Act of 1940 says, "*Open-end company* means a management company which is offering for sale or has outstanding any redeemable security of which it is the issuer." So, what is a "closed-end company"? Luckily, the Act clarifies that by telling us, "*Closed-end company* means any management company other than an open-end company."

So, open-end companies allow investors to redeem/sell the shares to the company for the net asset value (NAV, what they're currently worth). Closed-end companies might have the very same investment objective as an open-end fund (growth, income, etc.), but when you want to sell, you trade these shares exactly as you trade your shares of IBM, GE, or Walmart. You buy at the Asked price and sell at the Bid price. Sometimes the bid price is much lower than you'd like, unlike the open-end shares that simply pay out your fair share of the fund: the NAV. Oh well—that could be you putting in the bid, so you also get to buy closed-end shares at a discount, except when you have to buy them at a premium.

Remember, they trade like shares of stock on the NYSE, NASDAQ, etc. The open-end shares don't trade—instead, you sell them back to the issuer, which is called "redeeming" your shares.

Since we enjoyed that so much, let's look at the other two types of investment companies, and—please—keep this organizational chart clear in your mind. There are three types of investment companies. One type is called the "management company," and there are either open-end or closed-end management companies.

Another type is called the **face amount certificate company**. Here, the investor either pays installments or a lump sum into the investment program, and receives the higher face amount on the certificate on a future date. The exam might ask if these carry sales charges and/or management fees. The answer to both questions is yes. Sales charges cover the cost of marketing and selling the shares; management fees cover the cost of managing the investments in order to pay out more than they took in.

Then, there is the **Unit Investment Trust** or UIT. These are not actively managed/traded portfolios, so they don't charge a management fee. If it's a portfolio of bonds, they just let the bonds mature. So, like any trust, it just kind of sits there holding title to vast quantities of assets, and smiles all the way to the bank every time a big, fat dividend or interest check comes in the mail. Investors buy units of this investment trust, which is why the creative types just couldn't stop themselves from dubbing these things unit investment trusts. The units are redeemable, meaning they can be sort of "cashed in" for their current value.

The main point of this Act is that if you fit the definition of an "investment company," you will have to register your securities with the Securities and Exchange Commission. Of course, if you fail to register or leave out material (important) information in any report or document filed with the SEC, you will regret that lapse of judgment.

REGISTRATION OF INVESTMENT COMPANIES

Investment companies submit a registration statement to the SEC. The registration statement has two parts. The first part is called either "Part 1" or an "N1-A prospectus." To make sure it has at least three names, it can also be called a "summary prospectus." The second part of the registration statement is cleverly called "Part 2." Part 1 is what all prospects have to receive before purchasing a mutual fund. Part 2 contains more detailed information that must be made available but is not automatically provided. Part 2 is called the **statement of additional information**, or SAI.

Of course, the fact that a mutual fund or other investment company has been registered does not imply approval or endorsement by the SEC or any other regulator. The front cover of a mutual fund prospectus will make that very clear.

RESTRICTIONS

Unless the fund meets some very stringent financial and disclosure requirements, it is prohibited by the SEC from engaging in the following activities:

- Selling securities short (unlimited loss potential)
- Purchasing securities on margin (high-risk)
- Selling uncovered options (covered calls okay)
- Participating in joint investment or trading accounts
- Acting as a distributor of its own securities (use an underwriter, or a 12b-1 plan)
- Borrowing or lending money

If the fund wants to do any of the above, it must disclose the activities and explain the extent to which it plans to engage in them in the registration statement/prospectus. An open-end fund can borrow money from a bank but must maintain a 3-to-1 **asset-to-debt** coverage. And, the fund may not lend money to one of its officers or directors, no matter what it says in its registration statement. Finally, remember that open-end funds do not issue "senior securities" giving those investors higher claims. Open-end funds issue only common stock. It's the closed-end funds that can issue senior securities, as long as they follow the rules under the Investment Company Act of 1940.

We looked at the various players at a mutual fund: distributor, investment adviser, board of directors, transfer agent, and custodian. The Investment Company Act of 1940 stipulates that investment companies (e.g., The American Balanced Fund) cannot act as the distributor of their own shares unless they do so under SEC Rule 12b-1, which is why we've already discussed such 12b-1 fees, as an operating expense deducted against fund assets. As SEC Rule 12b-1 states:

A registered, open-end management investment company may act as a distributor of securities of which it is the issuer: *Provided,* That any payments made by such company in connection with such distribution are made pursuant to a written plan describing all material aspects of the proposed financing of distribution and that all agreements with any person relating to implementation of the plan are in writing." Also, the plan is only implemented when a majority of the outstanding shares, a majority of the board of directors, and a majority of the non-interested/independent board members approves it. The plan can also be terminated with a majority vote of the shareholders or a majority vote of the non-interested/independent board members. The plan has to be approved annually by a majority of the shareholders, a majority of the board of directors overall *and* within the board of directors, a majority of the non-interested/independent members of the board.

12b-1 fees cannot exceed .25% of the fund's average net assets if the fund wants to call itself "no load" and act as its own distributor. On the other hand, since I used the example of the American Balanced Fund, you would see quickly from their summary prospectus that the fund is distributed by American Funds Distributors and is not a "no load" fund. Basically, any fund family with B- and C-shares is not a "no load" fund family and has its shares marketed and sold by a separate-but-related distributor/underwriter.

Paying 12b-1 fees to broker-dealers and agents pursuant to a written agreement is fine, but a registered investment company cannot reward member firms for selling their shares by giving them portfolio securities or by giving them commissions when they agree to execute buy and sell orders through the broker-dealer. If the ABC Funds Distributors worked it out so that their related investment adviser executed the most transactions for the fund portfolios through the broker-dealers selling the most shares of the funds to their retail investors, this would be a violation. Without this rule, investors would end up being pitched mutual funds for reasons that have nothing to do with suitability. Each broker-dealer would end up using various mutual fund products as nothing but a way to generate trading commissions and profits from the mutual fund companies, at the expense of investors.

Open-end funds and their underwriter can only offer to exchange shares of one fund for shares of another based on the relative Net Asset Values (NAV) of the funds, unless they have first filed the offer with the SEC and gotten their approval of the terms. This rule does not cover the case where the majority of the shares of an open-end fund have voted to reorganize the fund into something different. We're talking about the case where the ABC Fund Family offers to exchange shares of their Growth Fund for shares of their new Growth and Income Fund. If they do that, the exchange must be based on the relative net asset values of the fund shares unless they have first presented the offer to the SEC and received its okay. This rule also applies among the types of investment companies, too, so if you get a question about a fund company offering to exchange shares of an open-end fund for units of a unit investment trust, or vice versa, same deal.

Open-end and closed-end funds, as well as unit investment trusts, frequently pay dividend distributions to their share or unit holders. When doing so, they must either pay the dividend only from their net income, or—if it is being paid from some other source—a written statement must accompany the payment of the dividend or special distribution. Why? Dividend distributions tend to be fairly steady and predictable; if an investor gets a one-time payment of $5 per-share, we don't want her to start making plans to keep on receiving it, right? Remember that dividend distributions are not paid from portfolio trading profits (capital gains), so when capital gains or other distributions are made to shareholders, the fund must go out of its way to clarify that this is not a regular dividend distribution. Also, investment companies do not distribute capital gains to shareholders more than once every 12 months under the Investment Company Act of 1940.

The pricing of investment company shares is subject to regulation. First, when an investor redeems shares of an open-end fund, the price he receives is based on the next calculated price, not yesterday's NAV. Mutual funds price their shares once a day Monday through Friday as long as the exchanges are open and there are actually requests from investors to turn their shares back into cash—**redemption orders.** The fund does not have to allow member firms to buy shares for their customers and then immediately redeem them; in fact, if that happens within a certain time frame, any sales charges earned will be forfeited. Member firms cannot purchase shares of open-end funds below the net asset value. Instead, they make part of the extra fee added to the NAV called a **sales charge.** As we saw, the sales charges are laid out in the breakpoint schedule shown in the summary or statutory prospectus for the fund. If the fund ever changes this sales charge schedule, it has to provide full disclosure to prospective and existing shareholders, revise its prospectus and Statement of Additional Information (SAI), and has to apply the new sales charge schedule uniformly to all investors who invest the certain stated amounts in the new breakpoint schedule.

Open-end funds and Unit Investment Trusts are both registered investment companies that issue redeemable securities. Under the Investment Company Act of 1940, they may only suspend the investor's ability to redeem or turn shares back into cash under limited circumstances and, otherwise, complete a redemption order within 7 days. As the Investment Company Act of 1940 states:

> No registered investment company shall suspend the right of redemption, or postpone the date of payment or satisfaction upon redemption of any redeemable security in accordance with its terms
>
> for more than seven days after the tender of such security to the company or its agent designated for that purpose for redemption, except—
>
> (1) for any period (A) during which the New York Stock Exchange is closed other than customary week-end and holiday closings or (B) during which trading on the New York Stock Exchange is restricted;

(2) for any period during which an emergency exists as a result of which (A) disposal by the company of securities owned by it is not reasonably practicable or (B) it is not reasonably practicable for such company fairly to determine the value of its net assets; or

(3) for such other periods as the Commission may by order permit for the protection of security holders of the company.

So, in general mutual funds and UITs have to redeem their investors' securities within 7 days. But, since investment company products are used as the investment vehicle for variable annuities, a rule had to be written to exempt them in the case where an annuitant is receiving payments under a "life contingency" payout option, e.g. a "life with period certain" settlement option.

The ways in which closed-end funds distribute and/or repurchase their shares is also regulated under the Investment Company Act of 1940. The same way that public companies such as ORCL or SBUX might decide to repurchase their shares on the secondary market, a closed-end fund could buy its shares back on the secondary market. If so, they must inform the existing shareholders at least six months ahead of time, and they must do so in a way that satisfies SEC requirements. For example, if their shares are listed on the NYSE, and they purchase them from investors through that medium, everything looks fine. But, if they quietly buy 1,000,000 of their shares from a hedge fund or secretive trader from Bora Bora, that wouldn't work. Closed-end funds also cannot issue their securities at special prices to member firms except in connection to an offering/underwriting of securities. In other words, when the fund is capitalizing or doing an additional offer of shares, then member firms can make customary underwriting fees. But, when the closed-end fund shares are trading on the secondary market, a broker-dealer does not get to buy shares from the fund at a deep discount. Rather, trades in closed-end funds yield either commissions (broker) or markups/markdowns (dealer) to member firms executing the transactions for or with their customers, as do trades in any other common stock issues. Also, closed-end funds may not issue their shares in exchange for services rendered or for property. Why not? If you were an existing shareholder, you would only want to see new owners come in if they contributed *money* to the fund, right? The fact that they did tax planning for the principals at the fund company wouldn't really help you much but would, rather, dilute your equity or devalue your ownership stake in the fund.

The names of funds and the words connected to them could end up being misleading, and we know how much the SEC hates it when investors are misled. Therefore, the Investment Company Act of 1940 stipulates:

It shall be unlawful for any person, issuing or selling any security of which a registered investment company is the issuer, to represent or imply in any manner whatsoever that such security or company—

(A) has been guaranteed, sponsored, recommended, or approved by the United States, or any agency, instrumentality or officer of the United States;

(B) has been insured by the Federal Deposit Insurance Corporation; or

(C) is guaranteed by or is otherwise an obligation of any bank or insured depository institution.

So, whether it's the investment company itself or anyone selling the shares, the fund is *not* guaranteed by the United States Treasury even if every single security in the portfolio is a U.S. Treasury security. The U.S. Treasury issues their bills, notes, and bonds to whomever; they do not guarantee mutual fund companies who might decide to buy such securities as part of their business model. Similarly, the money market mutual fund is basically a worry-free investment, but it is still not a bank product and, therefore, not backed up by the FDIC or any bank. Making statements or implications that the securities you sell are safer than they are in fact is exactly the sort of thing that FINRA finds "inconsistent with high standards of commercial honor." It's a deceptive sales practice that has gotten many an agent removed from the industry. And, if you think about it, why couldn't you sell a money market mutual fund without lying? Is there something scary about the product that would lead to mass resistance? Of course not. And that also seems to tick off the regulators no end—many of the little lies and deceits used by bad-boy agents and firms are completely unnecessary. If somebody wants to park some of their money in a safe, liquid account, it should not be that hard to tell them that they'll likely get a better yield here than at the bank but that the money is not FDIC insured. What if they decide to put their money in the bank rather than with you? Then, you won't be earning 12b-1 fees on that money, just as you won't be playing for the New York Yankees or the New York Philharmonic unless you already happen to be at this point. Life can be tough—lying seldom makes it better, as a long line of former Illinois governors could attest.

Finally, the Investment Company Act of 1940 lays out its own penalties for larceny or embezzlement of fund assets, just in case the police or FBI weren't already all over the case. The "Act" states, "Whoever steals, unlawfully abstracts, unlawfully and willfully converts to his own use or to the use of another, or embezzles any of the moneys, funds, securities, credits, property, or assets of any registered investment company shall be deemed guilty of a crime, and upon conviction thereof shall be subject to the penalties provided in section 49. A judgment of conviction or acquittal on the merits under the laws of any State shall be a bar to any prosecution under this section for the same act or acts." That means that if somebody working for the investment adviser to the ABC Growth Fund accidentally "converts" $500,000 for her own benefit, she could be prosecuted under the Investment Company Act of 1940 in federal court if the local District Attorney's office didn't feel like making an example of her. But, if the DA does file charges, then the Investment Company Act of 1940 is not used to take another swing at her.

What are the "penalties provided in Section 49"? A $10,000 fine and/or up to five years in federal prison. But, if the defendant sustains the burden of proving he had no actual knowledge of the rule, regulation, or order, then he won't be convicted under the Act.

TAXATION

As you probably know, people like interstate highways, public universities, national parks, a strong national defense, and maybe a lunar landing every decade or so just to show the world we still got it. Unfortunately, the federal government has no money to pay for any of that stuff unless taxpayers are willing to pitch in. Similarly, your state government provides roads, parks, state troopers, state fairs, etc., and they use the taxes you pay to fund that stuff. So, when you get a paycheck, both the federal and state governments insist on sharing some of it with you. As it turns out, they also insist on sharing the money you earn from investments.

BONDS

U.S. Treasury securities, which include T-bills, T-notes, T-bonds, I-bonds, and STRIPS, pay interest that is taxed at ordinary income rates, but only at the federal level. Much to their disappointment, state and local governments can't tax that interest. Capital gains are also taxable at the federal level, remember, and that includes the next type, municipal securities.

Municipal securities pay interest that is tax-exempt at the *federal* level. At the state level, it depends on where the bond was issued. If you live in Kentucky and buy a general obligation of Little Rock, Arkansas, Kentucky can tax the interest, and so can your local government. Of course, if you buy the general obligations of Louisville or the State of Kentucky, you'll get a break. Regardless, when you're selling municipal bonds and taking capital gains, those are still taxable as capital gains, either short-term or long-term depending on your holding period.

Corporate bonds, and also Ginnie, Fannie, and Freddie, pay interest that is taxable at all three levels: federal, state, and local.

And don't forget the funky zero-coupon bonds. These are issued originally at a discount, which is why the creative types named them original issue discount bonds, which immediately became OIDs to make sure the industry had enough acronyms. If you buy a zero coupon issued for $500 with a par value that will become $1,000 in 10 years, you basically report the $50 increase each year on a 1099 OID. Yes, the interest income you haven't collected yet is still taxable at this point.

STOCK

Mutual funds have been marketed so successfully that many people don't even realize they can, like, buy stock. But, of course, they can do exactly that. If they think companies such as General Electric, Home Depot, or Starbucks will continue to do well over their lifetimes, they can own little pieces of them by purchasing their stock.

Dividends

If and when companies pay dividends to shareholders, the shareholders are taxed. For most investors, the tax on "qualified dividends" is 15%, but low-bracket investors pay no tax on dividends, and people in the highest tax bracket (which we'll examine soon) actually pay 20%. But, the exam may not care about real-world tax rates, anyway. The exam would likely be more concerned with making sure you know that cash dividends are taxable, whatever the rate. Sometimes, the rate used is the ordinary income rate; recently, many dividends have been taxed at 15% (even 5% in some cases). The main point here for the exam would be that the dividend income is taxable. In case the exam surprises us and gets all "real world," please know that a qualified dividend is what you would receive from GE or Home Depot. Those companies pay the dividend after they've paid their taxes on the profits they made. So, why should the shareholders get fully taxed on their part of that profit that's already been taxed?

Turns out, Congress and a Republican President recently said they shouldn't, and the older I get the smarter that sounds. Earn a million dollars in qualified dividends this year and keep $850,000. Not too shabby, from what I understand. But, if the exam wants to play hardball, remember that there are still some dividends that are taxed at ordinary income rates. These are called, surprisingly enough, ordinary dividends. Real Estate Investment Trusts (REITs) pass through 90% of their net income to the shareholders, but the shareholders pay ordinary income tax on those fat dividends. What's the difference? At the time of this writing, ordinary income rates could be as high as 39.6%. So could mine, if people continue to buy Pass the 6™ products with the same enthusiasm they've shown so far. In any case, notice that there are few black-and-white statements that can be made about securities and taxation. If someone says that all dividends are taxed at 15%, he's way off. First, some people only pay 0%, and, second, there are ordinary dividends and even royalties that are paid to shareholders, and the taxation is different from the treatment of qualified dividends. Bottom line is that if you own stock inside a regular old brokerage account, the income those stocks pay to you will be taxable. Companies like GE, Home Depot, and Microsoft pay qualified dividends taxed at a low rate. If you own REITs or royalty trusts (oil & gas, for example), the taxation will be a little different. Either way, you'll receive a Form 1099-DIV to help you and your accountant deal with the tax implications. And, the tax rate on dividend income is in play as we go to press, so don't be shocked if the tax rates have changed by the time you read this. We update numbers at www.passthe6.com/updates, and we also assume that the exam is not about memorizing little factoids and spitting them back at the testing center. Still, to be on the safe side, we do provide the numbers that could show up on a test question.

Capital Gains

So, the income paid to shareholders is taxable. And, when the shareholders decide to sell their stock to other investors, they could end up selling for more than they paid, and nothing seems to get the IRS's attention faster. See, if you buy $10,000 of GE stock in, say, 1993 and have the audacity to sell that stock for $15,000 in 2013, you have "realized a capital gain" of $5,000. First of all, congratulations on making a profit and, secondly, don't forget your friends and mine at the IRS. At the end of the year when you figure your taxes, you'll have to report the $5,000 capital gain and maybe end up paying taxes on it.

Why just "maybe"? Because, if you're like most investors, you will have even more stocks that moved in the opposite direction. See, if you had purchased $15,000 of XYZ in 1999 and sold it for a whopping $1,000 in 2012, you would have realized a $14,000 capital loss, which would more than offset the gain you took on GE. Investors subtract their capital losses from their capital gains taken during the tax year. If they end up with more gains than losses, they have a "net capital gain" for the year. If the stock was held for at least 12 months plus one day, it is treated as a long-term capital gain. Those are taxed at a maximum of 15% currently, or 20% if you are in the very top tax bracket. If the capital gain had been taken on stock held one year or less, that's a short-term capital gain, taxed at the investor's ordinary income bracket just to keep things nice and simple the way the IRS and the United States Congress like it.

The "long-term" and "short-term" thing has to do with what the exam will call the investor's **holding period**. The holding period begins the day after the trade date and stops on the day the stock is sold. So, if you buy stock on November 5, 2014, you can sell it on November 6, 2015, for a long-term capital gain. But if you sell it sooner than that, it will be treated as a short-term capital gain.

To determine if the sale triggered a gain or loss, the investor compares the proceeds of the sale with the cost basis on the stock. The fancy phrase "cost basis" means all the money the investor has put into the thing up to this point. If you buy $5,000 of Microsoft common stock and pay a $25 commission, your cost basis is $5,025. The IRS has already taxed that money and won't tax it again. If you sell that stock later for $6,000 and pay another $25 commission, your "proceeds" will be $5,975. So, you would take the proceeds of $5,975 minus the cost basis of $5,025 for a capital gain of $950. If you held it for at least one year plus one day, it's a **long-term capital gain** taxed at the kinder, gentler rate. If your holding period was less than that, it's a **short-term capital gain**, which is probably taxed at a higher rate.

The exam might try to mess with you by mentioning **unrealized capital gains**, so let's take a look at that. If you buy 1,000 shares of Starbucks for $10 a share, and the stock is now trading at $55 a share, how much of a capital gains tax do you have to pay at this point?

Not a penny. This is just a gain on paper, called an "unrealized capital gain." It gives you major bragging rights around the water cooler, but you haven't sold anything yet. It's only when you "realize" your capital gain that the IRS gets concerned. To realize a capital gain means that you've sold the stock. Until you sell it, there are no capital gains taxes to pay.

But don't you have to sell the stock eventually? Not really. Some people hate the IRS so much that they will *never* sell it. Instead, the stock will pass to their children or grandchildren when they die. Or they'll just give the stock to somebody. Or, maybe they'll donate it to a charity.

Inherited Shares

Let's say that Grandma purchased 1,000 shares of Harley-Davidson back in 1983 for $10 a share. On the day she dies, November 15, 2014, the fair market value is $50 a share. If you inherit the shares, what is your cost basis?

$50 a share. So, if you sell it a few days later for $55, that's only a capital gain of $5 per share, not $45. It's also treated as a long-term capital gain, even if you sell it right away. The IRS actually explains this quite clearly at www.irs.gov:

> If you inherit investment property, your capital gain or loss on any later disposition of that property is treated as a long-term capital gain or loss. This is true regardless of how long you actually held the property.

See, they do have a heart at the IRS. Imagine if you had to take Grandma's original cost basis. First, that would have made the capital gains tax much, much higher. Secondly, where the heck did Grandma keep her trade confirmations? Doesn't matter. You just take the "fair market value" as of the date of death. And, again, you can sell it as soon as you want—it's still a long-term capital gain.

Gifts of Stock

Unfortunately, if the stock has appreciated Grandma will have to die in order to get you the nice tax break. See, if Grandma is still toolin' around on her Harley and just, like, *gives* you this stock that has risen about $40 a share, you'd have to take her cost basis of $10.

Charitable Donations of Stock

Maybe Grandma has a more worthy cause than you and decides to donate the stock to her favorite charity. If so, she can deduct the fair market value of the stock on the day of the donation from her ordinary income and reduce her tax bill that year. You, however, would get squat on that deal, so you may want to talk to her before she goes and gets all philanthropic suddenly.

Capital Losses

As mentioned, investors often end up selling stock for less than they paid, which sort of stinks. Then again, it's not the end of the world. When you sell stock for less than you paid, you get to use that capital loss to reduce the capital gains you may have taken on other sales. And that reduces your capital gains taxes for the year. Some people go overboard. If they take a $10,000 capital gain, they then take a $15,000 capital loss just to make sure they pay no capital gains taxes that year. That extra $5,000 "net capital loss" could be used in future years to offset capital gains. $3,000 of it can also be used to reduce the investor's ordinary income for the current tax year. So, if his adjusted gross income was going to be $50,000, now it's only $47,000. He would only save a percentage of that $3,000, remember. It's not a tax credit; it's a tax deduction. You have to lose a dollar in order to save 25 or 35 cents, in other words. I mean, it's nice, but I wouldn't make it a cornerstone of your long-term investment strategy.

Wash Sales

When the investor realizes the capital loss on his stock, the IRS is cool with that. But, he has to wait a full 30 days and not repurchase that company's stock until the 31ˢᵗ day. Otherwise, he can't use the loss. Also, he could not have purchased that company's stock 30 days before selling it at a loss. So, there is a 60-day window pointing 30 days before and after the sale. Stay out of the stock if you want to use the loss to offset gains for the year.

What if you promise not to buy the stock back for 30 days but simply can't stop yourself? First of all, I can recommend a good therapist, and, secondly, you simply can't use that loss. However, if you took a loss of, say, $5 a share that is now going to be disallowed due to the wash sale, you can add that $5 to your cost basis on the new purchase, meaning you will eventually get the benefit of that loss you tried to take this year.

Just to keep things nice and simple. The IRS, again, actually explains this all very clearly at www.irs.gov, which is becoming, like, one of my favorite websites lately:

```
If your loss was disallowed because of the wash sale rules,
add the disallowed loss to the cost of the new stock or secu-
rities. The result is your basis in the new stock or secu-
rities. This adjustment postpones the loss deduction until
the disposition of the new stock or securities.
```

Share ID, Average Cost, FIFO

When an investor sells shares of stock, she either realizes a capital gain or a capital loss. If the investor has 1,000 shares of ORCL in her portfolio, which shares did she sell when she entered her order to sell 100 ORCL the other day? It's up to the investor (and her tax preparer) to choose a method of figuring her cost basis and sticking with it. One method is called **share identification**, and it is exactly what it sounds like. The investor simply identifies the particular 100 shares and would probably choose the ones purchased at the highest price, as long as they've been held at least 12 months plus 1 day (long-term gain). Or maybe she identifies shares held short-term because she has short-term losses to use as an off-set. Hopefully, the exam won't get too crazy here, but you should know that "share identification" is one method of calculating your cost basis for purposes of reporting capital gains and losses. The exact shares have to be identified on the trade ticket, by the way, rather than determined later based on what works out best for the investor.

Another method has always seemed the most sensible to me—**average cost**. If I buy 1,000 shares of ORCL at 10 different prices, I just take the total amount invested (including commissions paid) divided by the 1,000 shares. If I buy another 100 shares, I take the new total amount invested divided by 1,100 shares. Pretty simple, right?

For some reason, the exam seems more likely to bring up the third method, **FIFO**, or "first-in-first-out," which is an accounting method in which the thing we just sold (first-out) is the thing we bought first (first-in). If you get a test question about the IRS making assumptions, remember that the IRS uses FIFO (first-in-first-out) when they make the determination of which shares an investor sold.

I could now give you a math problem in which an investor buys shares over three or four different purchases and have you calculate the average cost per share. But I tend to err on the side of caution when it comes to overwhelming Series 6 students with calculations. As you'll see, the calculator is not used that much at the testing center. Knowing concepts is king.

TRUSTS, ESTATES, GIFTS, AND OTHER CONCERNS

You have probably noticed how much the IRS enjoys taxing people while they're alive. Did you know they also enjoy taxing people when they die? Conservatives generally call this unfortunate reality the "death tax," while liberal politicians simply refer to it as the "estate tax," but, whatever we call it, the fact is that when someone dies, the IRS and state tax collectors may end up taxing the value of assets (house, farm land, bank account, IBM stock, etc.) that the deceased individual owned.

ESTATES

Elvis Presley is a not a person; however, the Estate of Elvis Presley *is* a person. As the exam might expect you to know, the following are not legal persons:

- Dead people
- Minor children
- Individuals declared mentally incompetent by a court

That means they can't open investment accounts or enter into binding legal contracts. So, a dead person, such as the king of rock 'n' roll, is not a legal person. However, the assets of a deceased individual such as Elvis Presley (Graceland, recording royalties, residuals from lame beach movies) go into a legal "person" known as an estate. The estate is an entity, a "legal person." Like a corporation, it has an FEIN (Federal Employee Identification Number). Also like a corporation, the assets of the estate are separate from the assets of the beneficiaries of the deceased person's will. So, if Grandma dies and somebody files a claim that she still owes him $800,000, what happens if all of Grandma's assets are only worth $100,000?

Dude should have tried to collect sooner. Maybe he'll get every last dollar of that 100 grand, but the children and grandchildren do not have to make up the difference—the estate is a separate legal entity, just like a corporation. Similarly, you might be able to sue one of Donald Trump's corporations or partnerships, but you aren't getting one dollar out of the Donald personally.

So, an estate (like a corporation, partnership, limited liability company, etc.) is a separate legal entity. When Grandma dies, her checking and savings accounts, CDs, real estate, life insurance, etc., all go into a new legal entity called an estate. If you were named the executor of the estate, it's your job to get several death certificates and do lots of paperwork required to transfer her checking and savings to a new bank account entitled, say, Jason Miller, Executor for the Estate of Maude L. Miller, Deceased. If Grandma owned stocks and bonds, they need to be re-titled in the name of the estate, as well. This will require affidavits, signature guarantees, stock powers, letters of office...the whole nine yards. When you effect these transfers of ownership, make sure you have plenty of original death certificates and that the court appointment/letters of office are no more than 60 days old.

Income of the Estate

An estate is generally open at least six months. What happens if the stocks, bonds, CDs, etc., earn interest/dividends in the meantime? That income is taxable to the estate. Of course, the legal fees charged by the estate attorney will often cancel that income out, but if the estate earns, say, $5,000 in dividend income when the legal bills are just $2,000, there is $3,000 of taxable income there.

Is the Estate Going to Pay Estate Taxes?

More important, before the assets of the estate are transferred to the beneficiaries, the IRS (who, as always, is here to help) may want to help the estate out of some of those assets. Will the estate be taxed? First, we start with the gross estate—the value of the assets before we start taking deductions. The following are included in the value of the gross estate:

- house, farm land, bank account, checking account, investment accounts, clothing, oil paintings, etc.
- includes value of insurance and annuity contracts!
- assets placed in revocable trusts
- does not include assets placed in irrevocable trusts (except certain property transferred within three years of death!)

So, we add up all of those values and then we start subtracting things to knock down the value of this estate enough to avoid estate taxes. The following will reduce the value of the gross estate:

- Funeral and administrative expenses
- Debts owed at the time of death
- Any charitable gifts made after death
- The marital deduction

The "marital deduction" means that husbands and wives pass their property to one another without paying estate taxes—it's when the assets then go from the "second to die" to the heirs that things get dicey. So, after we've added the value of all the assets (gross estate) and subtracted the first three bullet points above, maybe what's left is $1 million. Will we have to pay estate taxes?

No. Currently, there is a lifetime credit of $5 million indexed for inflation for estates and since the taxable estate is below that number, we avoid paying estate taxes. The assets distributed to the heirs are taxable to them on their individual income tax returns when they sell them, but we won't pay the estate tax.

How are the heirs taxed? Remember that when Grandma died, we took the fair market value of her securities as our cost basis—when we sell the stocks and bonds for more than that fair market value, that excess is a *long-term capital gain*. Please note that the test is not expected to hit people with precise numbers when those numbers are ever-changing in the so-called real world. The answer "$5 million indexed for inflation" would probably be precise enough for a test question. Similarly, we are now going to talk about an "annual gift tax exclusion" of $14,000, but the test might refer to that as "$10,000 indexed for inflation."

GIFTS

What if several months ago Grandma had gone in for her regular check-up and found out from her doctor that she had maybe two months to live? To avoid forcing her heirs to pay estate taxes, couldn't she just start handing out big, fat envelopes of cash to all the kids and grandkids?

Sure. In fact, the IRS is totally cool with that, to the extent that "IRS" and "totally cool" could ever go together. See, the gifts that Grandma gives while she is alive are also taxable if they are over a certain amount. That number is forever changing—used to be $13,000 per person per year for 2012, and is $14,000 for 2014. Whatever the amount is, there is an **annual gift tax exclusion**, which means that if Grandma gives anyone other than her husband (who died years ago) a gift worth more than that amount, she has to start chipping away at her **lifetime gift tax credit**, $5 million indexed for inflation. That number is currently closer to $5.25 million, but the test would likely just say "$5 million indexed for inflation," if it even asked such a question. The amount of the credit that was used up over her lifetime will reduce the amount of the credit you and the other beneficiaries can use when trying to reduce the size of the estate in order to avoid paying estate taxes.

Just to keep the tax code nice and simple, the way Congress and the IRS like it.

So, what is a **gift**?

The IRS defines a gift as "transferring property to someone else and expecting nothing in return." The IRS also points out that the following can be considered gifts:

- selling something at less than its value
- making an interest-free or reduced-interest loan

Wait, so when Grandma sold Uncle Bill the back forty for $70,000 below market value, that could have been considered a "gift" to Uncle Bill? Absolutely. So, when Grandma goes around giving people things worth more than the current annual exclusion, she files a return and tells the IRS that she's using part of her lifetime credit to avoid cutting a check at this time. What if the gift is worth no more than the current exclusion of $14,000?

Nobody cares.

In the following cases, no gift taxes would be due and no returns would have to be filed:

- Gifts made to a spouse
- Gifts that do not exceed current exclusion amount
- Paying tuition costs for someone else—payable directly to educational institution
- Paying medical costs for someone else—payable directly to the care provider
- Political, charitable donations

Gift Splitting

The IRS, believe it or not, is actually very clear on the exciting topic of **gift splitting**, so let's copy and paste from Publication 950 from www.irs.gov, which states:

> Harold and his wife, Helen, agree to split the gifts that they
> made during 2014. Harold gives his nephew, George, $21,000,
> and Helen gives her niece, Gina, $18,000. Although each gift
> is more than the annual exclusion ($13,000), by gift splitting
> they can make these gifts without making a taxable gift.

All that means is that half of $21,000 ($10,500) and half of $18,000 ($9,000) would be less than the annual exclusion of $14,000, so they can treat each gift as half from Grandpa and half from Grandma. No gift taxes are due and none of the lifetime credits have to be used up, but the IRS still requires that they file a return since they're getting pretty darned fancy with their little gift-splitting maneuver.

TRUSTS

Like an estate or a corporation, a **trust** is also a separate legal entity. The trust holds assets, just as a corporation or estate holds assets. The person who administers the trust is the trustee. The one who grants the assets to the trust is called the grantor. And the ones who benefit from the trust are cleverly called the "beneficiaries."

When an adult sets up an **UGMA/UTMA account**, the minor owns all the assets by age 21. But, if you set up a trust, you can specify all types of things in the trust agreement and, thereby, assure that your kids will be rich enough so that they can do anything, but not rich enough so that they can do nothing with the rest of their lives. The exam might point out other advantages of establishing trusts:

- Faster and less costly way to transfer property upon death compared to a will
- Avoid probate court process (time, expense), especially if property owned in several different states
- Eliminate challenges to estate—specifically disinherit anyone who posts a challenge to your wishes upon your death
- Keep transfer of property private—probate can expose assets to public
- Reduce amount of estate taxable to heirs

Revocable, Irrevocable

As we said, reducing the amount of the taxable estate will come down to the difference between revocable and irrevocable trusts. In general, assets placed in an **irrevocable trust** do not count as part of the estate, while the assets placed in a **revocable trust** do count. What's the difference? As always, let the words talk to you—if the trust is revocable, the person who set it up (grantor) can always take back (revoke) the assets. Therefore, not only are those assets still taxable to the grantor while he/she is alive, but when he/she dies, those assets do count towards the value of the estate. If a grantor sets up an irrevocable trust, the assets, obviously, cannot be revoked. Therefore, the assets are no longer taxable to the grantor while he/she is alive, and when he/she dies, the assets do not count towards the value of the estate that the heirs are hoping to keep below the amount that triggers estate taxes.

Except when they do. Even in an IR-revocable trust, certain property transferred within three years of death DOES count as part of the taxable estate. And, if the irrevocable trust states that income is to be used or held for the benefit of the grantor or the grantor's spouse, the grantor will be subject to taxation while he/she is alive.

Tax Liability

The irrevocable trust will either distribute income to the beneficiaries, or it won't. Either way, the interest, dividends, and capital gains generated are taxable. If the income is distributed to the beneficiaries, they include it on their own income tax forms. If the income is not distributed, it is taxable to the trust.

In a revocable trust, or even in an irrevocable trust where the grantor or grantor's spouse benefits from the income, the **grantor** is subject to taxation while he/she is still alive.

So, to sum up on estates and trusts, when the estate earns income, that income is taxable to the estate. And, if the estate is over a certain amount, estate taxes will be due. Either way, the **beneficiaries** will pay capital gains taxes on stocks and bonds sold above cost basis. Some folks establish a trust to simplify the process and maybe avoid the estate tax. If it's an irrevocable trust, generally, those assets don't get counted toward the estate for tax purposes. Of course, now there is a trust to think about—the interest, dividends, and capital gains earned by this trust will either be taxable to the trust if it all remains in the trust, or taxable to the beneficiaries when distributed to them.

AMT

If you're in a certain marginal tax bracket, you will be subject to an **Alternative Minimum Tax**, or "AMT." That means that even though people say that municipal bonds pay tax-free interest, you will actually report *some* municipal bond interest on your **AMT** form as a "tax preference item." Generally, municipal bonds that are considered "private purpose" by the tax code subject investors to reporting income on their AMT forms. That's why many tax-exempt mutual funds also buy bonds that are not subject to AMT taxes.

When the IRS gets hot, they really get hot, so let's just let them explain the AMT for us. The following comes from their page-turning thriller entitled *Publication 556 – Alternative Minimum Tax*:

The tax laws give preferential treatment to certain kinds of income and allow special deductions and credits for certain kinds of expenses. The alternative minimum tax attempts to ensure that anyone who benefits from these tax advantages pays at least a minimum amount of tax. The alternative minimum tax is a separately figured tax that eliminates many deductions and credits, thus increasing tax liability for an individual who would otherwise pay less tax. The tentative minimum tax rates on ordinary income are percentages set by law. For capital gains, the capital gains rates for the regular tax are used. You may have to pay the alternative minimum tax if your taxable income for regular tax purposes plus any adjustments and preference items that apply to you are more than the exemption amount.

I would expect to see mention of the fact that certain municipal bonds subject investors to AMT. If it's considered a "private purpose bond" under the tax code, the investor will actually end up paying some tax on that municipal bond interest that is usually thought of as "tax-free."

Just to keep things nice and simple.

A test question might also bring up the fact that the owner of a limited partnership interest will need to consult the instructions to his little K-1 and may have to add certain tax preference items such as "accelerated depreciation" to his AMT form. The test question might say that "straight line depreciation" would not be a tax preference item, just in case it hasn't already killed you with boredom.

INCOME TAXES

The exam will likely refer to taxation issues that are beyond just the taxation of investments or the special tax rules for different types of investment accounts. Income taxes are also fair game—the taxes you pay on the money you earn on the job. Believe it or not, most of us pay income taxes at several different rates due to the **graduated, progressive income tax system** in the United States. Did you know that the first so much of your income is taxed at 10%, the next at 15%, then 25%? In other words, you don't pay 25% on all your income just because you reach that bracket; you pay 25% on the amount of money you make above a certain amount.

Seriously.

If you start making decent money, the last dollars earned that year will be taxed at 28% or maybe 33%. And, if you're really making bank, some of your income (above approximately $400,000) will be taxed at the top rate of 39.6%. Ouch. But, again, even if some of your income is taxed at 39.6%, a lot of it was also taxed at 35%, 33%, 28%, 25%, 15%, and 10%, as well.

Let's see what the folks at the Internal Revenue Service have to say about it:

> The United States has a progressive income tax structure, meaning that different portions of taxable income are taxed at different rates with the "last" income received being taxed at the highest or marginal tax rate. From the inception of the individual income tax in 1913, tax rates have varied from as low as 1 percent to as high as 94 percent. Since 1916, the Internal Revenue Service has been publishing income and tax statistics based on information reported on Federal tax returns filed by U.S. individual taxpayers.
>
> For tax year 2008, there were six different tax rate classes ranging from 10 percent to 35 percent. The taxable income thresholds for each tax rate class varied depending upon the taxpayer's filing status (single, married, etc.). More than 85 percent of returns with income subject to tax were in the 10, 15 or 25 percent marginal tax rate classes. Different forms of income may receive different treatment under the

> tax laws. Items such as capital gains and certain dividends
> qualified for special tax treatment.

The IRS just answered a potential test question in that passage above when they wrote, "with the last income received being taxed at the highest or marginal tax rate." The exam could easily ask, "What is an individual's 'marginal tax rate'?" You would choose an answer such as "the rate of tax paid on the last dollar of income earned." Also, the reference to "2008" does not make this book "dated." That was just the most recent information the IRS had made public when we went to press recently. Those tax rates held from 2003 through 2012. Congress then tweaked things a bit by adding the 39.6% bracket and making people who hit that marginal bracket also pay 20% on qualified dividends and long-term capital gains.

The IRS mentioned above that there are different methods of filing income taxes, and these methods definitely affect the rate of taxes paid. For example, if you file singly/single filer, you will get pushed into the 15% tax bracket and then the 25% bracket at a certain dollar amount, while a married couple filing jointly would get to make twice those amounts before being pushed into the 15% and then the 25% bracket. On the other hand, if they choose "married-filing-separately," the dollar amounts are different, and this explains why politicians are forever promising to "simplify the tax code" and why CPAs are still paid relatively well for their tax planning services. In case the exam goes this far, a married couple choosing to file separately can each earn as much as actual single people filing singly...until we get to those middle tax brackets and, suddenly, they get pushed into the 28% and 33% sooner than if they'd stayed unattached.

In other words, there definitely is a so-called "marriage penalty" built into these tax brackets. At the lower brackets, it makes perfect sense for two people to get married from a tax standpoint—they can choose married-filing-jointly and make exactly twice as much as they could make if living apart before being pushed into the next bracket. Or, they could choose married-filing-singly and get the same effect, while likely sharing expenses, too. But, at the next few brackets, married couples get pushed into the next higher rate at much lower dollar amounts of income than if they were to live apart. And that holds true whether they file jointly or separately. I suppose this could almost make sense, except that at the top bracket, once again a married couple can make exactly twice as much as a single filer before that bracket kicks in whether they file jointly or separately.

Bizarre. Not sure if Congress intended it that way, but the way I read the tax code, it makes sense for people to get married if they're either scraping by or killing it financially. All the folks making the low six figures—from a tax standpoint, it makes more sense to stay single.

Wild. Why should the federal government encourage or discourage marriage at various income levels? No idea, but also not a testable point.

There is another method of filing called "head of household." If the test question says that your client is now raising two children orphaned when her sister was killed in a car crash, that individual should file as "head of household" versus "single filer." For a "head-of-household" filer, the dollar amounts of income allowed before being pushed into the next tax bracket are much higher compared to a single filer.

Whatever the marginal tax bracket, what we're talking about here is **ordinary income**. Ordinary income is made up of wages, salaries, bonuses, commissions, some dividends, and most forms of bond interest.

TOPIC QUIZ: TAXATION

1. **Which of the following items would be included in the gross estate for purposes of federal estate tax liability?**

    I.   Life insurance policy

    II. Value of the decedent's primary residence

    III. A house transferred to an irrevocable trust 24 months prior to death

    IV. A house transferred to a revocable trust

    A. I

    B. II, III

    C. I, IV

    D. I, II, III, IV

2. **Which of the following items would reduce the amount of the gross estate for the purposes of figuring the taxable estate?**

    I.   Funeral and administrative expenses

    II. Market value of municipal bonds

    III. Charitable gifts made after death

    IV. Marital deduction

    A. I, III

    B. I, II, IV

    C. III, IV

    D. I, III, IV

3. **Mr. Jeffries sets up a trust for the benefit of his adult daughter, Amber, from which his wife may withdraw only if necessary. Therefore, income on the trust will be taxed to:**

    A. Mrs. Jeffries as the contingent beneficiary

    B. Mr. Jeffries as the donor

    C. Amber as the primary beneficiary

    D. the trust because it is a separate legal entity

4. **Darlene has made the following gifts for Tax Year 2014: a $15,500 check to her brother, Virgil, for tuition at a state college, $8,000 to her husband, Cletus, for a second-hand four-wheel-drive pickup truck, $18,000 to her girlfriend, Becky Sue, and a $15,000 check to her mother's primary physician. Which of the following statements best describes the tax implications of these gifts?**

    A. the amount subject to gift taxes is $17,000

    B. no gift taxes are due

    C. the amount subject to gift taxes is $5,500

    D. the amount subject to gift taxes is $6,000

5. **One of your clients, Rachel, has inherited securities through her Aunt Jessica's will. Aunt Jessica purchased 1,000 shares of Harley-Davidson for $5,200 twenty years earlier. On the day Aunt Jessica died, the fair market value of Harley-Davidson common stock was $30 per share. If Rachel sells all shares four months later for $40 per share, the tax implications will be**

    A. $34,800 taxed at long-term capital gains rates

    B. short-term gain of $10,000

    C. $40,000 taxed at long-term capital gains rates

    D. long-term gain of $10,000

6. **Jarod Stevens had the following results on four stock sales this year:**
    $15,000 in long-term gains
    $5,000 in long-term losses
    $5,000 in short-term gains
    $13,000 in short-term losses
    Therefore, the tax implications are:

    A. short-term capital gain of $8,000

    B. long-term capital gain of $2,000

    C. short-term capital gain of $2,000

    D. long-term capital gain of $15,000

7. **Jarod Stevens had the following results on four stock sales this year:**
    $15,000 in long-term gains
    $23,000 in long-term losses
    $15,000 in short-term gains
    $5,000 in short-term losses
    Therefore, the tax implications are:

    A. short-term capital gain taxed at a maximum of 15%

    B. no net gains or losses

    C. short-term capital gain of $2,000 taxed at ordinary income rates

    D. long-term capital loss of $8,000, short-term capital gain of $8,000

8. **Jarod Stevens had the following results on four stock sales this year:**
    $15,000 in long-term gains
    $5,000 in long-term losses
    $5,000 in short-term gains
    $17,000 in short-term losses
    Therefore, the tax implications are:

    A. short-term capital gain of $2,000

    B. long-term capital gain of $2,000

    C. short-term capital gain of $5,000

    D. short-term capital loss of $2,000, which offsets ordinary income

9. **Within her IRA, Marla Mathers purchased 1,000 shares of ABC @14 on January 12, 2011. The next day, she also purchased 1,000 shares of XYZ @15. On January 11, 2013, she sells all her ABC stock for $19 per share and all her XYZ stock for $7 per share. Which of the following accurately describes the tax implications?**

    A. Marla may reduce her ordinary income by $3,000

    B. There will be no effect on taxation of this account

    C. The purchase of XYZ within 30 days of the ABC purchase triggers wash sale rules

    D. The amount of the capital loss depends on Marla's marginal tax rate

10. **Which of the following represents an accurate statement concerning gifts?**

    A. if a wife gives her husband $15,000 in Tax Year 2014, no gift taxes are due, but the amount above the annual exclusion must be reported to the IRS

    B. if an individual pays the tuition of another individual, the individuals must be related; otherwise, the payment is considered a taxable gift

    C. when utilizing "gift splitting," no taxes are due and no forms must be filed

    D. a gift of $28,000 can be considered half from the husband and half from the wife in order to avoid paying gift taxes for 2014

11. Which of the following statement(s) is/are accurate concerning wash sale rules?

    I.   It is illegal to sell common stock at a loss and then repurchase it within 30 days

    II.   If a loss is disallowed due to wash sale rules, the investor adds the loss to the cost basis on the re-purchase

    III. An investor may sell MSFT common stock at a loss and purchase MSFT preferred stock within 30 days and still claim the loss on the common stock

    IV. Wash sale rules do not apply to a Traditional IRA or Roth IRA

    A.   I

    B.   II, IV

    C.   II, III, IV

    D.   I, IV

ANSWERS

1. **ANSWER:** D

    WHY: that's the nature of a trick question. Assets placed in an irrevocable trust are not included, except when they are. A house transferred within 3 years of death would be included in the taxable estate.

2. **ANSWER:** D

    WHY: don't read too fast—yes, interest on municipal bonds is tax-free, but that has nothing to do with this question.

3. **ANSWER:** B

    WHY: a husband and wife are an economic unit, so if the wife can withdraw from this trust, that's the same thing as Mr. Jeffries being able to draw from it. Therefore, the income is taxable to him.

4. **ANSWER:** C

    WHY: since the IRS realizes how easy it would be for all the Darlenes and Virgils out there to say that a check was for "tuition," Darlene really needed to cut the check directly to the educational institution. Same thing for paying someone's medical expenses—to make sure it's a tax-free gift, cut the check directly to the provider. So, the $15,500 to Virgil is $1,500 over the annual exclusion, and the $18,000 to Becky Sue exceeds the current annual exclusion by $4,000, for a total of $5,500.

5.   **ANSWER:** D

WHY: keep it simple. For an inheritance of appreciated securities, the cost basis is the fair market value on the date of death. Any gain is long-term.

6.   **ANSWER:** B

WHY: step one, line up the long-term gains and the long-term losses, then line up the short-term gains with the short-term losses. Jarod ends up with $10,000 in long-term capital gains, but has $8,000 in short-term losses. That's a net gain of $2,000 and it's treated as a long-term capital gain. Why a long-term capital gain? Because it's the long-term net capital gain of $10,000 that triggered the capital gains tax.

7.   **ANSWER:** C

WHY: line up the long-term with long-term, and the short-term with short-term. You end up with a net long-term loss of $8,000 and a net short-term gain of $10,000. The $8,000 in losses brings the total capital gain down to $2,000, which will be taxed as a short-term capital gain. Why a short-term capital gain? Because it was the short-term net gain that triggered the tax.

8.   **ANSWER:** D

WHY: match up long-term with long-term and short-term with short-term, then net out your results. There is a net long-term gain of $10,000 and a net short-term loss of $12,000. That makes it a net loss of $2,000, which can be used to offset ordinary income. Too bad Jarod couldn't have lost another $1,000 on our lousy stock picks to take full advantage of our services, huh?

9.   **ANSWER:** B

WHY: as soon as you see "IRA," all notions of capital gains, losses, wash sales, etc., flew right out the window. Remember that in a retirement plan, gains, interest, and dividends just stay in the account growing tax-deferred. Some day the money will come out, and you will either pay ordinary income rates (never cap gains), or—in some cases—no tax at all (Roth, 529, Coverdell).

10. **ANSWER:** D

WHY: the IRS doesn't care about gifts between husband and wife. If you pay tuition for someone else, it makes no difference if the two of you are related or not. Just make sure you pay the educational institution directly. That way it's a non-taxable gift, and you don't even need to file a return. The wife could give somebody $28,000 and consider that as ½ from her, ½ from her husband. When you use gift splitting, no taxes are due, and you don't have to use up the lifetime credit. But, since you're getting fancy, you do need to file a return to let the IRS know what's up.

11. **ANSWER:** C

WHY: nothing illegal about repurchasing the security within 30 days, but—as another answer choice points out—you don't get to use that loss. Instead, you add it to the cost basis on the re-purchase in order to keep the tax code nice and simple. Preferred stock is a whole different animal from common stock, and so are bonds. Unless they are CONVERTIBLE bonds or CONVERTIBLE preferred stock—that stuff can be converted to common stock immediately in most cases. Finally, once you throw in the retirement-account angle all of this capital gain/capital loss stuff flies out the window.

TAX IMPLICATIONS FOR MUTUAL FUND INVESTORS

We looked briefly at tax issues for mutual funds already, but it makes sense to look at it in more depth here, too.

Stock Funds

If it's a stock fund, the taxation will be a little different from a bond or money market fund. We haven't gotten into the details of mutual funds yet, but they're really just gigantic portfolios of stocks, bonds, etc. You can buy little slices of the gigantic portfolio, which is much easier than picking your own stocks and bonds. Let the mutual fund do that—you'll just own a percentage of whatever they decide to invest in. The mutual fund portfolio will receive dividends from some of the stocks they own, and since they trade their stocks all the time, they'll usually end up with a capital gain for the year. Investors in the mutual fund receive dividends and capital gains distributions from the fund, and these are taxable. The **Form 1099-DIV** that the fund sends to investors will show how much they received in qualified versus ordinary dividends, and how much they received in capital gains distributions. Is it a short-term or long-term capital gain? The 1099 will tell you that, too. Remember, the holding period is based on how long the fund held the securities before trading them. It has nothing to do with how long the investor has been in the fund—the investor didn't sell anything. She's just receiving her fair share of the trading profits generated by the mutual fund portfolio.

Usually, the fund makes sure the gains distributed are long-term gains, since the tax rate is a lot easier to swallow than the ordinary income rate some folks pay on short-term gains. Can the fund distribute short-term capital gains? Absolutely. And when they do, they're taxable to the investors as short-term capital gains. But, that is unusual—we assume that all distributions of capital gains from a mutual fund are long-term—unless specifically told otherwise. The higher a fund's turnover rate the more likely it will generate short-term capital gains. But, really, all of the capital gains distributions from mutual funds to investors are long-term, except for the ones that are short-term.

Conduit Tax Theory

In a mutual fund, as we'll see, investors get charged for many expenses. The portfolio manager charges a management fee, and investors pay for that. The board of directors likes their six-figure salaries, and shareholders pay for that. There are legal and accounting fees, transfer agent fees, custodial fees, and 12b-1 fees that cover all the sales and marketing costs. How does the fund cover these expenses? They use the dividends they receive from the portfolio stocks and the interest payments from the bonds and money market securities that they hold. When the fund takes the dividends and the interest, then deducts all the expenses, they are left with net income. The IRS, who is here to help, generally likes to share profits with companies showing net income, but they will allow the fund to use something funky called the "**conduit**" or "pipeline theory." If the fund has, say, $1 million in **net investment income** this year, they can distribute 90% or more ($900,000+) to the shareholders and, thereby, avoid being taxed on that $900,000. The shareholders will get taxed on that money, instead. The fund only has to pay taxes on what they did *not* distribute—in this case, $100,000. The fund may also end the year taking more profits than losses trading the portfolio. If so, they realize a net capital gain and also distribute that to the shareholders. They usually only do that once a year, and usually in December.

What can you do with these dividend and capital gains distributions? A, you can tell them where to send the check and go shopping. B, you can automatically reinvest the money into more shares of the fund. So, the IRS would only tax you if you cashed the check, right? No. As it turns out, the IRS could sort of care less what you *do* with the distribution. Whether you cash the check or reinvest it into more shares, you get taxed on the distributions. People reinvest these things to avoid paying sales charges to the fund, but it doesn't help them in the least with their pals at the IRS. Remember that whether the dividend or capital gains distribution is paid in cash or reinvested into more shares, the investor is taxed. And that means that when you reinvest a dividend or capital gain, your cost basis rises by that amount. So, if the test question says that Melody has invested $10,000 into the Argood Aggressive Growth Fund and reinvested dividends of $2,000, her cost basis equals $12,000. **Cost basis** is basically the money you've put into an investment that the IRS has already taxed. The capital gain that may someday materialize is just the amount you manage to sell it for above that amount.

Should you be so fortunate.

Bond Funds

For bond funds, there is really nothing to add to our discussion of bonds held individually. The "dividends" paid are really coming from bond interest received by the portfolio. So, U.S. Treasury funds would pay dividends that are taxable as ordinary income on federal returns but exempt from state or local taxation. Tax-exempt Municipal Bond funds would pay dividends that are tax-exempt for federal returns but may be subject to state and local taxation. This is why some fund companies have rolled out, say, the Maryland Tax-Exempt Fund or the Tax-Exempt Fund of California. That way residents of those high-tax states can buy mutual funds that pay income exempt from both federal and state taxes. If you're in a state that wants, say, 14% of your income, it might be a good idea to avoid that whenever possible, right? Corporate bond funds, unfortunately, would pay dividends subject to taxation at all three levels.

Capital gains would also be taxable to investors, including capital gains distributions to investors in municipal bond funds. Municipal bonds pay *interest* that is exempt from federal taxation, but nobody said anything about capital gains. Those are still taxable at capital gains rates.

Money Market Funds

According to my trusted www.irs.gov website:

> Report amounts you receive from money market funds as dividend income. Money market funds are a type of mutual fund and should not be confused with bank money market accounts that pay interest.

TAX TREATMENT OF VARIABLE ANNUITIES

Remember that a variable annuity is basically a cross between a mutual fund, a retirement plan, and an insurance policy. In a non-qualified variable annuity, the investor contributes money that has already been taxed. Therefore, the money she puts into her annuity is her cost basis. The IRS won't tax the money she puts in; they'll only tax the money she takes out above that someday. The money grows tax-deferred, which means all the dividends and bond interest being paid to the investor will not be taxed until money is finally taken out. She put in a total of $10,000. Let's say at retirement, the annuity is worth $50,000. That means that $40,000 of earnings have accumulated. No matter how she takes the money out, she will pay ordinary income tax on that $40,000. The exam will probably call the $40,000 the "earnings" or "**the excess over cost basis,**" just to make you sweat a little. The annuitant can take a lump sum distribution, just like somebody who retires with a pension. Gimme all my money right now, please. Fine. But, she'll have to pay ordinary income rates on that $40,000, and that money might push her into a higher tax bracket. Since that might push her into a higher bracket, maybe she does a "random withdrawal" of $10,000. Here's where the exam is looking to snare a few insurance agents. Insurance agents might think that since she put in $10,000 and is only taking out $10,000, there will be no tax hassles. Unfortunately, the IRS, who is here to help, considers all of the money coming out to be the earnings portion first. The exam might call that **LIFO** for "**Last In-First Out.**" The earnings were the last thing into the account, so we consider them to be the first thing coming out. Why?

Because we can.

So, not only will this $10,000 random withdrawal be fully taxable as ordinary income, but also so will the next withdrawals that take us through the $40,000 of earnings.

Many people just "annuitize" the contract, which means they want to receive a monthly check for the rest of their lives. Depending on how long their life expectancy is, each monthly payment will represent part cost basis and part earnings. So, the exam wants you to know that part of each annuity payment is taxable, and part is considered a return of the cost basis.

When people annuitize the contract, they can choose to receive payments for as long as they live, or they can choose to cover a beneficiary. We'll talk about "period certain" and "joint with last survivor" later on. For now, just know that if the wife or the daughter is receiving annuity payments from the annuity purchased by a husband or parent, she is going to pay ordinary income tax on the "excess over cost basis," too. Somebody, in other words, always pays ordinary income tax on the amount above what the annuitant put into the contract. That's the deal you make in exchange for the tax deferral.

What if the annuitant dies while he's still putting money into the contract? This is known as the "accumulation phase," by the way, and if the annuitant has put in $10,000 when he dies, the death benefit will pay his beneficiary the greater of that $10,000 or whatever the contract is currently worth. So, if the annuity is worth $13,000 now, the beneficiary receives $13,000. If the value had dipped to $8,000 due to a tough stock or bond market, the beneficiary would still receive $10,000. And, as always, if the beneficiary receives more than the annuitant has contributed, that excess is taxable to her as ordinary income.

Someday you may meet up with a client who was sold a really lousy annuity from some sketchy company. You might be able to talk her into selling that one and exchanging it for an annuity that you sell. If so, she can do a **1035 tax-free contract exchange**. In other words, this is different from selling one mutual fund to buy the proceeds of another fund in the same family—that would still be a taxable event. But annuities are retirement plans, really, so there is a special provision here for tax-free exchanges, just as there is for life insurance.

Since they're retirement vehicles, the individual needs to wait until she's 59½ before taking money out. Otherwise, she'll pay not just her ordinary income rate on the excess over cost basis but also a 10% penalty to the IRS.

Loans

Some insurance companies allow contract owners to take a loan against the value of the annuity during the accumulation period. Usually, the interest charge is handled by reducing the number of accumulation units owned. If the owner pays back the loan in full, the number of units goes up again. Unlike a loan against a life insurance policy, however, a loan from an annuity is treated as a distribution. In other words, it is not tax-free.

1035 Exchanges

Both annuities and insurance policies allow people to exchange their contract for another without paying taxes. That's fine, just don't forget the surrender period. If somebody still has a 6% surrender fee (contingent deferred sales charge) in effect, and you push them to do a 1035 exchange, the IRS won't have a problem with it, but FINRA almost certainly will. Especially if you get caught.

Annuity Period

When the annuitant begins receiving monthly checks, part of each check is considered taxable ordinary income, and part of it is considered to be part of the cost basis. Once the annuitant has received all of the cost basis back, each additional annuity payment will be fully taxable.

Also, if the beneficiary is receiving annuity payments through a "life with period certain" or a "joint with last survivor" settlement option, she will pay ordinary income tax on part of each monthly check, too—as always, on the "excess over cost basis."

72(t) and Substantially Equal Periodic Payments

Speaking of early withdrawal penalties, remember that annuities are by nature retirement plans, and are subject to the 10% penalty for withdrawals made before age 59½ without a good excuse. One good excuse is to utilize IRS rule "72(t)." As with an IRA, an individual can avoid the 10% penalty if the withdrawal qualifies for an exemption. For example, if the individual has become disabled and can't work, or has certain medical expenses, money can be taken out penalty-free. Notice how I didn't say tax-free.

Basically, a reference to "72(t)" has to do with an individual taking a series of substantially equal periodic payments. Of course, the industry quickly turned that phrase into the acronym "SEPP." The IRS won't penalize the early withdrawal if the individual sets up a rigid schedule whereby they withdraw the money by any of several IRS-approved methods. Once you start your little SEPP program, stay on it. See, the IRS requires you to continue the SEPP program for five years or until you are the age of 59½, whichever comes last. So, if the individual is 45, she'll have to keep taking periodic payments until she's 59½. If the individual is 56 when she starts, she'll still have to continue for 5 years. Either that, or cut the IRS a check for the very penalties she was trying to avoid.

TAXATION OF LIFE INSURANCE

When you pay your life insurance premiums, you don't get to take a deduction against income, so they are made after-tax. They usually grow tax-deferred, however, which is nice. When the insured dies, the beneficiary receives the death benefit free and clear of federal income taxes.

But the death benefit will be added to the insured's estate to determine estate taxes. It's that simple when the beneficiary has the lump-sum settlement option, anyway. If we're talking about those periodic settlement options that generate interest, some of those payments could be taxed as interest income. Rather than take a loan, the policyholder can also do a "partial surrender," whereby the policyholder takes out some of the cash value, not enough to make the policy lapse, of course. Depending on how much has been paid in premiums, taxes may be due on the amount withdrawn. Unlike for variable annuities, the IRS uses FIFO here, assuming that the first thing coming out is the cost basis, not the earnings. Only the part taken out above the premiums paid would be taxed.

If a loan is taken out, there are no immediate tax consequences.

RETIREMENT PLANS

EMPLOYER-SPONSORED PLANS

If you're fortunate, you have a job where the employer sponsors a retirement plan. If you're really fortunate, your employer is old fashioned enough to offer a defined benefit pension plan, where the employer says something like, "After you put in 20 years of service we'll pay you 70% of your average salary over the last few years of your career when you retire." If the employer defines the benefit, they bear the investment risk, which explains why most companies have shifted the investment risk to their loyal employees with defined contribution plans. In a defined contribution plan, the company—get this— simply defines their contribution into the employee's account. How every- thing works out in retirement is left completely undefined although they do wish you the best of luck in most cases. A 401(k) plan defines the contribution your employer will make on your behalf. Usually, they will match your own contributions up to a certain percent of salary. Profit sharing plans are also a form of defined contribution plan where contributions are tied to profits. What happens if the company doesn't make a profit this year?

No sharing. So, the employer-sponsored plan either defines how much the company will put in on your behalf (contribution) or how much you'll receive (benefit) when you retire. If it defines the benefit, it bears the investment risk. If it defines only the contribution, you bear the investment risk, which I'm sure they mentioned in the brochure.

In a profit-sharing plan the company can skip the whole contribution thing if there are no profits, and they will certainly contribute more or less based on their ever-fluctuating profits. Well, with a **money purchase plan** things aren't quite so flexible. In a money purchase plan the employer contributes a fixed percentage of the employee's salary, regardless of the company's profitability. That means the company has to make contributions or pay a penalty, so these are not appropriate for all businesses.

Keogh Plans are for **sole proprietors**, not corporations, LLCs or partnerships. If the individual in the test question has side income or is self-employed, she can have a Keogh. She can contribute a certain percentage of her self-employment income into the Keogh.

How much? A lot. But, if the sole proprietor is taking care of himself, he has to take care of his employees, too. If he makes his maximum contribution, he has to make his employees' maximum contributions as well.

A small business (including a sole proprietor) could, instead, use a **SEP-IRA**, which stands for "**Simplified Employee Pension**" IRA. This allows the business owner to make pre-tax contributions for herself and any eligible employees, just like the Keogh. If the workers earn big salaries, the SEP would probably be ideal, since it lets them have a big percentage of their salary contributed into the plan, up to a maximum amount that is often six or seven times what's allowed in a Traditional or Roth IRA and maybe three times what's allowed in a 401(k) or 403(b) plan. Of course, you have to make a lot of money to be able to put a lot of money into your SEP. And, remember that only the employer (not the employee) makes contributions into a SEP-IRA.

If the workers aren't paid huge salaries, they might be able to put more money into a **SIMPLE IRA**. The SIMPLE IRA is for businesses with no more than 100 employees that have no other retirement plan in place. The participants don't have to make high incomes in order to put in the maximum contribution. The maximum contribution is lower than what's allowed in the SEP-IRA, but at least employees can make contributions to a SIMPLE IRA. Remember that in a SEP-IRA, only the employer makes contributions.

A **Section 457 plan** is a deferred compensation plan for state and local government workers. Employees can contribute part of their salary to reduce their tax burden now, and let the earnings grow tax-deferred. Of course, whenever you do this, you end up paying ordinary income tax on everything that comes out. But that's okay. Most people plan on being in a lower tax bracket when they retire, and their money grows faster when it isn't being depleted every year by cutting a check to the IRS.

Schools, hospitals and other nonprofit organizations often use **403(b) plans**, in which the investments are limited and are usually annuities. That's why they can be referred to as **tax-sheltered annuities** or TSAs, as well. On the exam, assume that these plans are funded with a pre-tax contribution, and the employees will pay ordinary income tax on all the money when they pull it out at retirement. Students don't qualify; janitors at the school do. Gotta be an employee to participate.

The phrase **qualified plan** refers to an employer-sponsored plan that has to meet IRS approval and follow all the rules of ERISA, which stands for the **Employee Retirement Income Security Act**. It governs retirement plans in the private (non-government) sector. ERISA spells out things like vesting, funding, disclosure, etc. **Vesting** means that at some point even the employer's contributions belong to the employee. Or, at least some percent of those contributions. If you're in a 401(k) and your employer has put in $10,000 in matching contributions, you'd walk away with only $3,000 if you were only 30% vested. If you were 70% vested, you'd probably forego the temptation to accidentally key your supervisor's car in the parking garage as you walk out with $7,000. And if you were 100% vested, you might even go back to meet a former colleague for lunch once in a while, as long as it's their treat. The vesting schedule has to be laid out. And it can't take longer than 7 years for an employee to become fully or "100% vested." There has to be money in the plan and the contributions are governed by the section on **funding**. The section on **reporting** makes sure that employees are provided regular updates on the account. The employee also gets to choose a beneficiary.

Who is eligible for these qualified plans? Gotta be 21 years old and work at least 1,000 hours a year.

That's ERISA in a nutshell, a really small nutshell.

INDIVIDUAL PLANS

The first thing you need to remember is: the I in "IRA" stands for Individual. An IRA is an **Individual Retirement Account**, so don't let the exam trick you into saying a husband and wife should open a "joint IRA." There is no such thing. If a spouse is non-working, an individual can contribute the current maximum contribution limit on his or her behalf in the spouse's Individual Retirement Account. They can do this if they file jointly for income taxes, that is, but under no circumstances can two people jointly own an IRA.

Who can have a Traditional IRA? Anyone with earned income. Earned income includes the money made through working and even includes the receipt of alimony payments. Earned income does not include dividends, interest, or capital gains, or passive income from, say, real estate rentals or limited partnerships. That means that rich folks living entirely on rental income, bond interest, and dividends are not allowed to make any contribution to their IRA account. IRA accounts are for people who are still working for a living and hoping to stop working someday. If you already make enough money to avoid working, what the heck—looks like you basically are retired.

How much can an individual with earned income contribute to her IRA? 100% of earned income up to the current maximum contribution limit. She might not get to deduct her contributions, but if she has earned income, she can contribute to an IRA, so don't let the exam trick you into saying a wealthy executive with a 401(k) is somehow prohibited from contributing to an IRA. Anyone with earned income can contribute to a Traditional IRA—not everyone can deduct the contributions made into the account.

There are (at least) two types of IRAs, Traditional and Roth. Traditional IRAs can be funded with pre-tax dollars. That means if you make $25,000 a year and contribute the current maximum contribution limit to your traditional IRA, you're taxed only on what remains of your income after that. In other words, you reduce your income to figure the "adjusted gross income" line on your 1040. That gives you a nice tax break now.

Of course, when you pull the money out at retirement, you'll pay ordinary income tax on all of it. See, with retirement plans, you either pay tax before it goes in, or when it comes out. Luckily, you don't have to pay tax on both ends. You generally shouldn't take any money out until you're 59½ years old because if you take it out before then, you'll pay a 10% penalty. Unless you:

- Die
- Become disabled
- Buy a first home for residential purposes
- Qualify for withdrawals due to certain medical, educational costs

Also, if an individual made her IRA contribution, but then decided she needed to pull it back out, she would not be penalized if she pulled it out before the deadline for making the contribution, which is the tax filing deadline. Why the exam would want registered representatives to know that and possibly encourage people to do that, I have no idea, but it's exactly the sort of esoteric thing the exam could ask just to be difficult. The contribution and any interest or dividends it earned would have to be removed by the April 15th deadline to avoid IRS hassles.

An individual generally shouldn't take any distributions from the account until he's 59½; he also has to start taking it out by the time he's 70½. If not, the IRS will slap a 50% insufficient distribution penalty on him, which seems a little harsh but is unfortunately how it is. To keep things nice and simple, it's not the year in which the individual turns 70½. It's April 1st (not the 15th, which would have made too much sense) of the year following the year in which the individual turns 70½. The exam might refer to the amount that must be taken out as an RMD or **required minimum distribution**. Basically, if your life expectancy is 20 years when you turn 70½, you would take out 1/20th of the account value. The next year, you'd take out 1/19th, then 1/18th and so on as you get closer and closer to that great retirement community in the sky. Sometimes the federal government will give folks a break and not require anyone to take a required minimum distribution, but that should not affect the exam questions much, if at all. For example, the federal government decided to give folks a break for 2009 (and maybe beyond) by not requiring anyone to take a required minimum distribution. But, that most likely would not change an exam question on RMDs. The exam focuses on concepts much more than current events.

The **Roth IRA**, on the other hand, is funded with after-tax or non-tax-deductible dollars. Therefore, the money comes out tax-free as long as the individual is 59½ years old and has had the account for at least 5 years. Notice how I underlined the word "and," which means if you start your Roth at age 56, you'll have to wait five years to take the money out tax-free. For the Roth IRA there is no requirement to start taking the money out at 70½. Since the IRS isn't going to tax that money, it couldn't care less when it starts coming out. In fact, if she has earned income, an individual can still contribute to her Roth IRA, regardless of her age. Make sure it's earned income, though, not bond interest or pension checks, etc.

A rather funky feature of the Roth IRA is that the IRS could sort of not care less about your cost basis. They'll let you have anything over and above what you put in tax-free as long as you abide by the 5 years and 59½ years old requirement. But, if you're only taking out the amount you put in, they don't care about that, not after you've had the account going 5 years or more. So, after the account has been open at least 5 years, your cost basis can be removed from the Roth IRA if you absolutely have to have the new Lexus. Of course, if you pull the $10,000 out, that's $10,000 that's not going to be earning interest and dividends or appreciating in value over time, but—hey—it's your money.

The contribution limits for both the Traditional and the Roth IRA are 100% of earned income up to the current maximum contribution limit. For people 50 and older an additional "catch-up provision" is allowed. If an individual has both a Traditional IRA and a Roth IRA, the current maximum contribution is the total between both accounts.

If the individual (or married couple filing jointly) earns a high income, he cannot make a contribution to a Roth IRA. But, many people do not realize that there are no income limits for the Traditional IRA. Don't worry about how much money somebody makes in the test question, or if she's covered by an employer plan. All that would change is the amount she can <u>deduct</u> from her contribution. See, nothing is simple. We'd like to say that all contributions to a Traditional IRA are pre-tax, but, if the individual is covered by an employer plan and makes what the IRS deems a high salary, she might get to deduct only some of her contribution, or even none of it.

So what?

Either way, she can *make* her maximum contribution. If she's covered by an employer plan and makes a certain amount of money, she'd just have to keep track of how much went in after-tax so she doesn't get taxed twice on that money when it comes out with everything else. So, if she has earned income, she can contribute to her Traditional IRA. She might not deduct 100%, or even any percent, of it, but it can still go in there. And, don't forget this: if she's <u>not covered</u> by an employer plan, she can deduct all of her contribution, *regardless of her income*. If you disagree with any of this, see IRS Publication 590 at <u>http://www.irs. gov/pub/irs-pdf/p590.pdf</u>.

Either way, remember that whether you deduct your contribution or not, the real beauty of these plans is that the earnings grow tax-deferred. In a regular old investment account if an individual is in the 35% tax bracket, that means every time he sells stock held less than a year for a profit, he has to give up 35% of the gain to the federal government. Whenever she receives dividends or bond interest, she has to pay tax on that, which reduces the amount she has invested. However, if the stock is owned inside an IRA, there are no taxes to pay until retirement. This allows your money to grow faster. When you retire, you'll pay taxes on all the money in your account at your ordinary income tax rate, which should be pretty low when you retire.

Right?

I'm not sure how many people end up *over*-funding their IRAs, but if the maximum contribution is, say, $6,000, and you accidentally put in $7,000, you have an excess contribution of $1,000. What can you do to fix it? One, you could remove the excess by the tax filing deadline to avoid hassles—and any interest or dividends the custodian determines are associated with it. Two, if you exceeded your 2011 contributions, you could re-characterize those contributions as being made for Tax Year 2012 by filling out the appropriate forms. Three, if you don't take either of those options, you'll have to pay a 6% tax on the $1,000 and any interest or dividends it generated.

Investment Restrictions

IRAs are not for speculation. Toward that end, there are to be no short sales or margin trading in these accounts. Also no collectible items (tangibles) or life insurance. It would also be a real bad idea to own municipal bonds or municipal bond mutual funds inside a Traditional IRA, or any plan that will leave you with taxable distributions. Municipal bonds pay tax-exempt interest, which is why their coupon payments are so low. All money coming out of the Traditional, SEP, SIMPLE, etc., is taxed, so the municipal bond's tax advantage is destroyed and all the individual is left with is a lower coupon payment.

And maybe an arbitration claim against you and your firm.

Transfers and Rollovers

I'm not sure why, but some people will take a **rollover** from an IRA and then plan to send the money to a new IRA custodian within 60 days. Remember that a rollover must be completed within 60 days, and an individual can only do one per year without IRS hassles. A true "rollover" is a situation where the individual has the current custodian cut her a check in her name. I guess she's planning a shopping spree, but she'll notice that her check is short by 20%, which is the withholding that the custodian will keep for their friends at the IRS. The individual would then need to make up the 20% shortfall when she cuts her check to the new custodian. Either that, or the IRS will treat the 20% shortfall as an early distribution subject to ordinary income tax and the 10% penalty.

So, most people would do a **direct transfer** of funds from the existing IRA custodian to the next. There are no limits here, since the individual does not cash a check, play with the money a while, and then roll it over into a new IRA.

This issue of what to do with existing retirement account balances is very common when someone leaves a job where they have a 401(k) or 403(b) account balance. If you leave your job and want to move the 401(k) balance to your own IRA, you can have the custodian cut a check to the IRA custodian and send the funds directly. Or, you can establish a new "rollover IRA," and there will be no tax problems. The amount from the 401(k) plan won't even count as a current year contribution. The 401(k) custodian will cut a check in the name of the IRA custodian "F.B.O. Your Name," and that would avoid the IRS hassles.

But, if you have the custodian just cut you a check in *your* name, and then you start procrastinating about establishing the new IRA, now you're doing what the exam calls a "rollover." You can do one rollover per year. You must complete it in 60 days. And, there will be the 20% withholding hassle.

Also, I'm not sure how precise an exam question would be, but there is a "rollover," and then there is a "direct rollover." If the question just uses the term "rollover" or "qualifying rollover," associate that with the 60 days and the 1-year waiting period. If it specifically brings up "direct rollover," know that this method avoids the 10% penalty and the 20% withholding because the check is payable to the IRA custodian F.B.O. the individual. The fact that the check is *sent* to the individual is not such a big deal, since the check is *payable* only to the custodian. The individual would fill out an IRA deposit slip and send that plus the check to the new custodian to complete the "direct rollover."

Converting a Traditional IRA to a Roth

Roth IRAs are funded with after-tax contributions. When the money comes out at retirement, no taxes are due, which makes budgeting much easier during retirement. So, if you wanted to turn your Traditional IRA into a Roth IRA, basically, you'd just have to pay ordinary income tax on the Traditional IRA's account value before making the Roth contribution with what are now after-tax dollars. That way, in retirement, you can take money out of the Roth without paying taxes.

Way too much strategizing for me, but clearly this is an option that many investors will consider, so the exam might bring it up.

Also, individuals and married couples who fall into the high-income bracket simply cannot make a contribution to a Roth account as of this writing. So, they would not be able to convert a Traditional to a Roth IRA if their income levels were above what the IRS considers to be decent or necessary. If the exam expects you to know the precise income level where people are phased out of their ability to make a Roth contribution, then we're all in a world of hurting. A question like that would imply that there is really no way anyone could ever know enough trivia to pass what is, essentially, an easy exam. And, remember, you can miss 30 questions and pass the Series 6.

SOLO 401(K)

The solo, or self-employed 401(k) plan is for sole proprietorships that have no full-time employees but self and spouse. Of course, that implies that the business can have part-time employees, but only the owner and the spouse work full-time. The self-employed 401(k) offers flexible contributions, and allows participants to take loans on the principal. The business can be a sole proprietorship, a partnership, or a C Corporation, S Corporation, or limited liability corporation. Why would a small business owner start a self-employed 401(k) over a Traditional IRA or a SIMPLE?

Higher contribution limits.

EDUCATION SAVINGS PLANS

These are not retirement plans, but we usually talk about them when discussing retirement plans because of the tax deferral.

529 Savings Plan

The **529 savings plan** allows investors to save/invest for education. Usually, it would be a family member socking away money for a nephew's or grandchild's education, but, actually, the beneficiary (unlike for a Coverdell) does not have to be a child and does not have to be a blood relative of the donor. The person who opens the account is the owner; the beneficiary is the person who will use the money for education. Contributions are made after-tax, and the withdrawals used for qualified education expenses are tax-free at the federal level. Notice how I said "federal level." The plans are state-specific, so some states may tax the withdrawals if little junior decides he's too good for any of the little colleges in his home state. Or, they might allow the donors who are residents to deduct their contributions for purposes of state income taxes. So, you don't want to buy into a 529 savings plan without first checking how it will be taxed by the state. And, even with the federal taxation, the withdrawals for education have to be qualified withdrawals that cover tuition, room & board, books and no more than seven pitchers of beer per week. Kidding with the last item—the expenses do need to be directly related to education; otherwise, you'll get hit just like you do for an early IRA distribution (10% penalty plus ordinary income tax). Once per year, the account can be transferred to a different 529 savings plan without tax hassles. Also, if the beneficiary decides he doesn't need the money, the account can name a second beneficiary without tax problems, as long as the second beneficiary is related to the first.

When Grandma, for example, is putting money into a 529 savings plan on behalf of her granddaughter, she is basically making a gift. Gifts over a certain amount are actually taxable to the one making the gift, as we just saw. That amount was $13,000 for 2012 and has recently been $14,000. With a 529 savings plan, Grandma can contribute up to the gift tax exclusion without incurring gift taxes and can even do a lump sum contribution for the first five years ($70,000) without incurring gift tax hassles. A married couple—grandpa and grandma, for example—could double that amount and contribute $140,000. This is a technique known as "gift splitting" for obvious reasons. Note that if somebody uses the five-year-up-front method, they can't make any more gifts to the beneficiary for the next five years without dealing with gift taxes.

Prepaid Tuition

If you're pretty sure that junior won't be too good for any of the colleges in your state, you might want to lock him in as a future Boilermaker, Hoosier, or Sycamore through a plan whereby you pay for his tuition credits now for any state school in the fine state of Indiana. I didn't say you were locking him into being accepted at Purdue or IU, but he would get to go to a state school with a certain number of credits already paid for.

What if he decided he wanted to be a Buckeye or Hawkeye, instead?

The financial penalties could be nasty in that case, which is why we need to be reasonably sure that the kid will end up going to school in-state. Also note that these credits cover tuition and fees only.

Coverdell Education Savings Plan

A **Coverdell plan** also allows for after-tax contributions, but the current maximum is $2,000 per year per child. Note the word "child." Unlike in a 529 plan, the beneficiary does need to be a child. The distributions will be tax-free at the federal level if used according to the plan guidelines. Unlike with the 529 plan the assets here can be used before post–high school education, so if parents wanted to use the plan to help pay for their daughter's private middle school, that would be okay. And, unlike with the 529 plan, the assets become the property of the beneficiary as soon as he/she becomes an adult.

NOTE: We have not included current maximum retirement plan contributions because we prefer to keep these numbers up-to-date. Please download the PDF at www.passthe6.com/updates.

Chapter 2 Review Quiz
(47 questions)

1. **If an employee transfers a 401(k) to a rollover IRA upon leaving a job,**

   A.   The employee must pay tax on the excess above cost basis

   B.   There will be no penalties or taxation to pay at this time

   C.   The employee must be 59 ½ to avoid penalties

   D.   The employee may only perform one transfer per year

2. **A 1035 contract exchange may not take place in which of the following ways?**

   A.   one annuity to another offered by a different company

   B.   one annuity to a life insurance policy issued by the same company

   C.   one insurance policy to another issued by a different company

   D.   one insurance policy to another issued by the same company

3. **A teacher participated in a tax-sheltered annuity for 20 years. During her employ-ment she and the school district contributed $30,000 into the plan. At retirement the teacher takes a lump-sum distribution of $50,000. What is the tax treatment of the distribution?**

   A. $20,000 taxed at long-term capital gains rates

   B. $50,000 taxed as ordinary income

   C. $50,000 taxed at long-term capital gains rates

   D. $20,000 taxed as ordinary income

4. **JoAnn originally invested $10,000 into the Argood Value Fund. She has since reinvested dividend distributions of $1,000 and capital gains distributions of $500. If JoAnn cur-rently holds 1,000 shares of the Argood Value Fund, her cost basis per-share is**

   A. $10.00

   B. $11.00

   C. $11.50

   D. $10.50

5. **Doris contributed $60,000 into a non-qualified variable annuity at age 41. Nine years later Doris takes a random withdrawal of $15,000 with the account value at $85,000. Her tax liability on the withdrawal is**

   A. Ordinary income tax on $15,000

   B. Ordinary income tax on $15,000, plus a $1,500 penalty tax

   C. None, as this represents a tax-free return of cost basis

   D. Ordinary income tax on $25,000

6. **Which of the following statements accurately describe(s) the tax implications of insurance contracts?**

   A. death benefits are not taxable to the beneficiary, but are includable in the insured's estate for purposes of estate taxes

   B. loans against the policy are charged interest, and both the principal and interest reduce the contract values

   C. the policyholder may surrender the part of cash value representing net premiums paid into the contract tax-free

   D. all choices listed

7. **Which of the following retirement plans are available only to sole proprietors?**

   A. SIMPLE IRA

   B. SEP-IRA

   C. KEOGH

   D. NON-QUALIFIED ANNUITY

8. **Which of the following may a 72-year-old not do regarding a Roth IRA account?**

   A. Change the beneficiary

   B. Elect to take no distributions

   C. Continue to make contributions from earned income

   D. Make deductible contributions from earned income

9. **Which of the following offers annual downside protection to an investor?**

   A. U.S. Treasury Bond

   B. Equity indexed annuity

   C. Variable annuity

   D. All choices listed

10. **Which of the following statements accurately describes SIMPLE Individual Retirement Arrangements?**

    A.   Employees are immediately vested

    B.   SIMPLE IRAs are for businesses with more than 100 employees

    C.   SIMPLE IRAs are for businesses with at least one other retirement plan option

    D.   Contributions are non-tax-deductible

11. **Which of the following retirement plans allow(s) for the least flexible contributions on behalf of the employer?**

    A.   Profit sharing

    B.   Defined benefit pension

    C.   SIMPLE IRA

    D.   Money purchase

12. **FINRA requires a reasonable-basis suitability standard for investment recommendations. Which of the following exemplifies a broker-dealer meeting this standard?**

    A.   An agent of the firm recommends a transaction that is suitable based on an inquiry of the customer's needs

    B.   The firm performs due diligence to determine that a new securities product may be suitable for some investors

    C.   An agent of the firm recommends a deferred annuity to an elderly client with high liquidity needs

    D.   The firm reviews the transactions within an agent's book of business to verify that an excessive number of transactions has not been executed, making otherwise suitable recommendations unsuitable when taken as a whole

13. **When a large state needs to raise capital in order to improve the highway system, the services of which of the following would be used?**

    A.   Retail bank

    B.   Investment banker

    C.   Investment adviser

    D.   The state must raise capital internally, and may not use the services of an outside party to raise capital for such projects

14. ABC Industries completed its IPO several years ago. If the company offers shares to investors this year, the offering could be accurately referred to as a/an

    A.   Subsequent primary offering

    B.   Secondary offering

    C.   Combined offering

    D.   Reg D offering

15. Which of the following securities issued by a corporation pays an income stream that is fixed as to the minimum but not as to the maximum?

    A.   Straight preferred stock

    B.   Participating preferred stock

    C.   Callable preferred stock

    D.   Cumulative preferred stock

16. Which of the following positions allows the investor to force another investor to buy her stock at a stated price?

    A.   Buy a call

    B.   Buy a put

    C.   Sell a call

    D.   Sell a put

17. GNMA (Government National Mortgage Association) pass-through securities make payments to investors in which of the following ways?

    A.   Interest is paid semi-annually with all principal paid at a stated maturity date

    B.   Interest is paid monthly with all principal paid on an uncertain maturity date

    C.   Interest and principal are paid monthly

    D.   Interest is paid monthly, principal is paid annually

18. Which of the following securities is offered with a relatively low rate of income but with potential capital appreciation/purchasing power protection?

    A.   Participating preferred stock

    B.   Callable preferred stock

    C.   Adjustable-rate preferred stock

    D.   Convertible preferred stock

19. **A 69-year-old annuitant would likely receive the highest monthly payment if choosing which of the following payout options?**

    A. Straight life

    B. Life with 15-year period certain

    C. Join-and-last survivor

    D. All choices would lead to equal monthly payouts

20. **You could accurately inform a customer that the death benefit offered through a deferred variable annuity contract works in which of the following ways?**

    A. During the accumulation phase the beneficiary would receive at least what the annuitant contributed to the contract upon his/her death

    B. Once annuitized the beneficiary will receive at least what the individual contributed to the account

    C. Once annuitized the beneficiary will receive a minimum number of payments

    D. During the accumulation period the beneficiary is assured of receiving a minimum rate of return on the annuitant's purchase payments

21. **What is true of the investment options offered to the policyholder of a variable life insurance contract?**

    A. The policyholder may invest no more than 50% of net premiums in the separate account

    B. The policyholder may invest no more than 50% of net premiums in equity-based subaccounts

    C. The policyholder may invest among the subaccounts as she sees fit

    D. During the first 24 months net premiums are automatically allocated to the general account

22. **Companies typically finance their short-term operations with the issuance of which of the following types of securities?**

    A. Commercial paper

    B. Banker's acceptances

    C. Treasury Bills

    D. Treasury stock

23. **Jennifer purchased shares of the ABC Balanced fund in January and redeemed them for more than she paid in December of that year. Virginia purchased shares of the same fund on the same day and then received a capital gains distribution from the ABC Balanced fund in December of that year. Therefore, which TWO of the following are accurate?**

    I.   Jennifer's capital gain is long-term

    II. Jennifer's capital gain is short-term

    III. Virginia's capital gain is long-term

    IV. Virginia's capital gain is short-term

    A.   I, III

    B.   II, III

    C.   I, IV

    D.   II, IV

24. **The ABC Fund Family is a front-end-load mutual fund complex that offers a "conversion/exchange privilege" to investors. Therefore, if a shareholder exchanges $20,000 of the Balanced Fund and immediately places the proceeds into the family's Growth & Income Fund, which of the following will occur?**

    A.   The investor will be relieved of any capital gains taxes on the sale of the Balanced Fund shares

    B.   The investor will be relieved of any front-end load on the purchase of the Growth & Income Fund shares

    C.   Both choices

    D.   Neither choice

25. **Which of the following is potentially a dis-advantage of automatically investing $100 into a mutual fund each month?**

    A.   Dollar cost averaging

    B.   Avoiding timing risk

    C.   Triggering wash sales

    D.   There are no dis-advantages to this practice

26. **Investors who re-invest dividend distributions from a mutual fund should be aware of which of the following?**

    A.   Reinvested dividends are taxable and do not add to the investor's tax basis

    B.   Reinvested dividends are not taxable but are added to the investor's tax basis

    C.   Reinvested dividends are taxable and are added to the investor's tax basis

    D.   Reinvested dividends reduce the investor's tax basis by the amount reinvested

27. **What is true of surrenders of cash value on a variable life insurance policy?**

A. The policyholder is taxed on any surrenders of cash value similar to the tax consequences on a non-qualified variable annuity

B. Surrenders up to the amount of premiums paid are not taxable to the policyholder

C. Surrenders must be for the full cash value of the policy in order to avoid tax consequences

D. Surrenders of cash value do not impact the amount of the policy's death benefit

28. **Several weeks after one of your elderly customers passed away you are meeting with the executor of the estate, who is also the sole beneficiary of a variable life insurance policy you sold to the now-deceased customer. All of the following statements to the executor are accurate EXCEPT:**

A. The death benefit is not taxable to the executor

B. The death benefit is includable in the value of the deceased customer's estate

C. The securities account can only be re-titled in the name of the estate after receipt of a death certificate, letters of office, affidavits, etc.

D. The death benefit is not includable in the value of the deceased customer's estate because the executor and beneficiary are one-in-the-same

29. **Individuals frequently take distributions from annuities and retirement plans prior to age 59 ½ and avoid penalties under which section of the tax code?**

A. 1035

B. 1031

C. 72(t)

D. 401(k)

30. **Contract owners of annuities and insurance policies are able to transfer contract values tax-free by utilizing which of the following sections of the tax code?**

A. 1031

B. 1035

C. 1099

D. 72(t)

31. **If a registered representative of a FINRA-member firm borrows money from a customer without violating FINRA rules, the most likely reason is that**

    A.   The member's written supervisory procedures permitted the activity

    B.   The customer was a bank

    C.   The customer was an immediate family member

    D.   The customer was a registered representative of an unaffiliated brokerage firm

32. **On vacation recently, you met a registered representative working for a different broker-dealer than yours and discovered that while the registered representative does not sell variable annuities, you do not like to sell open-end mutual funds. In order to work together, which of the following are you allowed to do without violating industry rules?**

    A.   Make an annual payment to the registered representative of $500

    B.   Make an annual payment to the registered representative of $500 only after receiving principal approval

    C.   Set up a referral arrangement and split the commissions 50/50

    D.   Make a gift of cash or goods not to exceed FINRA's annual limit

33. **One of your customers is 55 years old and ready to retire in the next few months. She owns a non-qualified variable annuity with a cost basis of $300,000 and a contract value of $442,000. Which of the following statements could you accurately make to this customer?**

    A.   A lump-sum withdrawal of $442,000 will be taxed as ordinary income in its entirety

    B.   If you annuitize the contract, the first two years' of payments will be tax-free

    C.   A random withdrawal of $75,000 would be subject to a penalty of $7,500

    D.   There is no way to avoid either income taxes or penalties on any withdrawal from this account due to your age

34. **An annuitant in her 40's is receiving generous dividend and capital gains distributions from the various subaccounts of her variable annuity to which her purchase payments have been allocated. What is true of the tax implications of these distributions?**

    A.   They will be reinvested into more accumulation units of the separate account

    B.   They may be received constructively currently without tax implications

    C.   The dividend distributions are tax-exempt while the capital gains distributions are taxed at long-term capital gains rates

    D.   The dividends are tax-exempt if the purchase payments are allocated to any municipal bond subaccounts

35. Which of the following is an accurate statement of guarantees as they relate to the securities industry?

    A.   No securities are guaranteed

    B.   U.S. Treasury—but not corporate—bonds may be described as "guaranteed"

    C.   Broker-dealers and agents may not guarantee customers against investment loss

    D.   All of these choices

36. For purposes of determining the suitability of an annuity switch transaction which of the following facts about the customer or the proposed transaction would most likely make the switch suitable?

    A.   The customer is 53 years old

    B.   The customer is female

    C.   The existing contract will charge a 6% surrender fee

    D.   The annuity offered will waive all surrender charges after two years

37. Your Aunt Allie Mae originally invested $25,000 into the ABC Balanced Fund. Over the years, she has reinvested $3,000 in dividends and $1,500 in capital gains distributions. When she dies, you inherit the shares, with the investment worth $48,000. What are the tax implications on your inheritance?

    A.   None currently except to establish a cost basis of $48,000

    B.   None currently except to establish a cost basis of $29,500

    C.   None currently except to establish a cost basis of $25,000

    D.   Long-term capital gains tax rates on $17,500

38. The only securities investment listed below that is NOT subject to heightened suitability requirements by FINRA is a/an

    A.   Collateralized Mortgage Obligation (CMO)

    B.   Unit Investment Trust (UIT)

    C.   Deferred Variable Annuity

    D.   All of these choices are subject to heightened suitability

39. Which of the following correctly describes the FINRA violation called "breakpoint selling"?

A.   Trying to guide investors toward investing in mutual fund shares at a higher dollar amount

B.   Intentionally trying to guide investors to combine investments within one family of funds

C.   Intentionally trying to entice investors to buy shares of a mutual fund in order to receive an upcoming dividend distribution

D.   Selling mutual funds in a way that prevents investors from receiving available breakpoints

40. The one accurate statement below of mutual fund sponsors is that

A.   They are federal covered investment advisers

B.   They may offer educational seminars to registered representatives based on their sales volume

C.   They may offer educational seminars to registered representatives, reimbursing their expenses as well as the reasonable expenses of one guest

D.   They must be FINRA-member firms in good standing

41. Under the Securities Act of 1933 the SEC is responsible for all of the following EXCEPT:

A.   Promotion of market efficiency

B.   Fostering capital formation through the primary market

C.   Encouraging competition among market participants

D.   Reducing paperwork for brokerage firms

42. FINRA would have regulatory concerns over which of the following compensation arrangements?

A.   Janet and Jill, registered representatives of ABC Brokerage Services, plan to do joint work and split commissions on mutual fund sales

B.   David, age 67 and retired, pursuant to a written agreement with his former employing member firm receives commissions on annuity business written several years ago

C.   Donna, registered with a Series 7 and Series 24, receives a percentage of the commissions received by the registered representatives under her supervision

D.   Myrtle agrees to rebate 1/3 of the commissions paid on a large variable annuity sale to the customer after receiving principal approval

43. **An example of market manipulation, prohibited under Rule 10b-5 of the Securities Exchange Act of 1934, is which of the following?**

    A.   An institutional traders sells 1,000 shares of ABC short without attempting to pay for the stock immediately

    B.   A broker-dealer executes in excess of 25 agency cross transactions on the same trading day

    C.   A retail investor establishes five separate LLCs under diverse names and stated purposes and spends the day trading an illiquid stock at progressively higher price and volume levels among the various controlled entities

    D.   Seven retail investors form an investment club for the express purpose of pooling their capital, knowledge, and experience

44. **While making a sales presentation to a wealthy customer, you discover that the customer's business is about to be acquired by a much larger player, with the announcement to come out the following afternoon after markets close for regular trading. At this point, what can you do concerning this information?**

    A.   Use it for your own personal trading, but not for recommendations to your customers

    B.   Do not use it for your own personal trading or for recommendations to your customers but inform investors who are not customers of your firm in the interest of full and fair disclosure

    C.   Contact FINCen immediately and/or complete a Suspicious Activity Report

    D.   Do not use the information for your personal trading, and do not divulge it to any other investor until it has been publicly released

45. **If a retail investor reads the summary prospectus for the ABC Value Fund and sees that no more than 15% of the fund's assets may be invested in companies that are neither domiciled in the U.S. nor included in the S&P 500. This policy exists as stated because**

    A.   The SEC requires that funds invest no more than 20% in such companies

    B.   FINRA requires that funds invest no more than 1/3 of total assets in such companies

    C.   The investment adviser has determined that this is a prudent investment policy

    D.   The board of directors has established this policy

46. **One of your customers is a 31-year-old single woman who is about to purchase a condominium. Which of the following statements could you accurately make to her concerning her Traditional IRA and this transaction?**

   A.   She can perform a qualifying rollover from her existing IRA to a new account if she completes it within 180 calendar days

   B.   She can withdraw up to $10,000 from the account and use it as a down payment without any tax implications

   C.   If she were purchasing a detached, single-family home she could withdraw up to $10,000 from the account and use it as a down payment without penalty

   D.   If this is her first purchase of a primary residence, she can avoid penalties on a withdrawal of up to $10,000 for a down payment on the property

47. **One of your mutual fund customers is ready to retire. She would like to receive $500 monthly through a systematic withdrawal plan. Which of the following statements is accurate of this situation?**

   A.   She should choose a fixed-share withdrawal plan

   B.   She should choose a fixed-dollar withdrawal plan in order to be certain of her money lasting a minimum amount of time

   C.   She should choose a fixed-dollar withdrawal plan provided she can live with the uncertain time frame implied by this choice

   D.   She should choose a fixed-percentage withdrawal plan

Chapter 2 Review Quiz Answers

(47 questions)

1. **ANSWER:** B

    WHY: transfers do not cause problems for the individual—it's the 60-day rollover that presents challenges. Also, there is no cost-basis in a retirement account funded with tax-deductible contributions.

2. **ANSWER:** B

    WHY: you can't turn an annuity into a life insurance policy since life insurance policies are subject to underwriting standards, health exams, etc. while an annuity is essentially an investment product.

3. **ANSWER:** B

    WHY: a "cost basis" would allow the teacher to avoid paying tax on her contribution. Since she's never paid tax on her contribution, she has no cost basis, or—more simply—all money coming out is taxed. Retirement money is *never* taxed at long-term capital gains rates. It is either taxed as ordinary income or—in some cases—tax-free upon distribution (Roth IRA, e.g.).

4. **ANSWER:** C

    WHY: distributions are taxed whether you reinvest them or cash the check. Since re-invested distributions are taxable, add that amount to the cost basis. Cost basis is the amount that has gone into an investment and has already been taxed once.

5. **ANSWER:** B

    WHY: she is subject to the 10% penalty until age 59 ½, and since there are earnings of $25,000, all of this distribution is taxable.

6. **ANSWER:** D

    WHY: annuities subject the contract owner to taxation upon withdrawal, but insurance contracts allow the policyholder to do as Choice C suggests. Many individuals take loans against cash value, which reduces the value of the policy, of course, unless/until repaid, with interest.

7. **ANSWER:** C

    WHY: the business must be organized/owned as a sole proprietor; any eligible employees can and must also be included in the plan along with the business owner.

8. **ANSWER:** D

    WHY: Roth IRA contributions are never deductible. Unlike with a Traditional IRA, this 72-year-old can decide to take no distributions and continue to make contributions (non-deductible) if she has earned income.

9. **ANSWER:** B

    WHY: the U.S. Treasury doesn't re-set the bond's market value the way an indexed annuity promises to increase by a minimum amount if the stock market index has a bad year.

10. **ANSWER:** A

    WHY: Choices B and C almost have it right—the business has no more than 100 workers and no other retirement plan in place. The contributions are made pre-tax or on a tax-deductible basis, reducing the amount of the participant's compensation that is subject to tax for the year it was made.

11. **ANSWER:** D

    WHY: the money purchase plan allows for large annual contributions but the contributions are mandatory for the employer. In a profit sharing plan, the employer can make no contributions if the company does not make a profit. The SIMPLE IRA offers several options to the employer, none of them more than a mild discomfort compared to the money purchase plan's requirements. Defined benefit pension plans are subject to various funding formulae that leave much flexibility to the employer.

12. **ANSWER:** B

    WHY: the firm must have some basis to believe the investment/product could be suitable to at least some investors to meet the "reasonable-basis" standard. Choice A is talking about the "customer-specific" standard and is, of course, a much more tempting answer than the one that turned out to be correct. The test loves to do that, by the way.

13. **ANSWER:** B

    WHY: investment bankers are broker-dealers who raise capital for their clients, the issuers of securities. Municipal bonds are underwritten by broker-dealers to raise capital for states, counties, cities, and school districts, just as common stock is underwritten by broker-dealers for companies raising capital by issuing bonds, preferred stock, common stock, etc. The issuer receives the proceeds of the sale, minus underwriting fees to the broker-dealers who brought the investors to the table.

14. **ANSWER:** A

    WHY: if the issuer gets the proceeds, it's a primary market transaction, and if the issuer does not get the proceeds, it's a secondary market transaction (non-issuer transaction).

15. **ANSWER:** B

WHY: preferred stock pays a fixed dividend that is fixed as to the minimum and the maximum amount—it will not be increased. It will not be increased, unless it is participating preferred stock, that is. So, all preferred stock is fixed as to the maximum amount received except participating preferred stock, whose dividend rises if the dividend paid to common stockholders rises.

16. **ANSWER:** B

WHY: the term "to put" a stock to someone means to make them buy it from you at the stated price. If you buy an ABC Apr 50 put, you have the right to force anyone who wrote that series of option to buy 100 shares of ABC for $50, no matter what they're actually worth. Some investors buy puts to protect shares they own. Some are just speculating that a stock is about to drop. Either way, they pay their premium and receive the right to sell their stock—yes, they buy the right to sell. It's okay—you'll get used to it the longer you stay in the industry

17. **ANSWER:** C

WHY: a CMO withholds all the principal payments until maturity, but GNMA, FNMA, and FHLMC mortgage-backed securities pass the homeowners' monthly payment of principal-and-interest to the investors. When will the principal be paid up? Nobody knows, and that is either prepayment risk (rates drop) or extension risk (rates rise).

18. **ANSWER:** D

WHY: the only type of preferred stock that would have the investor caring about increased profits at the company is convertible preferred stock, which is tied to the value of the issuer's common stock. All other preferred stock has the investor concerned about receiving the dividend, period. Common stockholders need ever increasing profits at the company while preferred stockholders (other than convertible) simply need the company to make enough profit to pay the promised, stated dividend. Both are owners of the company, but they have much different interests, as you can see.

19. **ANSWER:** A

WHY: when the individual dies, the payments stop. The payouts are not set up on some minimum period of 15 years or tied to more than one person's life expectancy. Those who picked Choice D need to cut it out. Quick. You know what I mean. Start reading each answer choice carefully, attempting to eliminate it. Don't just pick something in order to make the pain of the question go away.

20. **ANSWER:** A

WHY: the death benefit brings some peace of mind to the annuitant, who knows that if he gets hit by a bus during the accumulation (saving-up) phase, his beneficiary will receive at least what he contributed, even if he picked the worst subaccounts offered at the worst possible time. I'm not implying the cause of death has to be "hit by a bus" or even "accidental." Just making a point. Remember that when the contract is annuitized, the individual makes a choice of settlement options—straight-life, period-certain, joint-and-last-survivor, etc.

21. **ANSWER:** C

WHY: the investment options are mutual-fund-type accounts called "subaccounts." Your job is to help your customer choose wisely among these subaccounts, since their performance will determine the value of his investment, net of the many fees involved.

22. **ANSWER:** A

WHY: commercial paper is issued to money market mutual funds to help companies finance short-term operations. Importing/exporting activities are often financed with banker's acceptances. The U.S. Treasury issues Treasury Bills to finance government spending. Treasury stock has been issued and then repurchased by the company, often to boost the earnings-per-share for the common stock.

23. **ANSWER:** B

WHY: if an investor buys and sells the shares within 12 months, the gain or loss would be short-term. On the other hand, distributions of capital gains to investors are assumed to be long-term to all who receive them. Don't confuse buying and selling shares with owning a mutual fund and receiving your fair share of the net long-term capital gain realized by the investment adviser to the fund.

24. **ANSWER:** B

WHY: this is a feature some funds offer their investors—waiving the front-end sales charge. The IRS doesn't offer a lot of little deals like that.

25. **ANSWER:** C

WHY: if the investor buys new shares each month, any sale at a loss will become a wash sale in a regular, taxable account.

26. **ANSWER:** C

WHY: because the re-invested dividend is taxable, it is also added to the investor's cost basis on the mutual fund shares.

27. **ANSWER:** B

WHY: unlike with annuities, life insurance policies allow the policyholder to surrender up to the amount he's paid in without tax implications.

28. **ANSWER:** D

WHY: the beneficiary receives the death benefit tax-free, but the death benefit is also includable in the insured's estate.

29. **ANSWER:** C

WHY: although these early distributions are still taxable, the "72(t)" allows these individuals to avoid the penalty when they take out a series of substantially equal payments over several years.

30. **ANSWER:** B

WHY: the 1031 exchange is for real estate. 72(t) allows early distributions from retirement accounts without penalty. A 1099 is a form for a subcontractor, or a form showing dividends and interest received by the investor, among other things.

31. **ANSWER:** A

WHY: the firm doesn't have to allow registered representatives to borrow money from any customer. FINRA rules permit firms to allow borrowing in certain cases, but the registered representative must check the firm's supervisory procedures before engaging in borrowing with any customer to see what is allowed and what is required if the practice is allowed in the first place.

32. **ANSWER:** D

WHY: annual gifts to influence other members and their employees may not exceed the current maximum allowed by FINRA, which is currently _____.

33. **ANSWER:** C

WHY: because she is under 59½ years old, the withdrawal is subject to a 10% penalty. There are ways to avoid this, but none was presented in this question. The entire amount is not taxed—just the growth of $142,000.

34. **ANSWER:** A

WHY: she is far too young to be taking money out of the contract, so she will automatically reinvest into more shares/units.

35. **ANSWER:** C

WHY: a corporate bond or stock could be guaranteed if a third party promises to pay dividends, interest, and/or principal if the issuer cannot, but agents and their firms may not guarantee anyone against investment loss.

36. **ANSWER:** D

WHY: the first two choices don't tell us enough to draw any conclusions. Choice C would be a reason not to approve the transaction, but if the annuity company will waive surrender charges, that is a reason in favor of making the switch.

37. **ANSWER:** A

     WHY: for inherited shares, the recipient gets to "step up" the cost basis to their fair market value on the date of death, thereby avoiding capital gains that the deceased might have had to pay if he or she had, you know, not died.

38. **ANSWER:** B

     WHY: Both deferred annuities and CMOs have special suitability rules based on their complexity.

39. **ANSWER:** D

     WHY: the term "breakpoint selling" is a bit misleading, since the violation occurs when the registered representative does *not* sell mutual fund shares at the next breakpoint. But, as they say, it is what it is. Always encourage investors to consider breakpoints when investing into front-end-loaded mutual fund shares.

40. **ANSWER:** D

     WHY: sponsors of mutual funds are FINRA-member broker-dealers, and they may not reward registered representatives with lavish "educational seminars" given as rewards for selling the fund's shares to investors. They also can only reimburse the registered representative's travel expenses to any *legitimate* seminars provided.

41. **ANSWER:** D

     WHY: the Securities Act of 1933 states that the SEC's goals include choices A through C. We're not saying the SEC doesn't care about reducing paperwork—we just needed a false choice to make the question work.

42. **ANSWER:** D

     WHY: no sharing of commissions with unregistered persons allowed! Continuing commissions on former business written by a retired representative is also okay, as are the other two situations, of course.

43. **ANSWER:** C

     WHY: Choice C exemplifies "effecting a transaction in a security which involves no change in beneficial ownership," which means all the trades are being done to create the false appearance of trading activity, to the benefit of the individual manipulating the market.

44. **ANSWER:** D

     WHY: if you have material insider information, keep it to yourself until it's been announced.

45. **ANSWER:** D

     WHY: the board of directors establishes the investment policies of the fund. The investment adviser manages the portfolio in accordance with those policies.

46. **ANSWER:** D

    WHY: the withdrawal will be taxed, but if it's for the first-time purchase of a primary residence, the penalty will be avoided.

47. **ANSWER:** C

    WHY: no one knows how long the shares will last if the fund is liquidating enough of them to raise $500 cash each month. If the investor is okay with the uncertain time frame, the fixed-dollar plan is appropriate.

CHAPTER 3

Obtains, Verifies, and Confirms Customer Purchase and Sale Instructions

(Represents 10 of 100 Questions on the Series 6 Exam)

Once you are registered, you will open customer accounts, get to know your customers' investment profiles, and make suitable recommendations of mutual funds, variable annuities, and/or variable life insurance policies to your customers based on their goals and financial situations. Obviously, when your customers accept a recommendation to buy or sell a security, your job description is exactly what the title of this section of the outline indicates, "Verifies, enters and monitors orders in accordance with customers' instructions and regulatory requirements and reports trade executions to customers."

EXECUTING ORDERS

REGULATION T

With your Series 6 designation you will execute purchase and redemption/sale orders for open-end funds, variable annuities, and variable life insurance. However, your exam will likely ask questions about terms and processes that are actually only used by Series 7 licensees. For example, if you had your Series 7 designation, you could help a customer buy 1,000 shares of MSFT today and earn a commission for your trouble. If so, you would enter the transaction on the **trade date,** but the **settlement date** would not occur for three more business days. Transactions in stock, corporate bonds, and municipal bonds settle **regular way** on "T + 3," which means whatever the trade date is, count forward three business days to the settlement date, which is when both sides of the transaction complete their obligations to make payment and deliver the securities. If the trade date is Tuesday, the settlement date is Friday. If the trade date is Wednesday, the settlement date is Monday. Unless there is a holiday. As you would expect, weekends and holidays don't count.

If a customer enters an order to buy 500 shares of ABC on Tuesday, the broker-dealer would generally expect payment by the settlement date of Friday. Under the Federal Reserve Board's **Regulation T**, payment must be made within 2 business days of regular way settlement. If not, the firm must impose a **frozen account** status on the customer. That just means that while an account is "frozen" no purchase orders can be executed unless the customer already has the cash in the account—no more credit for 90 days. Besides being a slow payer, another way for a customer to get his little account frozen is to try something cute like this: buy 1,000 shares of MSFT on Monday for $30 a share, only instead of ever actually sending in $30,000, just go ahead and sell the shares for $31 on Wednesday, using the proceeds to cover the purchase side of the transaction. No—that is freeriding and will lead to an account freeze.

Broker-dealers don't have to extend credit to their customers at all. The one that I use, in fact, would reject any purchase order that involves more funds than I actually have in the account. If they wanted to let me slide, they would have to do so according to the requirements of Regulation or "Reg" T. Regulation T requires broker-dealers to get prompt payment from customers or request a formal extension. If the firm gets an extension and the customer still doesn't pay, that's really the firm's problem. They have to settle regular way with the other side of the transaction, so if they have to buy or sell securities at prices that cause a loss, yes, they can take that from the customer's account—or not. Either way, they have to settle up with the broker-dealer on the buy or sell side of the transaction and work things out with their customer on their own time and their own dime.

If you have a big customer—maybe the quarterback for your city's NFL franchise—what if he buys $80,000 worth of ABC common stock, but then goes out of town before he gets a chance to make payment? Couldn't you or your firm just float him a short-term loan of $80,000?

Not if there's any chance of getting caught. I actually know of a *former* agent who was caught lending customers money to buy his investment products, allowing him to make commissions-plus-interest, and hit his sales targets. That worked really well, for about four months. Not sure which industry he went into after his employer found out about his creative business practices.

ORDER TICKETS

Rules under the Securities Exchange Act of 1934 require that brokerage orders be evidenced by a written **memorandum** or **order ticket.** As the rules state, the firm needs to make and keep "a memorandum of each brokerage order, and of any other instruction, given or received for the purchase or sale of securities, whether executed or unexecuted." The "unexecuted order" might seem strange, but when trading individual shares of stock it is very common for investors to place an order to buy or sell shares at a certain price; if that price never materializes, the orders are unexecuted. The firm would still need records of these orders—limit and stop orders, for example.

What must be contained on such a "memorandum" or "order ticket"? Here we go:

> The memorandum shall show the terms and conditions of the order
> or instructions and of any modification or cancellation thereof;
> the account for which entered; the time the order was received;

> the time of entry; the price at which executed; the identity of
> each associated person, if any, responsible for the account;
> the identity of any other person who entered or accepted the
> order on behalf of the customer or, if a customer entered the
> order on an electronic system, a notation of that entry; and,
> to the extent feasible, the time of execution or cancellation.

If a test question asks what is *not* on the order ticket, a possible correct answer could be "the agent's commission" or "the rating of the bond." Or, of course, anything not in the list I just quoted. It's a hard test—you knew that, right?

Excellent.

The rule goes on to point out that:

> an order entered pursuant to the exercise of discretionary
> authority by the member, broker or dealer, or associated
> person thereof, shall be so designated.

As we saw in Chapter 2, broker-dealers need to keep a memorandum for each order executed for their own account. We'll leave the details that we already covered there.

Also note that order tickets/memoranda are basically for "trades" of securities. If securities are purchased on a subscription basis from the issuer of the securities, the firm can just keep a copy of the subscription agreement. An investor purchasing a limited partnership interest in a natural gas project, for example, would be signing a subscription agreement and attaching payment to the issuer of the securities. Not that you can sell limited partnership interests with a Series 6 license, but, again, the exam goes much wider and deeper than that.

So, whether you are selling shares of common stock or shares of mutual funds, the regulators require certain information be obtained and maintained for each order. They also require that members confirm transactions with their customers, as we see in virtually all other industries.

TRADE CONFIRMATIONS

An order ticket or order memorandum is an internal document of the broker-dealer. Once the order has been executed, a **trade confirmation** is sent to the customer in order to, yes, confirm the trade. FINRA and SEC rules require the confirmation to be delivered no later than settlement of the transaction. For corporate and municipal bonds and for common stock, settlement is T + 3. For U.S. Treasury securities, however, trades settle regular-way on the next business day (T + 1). In either case, trade confirmations must be delivered to customers, who are encouraged to review them for accuracy and keep them for their records. Trade confirmations must include the following information:

- Date and time of the transaction (or furnish the time upon request)
- Identity of the securities purchased or sold
- Price of the securities purchased or sold
- Number of shares/units

- Whether member acted as an agent or principal—if principal, indicate if acting as a market maker in the security
- If acting as agent: name of the person from whom security was purchased or to whom it was sold (or furnish upon request), and the amount of any remuneration received

BEST EXECUTION

The securities regulators do not allow member firms to gouge their customers. FINRA rules require broker-dealers and their agents to use "reasonable diligence to ascertain the best market for the subject security" and get the transaction done on terms "as favorable as possible under prevailing market conditions." The fairness of transactions with customers is a major regulator concern. To determine the fairness that a brokerage customer received, the following factors are taken into consideration:

- The character of the market for the security (price, volatility, liquidity, etc.)
- The size and type of transaction
- The number of markets checked
- Accessibility of the quotation
- The terms and conditions of the order as communicated to the member and associated persons

In other words, there are some stocks that trade infrequently and only on the "Non-NASDAQ Over-the-Counter Market." The liquidity and volatility of these stocks could easily justify a price not as good as the customer had hoped. On the other hand, a stock as liquid as MSFT should not involve large markups or markdowns to the customer.

FINRA rules also prohibit the violation known as **interpositioning.** This violation entails involving a third party in a transaction that is not necessary and in a way that hurts the customer. As FINRA rules state:

> In any transaction for or with a customer or a customer of
> another broker-dealer, no member or person associated with a
> member shall interject a third party between the member and
> the best market for the subject security in a manner incon-
> sistent with this rule.

The rule also says that when a firm has to use a third party to get the transaction done—as they often do for municipal bonds—the burden of showing the necessity of the third party and the benefit to the customer would be on the member, should FINRA ever get curious.

ACCOUNT STATEMENTS

Member firms have to send to their customers at least quarterly **account statements** that show the current values for cash and securities, and any activity that took place since the last statement in terms of purchases and sales or deposits and withdrawals of securities. As the NASD rule stipulates:

> Each general securities member shall, with a frequency of not
> less than once every calendar quarter, send a statement of
> account ("account statement") containing a description of any
> securities positions, money balances, or account activity to
> each customer whose account had a security position, money
> balance, or account activity during the period since the last
> such statement was sent to the customer.

The account statement also needs to contain a statement to the customer "that advises the customer to report promptly any inaccuracy or discrepancy in that person's account to his or her brokerage firm."

COMPENSATION TO REGISTERED REPRESENTATIVES

The Securities Exchange Act of 1934 requires broker-dealers to keep detailed records regarding the compensation paid to their registered representatives. As one of the rules under this Act stipulates, member firms must make and keep a record:

> as to each associated person listing each purchase and sale
> of a security attributable, for compensation purposes, to
> that associated person. The record shall include the amount
> of compensation if monetary and a description of the compen-
> sation if non-monetary. In lieu of making this record, a
> member, broker or dealer may elect to produce the required
> information promptly upon request of a representative of a
> securities regulatory authority.

The firm also needs a record:

> of all agreements pertaining to the relationship between each
> associated person and the member, broker or dealer including a
> summary of each associated person's compensation arrangement
> or plan with the member, broker or dealer, including commission
> and concession schedules and, to the extent that compensation
> is based on factors other than remuneration per trade, the
> method by which the compensation is determined.

Also, as a registered representative you may not share your commissions with anyone who is not a registered agent and who does not work for your firm or an affiliated firm. And, in any case, your supervisor would have to approve of the sharing of commissions or payment of referral fees. So, if you get a test question about a big customer who wants the agent to "rebate a third of his commissions" to him to help offset the large purchase price, remember that this is not an acceptable business practice.

NASD RULE. SUPERVISION

A member firm has to monitor its **registered principals**, who have to monitor their **registered representatives**. Both registered representatives and their principals/supervisors are "associated persons of a member firm." This rule is pretty clear all by itself:

> Each member shall establish and maintain a system to supervise the activities of each registered representative, registered principal, and other associated person that is reasonably designed to achieve compliance with applicable securities laws and regulations, and with applicable NASD/FINRA Rules.

WRITTEN PROCEDURES

> Each member shall establish, maintain, and enforce written procedures to supervise the types of business in which it engages and to supervise the activities of registered representatives, registered principals, and other associated persons that are reasonably designed to achieve compliance with applicable securities laws and regulations, and with the applicable Rules of FINRA/NASD.

> A copy of a member's written supervisory procedures shall be kept and maintained in each OSJ and at each location where supervisory activities are conducted on behalf of the member. Each member shall amend its written supervisory procedures as appropriate within a reasonable time after changes occur in applicable securities laws and regulations, including the Rules of this Association, and as changes occur in its supervisory system, and each member shall be responsible for communicating amendments through its organization.

> When a member firm violates the conduct rules, they usually get penalized for violating the rule and also for not having adequate supervisory systems in place that should have prevented what happened from happening.

The exam outline also mentions the definitions of **OSJ** and **branch office**, and I'm going to just let FINRA explain it by copying and pasting:

> (g) Definitions

> (1) "Office of Supervisory Jurisdiction" means any office of a member at which any one or more of the following functions take place:

> (A) order execution and/or market making;

> (B) structuring of public offerings or private placements;

(C) maintaining custody of customers' funds and/or securities;

(D) final acceptance (approval) of new accounts on behalf of the member;

(E) review and endorsement of customer orders, pursuant to paragraph (d) above;

(F) final approval of communications for use by persons associated with the member, pursuant to Rule 2210(b)(1); or

(G) responsibility for supervising the activities of persons associated with the member at one or more other branch offices of the member.

(2)(A) "Branch Office" means any location identified by any means to the public or customers as a location at which the member conducts an investment banking or securities business, excluding:

(i) any location identified in a telephone directory line listing or on a business card or letterhead, which listing, card, or letterhead also sets forth the address and telephone number of the branch office or OSJ of the firm from which the person(s) conducting business at the non-branch locations are directly supervised;

(ii) any location referred to in a member advertisement, as this term is defined in Rule 2210, by its local telephone number and/or local post office box provided that such reference may not contain the address of the non-branch location and, further, that such reference also sets forth the address and telephone number of the branch office or OSJ of the firm from which the person(s) conducting business at the non-branch location are directly supervised; or

(iii) any location identified by address in a member's sales literature, as this term is defined in Rule 2210, provided that the sales literature also sets forth the address and telephone number of the branch office or OSJ of the firm from which the person(s) conducting business at the non-branch locations are directly supervised.

(iv) any location where a person conducts business on behalf of the member occasionally and exclusively by

> appointment for the convenience of customers, so long as each customer is provided with the address and telephone number of the branch office or OSJ of the firm from which the person conducting business at the non-branch location is directly supervised.

There.

FINRA CODE OF PROCEDURE

We will look at many rules and regulations in Chapter 4, but we have already looked at several member conduct rules at this point. So, let's say somebody gets caught violating these rules—what happens then? FINRA investigates violations of the conduct rules through **Code of Procedure** (COP). When we mentioned words such as "suspend, expel, bar, and censure," those are all part of this Code of Procedure. Maybe a staff member of FINRA found out some rather disturbing information during a recent routine examination of a firm, or maybe one of your customers got ticked about losing 90% this year and then found out you were breaking rules along the way. Either way, you'll be notified and asked to respond to the charges in writing. That's why you would be referred to as the "respondent." All requests for information must be met within 25 days, so start writing. Remember that you have to cooperate with the investigation, producing documents or testimony as required. If you don't file a response or cooperate with the process, a disciplinary order will be issued without you—a **default decision**. And if it's decided that you broke a rule, you could be censured, fined, suspended, expelled, or barred. You would get to appeal, assuming you can afford the legal fees. The appeals first go to the **National Adjudicatory Council** (NAC), then to the SEC, and even into the federal courts.

But it would be easier if you didn't get in trouble in the first place.

Under **Acceptance, Waiver, and Consent**, or "AWC," the respondent chooses not to dispute the allegations. In that case the Department of Enforcement has the respondent sign a letter accepting a finding of violation, consenting to the sanctions imposed, and waiving the right to a hearing or to an appeal. If the respondent agrees, the letter is sent to the NAC for review. If accepted, it becomes final. If not, the next step is a formal hearing. Please note that if you read the disciplinary actions that FINRA posts at www.finra.org, you will find much use of the "acceptance, waiver, and consent" process. You will also find the exercise very useful in preparing for the Series 6 exam.

If the activity is considered a "minor rule violation," the maximum fine would be a relatively low amount, and the process would involve having the respondent sign a minor rule violation letter. When the respondent signs the letter, the settlement is final, and the NAC can tack on a limited fine and/or a letter of censure that will hang over the respondent's head like a dark cloud for a while.

Other times, the respondent makes an **offer of settlement**, in which he proposes what FINRA ought to do about his recent lapse of judgment.

In many cases a settlement can't be reached and there is a hearing. If so, the decision will be listed as **contested** when FINRA announces it on their website along with all the other recent disciplinary actions. Whether the punishment is arrived at through Acceptance, Waiver, and Consent, an offer of settlement, or through a contested hearing, any of the following penalties can be assessed:

- Censure
- Fine (any amount)
- Suspension (temporary)
- Expulsion (the firm is done)
- Barred (associated person is done)

If either side is unhappy with the decision of the hearing panel, an appeal can be filed to the NAC within 25 days. From there, the case can be appealed to the SEC (Securities and Exchange Commission) and even the federal civil court system from there.

FINRA RULE: PROVISION OF INFORMATION AND TESTIMONY AND INSPECTION AND COPYING OF BOOKS

As I mentioned, when FINRA wants to review your records or take down your testimony, you can either play along or find yourself a new career. As FINRA Rule 8210 makes clear:

> For the purpose of an investigation, complaint, examination, or proceeding authorized by the FINRA/NASD By-Laws or the Rules of the Association, an Adjudicator or Association staff shall have the right to:
>
> (1) require a member, person associated with a member, or person subject to the Association's jurisdiction to provide information orally, in writing, or electronically and to testify at a location specified by Association staff, under oath or affirmation administered by a court reporter or a notary public if requested, with respect to any matter involved in the investigation, complaint, examination, or proceeding; and
>
> (2) inspect and copy the books, records, and accounts of such member or person with respect to any matter involved in the investigation, complaint, examination, or proceeding.
>
> (c) Requirement to Comply
>
> No member or person shall fail to provide information or testimony or to permit an inspection and copying of books, records, or accounts pursuant to this Rule.

But, since they do have a heart, FINRA/NASD also stipulates that:

Inspection and Copying

A witness, upon proper identification, may inspect the official transcript of the witness' own testimony. Upon written request, a person who has submitted documentary evidence or testimony in an Association investigation may procure a copy of the person's documentary evidence or the transcript of the person's testimony upon payment of the appropriate fees, except that prior to the issuance of a complaint arising from the investigation, the Association staff may for good cause deny such request.

FINRA CODE OF ARBITRATION PROCEDURE

As in major league baseball, disputes in the brokerage industry are settled in **arbitration**. Member firms can't sue each other in civil court if an underwriting turns sour and one member of the syndicate is convinced they are owed $1 million from the managing underwriter, who promised more shares than they delivered. That sort of dispute must be submitted to **arbitration**, which means you get one shot, no appeals.

CUSTOMER CODE

The Code of Arbitration Procedure is separated into a code for customer disputes and a code for industry disputes. Let's look at the customer code first. As we saw earlier, firms get their customers to sign pre-dispute arbitration agreements, but they have to be very clear what arbitration means to the customer in the document they're getting the customer to sign. The rule stipulates that the warning has to look like this:

> This agreement contains a pre-dispute arbitration clause. By signing an arbitration agreement the parties agree as follows:
>
> (A) All parties to this agreement are giving up the right to sue each other in court, including the right to a trial by jury, except as provided by the rules of the arbitration forum in which a claim is filed.
>
> (B) Arbitration awards are generally final and binding; a party's ability to have a court reverse or modify an arbitration award is very limited.
>
> (C) The ability of the parties to obtain documents, witness statements and other discovery is generally more limited in arbitration than in court proceedings.
>
> (D) The arbitrators do not have to explain the reason(s) for their award.

(E) The panel of arbitrators will typically include a minority
    of arbitrators who were or are affiliated with the secu-
    rities industry.

(F) The rules of some arbitration forums may impose time
    limits for bringing a claim in arbitration. In some cases,
    a claim that is ineligible for arbitration may be brought
    in court.

(G) The rules of the arbitration forum in which the claim is
    filed, and any amendments thereto, shall be incorporated
    into this agreement.

Only by getting the customer to sign this agreement would your firm know that when somebody loses a bunch of money investing through you and your firm, somebody will not be able to drag them through civil court, with appeal after appeal. Arbitration is faster and cheaper for all involved. Claims under arbitration can be filed up to six years after the event, which is why written customer complaints are maintained on file for six years by broker-dealers. What if a customer loses money investing through a firm that goes bankrupt, or has its license canceled, suspended, or revoked? Then the customer would be free to sue the pants off of them in civil court. But, if you get a question like that on the exam, we would be somewhat surprised—though never shocked by FINRA. Oh, no. *You'll* see.

Anyway, when a claim goes before an arbitration panel, some of the arbitrators come from the industry, and some don't. The ones that don't come from the industry are called "public arbitrators." The ones that do come from the industry are called "non-public arbitrators." To simplify the rule, let's define the two types of arbitrators like this:

Non-Public Arbitrator
• is associated with a broker-dealer
• was associated with a broker-dealer within the past 5 years
• is a member of a commodities exchange or associated with a commodities firm
• is retired from a broker-dealer or commodities exchange/member firm
• is an attorney, accountant, or other professional who has devoted 20% or more of their professional work in the last two years to broker-dealers, commodities firms
• is an employee of a bank or other financial institution and either executes transactions in securities or supervises those who do for compliance

Public Arbitrator
• person who doesn't fit the bullet points above
• person who is not an investment adviser
• person is not the spouse or immediate family of anyone in the above list
• person is not an employee of any entity in the securities industry
• person is not a director or officer of any entity in the securities industry, or his/her spouse or immediate family member

HEARINGS

The arbitration panel will consist of various numbers and types of arbitrators, depending on the severity of the dispute. For a claim of $50,000 or less, FINRA will appoint one public arbitrator. If the claim is more than $50,000, the panel will consist of one arbitrator unless both parties agree to three. If three arbitrators are on the panel, two will be public and one non-public (from the industry). For claims over $100,000 or for claims of unspecified damages, or for claims seeking non-monetary awards, the default setting is three arbitrators unless both parties agree to only one. Note that even if there is only one arbitrator, FINRA still refers to him as a "panel." Why not? For FINRA, that barely even qualifies as "weird." And, since I know how much most readers love little bullet lists, here is another one, at no extra charge:

- Claims of $50,000 or less
  - □ 1 arbitrator, simplified arbitration
  - □ Public arbitrator, unless agreed in writing otherwise
- Claims > $50,000 up to $100,000
  - □ 1 arbitrator unless parties agree to 3
  - □ Public arbitrator if panel of 1, unless agreed in writing otherwise
  - □ 2 of 3 public arbitrators if panel of 3
- Claims > $100,000, or Unspecified/Non-$
  - □ 3 arbitrators unless parties agree to 1
  - □ 2 of 3 public arbitrators if panel of 3

Even though we're not in court here, smart respondents appear with attorneys and let them guide them through this potentially expensive process. Remember, arbitration can lead to a big payout to an aggrieved customer, which is something you would then have to disclose in your U4 information, which is then open to anyone using FINRA's broker-check system at www.finra.org. If you think about it, many of FINRA's rules would likely either confuse a customer or seem like something outside his concern, while, on the other hand, seeing that a registered representative has had to pay out large amounts to dissatisfied customers would likely hit home for most potential and/or former customers. Failure to appear is a bad idea, since the panel can decide to hold the hearing without you as long as proper notice was provided. The same thing happens for disciplinary hearings—if the respondent won't cooperate, the panel usually just reaches a default decision. And, for not cooperating, the panel usually makes sure the respondent is permanently removed from the industry.

SIMPLIFIED ARBITRATION

If the dispute is between a public customer and either an associated person or a member firm and also involves no more than $50,000, the customer submits a statement of claim in writing to the Director of Arbitration. In the statement of claim, the customer details the dispute, the relevant facts, the remedies sought, and whether she's so worked up she's demanding a hearing. See, if the customer doesn't request a hearing in writing, and the arbitrator doesn't call one, these things are usually just decided by the public arbitrator knowledgeable in the securities industry and appointed by the Director. The Director serves the other side a copy of the claim, and the other side (the "respondent") sends its written response to the Director and the customer within 45 days, including documentation to support his side of the story if he wants. The arbitrator examines the facts of the case and makes his decision promptly.

The amount of $50,000 is a big deal here, and if the amount of monetary damages rises above $50,000 during the process, the claim would no longer be eligible for simplified arbitration.

AWARDS

Arbitration is supposed to be as fast and painless as possible, so the arbitrator(s) "shall endeavor to render an award within 30 business days from the date the record is closed." The **award** is a document summarizing the dispute, the damages sought and damages awarded, and the names and signatures of the arbitrators. Surely, since it's FINRA arbitration it's a private matter, right? Not. As the FINRA manual states, "All awards and their contents shall be made publicly available." That's why the firms might want to settle—settlements are private affairs. How long would the respondent have to pay an award? 30 days. What if the other side doesn't cough it up right away? Oh, we'll get them to turn their heads and cough, all right. As the FINRA manual says:

```
An award shall bear interest from the date of the award: (1)
if not paid within thirty (30) days of receipt, (2) if the
award is the subject of a motion to vacate which is denied,
or (3) as specified by the arbitrator(s) in the award. Interest
shall be assessed at the legal rate, if any, then prevailing
in the state where the award was rendered, or at a rate set
by the arbitrator(s).
```

If the respondent simply won't pay, they will end up being disciplined by FINRA under Code of Procedure, and you can go after them like any other creditor, reporting the debt to the big credit reporting agencies.

Although, really, you'd probably rather just get the check and cash it.

FINRA rules require agents and broker-dealers to report within 30 days whenever the firm or an associated person has been found to have violated securities laws, rules, or regulations, has been named in a written customer complaint, or has been the subject of arbitration, litigation, or a settlement involving in excess of $15,000. See, as a registered representative, your Form U4 information is made public through FINRA's BrokerCheck system. Obviously, no registered representative wants disciplinary problems or arbitration awards paid out to angry customers being disclosed through the FINRA website. Unfortunately, any such situations *will* go into that system. If an agent fails to update his U4 information promptly, we will see that he has now been barred by FINRA for that and, most likely, for failing to cooperate with the disciplinary process that proceeds from these unfortunate oversights.

Some of the disclosures agents must make could happen outside the industry. For example, if an agent were charged with felony possession of a controlled substance with intent to distribute, he might be tempted to conceal that fact from his employer and FINRA. Unfortunately, when his employer and FINRA do, in fact, find out, there will be even more disclosures going into the CRD system, allowing the public to find the special report on this individual who *used to be registered* with a FINRA member broker-dealer.

The only way to get a customer dispute **expunged** from the Central Registration Depository (CRD) system is through the courts. As FINRA rules state, members or associated persons who want to get a customer dispute expunged "must obtain an order from a court of competent jurisdiction directing such expungement or confirming an arbitration award containing expungement relief." If a member or associated person goes to court seeking an expungement, they must name FINRA as one of the parties and serve FINRA with all appropriate documents—unless FINRA formally waives that requirement.

And, if you're talking about a criminal conviction being expunged, this is tricky. Although the conviction could be expunged by the courts, Form U4 still asks if the individual has ever been *charged* with any felony or any misdemeanor relevant to the securities industry. Therefore, even though the individual could say "No" to the question of whether he's ever been convicted of such a crime, he would still have to answer "Yes" to the question of whether he was ever charged with such a crime.

As you can see, criminal and regulatory problems, as well as customer disputes, lead to nothing good. The firm and/or the agent either properly disclose everything and live with the consequences, or they try to conceal the information and usually end up with a set of even worse consequences that usually involve a permanent vacation from the securities industry. As many parents would agree, making a mistake is seldom as bad as trying to conceal it from the powers that be.

INDUSTRY CODE

FINRA's Code of Arbitration Procedure for Industry Disputes requires industry members to settle disputes through arbitration.

(a) Generally

Except as otherwise provided in the Code, a dispute must be arbitrated under the Code if the dispute arises out of the business activities of a member or an associated person and is between or among:

* Members

* Members and Associated Persons

* Associated Persons.

(b) Insurance Activities

Disputes arising out of the insurance business activities of a member that is also an insurance company are not required to be arbitrated under the Code.

So, if you should ever have to leave a firm under a cloud of bitterness, where you feel you are owed money, you would not be able to sue. You would submit your claim to arbitration. If you fail to convince the arbitration panel that your firm owes you, you won't be getting anything out of your firm. But, if you do convince the panel that your firm owes you, say, $50,000, they will have to honor that award. Failure to honor an arbitration award, or to produce documents or attend a hearing are all examples of "conduct inconsistent with just and equitable principles of trade," which is the ultimate sin as far as FINRA is concerned. If the parties use mediation and reach a settlement, failure to honor the terms of that settlement would also be considered conduct inconsistent with just and equitable principles of trade. It is also considered a violation of just and equitable principles of trade for a broker-dealer to require agents to waive their right to settle disputes in arbitration. As FINRA states:

> Action by members requiring associated persons to waive the arbitration of disputes contrary to the provisions of the Code of Arbitration Procedure shall constitute conduct that is inconsistent with just and equitable principles of trade and a violation of Rule 2110.

The number of arbitrators based on the dollar amounts we looked at are the same for industry disputes as they are for customer disputes. However, the composition of the panel is different, depending on whether an associated person and a member are in dispute or if the dispute is between two members. If the dispute is between an associated person and a member firm, the composition of the panel is the same as it is for customer disputes. If it's just one arbitrator, it will be a public arbitrator (unless both sides agree in writing otherwise), and if the panel uses three arbitrators, two of them will be public arbitrators. On the other hand, if the dispute is between members, a panel of one arbitrator will consist of one non-public arbitrator (unless both sides agree in writing otherwise), and a panel of three all will be non-public arbitrators. As mentioned, the dollar amounts we saw for the customer code are the same, and simplified arbitration is available for amounts of no more than $50,000.

MEDIATION

Sometimes both parties will agree to try and avoid arbitration by using the **mediation** process. Here a mediator listens to both sides and delivers a non-binding settlement. But, if a settlement cannot be reached, the matter goes to arbitration. The mediator cannot sit on that arbitration panel, should the exam actually reach that deep into the test bank the day you take it.

Chapter 3 Review Quiz
(10 questions)

1. **How would you explain to a customer the significance of a "frozen account"?**

    A. An account that cannot buy or sell securities for 90 days

    B. An account that can sell but cannot purchase securities for 90 days

    C. A margin account that is under-collateralized

    D. An account whose credit has been cut off for 90 days

2. **Which of the following customer actions will lead to an account freeze under Regulation T?**

    A. A customer requests the full amount of the proceeds of a large stock sale within 5 business days of the transaction

    B. A customer enters an order to buy 500 shares of ABC, making payment for the purchase from the proceeds of the sale executed on the next business day

    C. A customer writes a covered call within 4 business days of purchasing the underlying stock within a cash account

    D. All choices listed

3. **Marcy purchases 300 shares of ABC common stock on the ex-dividend date; therefore, which of the following will occur?**

    A. Marcy will receive the declared dividend on the payable date

    B. The seller will receive the declared dividend on the record date

    C. The seller will receive the declared dividend on the payable date

    D. Marcy will receive the declared dividend on the record date

4. **If a brokerage customer wants to see the dividends and interest received on her account over the previous month, she should consult which of the following?**

    A. Form 1041

    B. Account statement

    C. Trade confirmation

    D. Proxy statement

5. Which of the following is an accurate statement of trade and settlement dates?

A. Stock transactions typically settle on the day of the transaction

B. Municipal bond transactions typically settle on the next business day

C. Closed-end fund transactions typically settle "T + 3"

D. Open-end fund transactions typically settle "T + 3"

6. A trade confirmation sent to a customer who has sold $100,000 par value of a corporate bond issue would list all of the following information EXCEPT:

A. Commission if executed on an agency basis

B. Net price if executed on a principal basis

C. CUSIP number of the bond

D. Credit rating of the bond

7. If a registered representative engages in excessive trading of a customer account, which of the following is accurate?

A. The registered representative is subject to disciplinary action only

B. The registered representative is subject to arbitration only

C. The registered representative is subject to arbitration and FINRA disciplinary action but may not be fired for cause by his employing broker-dealer

D. The registered representative is subject to arbitration, FINRA disciplinary action, and being fired for cause by his employing broker-dealer

8. Which of the following represents appropriate conduct by an agent of a FINRA-member broker-dealer responding to a written customer complaint?

A. Call the customer and invite him or her to a business lunch in which you will attempt to rectify the situation amenably

B. Offer to refund the purchase price, plus interest, for the security involved in the complaint

C. Immediately forward the complaint to the appropriate principal

D. All of these choices

9. FINRA's Code of Procedure (COP) would be used in which of the following situations?

A. An agent works outside the firm without written notification provided to his employing member

B. An agent claims that his employer owes him $10,000 in promised commissions

C. The member of a syndicate claims that the managing underwriter owes the firm $50,000 and/or 1,000 more shares of a recent securities offering

D. A customer feels that she is owed $45,000 due to poor recommendations from an inexperienced agent

10. An order ticket for a securities transaction would contain all of the following EXCEPT

    A.   Commission to the registered representative
    B.   Account number
    C.   CUSIP number of the securities purchased or sold
    D.   Trade and settlement dates

Chapter 3 Review Quiz Answers
(10 questions)

1. **ANSWER:** D

   WHY: a "frozen account" is not as dire as it sounds—the customer will simply need to have the cash in the account before a purchase order can be accepted and executed over the next 90 days.

2. **ANSWER:** B

   WHY: among these answer choices the only problem is trying to pay for a purchase by selling the stock—that's called freeriding and leads to an account freeze. Customers are entitled to their cash once the trade settles, and writing covered calls has nothing to do with frozen accounts.

3. **ANSWER:** C

   WHY: the term "ex-dividend" means the stock trades that day without the dividend—the seller will get the dividend, on the payable date, not the buyer.

4. **ANSWER:** B

   WHY: brokerage account statements show securities and cash balances, transactions, deposits and withdrawals, and dividends and interest received. Customers should review each statement for mistakes or unauthorized transactions.

5. **ANSWER:** C

   WHY: stock transactions and transactions in corporate and municipal bonds settle regular way "T + 3." Closed-end funds are shares of stock trading on the secondary market. Open-end funds, on the other hand, are issued and redeemed by the transfer agent.

6. **ANSWER:** D

   WHY: credit ratings are issued by three major agencies and several lesser-known services, so just choosing which rating to use would be problematic, while the other answer choices represent key terms of the transaction.

7. **ANSWER:** D

   WHY: churning is a violation of the member conduct rules, so it can lead to disciplinary action and being fired for cause. Also, customers who lose money due to their registered representative's mishandling of the account typically do file arbitration claims.

8. **ANSWER:** C

   WHY: there are a few reasons you don't want to try and handle the situation with a business lunch and a personal check slipped under the table. First, the customer will cash the check. Second, the customer will file a complaint. Third, you will be disciplined by FINRA. Fourth, you will often be fired for cause by your employer. Much simpler to just face up to the complaint and forward it to your supervisor.

9. **ANSWER:** A

   WHY: disputes are handled under arbitration, while violations of the rules are handled under Code of Procedure. Note that the agent whose customer feels she is owed $45,000 could *also* be subject to disciplinary action, but that's not quite what that answer choice was saying. If the customer "feels she is owed money," you have to conclude that's a matter for arbitration.

10. **ANSWER:** A

    WHY: the order ticket is used internally at the firm. While the trade confirmation sent to the customer would indicate any commissions charged, that information is not necessary when the trade is being executed at the firm. The registered representative's initials would be on the trade ticket, of course, if the question goes there.

CHAPTER 4

Regulatory Fundamentals and Business Development

(Represents 22 of 100 Questions on the Series 6 Exam)

At this point we have looked at what a registered representative does for a living in chronological order: opens a customer account, determines and makes suitable recommendations to the customer, and handles purchase and sale orders for the customer. Now, we need to look more closely at the federal securities Acts and rules made "thereunder," as well as FINRA, in terms of their structure, function, and important rules. FINRA still uses some NASD rules, while many former NASD rules have either been incorporated or retired. Don't worry about whether a particular rule is an NASD or FINRA rule; rather, learn the rule and try to understand its importance to customers and the regulators.

Let's start with the federal securities Acts, again, in chronological order.

SECURITIES ACT OF 1933

The exam outline lists some specific definitions from this "Truth in Securities Act," including:

- Issuer: every person who issues or proposes to issue any security.
- The term "sale" or "sell" shall include every contract of sale or disposition of a security or interest in a security, for value.
- The term "offer to sell," "offer for sale," or "offer" shall include every attempt or offer to dispose of, or solicitation of an offer to buy, a security or interest in a security, for value.
- Underwriter: any person who has purchased from an issuer with a view to, or offers or sells for an issuer in connection with, the distribution of any security, or participates or has a direct or indirect participation in any such undertaking, or participates or has a participation in the direct or indirect underwriting of any such undertaking.

Let's take them one at a time. First, an issuer is considered an issuer as soon as they propose to issue a security. In other words, once you declare your intentions by filing a registration statement or putting together an offering circular, you are an issuer and are subject to all the rules that issuers must follow. You can't take money from investors, for example, until the securities have been declared effective for sale. And, you had better not deceive anyone in any way in connection with the offer of these securities. Remember that an issue of securities could be something as legitimate as an IPO for a well-known company like Starbucks or just some promissory note issued by an individual with no intention of repaying you. Both Starbucks and the scam artist issuing worthless paper are "issuers" as soon as they propose to issue *any* security.

The definition of *sale* within the Securities Act of 1933 is exactly what you would expect to see on the Series 63 exam that most readers also have to take. You might think it would have been easier if they'd used the word "money," but that would have left a loophole that scam artists could exploit—as long as the buyer gave the seller of the security non-cash compensation, there would be no sale. Oh, no. By using the word "value," the regulators cast a much wider net. This way, if you transfer shares of stock in your S-corporation to me in exchange for my used Toyota Camry, you have made both an offer and a "sale" of securities. Every time you even attempt to interest me in exchanging a security for something of value, you have made an *offer to sell* a security. The regulators also don't allow anyone to play games with semantics here—if you solicit an offer to buy a security, you are offering to sell it. That means if you publish a website describing the offering with a link to request a prospectus, you have either offered to sell the security or solicited an offer to buy it. We can split hairs if you want to, but the regulators are saying the security needed to be registered first either way. And, that aside from regulation, you needed to provide full disclosure to all investors and probably didn't.

The definition of *underwriter* includes any individual or firm who has agreed to purchase securities from an issuer in order to offer or sell them to investors as part of a securities distribution. Many broker-dealers have underwriting departments that derive a large percentage of the firm's profits, while other broker-dealers simply execute trades for their customers on the secondary market, and still others sell mutual funds and variable annuities almost exclusively. While it is easy to remember that firms including Goldman Sachs and JP Morgan are "underwriters," the Securities Act of 1933 also makes it clear that investors who buy unregistered securities from the issuer and then quickly resell them on the secondary market would be acting as "underwriters," too. That's why there are very specific rules involved whenever an issuer does a **private placement**, which we'll look at below. Since those securities are unregistered, the SEC has many concerns about investors buying and then quickly releasing them into the secondary market, acting just like an "underwriter."

In order to offer securities to investors on the primary market, most issuers must file a **registration statement** with the Securities and Exchange Commission under the Securities Act of 1933. The registration statement discloses what the business is, what properties it owns, its financial documents, the important risks associated with the security being offered, and information on the officers and directors of the company.

In other words—exactly what you would want to know from a friend who might be asking you to invest in his company. What does his little company do? Does it make any money, and how does it plan to keep on making money? Who's in charge of this little company, and can I see the finances, audited and verified by a certified public accountant, please. That sort of thing.

Not all securities are subject to this registration requirement, however. The following securities are considered **exempt securities** not required to register under the Act:

- Security issued or guaranteed by the United States
- Security issued or guaranteed by any territory or state of the United States
- Note, draft, bill of exchange, or banker's acceptance which arises out of a current transaction with a maximum maturity of 9 months
- Security issued by a person organized exclusively for religious, educational, benevolent, fraternal, charitable, or reformatory purposes and not for profit
- Security issued by a savings and loan, building and loan, cooperative bank, etc.
- Insurance and annuity contracts (not variable contracts!)

Municipal bonds, commercial paper, and common stock in a savings & loan are examples of securities offered and sold to investors without registration statements being filed with the SEC. That saves the issuers time and money, but it doesn't imply the SEC has approved these securities or determined they are safer, better, or anything like that. In fact, while a Treasury bond might be safe, some religious or bank securities could turn out to be the shakiest things any fixed-income investor ever bought. The offering documents prepared for investors of church bonds would not be filed with the regulators, but the documents would still have to be very clear that no regulator has "passed upon" (rendered a judgment on) the merits of the securities being offered or the issuer itself. Any statement or implication to the contrary is fraudulent, and since securities are offered both through the mail and electronically, mail and wire fraud charges can be filed against slick operators trying to take money from people through deception. So, remember that an exempt *security* is still a *security* and an offer of exempt securities will often still include offering documents to investors. If any material facts are misstated or omitted from those documents, the issuers can be sued by investors and the SEC, and—in some cases—prosecuted for criminal offenses. Registration is a line of defense in the SEC's fight to protect investors, but the fact that a security escapes registration in no way implies that it escapes the anti-fraud regulations. If it is a security, it is subject to anti-fraud statutes. If it is an *exempt* security, it is not subject to registration requirements.

Remember that there are exempt *securities,* and then there are exempt *transactions*. U.S. Treasury Notes and State of Oregon municipal bonds are **exempt securities**. As we saw elsewhere, there are also **exempt transactions**. That just means that if you sell the securities in a certain way you can either avoid registration altogether, avoid registration with the SEC, or perhaps just do a "fast-track" method using a scaled-down disclosure document like an "offering memorandum" or an "offering circular" as opposed to the telephone-book-size standard registration statement or "S1."

Under **Reg A**, an issuer can sell up to $5,000,000 worth of securities in a year without having to jump through all the usual hoops. Rather than filing a standard registration statement, the issuer files an offering circular, a much more scaled-down document. This is a small offering, so think of a small, Caribbean island where they play lots of Reg-A. But, please save the rest of that fantasy until after passing the test.

The SEC is in charge of interstate commerce, meaning commerce among many states. Therefore, if the issuer wants to sell only to residents of one state, the SEC doesn't have to get involved—there is already a state securities regulator who can deal with this one. So, if the issuer agrees to sell the stock to residents of only one state, they will qualify for a **Rule 147** exemption. The issuer's main business is located in this state, and 80% of its assets are located here. Also, the buyers can't sell the security to a non-resident for nine months. The issuer registers with the state, rather than the SEC, since it's all taking place in that one state. This is also called an **intrastate offering**, which means it all takes place within (intra) one state.

The SEC is out to protect the average Joe and JoAnne from fast-talking stock operators pushing worthless paper. But, the SEC doesn't have to provide as much protection to big, sophisticated investors such as mutual funds, pension funds, or high-net-worth individuals. If anybody tries to scam these multimillion-dollar investors, they'll be in just as much trouble as if they scammed an average investor, but the SEC doesn't have to put up as much protection for the big, institutional investors, who can usually watch out for themselves to a large extent. Therefore, if the issuer wants to avoid the registration process under the Act of 1933, they can limit the sale to these big institutional, sophisticated investors. These investors are often referred to as **accredited investors**. They include institutions and the officers and board of directors of the company. Also if an individual or married couple meets the net worth or the income requirements, he or she is accredited. So, an issuer can place their securities under a **Reg D** transaction with as many of these folks as they want. This "private placement" is, by definition, not being offered to the general public, so the SEC eases up a bit. As much as the SEC ever eases up, anyway. So, a **Reg D/private placement** transaction is exempt from the Act of 1933's registration requirements because it is offered to an exclusive group of investors. To keep things as clear as mud, the regulators also allow the issuer and underwriters to sell to no more than 35 non-accredited investors. Either way, if the investor is an individual, he has to hold the stock for a certain time frame before selling it. Or, he has to hold it for "investment purposes" as opposed to buying it and immediately flipping it. After the holding period, a **non-affiliated investor** (not on the board, not an officer, doesn't own 10% or more of the company) would have to comply with volume limits on any sales of the stock for only a specified time period, while an **affiliated investor** (10% owner, officer, or director of the issuer) would have to comply with volume limits all the time because they're, you know, affiliated.

See, if you're an affiliate of the company, you always have to file Form 144 with the SEC, announcing that you intend to sell a certain amount of your stock over the next 90 days. We don't want the huge shareholders to dump too much stock at once, which usually drives the price down for everyone else who might want to sell. The volume to be sold over the 90-day period is limited to 1% of the shares outstanding or the average weekly trading volume over the four most recent weeks, whichever is larger. That's surprising, too, because you might think the SEC would stick you with the smaller number.

Go figure.

The securities offered and sold through a private placement don't have to be registered, but FINRA still requires member firms to file a copy of the **private placement memorandum (PPM)** with their Firm Gateway. The PPM has to be filed no later than 15 calendar days after the first sale is made. Or, if no PPM is going to be used in connection with the offering, that fact has to be reported to FINRA.

Rule 144 also covers both "restricted stock" and "control stock." Nothing different about control stock *per se*—it's the people who hold the stock that are different. If you're the CEO of a corporation, or the CFO, or the owner of a major chunk (10%) of the stock, you could control the success of the company and even the share price by buying and selling huge chunks of your stock at strategic times. Therefore, you tell the SEC what you're planning to do with your stock every time you think about selling some of it. You do this by filing a Form 144, which also covers **restricted stock**.

What is restricted stock, you may be wondering. Well, stock sold through a private placement (Reg D) is unregistered and therefore restricted. Restricted means its transfer or sale is restricted—investors have to hold it for a specified time period before selling it. Currently, investors not affiliated with the issuing company have to hold the stock for 6 months before selling, and then conform to volume limits until the first year is up, after which they can sell as many shares as they want. Affiliates of the company (officers, directors, 10% shareholders, immediate family of insiders) also have to hold restricted stock for 6 months and—as always—must report their sales, which are subject to the volume limits under Rule 144, always. This is one of those rules that is changed frequently, so see the updates at www.passthe6.com/updates before taking the exam, assuming the test will go this far into trivial pursuits. When selling restricted shares under Rule 144, investors must file a Form 144 with the SEC no later than concurrently with (at the time of) the sale. The filing is good for 90 days. Also, in case the Series 6 doesn't have enough trivia for you to memorize, you may be expected to know that if the transaction is not larger than 5,000 shares and $50,000, the sale can be made without reporting. Basically, a transaction that small does not make the regulators nervous as it won't impact the price of the stock due to the low volume of shares traded.

And, those people can never sell the company's stock short. They can't profit from their company's poor stock performance, in other words. And, if they make a profit on their company's stock held less than 6 months, they'll wish they hadn't. This is called a short-swing profit, and it has to be turned back over to the company with the gain still being taxed by the IRS.

FINRA is very concerned that agents and their firms sometimes help clients sell unregistered restricted securities, which violates federal securities law. In other words, if the customer does not conform to all the stipulations we just went over, but wants to simply take his unregistered restricted shares and sell them, firms need to be sure they don't help him skirt securities law in this manner. FINRA alerts its member broker-dealer firms that some customers are really companies trying to sell their shares illegally. If the customer deposits certificates representing a large block of thinly traded or low-priced securities, that's a red flag. If the share certificates refer to a company or customer name that has been changed or that does not match the name on the account, that's another red flag. If a customer with limited or no other assets under management at the firm receives an electronic transfer or journal transactions of large amounts of low-priced, unlisted securities, that's another red flag. Broker-dealer firms need to do a reasonable inquiry to make sure that they are not helping people get around securities law. The SEC has said that "a dealer who offers to sell, or is asked to sell a substantial amount of securities must take whatever steps are necessary to be sure that this is a transaction not involving an issuer, person in a control relationship with an issuer, or an underwriter." For this purpose, it is not enough for him to accept "self-serving statements of his sellers and their counsel (attorneys) without reasonably exploring the possibility of contrary facts."

Rule 144a allows the restricted securities that we just discussed to be re-sold to institutional investors including banks, insurance companies, broker-dealers, investment advisers, pension plans, and investment companies without meeting the usual registration requirements under the Securities Act of 1933. So, if an investor acquires restricted securities through a private placement, he/they can actually re-sell them to **qualified institutional buyers** such as those mentioned without messing up the exemption the issuer is claiming from the registration requirements. As usual, the regulators want to prevent the shares from being distributed in a general public offering without registration requirements being met. When the buyers are all (allegedly) sophisticated institutions, the regulators can ease up and let the professionals play hardball.

This SEC rule also states that the seller needs to be reasonably certain that the buyers are qualified institutional buyers, which generally means that the institution invests on a discretionary basis at least $100 million, or is a registered broker-dealer, an investment company, a bank, or a federal covered investment adviser. To check that the buyers are qualified institutional buyers, the SEC says that the seller can rely on the buyer's most recent publicly available financial statements, or a certification from the CFO or other officer of the institution.

CIVIL LIABILITY

Registration and disclosure help to protect investors, but whether an offer of securities had to be registered or not, the persons connected to the offering have civil liability to the investors if material facts are omitted or misstated. Think of that for a second—if you are a registered representative, maybe you help five customers purchase $1 million worth of an offering in a high-risk start-up company. What does "civil liability" mean in that sense? In terms of money, the Securities Act of 1933 is on the same page with state law, where you would be liable to the person you harmed for "the consideration paid for such security with interest thereon, less the amount of any income received thereon." So...did you happen to park $1 million plus interest in a little "errors and omissions" account? Probably not, huh? And, in a civil action, the burden would shift to you if you were the plaintiff. As the Securities Act of 1933 states, if you are connected with the offer of a security, and the purchaser relied on your statements and did not know they were bogus, you would be liable if you couldn't prove you didn't know any better and couldn't have. The phrase in the Securities Act of 1933 is "and who shall not sustain the burden of proof that he did not know, and in the exercise of reasonable care could not have known, of such untruth or omission."

Let's examine that notion quickly. If you had a Series 7 license, you might offer a few wealthy investors looking for tax shelter a limited partnership investment in several oil wells in Wyoming. Turns out, the offering documents for the investment—called a private placement memorandum—made some statements that were bogus. They claimed that two of the wells were in production when, in fact, they were not, and they overstated the production of the five wells that were currently producing. Can you sustain the burden of proving you didn't know the statements were bogus and could not have known even after exercising reasonable care? Depends. If there were red flags in the offering document, your firm—who is charged with reviewing the document to determine suitability of any recommendations—should have done some digging. However, if they rely on a seemingly reputable geological report, then they probably couldn't be expected to know or assume otherwise. But neither you nor your firm can simply shrug these things off as if the buyer has the burden of doing more digging on his own. No, you and your firm have huge suitability obligations to each customer. FINRA has a system of arbitration to handle agents and broker-dealers. But the officers and directors of a public company have civil liability to stock and bondholders who rely on the information contained in registration statements/prospectuses. If one is the CFO, it is one's job to know if the numbers presented in the prospectus are accurate, right?

SECURITIES EXCHANGE ACT OF 1934

Many securities are exempt from the registration requirements of the Securities Act of 1933, but that just means they don't have to register. Whether a security has to be registered is one concern. A much more important concern is that if the investment fits the definition of a **security**, it is subject to anti-fraud regulations. In other words, if you tell me that the exempt security known as a Treasury bond leaves me no chance of sustaining a loss, you're in big trouble. Treasury bonds have interest rate risk, so if I buy one from you at par, the market price could plummet if interest rates go up, and I could lose money. The fact that the T-bond escaped the registration hassles under the Securities Act of 1933 is irrelevant when determining if an investor has been misled. In this case, no one is trying to regulate the Treasury bond; they're regulating the actions of a registered representative who sold the thing deceptively. Similarly, if a religious organization issues debt securities to fund their mission programs, they would not have to register their securities with the SEC. However, they would still put together offering documents for investors, and if these documents overstated the money the organization currently has in the bank, or if the proceeds are diverted from the mission program to buy the minister a brand-new BMW 5 Series coupe, we are definitely looking at securities fraud.

ANTI-FRAUD PROVISIONS

Why? Because the **Securities Exchange Act of 1934** has anti-fraud provisions that apply to *any person* and *any security*. As the Securities Exchange Act of 1934 makes clear:

> It shall be unlawful for any <u>person</u>:
>
> - To employ any device, scheme, or artifice to defraud,
>
> - To make any untrue statement of a material fact or to omit to state a material fact necessary in order to make the statements made, in the light of the circumstances under which they were made, not misleading, or

- To engage in any act, practice, or course of business which operates or would operate as a fraud or deceit upon any person, in connection with the purchase or sale of <u>any security</u>

In plain English, the above **anti-fraud statute** is just saying that it would be a bad idea for anybody to say anything that isn't true, or leave out an important fact, when involved with the offer or sale of anything defined as a security.

What Is a Security?

So, what is a "security"? The "Exchange Act" supplies us with a very long and tedious list:

> The term "security" means any note, stock, treasury stock, security future, bond, debenture, certificate of interest or participation in any profit-sharing agreement or in any oil, gas, or other mineral royalty or lease, any collateral-trust certificate, pre-organization certificate or subscription, transferable share, investment contract, voting-trust certificate, certificate of deposit for a security, any put, call, straddle, option, or privilege on any security, certificate of deposit, or group or index of securities (including any interest therein or based on the value thereof), or any put, call, straddle, option, or privilege entered into on a national securities exchange relating to foreign currency, or in general, any instrument commonly known as a "security"; or any certificate of interest or participation in, temporary or interim certificate for, receipt for, or warrant or right to subscribe to or purchase, any of the foregoing; but shall not include currency or any note, draft, bill of exchange, or banker's acceptance which has a maturity at the time of issuance of not exceeding nine months, exclusive of days of grace, or any renewal thereof the maturity of which is likewise limited.

The few who actually read the above list may have noticed that "investment contract" is listed as an example of a security. Since attorneys often tried to argue that the investment their client was offering/selling was not even a security, the regulators went around and around until we finally reached the Supreme Court's **Howey Decision**. The Howey Decision defined an **investment contract** as:

- An investment of money
  - □ in a common enterprise
  - □ with an expectation of profits
  - □ derived through the efforts of others

That casts a wide net, doesn't it? It clearly describes shares of stock in Microsoft. If I purchase 1,000 shares of MSFT, that's an investment of money in a common enterprise whereby I hope to benefit through the efforts of others. But, the definition would also include some things you might not think of right off. For example, if an Iowa farmer needed to raise $500,000 to expand his soybean and hog farming operation, maybe he prints up 10 fancy-looking certificates. Each one costs $50,000 and gives the investor a 3% ownership stake in the farming operation's profits. That's an investment of money in a common enterprise whereby each investor hopes to benefit solely through the efforts of others—the farmer. The investors aren't getting up at 5 a.m. on a cold, February morning in Iowa to feed the livestock, right? They're neither farm hands nor managers, and what they just bought was an "investment contract," which is one example of a "security" as listed in the Securities Exchange Act of 1934. So, if the farmer gives the investors offering documents with inflated profits or exaggerated crop yields, he has probably committed securities fraud. Fraud can carry criminal penalties and civil liabilities to the investors. But, on the other hand, if the investment of money is not a security, it is not subject to anti-fraud statutes under securities law. The following investments are not securities:

- Fixed annuities
- Whole life, term life
- Commodities futures contracts

But, if those aren't securities, who is going to regulate them to make sure investors don't get burned? Luckily, we already have insurance regulators for the insurance products and commodities regulators for the commodities futures. The securities regulators only want to regulate *securities*.

So, why is a fixed annuity not a security when a variable annuity is? A fixed annuity is just an insurance contract guaranteed by an insurance company's general account. Money is not really at risk when you buy a fixed annuity—the insurance company guarantees a certain rate of return and has to live up to the guarantee. But, once they start tying contract values to the wild ups and downs of the stock and bond markets—look out. Anything can happen. This is no longer an insurance contract; it is an investment of money into various mutual-fund-like subaccounts, so it needs to be registered and regulated as a security.

The most important concept in securities regulations is that if the investment of money fits the definition of a "security," and this security is "offered" and/or "sold" through any deceptive or manipulative device, that constitutes " securities fraud," and the regulators simply will not tolerate it. In order to protect investors, the regulators make securities issuers fill out registration statements and pay fees before anybody does anything. Unless the security or the transaction is exempt, let's see the registration statements.

SECTION 17 – RECORDS AND REPORTS

This section of the Securities Exchange Act of 1934 dictates that broker-dealers must file a balance sheet and income statement certified by a registered public accounting firm and any other documents the SEC rules say are needed to determine if the firm is in sound financial condition. Broker-dealers also need to send a certified balance sheet to their customers and any other document the SEC decides ought to be sent, as well. Unless they don't have to, because the very next paragraph says that the SEC can exempt certain broker-dealers if it's "consistent with the public interest and the protection of investors."

DEFINITIONS UNDER THE ACT OF 1934

The exam may want you to distinguish a "**broker**" from a "**dealer**." The same question will likely appear on most Series 63 exams, as well. It's quite simple. A broker-dealer is a firm that can either help you buy and sell securities, or they can take the other side of the transaction with you. If they act as a "broker" that means they charge a commission for finding a buyer or seller for your security. They take no risk here, as they hold no inventory. Or, they could take the other side of the transaction for you, acting as a dealer. That means they can sell you some of their stock for a markup or buy some of yours at a markdown. When they send a trade confirmation, they will indicate whether they acted as a broker/agent, or as a dealer/principal. The textbook definition of "broker" is "any person engaged in the business of effecting transactions in securities for the account of others." The definition of "dealer" is "any person engaged in the business of effecting transactions in securities for its own account." Shockingly, the definition of "broker-dealer" is "any person engaged in the business of effecting transactions in securities for the account of others or its own account." Some firms are only brokers, carrying no inventory. If they're a broker-dealer, they can—get this—act as either a broker or a dealer on any particular transaction.

SECURITIES AND EXCHANGE COMMISSION

The **Securities Exchange Act of 1934** established the **SEC** as the ultimate securities regulator. Remember, these folks aren't just an SRO (**self-regulatory organization**) such as FINRA. These folks comprise a federal government entity. They're real close pals with the Attorney General's office, so if the SEC isn't satisfied with ruining your career and extracting vast sums of money from you in the form of civil penalties, they might just turn you over to the Attorney General for *criminal* prosecution.

Of course, you'd have to be going out of your way to get in that much trouble, but it's still something to keep in mind.

Registration of Securities Associations

In any case, Section 15A of the Securities Exchange Act of 1934 requires national securities associations to register with the SEC. That means that exchanges and associations such as the NYSE, NASDAQ, FINRA, CBOE, etc., have to register. When the SROs want to change a rule, it has to be signed off on by the SEC as well. These SROs may not allow members to join the association unless the members are registered. And, they don't necessarily let everybody who wants in, in. Section 15A talks about "statutory disqualification," which means that, by statute, FINRA, etc., can deny membership to a firm if it lacks financial strength or has engaged in "acts or practices inconsistent with just and equitable principles of trade." As you may have noticed, FINRA and other SROs can deny membership if a firm or associate fails to meet "standards of training, experience, and competence as are prescribed by the rules of the association." A possible test question would have you say that any felony or securities-related misdemeanor in the past 10 years will likely lead to a **statutory disqualification**. Please note that "securities-related misdemeanor" would include anything involving money or deception: forgery, bribery, perjury, shoplifting, embezzlement, counterfeiting, extortion, fraud, etc.

Let's see how the Securities Exchange Act of 1934 explains the SEC that it empowers:

> The rules of the association are designed to prevent fraud-
> ulent and manipulative acts and practices, to promote just
> and equitable principles of trade, to foster cooperation and
> coordination with persons engaged in regulating, clearing,
> settling, processing information with respect to, and facili-
> tating transactions in securities, to remove impediments to
> and perfect the mechanism of a free and open market and a
> national market system, and, in general, to protect investors
> and the public interest;

Fingerprinting

Rule 17f-2 of the Securities Exchange Act of 1934 requires officers and certain employees of member firms to submit fingerprints. As the Act says in its rather awkward syntax:

> …every member of a national securities exchange, broker,
> dealer, registered transfer agent and registered clearing
> agency shall require that each of its partners, directors,
> officers and employees be fingerprinted and shall submit, or
> cause to be submitted, the fingerprints of such persons to
> the Attorney General of the United States or its designee
> for identification and appropriate processing.

But, of course, not *everybody* has to submit fingerprints. Persons who fit the following descriptions are exempt from the fingerprinting rule:

- Is not engaged in the sale of securities;

- Does not regularly have access to the keeping, handling or processing of:

  1. securities,

  2. monies, or

  3. the original books and records relating to the secu- rities or the monies; and

- Does not have direct supervisory responsibility over persons engaged in the activities referred to in paragraphs (a)(1)(i)(A) and (B) of this section.

Also, the following verbiage exempts those firms who fit this description:

```
Is engaged exclusively in the sale of shares of registered
open-end management investment companies, variable contracts,
or interests in limited partnerships, unit investment trusts
or real estate investment trusts; provided, that those secu-
rities ordinarily are not evidenced by certificates. Imagine
how much money could be made illegally if you and a friend
could figure out how to print up certificates representing,
say, 10,000 shares of GOOG, which recently closed around $800
a share. If you could sell "shares of Google" but present
bogus documents printed on a high-end color laser printer…
well, this is the sort of thing that makes the regulators
insist on fingerprinting and background checks.
```

SECURITIES ACT OF 1933 AND INVESTMENT COMPANIES

A public company such as Starbucks or Microsoft would register their offerings on a standard registration form called an **S-1**. Investment companies use registration **Form N-1A** to accomplish two things at once: register the fund under the Investment Company Act of 1940 and register their shares under the Securities Act of 1933. Form N-1A has two parts. Part A of the registration statement becomes the prospectus that will be used to sell the fund shares to investors. The SEC declares that the prospectus should "disclose fundamental characteristics and investment risks of the Fund, using concise, straightforward, and easy-to-understand language." Part B of the form provides a statement of additional information, which is why they named it the "statement of additional information" or SAI for short. The SEC explains that the SAI should "provide additional information about the Fund that the SEC concludes is not necessary to be in the prospectus, but that some investors may find useful."

In general, the prospectus should:

- emphasize the fund's overall investment approach and strategy
- elicit information for an average or typical investor who may not be sophisticated in legal or financial matters
- help investors evaluate risks of an investment and decide whether to invest in a fund by providing a balanced disclosure of positive and negative factors

Specifically, the following information is required:

- Objectives and goals, risk, performance
- Fee table
- Management of fund
- Purchase and sale of fund shares
- Tax information
- Financial intermediary compensation
- Objectives, strategies, related risks, overview of portfolio holdings

- Management, organization
- Financial highlights

The prospectus is all that is legally required to sell a mutual fund to an investor, but to get the investor's interest supplemental sales materials are often used as well. When they are used, these materials must point out how important it is for an investor to read the *prospectus* before investing money in the fund. If you listen closely to a radio advertisement for a mutual fund, you will hear this caveat at the end being read quickly, as if the studio has suddenly caught fire. What's the big deal about reading a prospectus? A prospectus is a disclosure document completely void of advertising slogans. Its only aim is to inform a prospective investor of all relevant facts he might need to know before investing money in the fund. If we let investors simply watch a 30-second TV ad and then send their money into the investment company—without even requesting a prospectus—that would sort of negate the Securities Act of 1933's requirement that investors receive full disclosure, right? I mean, we can't force the investor to actually READ the thing, but you do have to deliver it and at least encourage her to read it.

Remember that the prospectus is what it is; do not highlight it and do not make your own written summary of it for a customer, no matter how nicely she asks or how wealthy she is. If you highlighted sections of the prospectus, some customers would conclude they were supposed to ignore the rest of the document. And, if you wrote your own summary of a prospectus, imagine all the material facts you could end up leaving out, and all the statements you might end up making that have never been reviewed by FINRA or the SEC. Lawyers have already generated bazillions of billable hours putting these things together, so let's not try and reinvent the wheel here. Just make sure you deliver an unaltered, un-highlighted prospectus to the investor either "at or before solicitation" of the investment. In other words, either before or when you sit down to start selling the product, the customer has already received the prospectus. Your job is to answer any questions the customer might have and help him or her understand the terminology used in the prospectus—making your own written summary would be quite different from that, right? So, yes, walk your customer through the prospectus if he or she will pretend to listen for a few minutes, but do not alter, highlight, or rewrite the prospectus, ever.

In the prospectus an investor can quickly see what the fund is trying to achieve and what the important risks are. He can see the performance record for 1, 5, and 10 years, depending on how long the fund has been around. Right up front, the sales charges and expenses are laid out so investors can compare funds and fund families. While the mutual fund's portfolio is described in the prospectus, an investor often comes away with only a vague sense of what the individual securities are—9% financials, 8.2% consumer discretionary, 11.1% healthcare, etc. As the SEC notes, some investors might find it useful to see the statement of additional information, especially when it comes to looking at what's in the mutual fund portfolio.

The Statement of Additional Information includes a list of each security held in the portfolio and a recent value of the fund's total position in that stock, bond, etc. The prospectus would tell us what percentage of assets are devoted currently to financial companies, and might tell us that Wells Fargo is one of their ten largest holdings. But it wouldn't tell us how many shares of Wells Fargo are owned and what their total market value is. On the other hand, if the fund owns 41,235,800 shares of Wells Fargo (WFC) recently valued at $1.27 billion, the SAI lists that information along with each other position and its value. Any debt securities the fund holds are also listed, including both the par value and the current market value. So, while the prospectus might state that the balanced fund devotes 29% of assets to fixed-income investments, the SAI, on the other hand, would tell you every debt security held by the fund—the issuer, the nominal yield, the par value, and the current market value. In other words, if the fund holds $10 million par value (currently trading at $10.12 million) of 4.5% ABC subordinated debentures maturing in 2019, the SAI will tell us so.

The SAI also includes financial statements—both a balance sheet and an income statement—for the fund portfolio. An investor can, therefore, see what all the assets are worth—minus any liabilities—on the balance sheet, and can see how much money is generated by the portfolio and how much is left for investors after all expenses have been pulled out. The assets are the securities values and any cash the fund is sitting on, while the liabilities are usually minimal and include borrowings used to pay out investors who want to sell/redeem their shares. From the income statement an investor can see how much income the portfolio securities generated through dividends and interest payments, minus all the expenses of the fund for all the parties involved with running it: investment adviser, distributor, transfer agent, custodian, etc.

The SEC requires the following information in the SAI:

- Fund history
- Fund policies, e.g., borrowing, issuing, underwriting securities, etc.
- Is majority of shareholder approval required to change any of these policies?
- Detailed information on officers and directors
- Detailed information on all advisers and related entities
- Brokerage allocation
- Audited financial statements (income, balance)
- Portfolio securities in detail

The two documents come together again on the back cover of the prospectus, which must disclose how to obtain an SAI by calling a toll-free number, visiting the company's website, or mailing in a request. Having little patience, myself, I tend to just go to the mutual fund company's website and download the SAI in a few seconds. The one I'm looking at now for the American Balanced Fund is 111 pages long, and it shows exactly what is in the fund's portfolio and exactly how much money it generated for investors and for all the entities running the fund. For example, for the most recent year, the American Balanced Fund portfolio generated about $1.37 billion in dividends and interest and then took about $397 million of that to cover operating expenses before sharing what was left—about $978 million—with investors. That, I got from the income statement. The balance sheet tells me that the securities and cash, minus all liabilities, left the fund with just under $60 billion in net assets.

If you visit an investment company's website, you will find the prospectus and SAI for each mutual fund. You will also find links to the **semiannual report** and the **annual report** to shareholders. Note that while public companies report quarterly to shareholders, mutual funds report only twice per year, with the annual report audited by an independent accountant.

As with public companies, only the annual report for a mutual fund has to be audited, not that the other reports can be bogus or anything. It's just that a certified public accountant needs to certify that the numbers presented in the annual report have been verified.

The **summary prospectus** is the most scaled-down document used to offer and sell an open-end fund. The document must be clearly identified as a summary prospectus and on the cover page or toward the beginning of the document the following statement must be made:

> Before you invest, you may want to review the Fund's prospectus, which contains more information about the Fund and its risks. You can find the Fund's prospectus and other information about the Fund online at [____]. You can also get this information at no cost by calling [____] or by sending an e-mail request to [____].

To assist investors in getting the full or statutory prospectus, the summary prospectus must have a toll-free phone number, an email address, and a website address for obtaining the more complete document. The website address has to take the user directly to the document, too, should the test get that detailed. Finally, since this is a summary of the statutory prospectus, the information that is contained in both documents must be the same—in other words, the summary prospectus contains less information than the statutory prospectus—not a different set of facts.

GENERIC ADVERTISING

Generic advertising is defined as any type of notice that does not specifically refer by name to the securities of a particular investment company or to the investment company itself. Generic advertising would include communications that:

- relate to securities of investment companies generally or to the nature of investment companies, or to services offered in connection with the ownership of such securities
- mention or explain different types of funds, for example—growth, value, blend, bond, no-load, variable annuities, etc.
- invite the reader to inquire further

Generic advertising needs to contain the name and address of a registered broker or dealer or other person sponsoring the communication. What this all means is that generic advertising is not considered an offer for sale and, therefore, falls under different rules from, say, a prospectus or advertisement for a specific mutual fund.

SALES LITERATURE MUST NOT BE MISLEADING

As always, it would be a real bad idea to say or write anything misleading in connection with the offer or sale of any security. The Securities Act of 1933 specifically mentions that **sales literature** for investment company shares must not be misleading, either by making untrue statements of material fact or omitting material facts that need to be included to avoid misleading investors. For example, if the aggressive growth technology fund wants to brag about a 20% total return, they need to compare that to the appropriate technology index. If a technology fund is up 20% when the NASDAQ 100 is up 35%, the investor needs the whole story, right? And, of course, whenever past returns are mentioned, the sales literature needs to also point out that this does not imply that future results are somehow implied or predicted. Also, inappropriate comparisons among funds are prohibited. For example, if an aggressive growth fund tries to compare its 5% return to the 2% return on a money market fund, that would be misleading. See, the money market fund is about 1,000 times safer than the aggressive growth fund. So, the literature should take great pains to compare the aggressive growth fund to other aggressive growth funds and an appropriate index—not to bank CDs, T-bills, money market funds, or even growth & income funds.

Benefits of investing in securities and, particularly, the securities of the fund being promoted can be listed. This is, after all, sales literature. It's just that whenever a benefit is mentioned, a statement of risk can't be far behind. The prospectus I'm looking at tells the reader:

> Your investment in the fund is not a bank deposit and is not insured or guaranteed by the FDIC or any other government agency.

In case that didn't make the point, the next statement is:

> You may lose money by investing in the fund. The likelihood of loss is greater if you invest for a shorter period of time.

So, I guess mutual funds don't just go up once you buy them?
Hmm.

ADVERTISING

The Securities Act of 1933 authorizes the SEC to consider the purpose of each offering when writing requirements for the prospectus. As Section 10 of the Act states: the Commission shall have the authority to classify prospectuses according to the nature and circumstances of their use or the nature of the security, issue, issuer...and to prescribe as to each class the form and contents which it may find appropriate and consistent with the public interest and the protection of investors.

When an investment company advertises its products in a magazine, or on TV and radio, they are omitting many material facts contained in the prospectus; therefore, such an advertisement for a mutual fund may be referred to as an **omitting prospectus.**

An advertisement—which, by definition, excludes many material facts investors need to know—must include a statement that advises an investor to consider the investment objectives, risks, and charges and expenses of the investment company carefully before investing. The ad also needs to explain that the prospectus contains this and other information about the investment company, and it needs to identify a source from which an investor may obtain a prospectus. If it's a radio ad, these are the statements that the person reads as if the recording studio is on fire.

An advertisement containing performance data must include a legend disclosing the following:

- the performance data quoted represent past performance
- past performance does not guarantee future results
- the investment return and principal value of an investment will fluctuate so that an investor's shares, when redeemed, may be worth more or less than their original cost
- current performance may be lower or higher than the performance data quoted

The legend should also identify a toll-free telephone number or a website where an investor may obtain performance data current to the most recent month-end. If a sales load or any other nonrecurring fee is charged by the fund, the advertisement must disclose the maximum sales charge, and it must be clear whether the performance figures cited are including the deduction of sales loads. If they aren't including that, there must be a statement pointing out that returns would be reduced if we actually decided to factor in the sales loads.

An advertisement for a money market fund that presents itself as maintaining a "stable value" must include the following statement:

> An investment in the Fund is not insured or guaranteed by the Federal Deposit Insurance Corporation or any other government agency. Although the Fund seeks to preserve the value of your investment at $1.00 per share, it is possible to lose money by investing in the Fund.

Of course, if you end up losing money on a money market fund you might want to consult a qualified astrologer as to how, when, and why the planets decided to align against you like that—a loss on a money market fund investment could happen, but it almost certainly isn't going to happen. Most investors alive today have only heard of such craziness one time in their lives, no matter how old they might be. So, think of a money market mutual fund investment as a "safe-money investment" that isn't guaranteed by a bank, an insurance company, or the United States Treasury. It's backed up by the prudence of the portfolio managers buying the highest quality short-term debt securities they can buy that will also generate some sort of yield for the investors. If the exam asks you to compare the safety of a money market mutual fund and, say, a U.S. Treasury Note, or a $125,000 bank CD, remember that the T-note and the CD are in an entirely different world of safety—investors are not going to experience a default on these unless the United States Government basically just gives up and rolls over like a beached whale. A money market mutual fund, on the other hand, could end up being run by a group of guys who turn out to be, contrary to popular belief, maybe only the *second* or *third* smartest guys in the room—if the portfolio managers buy commercial paper in companies that then go belly up, the fund may not be able to keep the share price at $1. Once that news got out, investor redemptions would probably skyrocket, and the panic could force the fund to liquidate all kinds of holdings at fire-sale prices, further worsening the problem. So, as an investor, please tell me you don't actually worry about such an outcome, but, as a registered representative, please make sure your customer understands what could happen and why some safe-money investments are much safer than others. An investment guaranteed by the United States Treasury is always the safest thing out there, and that includes any FDIC-insured bank deposit. Insurance companies and mutual fund companies also offer products that provide a more stable principal and an extremely low chance of loss-of-principal.

DEFINITIONS UNDER INVESTMENT ADVISERS ACT OF 1940

A "broker-dealer" makes money through transactions in securities. So, of course, the investment in question would have to be a "security" as defined by law, not a fixed annuity, whole life insurance policy, etc. But if any "person" is effecting transactions for the accounts of others in "securities," they fit the definition of "broker-dealer." These transactions can take place on the primary market, as with IPOs, or on the secondary market, when an investor decides to buy or sell securities trading back and forth among investors.

An **investment adviser**, on the other hand, does not necessarily make money because somebody is buying or selling securities. Would you believe that an investment adviser is compensated for providing investment advice? If I draw up a detailed financial plan for you and charge you $3,000, I just got compensated for investment advice. If I tell you to buy five stocks and you decide not to, oh well—I'm getting compensated just for advising you.

The **Investment Advisers Act of 1940** defines an investment adviser as:

> ...any person who, for compensation, engages in the business of advising others, either directly or through publications or writings, as to the value of securities or as to the advisability of investing in, purchasing, or selling securities, or who, for compensation and as part of a regular business, issues or promulgates analyses or reports concerning securities.

And, boy, that sure clears things up, huh? What the law is trying to say is that if you get compensated for advising others on securities, you are acting as an investment adviser. What if you're advising them on fixed annuities? Those aren't securities, so you wouldn't be an investment adviser. If you did something stupid, you'd have to be busted under insurance laws. An investment adviser often does more than simply tell someone what he or she ought to do. Many investment advisers are really portfolio managers who trade their clients' accounts in exchange for a percentage of the account value. So, the number of transactions has no bearing on their compensation—their motivation is to make the account value rise. Which, as it turns out, is usually what their clients want, too. Even when an investment adviser places a buy or sell order for their client's account, that trade is executed at a broker-dealer. Some clients bypass the investment adviser and simply ask their registered rep what to do before making their own decision—if they buy or sell, the registered rep makes a commission. Some clients like using a portfolio manager to decide what to do, knowing the portfolio manager/investment adviser only gets paid more money if the client's account value rises.

INVESTMENT ADVISER REPRESENTATIVES

When investment advisers hire people to sell the services of the firm or manage customer accounts, those people have to be registered, too. These folks would be considered to represent the investment adviser, so the creative types in this industry decided to get a little crazy and call them **investment adviser representatives**. The investment adviser registers either with the SEC or particular states. When they do so, they use Form ADV and indicate whether they're registering with the federal regulators or the state regulators. They submit Form **U4** applications to the states in which their investment adviser representatives need to be registered, too. The exam might say that employees of an investment advisory firm would be considered representatives if they:

- manage accounts
- sell the services of the firm
- determine recommendations for clients
- make recommendations to clients
- supervise those who do any of the above

So, the receptionist or IT guy would not have to pass the 65/66 and get licensed, in other words. The regulators might call the folks who don't have to register "ministerial personnel" in order to scare you away from a perfectly good answer. Just use common sense—they want to regulate anybody meeting with clients or having any say whatsoever over their investment account at the firm. The guy still promising to take a look at your printer, he doesn't have to register.

FINRA (AND NASD) RULES

COMMUNICATIONS WITH THE PUBLIC

As we've seen, communications with the public have to be approved or at least monitored by a principal, with copies of certain materials kept in a separate file at the firm. Communications going out to retail investors not only have to be pre-approved and filed internally by the firm, but a copy of the material must also be filed with FINRA. Since these communications are regulated so tightly, it's important that each firm have sufficient written supervisory procedures governing the whole process. One of the more frequent violations that firms get nailed for is inadequate written supervisory procedure.

Let's look at the important definitions involved here. First, a "communication" is defined as "correspondence, retail communications and institutional communications," reducing the number of categories to just three. Let's look at the definitions for these categories then:

- Correspondence: any written (including electronic) communication that is distributed or made available to 25 or fewer retail investors within any 30 calendar-day period.
- Institutional Communications: any communication that is distributed or made available only to institutional investors. NOTE: **Institutional investors** (as opposed to retail investors) include: a bank, savings and loan association, insurance company,

registered investment company, registered investment adviser, any other entity (whether a natural person, corporation, partnership, trust, or otherwise) with total assets of at least $50 million, a governmental entity or subdivision thereof, a 403(b) or Section 457 plan that has at least 100 participants, a qualified plan that has at least 100 participants, a FINRA member or registered associated person of such a member, and a person acting solely on behalf of any such institutional investor.

- Retail Communications: any written (including electronic) communication that is distributed or made available to more than 25 retail investors within any 30 calendar-day period

So, correspondence is any written communication going to 25 or fewer retail investors. Whether these investors are prospects or existing customers makes no difference—FINRA is now only focused on the number 25 (or fewer). Correspondence does not have to be pre-approved by a principal or filed with FINRA, so that number 25 is a big deal. For example, if your test question says that a registered representative provides a handout at a live seminar for 22 investors, that material is merely correspondence. But if it is handed out to, say, 32 investors, it is now a "retail communication." Who cares? Well, retail communications have to be pre-approved and filed internally by a principal, with a copy also filed with FINRA. Failure to file these communications will lead to disciplinary action. Even though FINRA has changed the names of their categories, the following are still examples of written communications that could either be considered correspondence or retail communications, depending on whether they're delivered to 25 or fewer (correspondence) or more than 25 retail investors (retail communications):

- Form letter
- Computer slide show
- Brochure
- Market letter making investment recommendations
- Independently prepared reprint

For that last item, the "independently prepared reprint," remember that if a registered representative sends a copy of a favorable magazine or newspaper article to 20 retail investors, that is still correspondence, but if it goes to more than 25 retail investors, it is considered a retail communication.

Clearly, the written communications going to institutional investors are not regulated as tightly as those going to folks who often don't know much about investing. Communications to banks, pension funds, etc., cannot be misleading, of course, but the audience is not so unsophisticated that everything has to be pre-approved and/or filed with FINRA.

No matter how we define the communications with the public, it all comes down to this idea:

```
All member communications with the public shall be based on
principles of fair dealing and good faith, must be fair and
balanced, and must provide a sound basis for evaluating the
facts in regard to any particular security or type of security,
```

industry, or service. No member may omit any material fact
or qualification if the omission, in the light of the context
of the material presented, would cause the communications to
be misleading.

The communications put out by a member firm are a very big deal, which is why most of them have to be approved internally by a compliance principal and many require that a copy also be filed with FINRA. Retail communications have to be approved by a principal before they are used. This would include, for example, a form letter to prospects, a display ad in a local business directory, handouts from your investment seminar, or even an independently prepared reprint of a magazine article sent to more than 25 retail investors. Basically, what FINRA used to call "sales literature" or "advertising" would be examples of what they now call "retail communications." We used to have to split hairs between whether the communication was broadcast out to a general audience (advertising) or delivered to a controlled audience (sales literature). Either way, the stuff had to be pre-approved and filed internally and with FINRA. It still does, but it's now considered "retail communications," and you'll notice it's based on the sophistication level of the audience rather than the delivery method of the message, which seems smart to me though FINRA could not possibly care less about that.

The reason the test might sweat you on the difference between "correspondence" and "institutional communications" on one hand and "retail communications" on the other is that correspondence and institutional communications must be monitored, while retail communications must be approved by a principal internally before they are used, and filed with FINRA within 10 days of first use. Also note, though, that if materials have already been filed with FINRA, they do not need to be filed again as long as they are not being altered by the firm using them. In other words, the sponsor for a mutual fund files virtually all communications connected to it; from there, member firms selling the fund just need to be sure they use the material as it was filed. There is a big difference between a registered representative using a piece of supplemental sales literature on a mutual fund that was filed with FINRA long ago and that same registered representative creating his own PowerPoint slide show on the benefits of mutual fund investing. Right?

Retail communications have to prominently disclose the member firm's name and if any other entity is named, the communication must reflect the relationship between the member firm and that entity and make clear which products and services are offered by the member firm itself. Retail communications include advertising, which is why all TV and radio ads name the broker-dealer. The exception to that rule is a "blind recruitment ad" looking for employees—in these the firm can leave its name off the ad and ask candidates to submit their information to a nondescript mailing address. This makes sense, as a well-known firm might not want 10,000 aggressive sales professionals clogging up all lines of communication once they know who is hiring. A new member broker-dealer is required to file its retail communications before they are used. Established companies file most communications with FINRA within 10 days of first use—meaning no later than 10 days *after* the stuff already went out. But, certain materials would have to be pre-filed with FINRA even if the member broker-dealer is established. If the communication, for example, includes investment company rankings that are either not generally published or are created by the investment company itself or an underwriter/affiliate, the material must be filed before it's used. *What else must be pre-filed?*

When a member firm files copies of retail communications with FINRA, they provide the following information:

- Date of first use
- Name, Title, CRD # of principal approving it
- Date approval given

Not surprisingly, institutional communications are not regulated as tightly as retail communications are. As FINRA explains in a fairly recent notice to member firms, the rules on communications "permit a firm to distribute an institutional communication without having a registered principal approve the communication prior to distribution, provided that the firm establishes and implements certain written procedures for the supervision and review of such communications." So an institutional communication is treated similarly to correspondence—monitor it, have a procedure in place to supervise it, but prior principal approval is not required. A retail communication, on the other hand, is subject to internal principal pre-approval, with a copy usually also filed with FINRA. Correspondence, as opposed to retail communications, comes down to the number 25, remember. So, a seminar handout provided to 25 or fewer retail investors within a 30 calendar-day period would be considered correspondence under the new definition. Under the old definition, it would have been considered "sales literature." Either way, the materials need to conform to the rules on communications of a member firm.

TYPE OF COMMUNICATION	MONITORED?	PRIOR APPROVAL?	FILED WITH FINRA?
Correspondence	Yes	No	No
Retail Communications	Yes	Yes	Usually
Institutional Communications	Yes	Not usually	No

COMMUNICATIONS REGARDING VARIABLE CONTRACTS

Communications regarding variable contracts are subject to the same FINRA standards for communications, plus a few that are specific to these products. First, a customer must understand clearly whether she's being offered a variable annuity or variable life insurance (VLI). And in neither case is she being offered a mutual fund, even if there are similarities. Liquidity is not really available on most variable contracts, so if a customer is sold a variable annuity or variable life policy believing it makes a good short-term investment that can be liquidated for a good price, that's a problem. Contingent deferred sales charges and tax ramifications have to be made clear to the customer, since cashing in a variable annuity can subject the investor to a 10% penalty plus surrender charges/contingent deferred sales charges. There are "guarantees" offered in variable contracts, such as the minimum guaranteed death benefit on a VLI policy, or the death benefit offered on a variable annuity. But, these guarantees are subject to the insurance company's ability to pay claims. Make that clear to the customer. Even though variable life insurance ties cash value and death benefit values to the ups and downs of the investment markets, it needs to be marketed first and foremost as a life insurance product. If the regulators feel that you're selling VLI primarily as a way to invest in the stock and bond market, you could have problems. To that end, don't compare VLI to mutual funds, stocks or bonds; compare it to other types of insurance, including term, whole life, or variable universal life (VUL). Unlike when you sell a mutual fund —where you *never* even *imply* what future results *might* be—when selling insurance, illustrations are routinely used. Chances are, you will be showing illustrations that show a whole life insurance policy compared to a VLI and perhaps a VUL policy. The illustrations are not guarantees, and the insurance company has to be very careful how they present this information. Believe it or not, they can show a hypothetical illustration as high as a "gross rate" of 12%, as long as they also show how things would work out with a "gross rate" of 0%. Whatever the maximum rate used is, it must be reasonable given recent market conditions and the available investment options. Since mortality and expense charges reduce returns, illustrations must be figured using the maximum charges. Current charges may also be included.

INVESTMENT COMPANY RANKINGS

Broker-dealers sell mutual funds for compensation. Obviously, it is easier to sell a mutual fund described as being "number one," "best in its class," "5-star-rated," or some other attention-grabbing superlative. FINRA is concerned that investors could be misled by mutual fund rankings if the broker-dealers sponsoring the funds were also allowed to determine and publish the rankings on those funds.

Or, a broker-dealer could set up an affiliated company specializing in issuing such rankings and start putting out "objective" communications about the rankings determined by some "independent third party," who would, clearly, be anything *but* independent or objective.

FINRA says that member firms may use mutual fund rankings in their communications that were published by a **ranking entity** or an affiliated company using performance measures done by a ranking entity. A "ranking entity" is defined as an "entity that provides general information about investment companies to the public, independent of the investment company and its affiliates, and whose services are not procured by the investment company or any of its affiliates to assign the investment company a ranking." Three well-known "ranking entities," then, would be Lipper, Barron's, and Zacks Investment Research. If one of those independent entities places a fund as "number 1 in its class," that can be communicated to investors and prospects, as long as certain disclosures are provided, including:

- past performance is no guarantee of future results
- if there are sales loads, whether taken into account
- if fees waived or expenses advanced during the period on which ranking based, and the waiver or advancement had a material effect on the total return or yield for that period, a statement to that effect

- the publisher of the ranking data (e.g., "ABC Magazine, June 2014")
- if the ranking consists of a symbol (e.g., a star system) rather than a number, the meaning of the symbol (e.g., a four-star ranking indicates that the fund is in the top 30% of all investment companies)

As we saw in Chapter 2, there are many categories of mutual funds: large cap value, small cap growth, long-term bond, etc. Retail communications can certainly mention how a mutual fund was ranked in its category by these independent ranking entities in terms of its performance, but must not use any category based on asset size of an investment company or family, whether or not it was created by a ranking entity. In other words, FINRA does not want any investor to think that he is likely to achieve superior results simply because a lot of other investors seem to agree by putting in their money, too. As we also saw in Chapter 2, the only way for an investor to make money on a mutual fund investment is for the shares of the fund to rise in value or when they pay out dividends or capital gains to him. The number of shares or shareholders is virtually meaningless to an investor, though we could probably imagine a few unscrupulous broker-dealers trying to imply otherwise. If FINRA let them get away with it, that is, which they don't. Remember that the NAV is figured *before* any purchase or redemption orders are processed.

BOND MUTUAL FUND VOLATILITY RATINGS

As we saw in Chapter 2, bond prices react to interest rates and credit quality concerns. Many investors are deeply concerned about the volatility (price swings) of their bond holdings, which are usually achieved through bond mutual funds. Independent entities issue ratings based on the volatility of bond funds, and, as usual, FINRA has a few concerns.

Of course, the ratings would have to be issued by independent entities—not some office down the hall that the broker-dealer set up to help "support the sales team." And, FINRA rules declare that the "Use of supplemental sales literature containing bond mutual fund volatility ratings must be accompanied or preceded by a prospectus for the mutual fund." So, broker-dealers can put out sales literature that touts the bond fund's volatility rating, as long as they provide the full story on the fund by delivering a prospectus, too. The sales material also needs to provide:

- Name of entity issuing rating
- Most current rating and date plus explanation for any change since previous rating
- Description of rating in narrative form

INVESTMENT ANALYSIS TOOLS

Some broker-dealers provide investors with tools that can run simulations of hypothetical investment results based on the data the user inputs. Right there, FINRA has concerns, since these are all hypothetical outcomes that may not come close to reality if implemented. Member firms are allowed to offer **investment analysis tools** as long as the communication:

- Describes criteria and methodology used, including tool's limits and key assumptions

- Explains results may vary with each user
- Discloses hypothetical nature of results

FINRA defines an investment analysis tool as an:

> interactive technological tool that produces simulations and statistical analyses that present the likelihood of various investment outcomes if certain investments are made or certain investment strategies or styles are undertaken, thereby serving as an additional resource to investors in the evaluation of the potential risks and returns of investment choices.

Within 10 days of first use the firm must provide FINRA with access to the analysis tool and provide them with a template for any written reports or retail communications connected to the tool. Firms are prohibited from stating or implying that FINRA has approved the tool or any recommendations associated with it. If an investor were curious about investing in options, for example, the firm could provide him with an online simulation that shows hypothetical outcomes for various puts and calls he buys or sells with the pretend money in his little pretend options account. As long as he understands that any outcomes here are just hypothetical and that results may vary with each user, etc., everything should be fine. FINRA will simply want to review the tool and the communications connected to it after the firm's compliance officers have already vetted both internally. And, remember, that doesn't imply that FINRA thinks broker-dealers are bad people. It just means that human beings can get overly excited when rolling out a new product. FINRA's job is to make sure investors don't get hurt just because a broker-dealer got overly excited. I mean, broker-dealers are in general a very excitable bunch. If an investor got hurt every time a broker-dealer got overly excited, we'd have a real mess on our hands, wouldn't we?

PAYMENTS INVOLVING PUBLICATIONS THAT INFLUENCE THE MARKET PRICE OF A SECURITY

Advertising in a magazine is just fine, provided the member firm follows all the SEC and FINRA requirements. What is not fine is for a member firm to get a magazine or website to write favorable reviews of the member's family of mutual funds in exchange for cash or anything of value. The Securities Act of 1933 requires that any communication put out to influence the market price of a security must include disclosure that the person putting it out is receiving compensation. Research reports put out by broker-dealers are covered under different rules. A research report is really used to increase business for the broker-dealer as opposed to prop up the price of the stock that is being researched and possibly rated highly by the firm.

OUTSIDE BUSINESS ACTIVITIES OF AN ASSOCIATED PERSON

Many students seem shocked when I tell them that they'll need to notify their employing broker-dealer before doing any type of work outside the firm. As this rule stipulates:

> No person associated with a member in any registered capacity shall be employed by, or accept compensation from, any other person as a result of any business activity, other than a passive investment, outside the scope of his relationship with his employer firm, unless he has provided prompt written notice to the member. Such notice shall be in the form required by the member.

Notice that a "passive investment" does not count here. So, if you get a question about a registered representative who owns a vacation property that he rents out each summer, that is not covered under this rule. That is a passive investment.

PRIVATE SECURITIES TRANSACTIONS OF AN ASSOCIATED PERSON

Some people who attend my live classes seem to imagine that they'll be maintaining their independence and autonomy even after associating with a member firm. They can't believe they'd have to tell the firm about the landscaping business they're planning to open with their brother-in-law Joey next spring. They're appalled that, say, Ameritrade would have the audacity to inform their employer that they just opened an investment account at their firm. They also don't see why they can't join up with a member firm but continue to offer whatever type of investment opportunity comes up to their clients.

Well, FINRA wants all activities of a registered representative to be monitored, so if the registered representative is sitting in his office offering investors a chance to invest in his sister's new diner down the street without telling his firm, there is no way the firm could monitor his wacky sales activities. That could even be the answer to a Series 6 question asking why **selling away** is a violation—because it gives your principal/firm no opportunity to supervise your activities. It also gives them no opportunity to say, "Are you out of your f*#*#in' mind, you little piece of #*#*?" before calmly explaining the spirit and applicability of the FINRA Rule to your renegade little attitude. So, a registered representative cannot be offering securities to investors that his firm knows absolutely nothing about. As this rule makes clear:

> No person associated with a member shall participate in any manner in a private securities transaction except in accordance with the requirements of this Rule.
>
> (b) Written Notice
>
> Prior to participating in any private securities transaction, an associated person shall provide written notice to the member with which he is associated describing in detail the proposed transaction and the person's proposed role therein

and stating whether he has received or may receive selling
compensation in connection with the transaction.

Once you've provided written notice to your employer, they can either approve or disapprove of your little plan. If they approve your activities, the transaction must be recorded on the books and records of the member, and the member has to supervise your participation in the transaction as if the transaction were executed on behalf of the member. In other words, your boss is going to be enjoying free meals at your sister's diner for perpetuity, on the odd chance that he'll let you offer shares in the company at all. What if the firm says they disapprove of your activity?

Don't do it. And if you do it, don't get caught.

TELEMARKETING

So, you'd like to spend your day smiling and dialing, huh?

Careful. As you may have noticed, there has been a major backlash against telemarketing in general, and FINRA has codified how the smile-and-dial process needs to be approached. Let's bring up a few quick facts:

- Don't call the residence of any person before 8 a.m. or after 9 p.m. in the prospect's local time zone, unless that person has given express written/signed permission, is an established customer of your firm, or is a broker-dealer
- Check your firm's specific do-not-call list. If the prospect is on that list, should you go ahead and dial them anyway? Only if you're planning an early retirement
- Check the Federal Trade Commission's national do-not-call list and do not call anyone on that list
- A member or person associated with a member making a call for telemarketing purposes must provide the called party with the name of the individual caller, the name of the member, an address or telephone number at which the member may be contacted, and that the purpose of the call is to solicit the purchase of securities or related service. The telephone number provided may not be a 900 number or any other number for which charges exceed local or long distance transmission charges
- The provisions set forth in this rule are applicable to members telemarketing or making telephone solicitations calls to wireless telephone numbers
- If a member uses another entity to perform telemarketing services on its behalf, the member remains responsible for ensuring compliance with all provisions contained in this rule

Prior to engaging in telemarketing activities, the firm needs to:

- Create a written policy for maintaining a do-not-call list
- Train personnel who will be smiling and dialing
- If anyone requests to be put on your firm-specific do-not-call list, put 'em on the list
- Identify all callers—who you are, who you work for, the fact that you are trying to interest them in securities

Tape-Recording Rule

Obviously, this whole do-not-call stuff is a major pain in the neck. For some firms, the pain is even greater. If certain sales representatives have an employment history that includes working at a "disciplined firm," the firm is going to have to start tape-recording all telephone conversations between the member's registered persons and both existing and potential customers. The firm will have to establish procedures for reviewing the tape recordings and will have to maintain the recordings for three years. At the end of each calendar quarter, such firms have to report to FINRA on their supervision of the telemarketing activities. The reporting is due within 30 days of the end of each quarter.

What is a disciplined firm? Basically, any firm that has been busted by the SEC, any SRO, or the Commodity Futures Trading Commission. So, if a certain number of registered reps used to work at disciplined firms, break out the tape recorder and start taping. You can probably find a list of firms currently subject to this rule at www.finra.org.

SELLING DIVIDENDS

As any mutual fund prospectus explains, there is no reason to hurry up and buy the fund simply because it's about to pay a dividend. The share price will drop by the amount of the dividend, and the investor will be taxed. So, if you push your customer to hurry up and buy the fund or the common stock in order to receive the next dividend, that's a violation cleverly called **selling dividends**. Don't do that, especially if you might get caught. As the prospectus on my desk informs investors:

> On the ex-dividend date for a distribution, a fund's share price is reduced by the amount of the distribution. If you buy shares just before the ex-dividend date, in effect, you "buy the dividend." You will pay the full price for the shares and then receive a portion of that price back as a taxable distribution.

USE OF MANIPULATIVE, DECEPTIVE OR OTHER FRAUDULENT DEVICES

As we mentioned, the Securities Exchange Act of 1934 prohibits the use of fraud/deception in connection with the offer, sale, or purchase of *any* security. When you sit for the Series 63 exam, you'll see that state securities law is not just on the same page but sounds like an echo of the federal act. FINRA is also on the same page, which is why they decided to make it a violation of FINRA rules to mislead the heck out of investors and take their hard-earned money under false pretenses. As this rule states:

> No member shall effect any transaction in, or induce the purchase or sale of, any security by means of any manipulative, deceptive or other fraudulent device or contrivance.

Coming up with examples of "manipulative, deceptive, or other fraudulent devices" is not difficult, but it's impossible to think up all the crazy things people will do when trying to get money from investors. For example, if you needed $3 million to execute a business plan based on a communications device that is not quite ready for production, you could present a prototype to large investors with a phony report touting its many benefits and maybe a production engineer's assertion that the product can be made this quickly for this amount of money. You could do all this, that is, if you were reasonably sure the investors won't mind losing their money while you drive around in a new Cadillac CTS. I never seem to forget about an agent who took $70,000 from a 75-year-old widow, told her he was investing it in a specific mutual fund, but actually put the money into his own day-trading account, where whatever he didn't lose on bad tech-stock picks was eventually spent on personal items at the local mall.

That's manipulative, deceptive, or fraudulent. That's a career-ender, people.

TRANSACTIONS, ACCOUNTS AND ASSOCIATED PERSONS

On a new account form, you ask if the customer is associated with a member firm. If your broker-dealer knows that the customer is associated with a member firm, or if an associate of a member firm has discretion over the account, your firm must:

- notify the employer member in writing, prior to the execution of a transaction for such account, of the executing member's intention to open or maintain such an account;
- upon written request by the employer member, transmit duplicate copies of confirmations, statements, or other information with respect to such account; and
- notify the person associated with the employer member of the executing member's intention to provide the notice and information required

Broker-dealers have to go a little farther than just notifying the other firm that an employee is going to start executing transactions through the firm. All member firms have a duty to determine that any transaction entered for an employee of another member will not adversely affect (harm) the other member. The rule on adverse interest requires the executing member to use reasonable diligence to determine that a transaction will not adversely affect the employer member firm. Notice how FINRA puts the burden on the executing member firm to determine that the transaction will not harm the other member as opposed to forcing the other side to prove they've been harmed. These regulators—they think of everything.

You will soon be an associate of a member firm, so when you want to open an investment account with another firm, first of all rules state:

> A person associated with a member, prior to opening an account
> or placing an initial order for the purchase or sale of secu-
> rities with another member, shall notify both the employer
> member and the executing member, in writing, of his or her
> association with the other member; provided, however, that

> if the account was established prior to the association of
> the person with the employer member, the associated person
> shall notify both members in writing promptly after becoming
> so associated

Not only must you inform your employing broker-dealer about other brokerage accounts, but also FINRA requires employees to notify their employer in writing prior to any transactions in an account with an investment adviser, bank, or other financial institution. Upon written request from the employing member firm, the employee must request in writing and assure that the investment adviser, bank, or other financial institution provides the employer member with duplicate copies of confirmations, statements, etc.

FINRA RULES, PROCEDURES

We've looked at some specific FINRA and NASD rules. Now, let's look at the basic rules your test will be very interested in talking about. The phrase to *always* keep in mind is the essential rule for the conduct of member firms. This rule states that "A member, in the conduct of his business, shall observe high standards of commercial honor and just and equitable principles of trade." So, if the conduct is inconsistent with high standards of commercial honor and isn't fair to customers, FINRA sort of has a real problem with that. What can they do about it? As we'll see, they can fine violators serious money, and they can end their careers.

REGISTRATION

As we mentioned briefly, if a firm tries to register with FINRA, or if they try to hire an agent or principal, they could get shot down by what's called a "statutory disqualification." What that means is that, by statute, this firm or individual is disqualified. If you started a soccer league for your kids and their school friends, maybe you and the other parents write a statute that says any child older than 12 or any child with any weapons violations will not be allowed to play. Similarly, FINRA says, basically, that if the firm, the principal, or the agent has a real shaky past, they're disqualified. If the person trying to get registered has already been suspended by a securities regulator, his chances aren't looking too good. If they've been convicted of any felony or any securities-related misdemeanor in the past 10 years, thanks—but no thanks. A "securities-related misdemeanor," by the way, is much broader than it sounds. The FINRA manual explains that if the misdemeanor "involves the purchase or sale of any security, the taking of a false oath, the making of a false report, bribery, perjury, burglary, any substantially equivalent activity however denominated by the laws of the relevant foreign government, or conspiracy to commit any such offense," things aren't looking too good for the applicant.

Remember that selling securities is not a birthright; it's a privilege. Your firm belongs to a self-regulatory organization known as FINRA. If they break FINRA's rules, FINRA can kick them out, just like an Olympic committee or NCAA authorities could sanction athletes, trainers, and teams who violate the rules.

FINRA makes it clear that filing bogus or misleading information would be a really bad idea:

Filing of Misleading Information as to Membership or Registration

The filing with the Association of information with respect to membership or registration as a Registered Representative which is incomplete or inaccurate so as to be misleading, or which could in any way tend to mislead, or the failure to correct such filing after notice thereof, may be deemed to be conduct inconsistent with just and equitable principles of trade and when discovered may be sufficient cause for appropriate disciplinary action.

If FINRA is out to protect investors from dishonest financial services professionals, and they receive a dishonest application, that would be sort of a red flag. Individuals who try to conceal felonies or investment-related misdemeanors are filing misleading information and will be removed from the business when they are found out.

Failure to Register Personnel

The failure of any member to register an employee, who should be so registered, as a Registered Representative may be deemed to be conduct inconsistent with just and equitable principles of trade and when discovered may be sufficient cause for appropriate disciplinary action.

Secretaries and receptionists working for member firms don't have to be registered, but any employee who is selling mutual funds, annuities or other securities simply has to be registered.

Here's how FINRA puts it:

All Representatives Must Be Registered

All persons engaged or to be engaged in the investment banking or securities business of a member who are to function as representatives shall be registered as such with FINRA/NASD in the category of registration appropriate to the function to be performed as specified in Rule 1032. Before their registration can become effective, they shall pass a Qualification Examination for Representatives appropriate to the category of registration as specified by the Board of Governors.

How does FINRA define a "representative," such as you? Like this:

Definition of Representative

Persons associated with a member, including assistant officers
other than principals, who are engaged in the investment
banking or securities business for the member including the
functions of supervision, solicitation or conduct of business
in securities or who are engaged in the training of persons
associated with a member for any of these functions are
designated as representatives.

There are different categories of "registered representative," too. A General Securities Representative has a Series 7 and can sell individual stocks, bonds, municipal securities, options...generally just about anything. A person with a Series 6 is called a Limited Representative—Investment Company and Variable Contracts Products. This allows the individual to sell only mutual funds and variable contracts, plus something that seldom gets mentioned: a Series 6 holder can also be part of an underwriting for a closed-end fund. Just the underwriting, though, which is done through a prospectus.

Once they start trading in the secondary market between investors, they're just shares of stock, and a Series 6 holder can't sell individual shares of stock. Everything they sell has to come with a prospectus. It's basically the difference between selling securities à la carte (Series 7) or selling securities as a complete dinner package complete with a menu called a prospectus (Series 6).

Many people in my classes ask, "If I stop selling for a while, can't I just park my license at the firm until I'm ready to use it again?"

Here is how FINRA answers that:

No.

Actually, they go into more detail:

A member shall not maintain a representative registration
with FINRA/NASD for any person (1) who is no longer active
in the member's investment banking or securities business,
(2) who is no longer functioning as a representative, or (3)
where the sole purpose is to avoid the examination requirement
prescribed in paragraph (c).

So, if you're out for two years or more, you have to take this exam again, so (3) is saying that your firm had better not pretend you're associated just so you can skip the Series 6 requirement.

A broker-dealer also could not sponsor someone for the Series 6 exam just so the person could sit for the test. As the rules say:

A member shall not make application for the registration
of any person as representative where there is no intent

to employ such person in the member's investment banking or securities business.

Many of my students continuously remind me during the class, "But, Bob, I'm not actually going to be selling." To which FINRA says, "Close enough." An "assistant representative" will also have to get a license, because of the following:

All Assistant Representatives-Order Processing Must Be Registered

All persons associated with a member who are to function as Assistant Representatives-Order Processing shall be registered with the Association. Before their registrations can become effective, they shall pass a Qualification Examination for Assistant Representatives-Order Processing as specified by the Board of Governors.

(b) Definition of Assistant Representative-Order Processing

Persons associated with a member who accept unsolicited customer orders for submission for execution by the member are designated as Assistant Representatives-Order Processing.

Persons Exempt from Registration

(a) The following persons associated with a member are not required to be registered with the Association:

(1) persons associated with a member whose functions are solely and exclusively clerical or ministerial;

(2) persons associated with a member who are not actively engaged in the investment banking or securities business;

(3) persons associated with a member whose functions are related solely and exclusively to the member's need for nominal corporate officers or for capital participation; and

(4) persons associated with a member whose functions are related solely and exclusively to:

  (A) effecting transactions on the floor of a national securities exchange and who are registered as floor members with such exchange;

  (B) transactions in municipal securities;

  (C) transactions in commodities; or

> (D) transactions in security futures, provided that any
> such person is registered with a registered futures
> association.

So, if you're just doing filing/temp work, you're not involved with underwriting or trading securities, you're just sitting on the board for a golfing buddy, or you're a member of a futures or stock exchange filling orders for the firm, you don't have to register as a "registered representative." Also, before becoming a registered representative, the individual cannot take or execute trades, send research reports to clients, or accept unsolicited orders from clients. He or she could "compile a prospect list," because that would just involve somebody sitting at a computer looking up names and numbers.

FINRA also now requires registrations to be made electronically, and member firms must identify a principal or corporate officer responsible for supervising the registration process.

EXAM CONFIDENTIALITY

Some individuals become upset when they discover that my practice questions can only mimic the actual exam—I didn't actually pay a fraternity brother to, like, steal an old exam for me. How serious is FINRA about protecting the surprise element in their exams? Let's see:

> FINRA/NASD considers all of its Qualification Examinations
> to be highly confidential. The removal from an examination
> center, reproduction, disclosure, receipt from or passing to
> any person, or use for study purposes of any portion of such
> Qualification Examination, whether of a present or past series,
> or any other use which would compromise the effectiveness of
> the Examinations and the use in any manner and at any time of
> the questions or answers to the Examinations are prohibited
> and are deemed to be a violation of Rule 2110.

Since that's the case, I decided to start a little business whereby I'd text message certain "premium-level" clients during their exams for $50 per word. Unfortunately, FINRA says:

> An applicant cannot receive assistance while taking the
> examination. Each applicant shall certify to the Board that
> no assistance was given to or received by him during the
> examination.

FORM U4, FORM U5, AND CRD

When a broker-dealer hires a securities agent, the **U4** form must be completed. When an agent in training fills out the U4, he needs to be very sure that what he's filling out is the truth, the whole truth, and nothing but the truth. I have seen scores of agents lose their licenses for omitting criminal convictions or arbitration awards when asked about them on Form U4. As FINRA rules state:

> Every initial and transfer electronic Form U4 filing and any
> amendments to the disclosure information on Form U4 shall be
> based on a manually signed Form U4 provided to the member or
> applicant for membership by the person on whose behalf the
> Form U4 is being filed. As part of the member's recordkeeping
> requirements, it shall retain the person's manually signed Form
> U4 or amendments to the disclosure information on Form U4 in
> accordance with SEA Rule 17a-4(e)(1) and make them available
> promptly upon regulatory request. An applicant for membership
> also shall retain in accordance with SEA Rule 17a-4(e)
> (1) every manually signed Form U4 it receives during the
> application process and make them available promptly upon
> regulatory request.

Note that "SEA Rule" means "Securities Exchange Act Rule." Under each of the federal securities Acts, the SEC has the authority to make rules, and they have made mountains of rules under the "SEA of 1934."

As you can see, your Form U4 filing is a big deal. Form U4 is filed by the broker-dealer on behalf of the agent, but the agent must complete and sign (manual signature) several sections involving information such as:

- Name, address, any aliases
- 5-year residency history
- 10-year employment history
- Information on any charges of any felony or any "securities-related misdemeanor" such as fraud, forgery, theft, counterfeiting, extortion, embezzlement, etc.

Note that after a member firm submits U4 information on an individual, they must also promptly submit fingerprint information. If the fingerprint information is not provided to FINRA within 30 days of application, the registration will be deemed inactive.

Now, an exam question might need to add a couple of incorrect choices, so remember that on Form U4, you will not need to disclose your marital status or your education. Of course, if you get caught accidentally removing money from client accounts or executing purchase orders nobody ever ordered, you would be fired for cause, and the broker-dealer would indicate that on **Form U5**, the form used to terminate a registered representative. In other words, we'll be able to see it in FINRA's **BrokerCheck** for two years after your registration is revoked. With any luck, when an agent is terminated from a broker-dealer it's because he is retiring, or getting a job at another firm or in another industry. The broker-dealer would have nothing nasty to indicate in the Form U5 that way. When an agent leaves one broker-dealer to work at another firm, the broker-dealer fills out a U5 within 30 days of the agent's termination date. Then, the agent can do the whole U4 process all over again with the new firm. In other words, an agent's registration is not transferred from one firm to the next. U5 out. U4 in. The hiring broker-dealer would be required to get a copy of the agent's U5 filed with FINRA's **Central Registration Depository** or **CRD**, or they could require the agent to provide a copy, in which case he would have to do so within two business days of the request. Member firms have to keep their U5 records for three years, two years in an easily accessible place. The U5 information, remember, is just as important to the regulators as is the U4 information. Why? Because if an agent has a history of getting fired for bad deeds, the public needs to know that. In fact, it might be the biggest benefit provided by the BrokerCheck system.

Speaking of BrokerCheck, remember that FINRA only releases information considered relevant to the investing public. While you do provide your residential history on Form U4, FINRA does not provide that to the public. Nor do they provide your physical description, which is really good if you happen to make a bunch of really bad recommendations.

Remember that the "CRD" is a place that maintains information on all persons registered with FINRA, including information on customer complaints and disciplinary history. If you know somebody you don't like at the firm, it might be fun to see if you can find any dirt on him at FINRA's broker check at www.finra.org. It's public information; you would not be "spying." Member firms need principals who supervise the registered representatives, review correspondence and other communications going out to investors, approve every account, initial order tickets, handle written customer complaints, and make sure there's a written supervisory manual for the office to use to stay in compliance with regulations. In other words, somebody at the firm is ultimately responsible for the business of the firm—that person is the principal.

FINRA puts it like this:

All Principals Must Be Registered

All persons engaged or to be engaged in the investment banking or securities business of a member who are to function as principals shall be registered as such with FINRA/NASD in the category of registration appropriate to the function to be performed as specified in Rule 1022. Before their regis-tration can become effective, they shall pass a Qualification Examination for Principals appropriate to the category of registration as specified by the Board of Governors.

TRANSLATION: those of you who have been asked to take the Series 26—that would make you one of these principal-type-people.

Here is how FINRA defines a "principal":

Definition of Principal

Persons associated with a member who are actively engaged in the management of the member's investment banking or secu-rities business, including supervision, solicitation, conduct of business or the training of persons associated with a member for any of these functions are designated as principals.

Also note that, in general, each member must have at least two principals taking care of the stuff that principals are supposed to take care of. It probably wouldn't surprise you to hear that registered representatives have to, like, register.

CONTINUING EDUCATION

Registered representatives have to complete continuing education requirements including the **regulatory element** and the **firm element**. The regulatory element requires registered representatives to participate in a training exercise that must be completed within 120 days after a person's second registration anniversary, and every three years thereafter. If the rep does not complete the regulatory element, his registration can become inactive, meaning he can't do any business. If the registration remains inactive for two years, it is terminated. A test question might ask what would happen if a registered rep left his firm, and then re-associated with another firm, say, 15 months later—when would he need to complete the regulatory element? If so, tell the test that the regulatory element would be based on his initial registration date with the previous firm, not the new date of hire.

The firm element is completed annually. Member firms design a written training program that is interactive and covers the following topics:

- Regulatory requirements that apply to business performed
- Suitability and ethical sales practices
- Overall investment features and related risk factors

NASD RULE. PERSONS SERVING IN THE ARMED FORCES OF THE UNITED STATES

What happens when a registered representative volunteers or is called into active military duty? If he or she is away from the firm more than two years, does the license expire? Does he have to take continuing education courses in some cave in Afghanistan? Does she lose all the commissions she could have made on her "book of business"?

Not surprisingly, FINRA and the SEC are extremely accommodating when a registered representative or principal is called away from the firm to serve Uncle Sam. Here are the basic facts:

- license is placed on "inactive status"
- continuing education requirements waived
- dues, assessments waived
- two-year expiration period does not apply—exam might refer to this as "tolling"
- can earn commissions, usually by splitting them with another rep who will service the book of business
- the "inactive" representative cannot perform any of the duties of a registered rep while on inactive status

You could see a question about a "sole proprietor" called into active military duty. If so, tell the test that the same bullet points above would apply.

ANNUAL COMPLIANCE REVIEW

All registered representatives and principals must participate in an **annual compliance review**, which is separate from continuing education requirements. The venue for this compliance meeting needs to insure that participants can get their questions answered in a timely fashion. The meeting does not have to be in a live, physical venue—a webcast is okay, as long as, again, the participants can get their questions answered promptly either by telephone or email. Questions that are telephoned or emailed in must be recorded, with the recording or "archive" announced and made easily available to the participants. If it seems that a webcast might lead to registered representatives goofing around and drifting off, I suppose you're right. I'm just not sure how it differs from a live meeting in an auditorium.

FEES TO FINRA

If you get a test question asking how FINRA determines how much member firms must pay in fees, tell it that the fees are based on the number of registered representatives employed by the firm, and the number of branch offices the firm has.

USE OF THE FINRA NAME

Members cannot use the FINRA name in any way that might falsely imply that FINRA has endorsed them. For example, printing up business cards with the phrase "a FINRA-approved brokerage firm" would be a violation. The firm should simply state "member of FINRA" in a way that places no undue emphasis on that simple statement of fact. You will have business cards printed, and on these cards you may not print your name and contact info in a small font with "FINRA Registered Representative" in a big font. Doing so might imply that you belong to some rare group of registered representatives who belong to FINRA, or that, perhaps FINRA is giving you credentials like "CFP" or "CPA."

FEDERAL RESERVE BOARD'S REGULATION T, REG U

The Federal Reserve Board was granted the authority to regulate the extension of credit by broker-dealers under the Securities Exchange Act of 1934. Broker-dealers extend credit to customers by letting them buy securities on credit. The collateral backing the loan is the current market value of the securities the customer bought on credit.

No, seriously. If you want to buy $100,000 of stock today, you surely do not have to have $100,000 to do it. Heck no. Get yourself set up with a margin account, and your broker-dealer will spot you half. You put down $50,000, they put down $50,000. Bet you didn't realize broker-dealers were such philanthropists.

Oh, that's right—they charge interest on that $50,000 loan, just like the credit card company does when you take a cash advance. In fact, a margin account is a lot like a credit card, only you usually get a better interest rate because there is some collateral here, even if its value can fluctuate big time. So, **Reg T** regulates the extension of credit from a broker-dealer, and the percentage of the stock's value that the firm can lend the customer has been 50% for quite some time.

In a cash account, customers need to make full payment for securities purchases no more than two business days after regular way settlement. So, when you purchase stock in a regular ol' cash account, regular way settlement is T + 3, and it would be very polite to make full payment by then. Regulation T says that you can actually make payment within two full business days of that. And, if you're really a deadbeat, the firm can request an extension from FINRA or another self-regulatory organization, who will usually grant it. But, if the firm bends over backwards and you let them down, or if they're just tired of bending over backwards for your slow-paying attitude, they can put a 90-day freeze on the account. That just means that for the next 90 days, they won't take any buy orders from you unless the cash is already sitting in the account.

Regulation U regulates the extension of credit by a bank to a broker-dealer. In a margin account, your securities are being pledged as collateral to a bank, who is providing the loan to the broker-dealer, who is going to mark it up a few points to you. Reg U dictates how much credit a bank can extend in this situation.

SIPC

We mentioned that broker-dealers have to indicate if they are not members of **SIPC** on trade confirmations. That's because being a member of SIPC protects a customer's assets against a broker-dealer going belly up. The broker-dealer holding the customer's cash and securities could end up going under. If the creditors seize those assets, the customer is still protected by SIPC, which is the "Securities Investor Protection Corporation." A quick visit to their website (www.sipc.org) will explain that they are *not* the FDIC. If you buy $100,000 of stock that quickly becomes worthless, SIPC would like you to know that you really shouldn't have done that. They only protect your assets from broker-dealer bankruptcy. Rather than having to fight to get your cash and securities back for years in court, SIPC will distribute money to you.

Basic coverage is $500,000 per account, of which no more than $250,000 can be un-invested cash. So, if the question says that the customer's securities are worth $220,000 and there is $280,000 of cash in the account, she is not covered up to the full $500,000. Rather, SIPC covers the $220,000 of securities and the maximum $250,000 of cash, for a total of $470,000. What about the other $30,000? Get in line, honey—you're a general creditor.

Since SIPC does *not* cover against fraud or really stupid purchases, it is very important that registered representatives never tell a customer that SIPC and FDIC are basically the same thing. An investment covered by FDIC simply can't fail on you. The low interest rates you earn can annoy the heck out of you, but the CD you bought from the bank is a fully insured investment. SIPC is something completely different.

Chapter 4 Review Quiz
(22 questions)

1. **A registered representative of a FINRA member broker-dealer must update which of the following upon executing a "short sale" on his personal residence?**

   A. Form U4

   B. Form U5

   C. None, as this is a non-securities-related misdemeanor

   D. None, as this is a non-investment-related property

2. **Which of the following activities may a registered representative with a Series 6 license perform?**

   A. Approving retail communications if working at an OSJ (Office of Supervisory Jurisdiction)

   B. Approving the opening of a Joint Tenants In Common customer account

   C. Executing transactions in equity options (puts and call)

   D. Engaging in a primary market transaction for a non-diversified closed-end fund

3. **A new-hire of a FINRA member broker-dealer is completing her Form U4. Seven years ago, she was convicted of misdemeanor shoplifting and subsequently had the conviction expunged. How should she answer the question asking if she has ever been charged with a misdemeanor that is investment-related?**

   A. No

   B. Yes

   C. Nolo contendere

   D. Pass

4. **A registered representative must update her Form U4 information for which of the following?**

   A. Completion of her college degree (baccalaureate) from an accredited university

   B. Receiving her certification as a massage therapist

   C. Agreeing to satisfy a debt by paying $11,000 of a $19,000 balance

   D. Executing a call or put purchase transaction for any retail customer

5.   Which of the following activities may a registered representative engage in without notification to her firm?

   A.   Coaching a youth basketball team on a volunteer basis

   B.   Opening a brokerage account with another member firm

   C.   Opening a checking account with an unaffiliated bank

   D.   Giving piano lessons for modest remuneration

6.   FINRA's "BrokerCheck" system is accurately explained by which of the following?

   A.   A registration depository for agents of broker-dealers accessible by FINRA and the SEC only

   B.   A registration depository for agents, principals, and FINRA-member broker-dealers accessible by the general public

   C.   A system of credit for new agents and new FINRA members funded by industry assessments

   D.   An electronic system accessible by the general public showing the scores and number of attempts on each license exam for a particular broker

7.   An agent of a FINRA member firm could engage in which of the following activities without notifying her employing member firm?

   A.   Helping her sister find 10 investors—none of whom have accounts with the employing broker-dealer—for a bakery she is opening formed as an LLC

   B.   Helping her brother-in-law find 9 investors—5 of whom have accounts with the employing broker-dealer—for an auto body repair business formed as an S-Corporation

   C.   Directing a church choir for no more than $100 weekly

   D.   Joining a local health club when the firm has equal-or-greater facilities on premises

8.   Identify the one accurate statement below concerning securities accounts/transactions for agents of FINRA member firms?

   A.   Agents must notify their employer of their intention to open an account and the executing member of their affiliation with their employing firm

   B.   Agents may not open accounts except with their employing broker-dealer

   C.   While employed with a member firm, agents may purchase only mutual funds and annuities if they hold a Series 6 license, and only through an independent firm

   D.   Agents may not engage in options transactions unless the account is held by a non-FINRA-member firm

9. **An accurate statement of FINRA pre-licensing exams is that:**

    A. Only a handful of licensed vendors are allowed to send their instructors to regularly take the exams and only if the instructors teach a live or online course on the exam being taken

    B. FINRA discloses the exam content to no vendor or member firm in a way that would compromise the integrity of the exams

    C. Any licensed vendor is allowed to send their instructors to regularly take the exams as long as the instructor identifies him or herself to staff personnel as a FINRA member

    D. Old exam questions are available online at www.finra.org

10. **Marcy was hired as an agent of a FINRA-member firm two years ago. She recently opened a "total financial planning business" at a local strip mall in order to boost sales of the annuities and mutual funds she sells on behalf of her broker-dealer. Which of the following is a true statement of this situation?**

    A. Provided Marcy has the CFP distinction, no notification to the employing broker-dealer is required, but she would have to pass the exams required of investment advisory personnel

    B. Marcy may open a financial planning business, provided she first informs her broker-dealer in writing, without further securities licensing requirements

    C. Provided Marcy has the CFP distinction, no registration as an investment adviser is required, but notification to her employer would still be required

    D. Marcy would have to meet registration requirements for investment advisers and would have to notify her broker-dealer in writing, who would have the ability to restrict or prohibit this activity

11. **If a customer asked you what functions are provided by a "registered investment adviser," you could accurately inform her that registered investment advisers engage in all of the following EXCEPT:**

    A. Manage mutual fund portfolios

    B. Provide financial planning services for an hourly rate

    C. Manage private client portfolios for a percentage of assets

    D. Execute securities transactions for clients

12. **If a customer asked you what a Self-Regulatory Organization (SRO) is, you could accurately list all of the following as examples of SROs EXCEPT:**

    A. The SEC

    B. FINRA

    C. CBOE (Chicago Board Options Exchange)

    D. NASDAQ

13. **Now that you are a registered representative, many of your friends and family consult you on financial matters of all type. Which of the following people would you advise to treat the investment offered as a "security" subject to registration requirements and anti-fraud statutes?**

   A.   Uncle Lester, who owns a valued thoroughbred, and proposes to sell for $10,000 the right to breed one mare with the horse per year

   B.   Cousin Candace, who is allowing 12 investors to purchase interests in her remodeling company, organized as an S-Corporation, where the investors have no management responsibilities

   C.   Aunt Ginny, who wants to reward her long-time chef at the restaurant Ginny started years ago, with a 10% managing-member ownership interest in the LLC

   D.   Cousin Chester, who proposes to sell a prize-winning stallion to a neighbor for $25,000

14. **One of your customers has called to ask how dividends and interest payments within a mutual fund portfolio are allocated. You could accurately respond with which of the following?**

   A.   The mutual fund company typically keeps such distributions after covering all reasonable operating expenses under the "conduit theory"

   B.   The dividends and interest payments are the gross investment income that covers the fund's operating expenses, with the net income distributable to shareholders under the "conduit theory"

   C.   The mutual fund company allocates interest payments received to operating expenses and distributes regular dividends to shareholders through capital gains on sales of portfolio securities held long-term

   D.   Dividends and interest payments received by the fund are first disbursed to an independent escrow agent, who distributes such payments to shareholders on a pro rata basis

15. **FINRA's concerns about so-called "networking arrangements" include which of the following?**

   A.   If a member operates on the premises of a retail bank, all products must come with an implicit guarantee by the bank

   B.   If a member operates on the premises of a retail bank, all associated persons must also be bank employees

   C.   The firm must make oral and written disclosure that brokerage products are not obligations of the bank

   D.   With the passage of Dodd-Frank, all special disclosure obligations have been rescinded

16. **Which of the following communications by an agent of a FINRA-member broker-dealer would require pre-approval by a principal?**

    A. A brochure detailing the risks and rewards of margin accounts sent to 30 retail investors

    B. A computer slide show presented to 30 retail investors at an investment seminar

    C. Handouts for an investment seminar with 30 retail investors attending

    D. All choices listed

17. **If a customer asks what a "regulated investment company" under Internal Revenue Code Subchapter M is, you would accurately respond with which of the following?**

    A. A mutual fund that distributes a minimum of 90% of net investment income

    B. A mutual fund that is registered under the Investment Company Act of 1940

    C. An unregistered, continuously offered, non-diversified closed-end fund

    D. A mutual fund that distributes dividends regularly to shareholders

18. **Who may be called before 8 a.m. in their time zone by an agent of a FINRA member broker-dealer?**

    A. Another broker-dealer

    B. A prospect who indicated his preferred time to receive a phone call was before 8 a.m.

    C. An existing customer

    D. Any of these choices

19. **An accurate statement of retail communications containing mutual fund rankings is that**

    A. The mutual fund sponsor must indicate the publisher of the ranking and, if there are sales loads, whether they have been factored into performance

    B. No such rankings may be included in any advertisement, as they are considered inherently misleading

    C. Only affiliated entities of the mutual fund sponsor may prepare such rankings

    D. Projected returns may not include illustrations in excess of 12% unless a projecting using 6% is also used

20. Which of the following statements is accurate of communications concerning variable contracts?

A. An advertisement for a variable annuity may use the product's proprietary name without specifically identifying it as a variable annuity

B. An advertisement for a variable insurance contract—but not a variable annuity—may use the product's proprietary name without specifically identifying it as a variable contract

C. A sales presentation for a variable life insurance policy must emphasize the contract's insurance features as opposed to any related investment features

D. An advertisement for a variable annuity may emphasize liquidity provided there is some access to the annuitant's funds without a surrender charge within one calendar year

21. The only accurate statement below concerning a sales presentation for a variable life insurance policy is that

A. Illustrations may show a maximum return of 12% if a return of 0% is also represented

B. No projections of investment performance of any kind are allowed

C. Illustrations may show a maximum return of 15%

D. As long as the illustrations are marked "hypothetical" any reasonable illustration may be used

22. Under the Investment Company Act of 1940, which of the following meets the definition of a "management company"?

A. Any investment company with > 40% of its assets held in securities not including cash and U.S. Treasury securities

B. Any "unit investment trust"

C. A non-diversified, continuously offered closed-end fund

D. A Real Estate Investment Trust (REIT)

Chapter 4 Review Quiz Answers

(22 questions)

1.   **ANSWER:** A

   WHY: Form U4 is used to apply for registration, and is kept current by the employing firm and the agent. Form U5 is used when the agent leaves the firm or stops functioning as a registered representative.

2.   **ANSWER:** D

   WHY: Series 6 licensees can sell the primary offering(s) for a closed-end fund. Most, of course, only sell open-end funds, but that is a different matter.

3.   **ANSWER:** B

   WHY: as FINRA explains on their website, although a conviction has been expunged, the fact is that the individual was still *charged* with the crime. And, of course, any financial crime is relevant or considered "investment-related" and subject to disclosure.

4.   **ANSWER:** C

   WHY: there are a few professional certifications that would have to be indicated, but massage therapist is not one of them. Compromises with creditors must be disclosed promptly.

5.   **ANSWER:** A

   WHY: any work for compensation requires notification, as does the opening of financial accounts. Volunteer work is an exception.

6.   **ANSWER:** B

   WHY: the key parts of your U4 and U5 information are available to the public through FINRA's BrokerCheck. For fun, look up some of the people you know working (or formerly working) in the industry. And, try to avoid ever having any disclosure events yourself.

7.   **ANSWER:** D

   WHY: try not to be needlessly intimidated or confused by fancy language—the fact that phrases such as "equal-or-greater facilities on premises" appear in the question does not make them true. Remember that selling investments without your firm's knowledge is a violation called "selling away."

8. **ANSWER:** A

   WHY: agents can open accounts outside the firm as long as they notify the firm and identify their affiliation to the firm about to open their account. Your license allows you to *sell* certain investment products to customers, but investors do not need licenses to invest in securities. So, if you want to lose money really fast, you could certainly open yourself an options account, even though you couldn't sell options to customers without first getting a Series 7.

9. **ANSWER:** B

   WHY: not sure why so many candidates assume that some "vendors" are privileged or that "old test questions" are floating around out there, but both are urban legends at best. FINRA doesn't help any vendor or member firm by revealing the confidential content of the exams.

10. **ANSWER:** D

    WHY: a "CFP" distinction might lead to a waiver of the exam required of investment advisers (Series 65/66), but if a Certified Financial Planner (CFP) wants to open an advisory business, he or she is subject to registration requirements. And, if you're an agent of a broker-dealer, you can't work outside the firm without written notification, which is subject to their yea or nay.

11. **ANSWER:** D

    WHY: securities transactions are executed by broker-dealers, like the one you will soon represent. Investment advisers may perform any of the other services for compensation.

12. **ANSWER:** A

    WHY: under the Securities Exchange Act of 1934, exchanges and SROs must register with the SEC—obviously the SEC is above the mere SROs like FINRA, CBOE, and NASDAQ, then.

13. **ANSWER:** B

    WHY: looks like Cousin Candace is taking money from investors who will profit through the efforts of others. Uncle Lester is, essentially, renting out "equipment" to be used by others for potential profit-making enterprises. Aunt Ginny's chef has managerial control over the business. And Cousin Chester is merely selling a horse.

14. **ANSWER:** B

    WHY: the fund securities produce dividend and interest income (gross income) used to cover all operating expenses. After that, the net income can be distributed to shareholders— if 90% or more, the fund is utilizing the "pipeline" or "conduit theory" under the tax code.

15. **ANSWER:** C

    WHY: the brokerage products are securities and are not guaranteed by any bank, the FDIC, etc.

16. **ANSWER:** D

    WHY: retail communications must be pre-approved by a compliance principal, and any communication delivered to more than 25 retail investors is considered a "retail communication."

17. **ANSWER:** A

    WHY: if the fund funnels 90% or more of its net investment income to the shareholders, it is acting as a pipeline/conduit to the shareholders and, therefore, is not taxed on that income.

18. **ANSWER:** D

    WHY: as with all rules, there are exceptions, and in this question we see three of them. For *everyone else,* however, be careful what time it is in their time zone before commencing with the morning's smiling-and-dialing activities.

19. **ANSWER:** A

    WHY: always use logic—obviously, mutual fund rankings *can* be used, or we wouldn't have discussed them in the book. Also, if the entity is an affiliate of the fund, how happy could that possibly make the regulators, who favor transparency and integrity? No projected returns for mutual funds—we just tried to confuse you with something concerning a variable life insurance presentation.

20. **ANSWER:** C

    WHY: variable life insurance first has to be suitable as a life insurance policy—the investment features are secondary. Although the product's proprietary name can be used, it also has to be identified as what it is—a variable contract. Advertisements may not overemphasize the ease of access to account funds during the surrender period—*some* access isn't the same thing as liquidity.

21. **ANSWER:** A

    WHY: even though mutual fund performance is never projected, life insurance presentations do involve illustrations. For variable life insurance, remember what Choice A is saying here. And, of course, there would also have to be disclosure that this is all hypothetical so that the client doesn't start making plans.

22. **ANSWER:** C

    WHY: a "management company" is either an open-end or closed-end fund.

Practice Exams

Practice Exam 1

1. **Which of the following actions by the Federal Reserve would tend to stimulate the economy?**

   A. raising the discount rate

   B. increasing the reserve requirement for member banks

   C. selling U.S. Treasuries

   D. purchasing U.S. Treasuries

2. **Which of the following securities is typically not found in the portfolio of a money market mutual fund?**

   A. commercial paper

   B. negotiable CDs

   C. debentures

   D. banker's acceptances (BAs)

3. **Which of the following represents an inaccurate statement of investment bankers?**

   A. purchase securities from issuers and re-offer the securities to investors

   B. raise capital for state and local governments

   C. raise capital for corporations

   D. provide firm quotes for secondary market trading

4. **Inflation generally occurs because:**

   A. the Federal Reserve Board tightens the money supply

   B. demand for goods and services exceeds supply

   C. supply of goods and services exceeds demand

   D. all choices listed

5. **Advantages of owning common stock do NOT include:**

   A. claim on earnings

   B. claim on dividends

   C. safety of principal

   D. right to vote on mergers, acquisitions

6. What is true of the difference between the terms "BID" and "ASK"?

  A.   market makers sell at the bid, buy at the ask

  B.   market makers buy at the bid, sell at the ask

  C.   customers buy at the bid, sell at the ask

  D.   the terms are synonymous

7. An investor purchases a corporate bond on the secondary market for more than the bond's par value. Therefore:

  A.   the investor's nominal yield will be lower than the stated rate of return

  B.   the investor's yield to maturity will be higher than the nominal yield

  C.   the investor's yield to maturity will be lower than the current yield

  D.   the investor's current yield will be the same as the nominal yield

8. All of the following issue ratings for the creditworthiness of bond issues EXCEPT:

  A.   S&P

  B.   Fitch

  C.   Moody's

  D.   AM Best

9. Eileen resides in Richmond, Virginia. If Eileen purchases a tax-exempt municipal bond mutual fund from Rory, an associated sales agent of a FINRA member firm, which of the following accurately describes the tax implications?

  A.   if Rory is licensed in Virginia, Eileen will pay no state income taxes on the investment

  B.   when Eileen receives dividend distributions, they will likely be tax-exempt from federal income taxes

  C.   when Eileen receives capital gains distributions, they will likely be tax-exempt from federal taxes

  D.   when Eileen receives dividend distributions, they will be tax-exempt from Virginia state taxes

10. **Rule 17f-2 of the Securities Exchange Act of 1934 requires officers and certain em-ployees of member firms to submit fingerprints. Which of the following is/are subject to this rule?**

    I.   Director of a NYSE-member broker-dealer

    II.   Officer of a FINRA-member broker-dealer

    III. Registered representative of a FINRA-member broker-dealer

    IV. Employee of a FINRA-member broker-dealer not involved in sales or clearing of transactions

    A.   I

    B.   I, II, III

    C.   III

    D.   I, II, III, IV

11. **Which of the following is an accurate statement of FINRA rules on the suitability of investment recommendations?**

    6.   such rules cover recommendations to buy or sell securities only

    7.   such rules cover recommendations to buy or sell securities, or to pursue investment strategies only

    8.   such rules cover unsolicited orders only

    9.   such rules cover recommendations to buy, sell, or hold securities as well as to pursue investment strategies

12. **The registration statement for an issue of securities has just been declared effective by the SEC. This means:**

    A.   the SEC has declared the issue an effective investment opportunity for non-institutional investors

    B.   the SEC has reviewed the registration statement and is allowing sales to commence

    C.   the SEC has approved the securities

    D.   the SEC has determined that the disclosure provided in the registration statement is complete and most likely accurate

13. **Aunt Mildred purchased 392 shares of the XLT Value Fund in 1983, with the NAV at $9.92 and the POP at $ Aunt Mildred dies and wills all shares to you. On the date of death the NAV is $ If you redeem the shares 4 months later with the NAV at $00 and the POP at $25, your capital gain will be:**

    A.   short-term gain of $3.00 per share

    B.   long-term gain of $1.00 per share

    C.   long-term gain of $3.33 per share

    D.   short-term gain of $1.00 per share

14. **Mason Myer purchased 1,000 shares of MMM on January 1 of last year. On December 31 of last year, Mason sells the shares for a $300 capital gain. If the trade settles on January 4 of this year, which of the following accurately describes the tax consequences?**

    A.   the gain will be considered long-term

    B.   the gain will be considered short-term

    C.   Mason will report the gain or loss for this year's taxes

    D.   the gain will be treated as dividend income

15. **If an investor elects to have dividend and capital gains distributions from a mutual fund paid in cash, rather than reinvesting into new shares, within a 401(k) or Traditional IRA plan, which of the following best describes the tax ramifications of this decision?**

    A.   the decision will have no ramifications

    B.   the dividends will be taxed as long-term capital gains

    C.   the long-term capital gains will be taxed as long-term capital gains

    D.   dividends will grow tax-deferred, but capital gains will be taxed annually

16. **If the owner of a variable annuity contract dies during the accumulation phase:**

    A.   the surrender value is maintained in the separate account in order to offset miscalculations of mortality risk on the part of the actuary

    B.   the beneficiary receives proceeds tax-free

    C.   the beneficiary must pay tax on the proceeds

    D.   the beneficiary must pay tax at her ordinary income rate on the excess above cost basis

17. **Withdrawals from a Traditional IRA must begin:**

    A.   when the individual turns 59½

    B.   when the individual turns 70½

    C.   on April 1 of the year that the individual turns 70½

    D.   on April 1 of the year following the year that the individual turns 70½

18. **Heather is a college student who earned $1,300 last year waiting tables and also earned $600 selling online classified ads. If Heather also received $1,400 in T-note interest, she may contribute how much to her Roth IRA?**

    A. $3,300

    B. $600

    C. $1,900

    D. $5,500

19. **You have contributed to your Traditional IRA for each of the past four years. You recently took a job with an employer paying you $27,000 per year. If you participate in the employer's defined benefit pension plan, what is true of your IRA?**

    A.   it must be closed

    B.   it may remain open, but no contributions are allowed for five years

    C.   you may continue to make pre-tax contributions to your IRA

    D.   you may make only after-tax contributions to your IRA

20. **Your client's 73-year-old mother passes away, with your client named as beneficiary on the IRA account. Your client may receive the proceeds:**

    A.   over the life expectancy of his mother

    B.   over his own life expectancy

    C.   the longer of his life expectancy or that of the account owner's

    D.   tax-free

21. **Jill originally invested $9,000 into the VanWhitman Value Fund. She has since reinvested dividend distributions of $1,000 and capital gains distributions of $500. If Jill currently holds 1,000 shares of the fund, her cost basis is:**

    A.   indeterminable

    B. $10.50 per share

    C. $10.00 per share plus sales charges

    D. $11.50 per share plus commissions

22. **Which of the following statements accurately describes the taxation of capital gains?**

    A.   a profit realized on a stock held for 11 months is currently taxed at the investor's ordinary income rate

    B.   a loss realized on a bond held for 13 months is treated as a short-term capital gain

    C.   commissions are subtracted from the purchase price and added to the sales price of stock to determine cost basis and proceeds

    D.   investors offset long-term gains with short-term losses, and short-term gains with long-term losses

23. Daniella contributed $50,000 into a non-qualified variable annuity at age Nine years later Daniella takes a random withdrawal of $15,000 with the account value at $75,000. Her tax liability on the withdrawal is:

    A.   none, as her contributions exceed the amount withdrawn

    B.   none, as she has held the investment longer than 12 months plus 1 day

    C.   partially subject to ordinary income rates

    D.   ordinary income rates on $15,000

24. Which of the following statements accurately describe(s) the tax implications of insurance contracts?

    A.   the policyholder may surrender the part of cash value representing net premiums paid into the contract tax-free

    B.   loans against the policy are charged interest, and both the principal and interest reduce the contract values

    C.   death benefits are not taxable to the beneficiary, but are includable in the insured's estate for purposes of estate taxes

    D.   all choices listed

25. Which of the following professionals least likely meets the definition of "investment adviser"?

    A.   person providing advice on Real Estate Investment Trusts for a flat fee

    B.   person providing advice on fixed annuities for a flat fee

    C.   person providing portfolio management for 150 basis points

    D.   person selling reports on small cap equities to certain large pension funds

26. An omitting prospectus for a mutual fund containing performance data must include a legend disclosing all of the following EXCEPT:

    A.   The performance data quoted represent past performance

    B.   Past performance does not guarantee future results

    C.   The investment return and principal value of an investment will fluctuate so that an investor's shares, when redeemed, may be worth more or less than their original cost

    D.   The fund has less than a 30%% chance of finishing in the top 3.0% of its peer group

27. What is true of guarantees in the securities industry?

    A.   Broker-dealers may not guarantee customers against losses on securities investments

    B.   The word "guaranteed" may not be used in connection with any security

    C.   The word "guaranteed" may be used by agents and broker-dealers but not by investment advisers or investment adviser representatives

    D.   Only U.S. Treasury bonds may be described as "guaranteed" and only as to their guarantee against market risk or investment loss

28. Which of the following would be associated with a 50% insufficient withdrawal penalty?

    A.   non-qualified variable annuity

    B.   Traditional IRA

    C.   529 Plan

    D.   Roth IRA

29. Which of the following investment companies is considered a management company?

    A.   open-end fund

    B.   closed-end fund

    C.   neither choice listed

    D.   both choices listed

30. Julianne held 1,000 shares of ABC for 13 months before selling them for a loss of $1,000. If Julianne repurchases 1,000 shares of ABC 27 days later, which of the following accurately describes the tax implications?

    A.   Julianne can be fined by the FINRA

    B.   Julianne can be sued for tax fraud by the IRS and/or FINRA

    C.   the loss is disallowed

    D.   the loss is disallowed but is added to the cost basis of the new purchase

31. Which of the following offers no tax deferral?

    A.   non-qualified variable annuity

    B.   non-qualified fixed annuity

    C.   municipal bond mutual fund

    D.   401(k) plan

32. One of your clients calls to inquire about an equity income fund that your firm sells and requests a prospectus. Since her objectives perfectly match the objectives of the fund, you explain the risks involved and discuss the various methods of reducing the front-end sales charges on A-shares. The client invests $3,000 in the fund. Therefore:

    A.   you have complied with suitability requirements

    B.   no violations have occurred, provided the client does not lose more than 3% of her principal

    C.   a prospectus is not required for an unsolicited order such as this

    D.   you have violated prospectus delivery requirements

33. Which of the following is NOT found in the prospectus for a mutual fund?

    A.   investment performance figures for 1, 5, and 10 years plus/or "life of fund"

    B.   information on the investment adviser

    C.   investment objectives and policies established by the board of directors

    D.   estimate of performance for the year ahead with the maximum offering price used

34. Which of the following represents an accurate statement of FINRA rules on communications with the public?

    A.   a research report delivered to 50 existing retail customers is considered correspondence not subject to prior principal approval

    B.   a letter to 11 prospects is considered a retail communication subject to prior principal approval

    C.   institutional communications do not need to be reviewed or approved by a principal

    D.   a form letter to 300 retail investors is a retail communication subject to prior principal approval

35. All of the following information is typically found in a mutual fund prospectus EXCEPT:

    A.   list of portfolio holdings

    B.   dividend and capital gains distribution policy

    C.   investment policies

    D.   all fees and expenses

36. Which of the following securities would be exempt from registration requirements under the Securities Act of 1933?

    A.   open-end investment company shares

    B.   shares of beneficial interest in a newly created UIT

    C.   municipal bond mutual fund

    D.   commercial paper maturing in 270 days

37. Which TWO of the following are considered retail communications by FINRA?

    I.   A registered representative participating in a chat room on investing

    II.   Letter sent to a client discussing the client's securities positions

    III. Group e-mail sent to 37 retail investors

    IV. Computer slide show for a seminar given to 45 retail investors

    A.   I, II

    B.   III, IV

    C.   II, IV

    D.   I, III

38. Which of the following statements is true concerning sales charges and 12b-1 fees in connection with open-end funds?

    A.   money market mutual funds may charge a front-end sales charge of no more than 8.5%

    B.   money market mutual funds may not impose a 12b-1 fee

    C.   12b-1 fees are typically used to cover management fees

    D.   money market mutual funds may impose a 12b-1 fee not to exceed .25% of assets

39. A registered representative calls several clients in her book of business to interest them in an opportunity to invest in her brother-in-law's new restaurant. The investment contracts are properly registered in the state and, therefore, the registered representative offers and sells them without informing her principal. Which of the following best addresses this situation?

    A.   since the security was properly registered, no violation has occurred

    B.   this is a violation known as "interpolation"

    C.   this represents a "wash sale"

    D.   this is a violation of FINRA conduct rules because the registered representative gave her employer no opportunity to supervise her activities

40. One of your customers would like to redeem shares of the Greenwald Growth Fund. She may redeem the shares in which of the following methods?

    A.   through the Greenwald Fund Family website

    B.   by telephone

    C.   by fax

    D.   all choices listed

41. Which of the following statements is/are true concerning signature guarantees and mutual fund redemptions?

    A.   the fund reserves the right to require a signature guarantee on any redemption request

    B.   funds typically require the signature guarantee if the check is to be made payable to someone other than the registered shareholder

    C.   funds typically require the signature guarantee if the check is to be sent to an address different from the address of record

    D.   all choices listed

42. Claire is an associated person of a FINRA-member broker-dealer. Claire sells mutual funds and variable annuities on behalf of the member firm. Recently, Claire helped a college friend launch a marketing consulting business by selling ownership stakes representing 5% in exchange for only $10,000. Which of the following statements best addresses this situation?

    A.   as long as the investors are not customers of the member firm, no violation has occurred

    B.   as long as Claire did not mention the name of her employer when speaking to investors, no violation has occurred

    C.   Claire has violated FINRA rules by not informing her firm of her outside activities

    D.   as long as Claire is not also insurance licensed, no violation has occurred

43. An office of a FINRA member firm is considered an "OSJ" or "Office of Supervisory Jurisdiction" if which of the following take place at that location?

    A.   order execution

    B.   structuring of primary offerings of securities

    C.   maintaining custody of customer funds and/or securities

    D.   all choices listed

44. A "branch office" is defined as:

    A.   any location identified by any means to the public or customers as a location at which the member conducts an investment banking business

    B.   any location identified by any means to the public or customers as a location at which the member conducts a securities business

    C.   both choices listed

    D.   neither choice listed

45. Which of the following statements is NOT true concerning FINRA rules on customer complaints and arbitration awards?

    A.   FINRA member firms must maintain a separate file of all customer complaints at each OSJ and a record of the action taken

    B.   FINRA member firms must maintain the correspondence connected to any customer complaint

    C.   any pre-dispute arbitration clause that the customer signs must prominently and clearly explain the nature of FINRA Arbitration

    D.   unfavorable awards may be directly appealed to the NAC, the SEC, and the federal courts, respectively

46. Which of the following statements concerning a member firm's holding of customer mail is NOT accurate?

    A.   the firm must have written instructions from the customer in order to hold mail

    B.   if traveling domestically, the customer's mail may be held at the firm for a period of two months

    C.   if traveling abroad, the customer's mail may be held at the firm for a period of three months

    D.   holding of mail is a service performed exclusively for discretionary accounts

47. When opening a customer account, a FINRA member does NOT need to obtain and maintain which of the following information?

    A.   signature of the registered representative introducing the account

    B.   whether customer is of legal age

    C.   names of persons authorized to trade on behalf of a business entity, i.e., corporation or partnership

    D.   educational background

48. The principal of a FINRA member firm is responsible for which of the following?

    A.   supervising the sales activities of registered representatives

    B.   approving new customer accounts

    C.   approving and filing communications of the firm

    D.   all choices listed

49. **Which of the following is an accurate statement concerning the outside business activities of a registered representative of a FINRA member firm?**

A. as long as the representative is not paid more than $100, there is no duty to report the activity to the member firm

B. as long as the compensation is securities-related, there is no duty to report the activity to the member firm

C. the firm must be notified of, but may not restrict, the representative's ability to participate in the outside activity for compensation

D. if the representative receives any compensation for the activity, the activity must be reported to the member firm

50. **If Andrea's investment appreciates 2% during a period in which the CPI decreases 2%, her real rate of return is:**

A. flat

B. 4%

C. 3%

D. −2%

51. **If an investor inquires about the purchase of a bond mutual fund, which of the following risks would you LEAST likely explain to her?**

A. credit risk

B. interest rate risk

C. reinvestment risk

D. obsolescence risk

52. **Which of the following mutual funds typically subjects investors to the greatest political risk?**

A. corporate bond funds

B. tax-exempt bond funds

C. conservative income funds

D. emerging market funds

53. **Which of the following risks is reduced through dollar cost averaging?**

A. political

B. default

C. timing

D. all choices listed

54. **Sector funds concentrate on particular industries. In which of the following sector funds would an investor be especially interested if she anticipated an economic downturn/recession?**

    A.   pharmaceuticals

    B.   communications

    C.   automotive

    D.   aerospace

55. **Your client invests primarily in blue-chip stocks, reinvesting all dividends. This morning, while your client is traveling abroad, you see a tombstone for a primary offering of a new ETF tracking a blue chip index. Since the ETF is offered by a low-cost provider, you purchase a small amount on the effective date. Which of the following best addresses this situation?**

    A.   since the investment was suitable, you acted properly

    B.   since the investment was inherently unsuitable, you acted improperly

    C.   this is an example of an unauthorized transaction, a violation of FINRA conduct rules

    D.   this is a violation known as selling away

56. **Which of the following is NOT an asset to an investor?**

    A.   market value of a home

    B.   401(k) balance

    C.   credit card balance

    D.   variable annuity

57. **Which of the following types of mutual funds probably requires that the investor be able to withstand the largest amount of price volatility?**

    A.   equity income

    B.   growth fund

    C.   short-term U.S. Treasury fund

    D.   long-term corporate bond fund

58. To which of the following investors would a registered representative most likely recommend an aggressive growth fund?

    A.   investor with a short time horizon

    B.   45-year-old investor whose primary objective is income and secondary objective is growth

    C.   47-year-old investor whose insurance needs are adequately met and who participates in a defined benefit pension plan

    D.   45-year-old investor with a 16-year-old daughter hoping to attend private college

59. An investor is convinced that the asset allocation of his portfolio is underweighted toward equities, even though he plans to retire in two years. He would like to increase the equity allocation but has only $3,000 to invest. Which of the following best addresses suitability in this example?

    A.   an investor should never invest in equities—even a small percentage—for a period of less than 10 years

    B.   Treasury bonds are the most suitable investment for the entire portfolio

    C.   C-shares of a conservative equity income fund might be suitable

    D.   ETFs would not be suitable, due to the high management fees

60. Barb is 53 and plans to retire at age She is fully vested in a defined-benefit plan but is concerned about purchasing power. Her mortgage will be paid off over the next two years, and her husband has a life insurance policy with a $500,000 death benefit. Which of the following statements best addresses suitability for this investor?

    A.   U.S. Treasury securities are suitable for investors in Barb's age bracket

    B.   Barb should invest almost exclusively in money market mutual funds

    C.   A growth & income fund with a conservative investment approach may be suitable

    D.   Barb should open an IRA and purchase a variable annuity

61. Recently, the Japanese yen has depreciated versus the U.S. dollar. Therefore, which of the following statements is accurate?

    A.   American exports to Japan will be more competitive in Japanese markets

    B.   American imports from Japan will be more competitive in the American marketplace

    C.   Holders of the Toyota Motor Company's ADR will not be affected

    D.   The yen cannot fluctuate in value versus the U.S. dollar under the USA Patriot Act

62. **An investor purchasing an emerging market equity mutual fund is LEAST exposed to which of the following risks?**

    A. liquidity
    B. political
    C. business
    D. currency exchange

63. **Which of the following represent(s) accurate statements concerning various share classes of mutual funds?**

    A. A-shares carry front-end sales charges and lower operating expenses compared to B- and C-shares
    B. B-shares carry no front-end sales charges but do carry a declining back-end sales charge and higher operating expenses than A-shares
    C. C-shares are only suitable for the short-term holding period
    D. all choices listed

64. **Which of the following represents a true statement concerning a customer redemption order for a mutual fund investment?**

    A. customers receive the public offering price as next computed by the fund
    B. customers receive the Asked price as next computed by the fund
    C. customers receive the Net Asset Value as next computed by the fund, minus any back-end sales charges and/or redemption fees
    D. customers receive the Net Asset Value as last determined by the fund

65. **Which TWO of the following are advantages of mutual fund investing compared to investing in common stock directly?**

    I.   Professional portfolio management
    II.   12b-1 fees
    III. Redemption fees
    IV.   Diversification

    A. I, III
    B. I, IV
    C. II, III
    D. II, IV

66. **If an investor were reading a prospectus profiling all of the mutual funds offered within a mutual fund complex, she would expect to see which of the following categorized as having the highest price volatility?**

    A.   growth

    B.   bond

    C.   balanced

    D.   growth & income

67. **One of ABC's equity funds focuses on investing in the stocks of companies with long track records suffering temporary setbacks. This fund is a:**

    A.   growth fund

    B.   value fund

    C.   specialty fund

    D.   sector fund

68. **All of the following represent operating expenses to a mutual fund EXCEPT:**

    A.   management fees

    B.   12b-1 asset-based distribution fees

    C.   legal and accounting services

    D.   sales charges

69. **Open- and closed-end funds share all of the following characteristics except that open-end funds do NOT:**

    A.   provide clearly stated investment objectives

    B.   invest in debt securities

    C.   trade on the secondary market

    D.   need to be diversified

70. **All of the following are associated with money market mutual funds EXCEPT:**

    A.   sales charges

    B.   operating expenses

    C.   low rates of return

    D.   stable value

71. **An investor has received a prospectus for the Winthorp World-Class Equity Appreciation Fund. She notes that the fund offers both A-shares and B-shares. The main difference between the two types of shares, you would inform her, has to do with:**

    A.   amount of the management fee

    B.   investment policies and restrictions

    C.   method of paying sales charges

    D.   number of securities represented in the portfolio

72. **Which of the following statements concerning life insurance is false?**

    A.   the death benefit paid to the beneficiary would be reduced by any outstanding loans and unpaid premiums

    B.   the death benefit paid to the beneficiary is not subject to income taxes

    C.   the death benefit is not included in the estate for purposes of estate taxes

    D.   the death benefit is guaranteed on a whole life policy

73. **Which of the following fixed-income mutual funds likely has the longest average duration?**

    A.   short-term U.S. Treasury fund

    B.   intermediate-term investment-grade fund

    C.   long-term tax-exempt fund

    D.   money market mutual fund

74. **An investment in which of the following equity mutual funds generally requires the highest risk tolerance?**

    A.   small cap growth

    B.   mid-cap value

    C.   large cap growth

    D.   large cap value

75. **Which of the following is NOT an advantage to mutual fund investing?**

    A.   your investment is managed by a professional investment adviser

    B.   diversification can be achieved with a small minimum investment

    C.   your investment is FDIC insured

    D.   transfer agent provides safekeeping of securities

76. Which of the following statements concerning loan provisions for variable contracts is false?

A.   if an annuitant in the accumulation phase takes a loan, the number of accumulation units is reduced

B.   if an annuitant in the accumulation phase takes a loan, the IRS considers it a distribution

C.   if the policy owner takes a loan in a VLI policy, this will have no effect on cash value

D.   after three years, a VLI policy owner may take loans of at least 75% of cash value

77. In a variable life insurance policy, the policy owner should know that:

I.   Death benefit is calculated annually

II.   Death benefit is tied to AIR vs. actual performance of the separate account

III. Minimum cash value is guaranteed by the insurance company's general account

IV.   Cash value is calculated daily

A.   I

B.   II

C.   I, II, IV

D.   II, III, IV

78. Which TWO of the following represent accurate statements concerning variable annuity contracts?

I.   Number of accumulation units is fixed

II.   Number of accumulation units varies

III. Number of annuity units is fixed

IV.   Number of annuity units varies

A.   I, III

B.   I, IV

C.   II, III

D.   II, IV

79. Which TWO of the following operating expenses in a variable annuity contract allow the insurance company to guarantee an income stream for life while keeping expenses level?

I. Management fee

II. Mortality risk fee

III. Expense risk fee

IV. Appraisal fee

A. I, IV

B. I, III

C. I, II

D. II, III

80. Which of the following statements is inaccurate concerning mutual funds?

A. may not close off purchases to new investors

B. may impose both a sales charge and a 12b-1 asset-based distribution fee

C. must redeem shares within 7 days

D. do not trade on the secondary market

81. Variable annuities and mutual funds would generally both offer investors:

I. Investment options including growth, value, index, fixed-income, etc.

II. Tax deferral

III. 1035 contract exchanges

IV. Right to vote on changes to investment policy

A. I

B. III

C. I, IV

D. I, II, III, IV

82. Dale purchased an annuity through Strunk & White Broker-Dealers and received his first payment 30 days later. Dale purchased which type of annuity?

A. periodic-payment deferred annuity

B. single-payment immediate annuity

C. single-payment deferred annuity

D. periodic immediate annuity

83. Which of the following statements is NOT accurate concerning fixed annuities?

A.   the insurance company guarantees a minimum rate of return

B.   the insurance company bears the investment risk through its general account investments

C.   a Series 6 license is not required to sell the contracts

D.   an insurance license is not required to sell these products if the individual obtains a Series 7

84. Which TWO of the following statements are accurate of variable annuities and variable life insurance?

I.   The insurance company bears all investment risk

II.   Purchase payments are allocated to the separate account

III. The main advantage over fixed contracts is the potential protection from inflation

IV.   They are not defined as securities

A.   I, III

B.   I, IV

C.   II, III

D.   III, IV

85. Which of the following is the major reason for purchasing variable life insurance?

A.   tax deferral

B.   ability to protect purchasing power

C.   death benefit

D.   loan provisions

86. Mordecai has just annuitized his variable annuity contract at age 69½. Mordecai is assured of receiving a monthly income for the rest of his life because of which of the following contract features?

A.   payout guarantee

B.   mortality guarantee

C.   death benefit

D.   mens rea

87. **All of the following statements concerning the insurance company's separate account are true EXCEPT:**

    A. if the insurance company goes bankrupt, creditors can attach the assets

    B. must be registered under the Investment Company Act of 1940

    C. usually comprised of various sub-accounts representing different investment options

    D. other than a fixed-rate sub-account, the insurance company does not guarantee a rate of return

88. **Heather is 49 years old. Having purchased a single-payment deferred annuity two years ago, Heather would now like to surrender the contract. Heather will most likely pay all of the following except for:**

    A. surrender charges to the insurance company

    B. ordinary income tax on the excess over cost basis

    C. 10% penalty tax on the excess over cost basis

    D. gift taxes

89. **According to the Federal Reserve Board's Regulation T, in order to purchase shares of stock trading on NASDAQ, the customer in a new margin account must deposit:**

    A. at least 10% of the current market value

    B. 50% of the current market value

    C. 35% of the current market value

    D. 100% of the current market value

90. **Under FINRA's Code of Arbitration Procedure, which of the following statements accurately describes the ramifications of a member's refusal to honor an arbitration award?**

    A. this represents a felony subject to a mandatory 5 years in prison

    B. this is a matter for civil courts and not a violation of FINRA Rules

    C. this is considered conduct inconsistent with just and equitable principles of trade

    D. payment would be required upon court order

91. **Which of the following customer requests would be considered a discretionary order?**

    A. buy 1,000 shares of JDSU at the best price you think we can get today

    B. sell 1,000 shares of ORCL this afternoon

    C. buy 200 shares of a software company today

    D. all choices listed

92. Which of the following would protect an investor against missing assets due to the failure of her broker-dealer firm?

    A.   FDIC

    B.   CBOE

    C.   FINRA/NASD

    D.   SIPC

93. All of the following statements are accurate concerning UTMA accounts EXCEPT:

    A.   the minor's social security number is listed

    B.   income may be subject to taxation in the year received

    C.   if the minor dies, assets pass to the parents

    D.   gifts are irrevocable and indefeasible

94. In which of the following cases must a member firm file a currency transaction report to FinCEN?

    A.   a customer deposits $2,000 in cash

    B.   a customer deposits $50,000 in bearer bonds

    C.   a customer purchases $12,000 of stock with cash

    D.   a customer writes a check for $12,000 to a mutual fund company

95. A client deposits $6,000 at 10 a.m. If the client deposits $5,000 at 4:00 p.m., your firm would file:

    A.   no report at this time

    B.   a currency transaction report

    C.   a suspicious activity report

    D.   a Reg T extension request

96. Which of the following account types is typically for very short-term investing?

    A.   trust

    B.   UGMA

    C.   estate

    D.   corporate

97. **If a customer refuses to provide a social security or tax identification number, which of the following best explains the ramifications?**

    A. the account may not be opened

    B. a backup withholding may result

    C. the customer must be audited by a CPA

    D. an SAR-SF/Suspicious Activity Report should promptly be filed

98. **A Currency Transaction Report must be filed with FinCEN for any cash transaction exceeding:**

    A. $2,000

    B. $3,000

    C. $5,000

    D. $10,000

99. **FINRA requires members who belong to SIPC to maintain fidelity bonds. Fidelity bonds protect against:**

    A. lost, misplaced securities

    B. forgery

    C. fraudulent trading

    D. all choices listed

100. **A Series 6 licensee is authorized to engage in which of the following activities?**

    A. perform work outside the firm provided it pays under $100 per incident

    B. receive compensation for offering a closed-end fund on the primary market

    C. offer financial planning advice and execute securities transactions

    D. sell securities, including common and preferred stock, and mutual fund products

Answers to Practice Exam 1

1. **ANSWER:** D

   WHY: if the "Fed" is buying Treasuries, prices will rise/rates will drop, which helps the economy. The other actions fight inflation.

2. **ANSWER:** C

   WHY: money market = short-term debt. A bond/debenture is a long-term obligation.

3. **ANSWER:** D

   WHY: investment bankers raise capital for issuers by purchasing their securities and re-offering them to investors on the primary/capital market. Even though many famous investment banking firms also act as market makers, the two business models are different. Knowing the difference between the primary (new issue) and secondary (trading) markets is important on the exam.

4. **ANSWER:** B

   WHY: when the demand for something grows faster than its supply, prices rise. When a hurricane knocks out the refineries that turn oil into gas, the demand for gas is still high, but since the supply is tight, you're suddenly paying $3 or $4 per gallon.

5. **ANSWER:** C

   WHY: if you buy common stock, let's hope you aren't afraid of watching your initial investment go down, say, 35–50% really fast. If you are, buy something else, anything but common stock.

6. **ANSWER:** B

   WHY: there is a market for a particular stock because a market maker will let you sell at one price and let you buy at the higher price. The customer can sell at the bid price because the market maker will buy their stock at that price. But, the market maker will sell at the asking price if the customer is willing to pay it.

7. **ANSWER:** C

   WHY: if the price is up, the yields are down. So, when a bond is purchased above par, the current yield and yield to maturity both go down. The nominal yield is the fixed rate of interest paid by the bond, and it never changes. If it's a 5% bond, it pays 5% of par every year, end of story. The current yield and yield to maturity fluctuate with interest rates, but the nominal yield is fixed. Just like a fixed-rate mortgage, the borrower has locked in a rate over the life of the loan.

8. **ANSWER:** D

    WHY: AM Best rates the strength of insurance companies; the other three rate bonds issued by corporations and municipalities.

9. **ANSWER:** B

    WHY: dividends paid from bond mutual funds come from the interest payments on the bonds. If it's a tax-exempt bond fund, the dividends are treated just like the interest paid on the municipal bonds—tax-exempt at the federal level. Now, the state can tax you on municipal bond interest, unless you buy the bonds your state won't tax—the ones issued by them or a municipality in that state. So, a Maryland resident needs to buy a Maryland Tax-Exempt Bond Fund to escape both federal and state taxation of the dividends. Capital gains are simply taxable, period.

10. **ANSWER:** B

    WHY: only the people selling and dealing with customers' money/assets need to be fingerprinted. They, and their principals/supervisors/higher-ups, that is.

11. **ANSWER:** D

    WHY: Suitability rules cover the recommendations to buy, sell, or hold securities, or to pursue certain investment strategies, e.g., margin trading.

12. **ANSWER:** B

    WHY: look at the disclaimer on the front cover of a mutual fund prospectus, which tells you how the SEC feels about the securities registered with the SEC. No value judgments of any kind—the security has been registered, period.

13. **ANSWER:** B

    WHY: don't assume the IRS is always out to get us. They let you inherit securities and sell them for a long-term capital gain, no matter how quickly you sell them. The cost basis is the fair market value on the date of death, and the gains are long-term, regardless of how long the heirs hold the stock.

14. **ANSWER:** B

    WHY: is there any way that you could hold a stock for one year plus one day if you bought and sold it in the same calendar year? Not even on *Star Trek*, right? The holding period stops when you sell the stock and includes that day, too.

15. **ANSWER:** A

    WHY: the money would stay in the tax-deferred account, so there would be no tax ramifications. The investor could either automatically reinvest into more shares, or let the money accumulate until she's ready to buy whatever the heck she wants to buy with the dividends that have built up nicely over the past year or so. Either way, it all stays inside the protective layer of the tax-deferred account.

16. **ANSWER:** D

    WHY: it's not necessarily taxable or tax-free, but if the beneficiary receives more than the contract owner put in, that excess is taxed as ordinary income.

17. **ANSWER:** D

    WHY: memorize this. Remember that 59½ is the age when withdrawals may begin without penalty.

18. **ANSWER:** C

    WHY: it has to be EARNED income, not bond interest, dividends from stock, or rental income.

19. **ANSWER:** C

    WHY: you would have to be making a lot more money before you'd have a problem making your maximum pre-tax contribution to your IRA.

20. **ANSWER:** C

    WHY: something else to memorize.

21. **ANSWER:** B

    WHY: she has invested $10,500 into the fund. Divided by 1,000 shares = $10.50 per share. The IRS already collected taxes on all that money, so that is her cost basis.

22. **ANSWER:** A

    WHY: using process of elimination, you can find three false statements here. We don't turn losses into gains. There's no reason to match up long-term with short-term and vice versa. And, commissions paid to buy the stock are added to the investor's cost-basis; commissions paid to sell the stock are subtracted from the investor's proceeds when reporting a capital gain or loss.

23. **ANSWER:** D

    WHY: the earnings here are $25,000, so the first money coming out is part of that $25,000 "excess over basis." This $15,000 and the next $10,000 will all be considered the earnings, taxed as ordinary income. The rest is treated as a return of cost basis.

24. **ANSWER:** D

    WHY: three good things to know about insurance. If you borrow against the policy, you reduce the value of the policy, if you can believe such a thing, and, yes, the insurance company generally likes to collect interest on any money it lends out for any length of time. The beneficiary receives the death benefit free-and-clear, but the value of the policy could trigger estate taxes if proper estate planning was not performed. A nice thing about life insurance vs. annuities is that withdrawals of cash value are treated first as if they represent the cost basis. For annuities, remember, if you take money out, the IRS considers that to be part of the taxable earnings.

25. **ANSWER:** B

    WHY: the advice has to be on securities—a fixed annuity is not a security, and neither is whole life insurance or a commodity futures contract.

26. **ANSWER:** D

    WHY: projections of future performance are not allowed.

27. **ANSWER:** A

    WHY: Broker-dealers and agents do not guarantee against losses. Both U.S. Treasury securities and some corporate bonds are guaranteed, but the meaning has to be made clear to investors. People can and do lose money on "guaranteed securities."

28. **ANSWER:** B

    WHY: you're required to take a minimum distribution from your Traditional—not your Roth—IRA soon after you turn 70. Otherwise, the IRS will remind you by hitting you with a 50% penalty.

29. **ANSWER:** D

    WHY: there are three types of investment companies under the Investment Company Act of 1940: UIT, face-amount, and the management company. Management companies are either open- or closed-end funds. Memorize that, please.

30. **ANSWER:** D

    WHY: memorize this, as I expect at least one question on "wash sales." It's not a violation—it's just bad news from your accountant that the loss you thought you were going to use cannot be used now since you bought the stock too close to your sale date.

31. **ANSWER:** C

    WHY: if you want tax deferral, you need a retirement plan, annuity, or insurance. Mutual funds offer no tax deferral in and of themselves. I think the Series 6 will be very pleased if you know that.

32. **ANSWER:** D

    WHY: refusing to give the investor a prospectus? That's called "omitting material facts," or "securities fraud."

33. **ANSWER:** D

   WHY: you need to know what's in a mutual fund prospectus, and you need to know that predictions of performance are not allowed.

34. **ANSWER:** D

   WHY: communications to 25 or fewer retail investors = correspondence, which must be monitored. Institutional communications must be reviewed but are not necessarily subject to prior principal approval. A form letter delivered to > than 25 retail investors is a retail communication.

35. **ANSWER:** A

   WHY: the prospectus gives prospects an overview of the portfolio—maybe the top ten holdings and the percentages allocated to each industry sector. If you want a detailed list of portfolio securities, get the Statement of Additional Information or a shareholder report from the fund company's website.

36. **ANSWER:** D

   WHY: short-term debt securities (commercial paper, banker's acceptance) are generally exempt from the Securities Act of 1933's registration requirements. Which is good, since you're trying to borrow at current short-term interest rates. If you had to go through the registration process, who knows where rates will even be by the time you got the release date from the SEC? Remember that the SEC is out to protect investors but not to such extent that they choke off the free-flow of capital to companies and governments who need to access it through the capital markets.

37. **ANSWER:** B

   WHY: written communications to > 25 retail investors = retail communications. The chat room = a public appearance subject to monitoring appropriate for the firm. One letter sent to a customer = correspondence, which also must be monitored but neither pre-approved nor filed by a principal.

38. **ANSWER:** D

   WHY: money market mutual funds meet the definition of "no load," which means the 12b-1 fee can't exceed .25% of assets. See, if it exceeds that, then it's really a "load" whether you charge it upfront or a little bit every year. Keep it down to .25%, and that's not high enough to be a "load" on the investor. Management fees are separated from 12b-1, as anyone who has taken my advice and read a few prospectuses already knows.

39. **ANSWER:** D

   WHY: I just read about an agent in my state who was barred by FINRA and whose license was revoked by the state because he was selling securities without letting his firm know. I'm sure he enjoyed the extra income; trouble is, his career is now over. So, great short-term strategy. Not so profitable in the long-term.

40. **ANSWER:** D

WHY: mutual fund companies make it very easy for investors to redeem/sell back their shares. Another answer here could be that the customer can call you or your assistant and make you help. Always a drag to execute big sell orders when you were just getting used to collecting 12b-1 fees on those assets, but, what are you gonna do—it's the client's account. All you can do is make suitable recommendations and hope for the best.

41. **ANSWER:** D

WHY: just three things to know about signature guarantees and mutual fund redemptions. In other words, this topic seems less likely to show up on the test than many others that we go into with more detail. Still, it's testable, and this question probably covers what the exam would want you to know about the topic.

42. **ANSWER:** C

WHY: try to think in terms of what the regulators want you to prove that you know before turning you loose with a license, a cell phone, and goodness knows what sort of intentions.

43. **ANSWER:** D

WHY: these three activities are clearly major activities that a broker-dealer would perform: structuring offerings of securities, maintaining custody of customer assets, and executing buy/sell orders for securities. Remember that the OSJ is a major office of the broker-dealer firm with responsibility for supervising various branch offices.

44. **ANSWER:** C

WHY: remember that a broker-dealer is either involved with investment banking (primary market), executing trades (secondary market), or—usually—both.

45. **ANSWER:** D

WHY: disciplinary decisions can be appealed, but arbitration decisions are final and binding.

46. **ANSWER:** D

WHY: chances are, you will have few if any discretionary accounts, but you might have customers who don't want their trade confirmations, account statements, proxy voting materials, annual reports, etc., coming to their house while they're on vacation. If so, your firm can hold mail for 2 months if the customer is traveling domestically, 3 months if traveling abroad. And, the firm can't do it without a written request from the customer. Customer communications like these are crucial, so withholding them can only be done at the direction of the customer, and even then, only for a brief time period.

47. **ANSWER:** D

   WHY: the customer's level of education is not considered a material piece of information, and I can't imagine why it would be. What sort of "education" helps people understand and select mutual funds? Finance classes? Statistics? Common sense? Who knows?

48. **ANSWER:** D

   WHY: the word "principal" can mean many things on this exam, but here it means the supervisors of a broker-dealer with responsibility for these and other aspects of the member firm's business.

49. **ANSWER:** D

   WHY: the rule requires the representative to notify the employer of any outside business activities. The firm could also limit the rep's ability to participate in the activity, or even tell him not to do it.

50. **ANSWER:** B

   WHY: now that's a tough question. The word "real" means "above inflation." How much did the investment advance compared to inflation? It went up 2%, and inflation went down 2%… for a total of 4% above inflation.

51. **ANSWER:** D

   WHY: Obsolescence risk is an un-systematic risk usually associated with buying stock in companies whose products could become obsolete (VCR manufacturers, makers of the "Walkman," etc.).

52. **ANSWER:** D

   WHY: if the market is still emerging, chances are the social/political environment is just a little shaky. Tip—if you see crowds burning American flags and hanging rag dolls that look like our President on CNN with regularity, an investment in that country could be just a little, um, volatile.

53. **ANSWER:** C

   WHY: you don't want to end up buying all your stock or mutual fund at one price, since that could turn out being the highest price it reaches in 10 years. If you put in a fixed dollar amount regularly, you will avoid timing risk. Your average cost per share will be better than if you had purchased all at once or purchased equal numbers of shares each time.

54. **ANSWER:** A

   WHY: which industry would weather the storm of a recession the best? In other words, if times were tight, which of the following could you put off the longest: brand new SUV, or a refill for you daughter's asthma medicine?

55. **ANSWER:** C

WHY: doesn't that just look like an unauthorized transaction? I mean, it was a transaction, and I don't see any authorization for it, so...it's a great way to end a financial services career. Spending your customer's money without telling them? Huh?

56. **ANSWER:** C

WHY: if you thought your credit card balance was an asset, you are in good company but incorrect nonetheless. A credit card balance, like a mortgage balance, represents a liability, not an asset.

57. **ANSWER:** B

WHY: growth stocks and U.S. Treasuries sit as far apart on the investment continuum as the North Pole sits from the South Pole. If you chose equity income funds as being more volatile than growth, please remember that when a security provides consistent income, that takes a lot of the wildness out of the wild ride. A growth investment is all specula- tion, often for decades. One day it looks great, the next it looks scary, but you're getting NOTHING you can spend at the store in the meantime.

58. **ANSWER:** C

WHY: use process of elimination. Growth funds require investors to have long time horizons. If income is the obective, put them in an equity income (or bond) fund. If the daughter is two years away from college, that is a very short time-horizon. Buy a 2-year T-note, or—if they prefer paying sales charges and expenses—put them in a short-term U.S. Treasury fund and call it a day.

59. **ANSWER:** C

WHY: this is about the only nice thing I can think to say about C-shares. If you have just a little bit of time and a little bit of money and you simply have to have this investment, buy the C-shares. Whenever the investor has a long time horizon and plenty of money to invest, put him in the A-shares.

60. **ANSWER:** C

WHY: FINRA generally hates to hear that an investor was told to "buy an annuity inside an IRA," since that would be redundant. She says she's worried about purchasing power, so she has to buy stock. Money market and Treasury securities are for wimps looking for income. Eliminate those two and you're done with this question.

61. **ANSWER:** B

WHY: the stuff we make is priced in dollars; the stuff they make is priced in yen. If their yen goes down in value, our dollars can buy more of their stuff, and their yen can buy less of our stuff.

62. **ANSWER:** A

WHY: if you own a mutual fund, your investment is redeemable at the NAV whenever you get tired of holding it, so there is no liquidity risk. There is liquidity risk on the closed-end fund shares, but not on the open-end fund shares.

63. **ANSWER:** D

WHY: A-shares end up being the most frequently purchased and are suitable for anyone with a long time horizon and enough money to reach a breakpoint. B-shares are good for people with a long time horizon but not enough $ to reach the breakpoints offered on A-shares. C-shares have the high "level load" or 12b-1 fee, so they only work if the investor intends to exit after a few years.

64. **ANSWER:** C

WHY: the "ask" is also called the public offering price. Either way, that would represent what a customer pays, not what a customer receives when selling. Use forward pricing—the price next computed by the fund.

65. **ANSWER:** B

WHY: 12b-1 fees and redemption fees are not advantages—they are the price you pay for getting benefits such as diversification, professional management, and one 1099 DIV that makes it more convenient to do taxes compared to receiving dividends from 20 different companies and keeping 20 different 1099s straight.

66. **ANSWER:** A

WHY: growth funds are the most volatile, then growth & income, then equity income, then balanced, then bond, then money market.

67. **ANSWER:** B

WHY: I don't care what people are saying about the price of Walmart stock right now—it's a great company with a stock trading on the cheap. Talk about a VALUE opportunity.

68. **ANSWER:** D

WHY: any mutual fund prospectus for a fund charging a sales charge will show that a sales charge is deducted from the investor's check when she buys (A shares) or when she sells (B shares). Operating expenses are in a different table, a whole different ball of wax. Whether a fund has a sales charge or not, it will have operating expenses.

69. **ANSWER:** C

WHY: the main thing that separates the open-end and closed-end fund is that you redeem your open-end fund to the company, who pays you the NAV, while you have to trade your shares of your closed-end fund exactly as you would trade shares of Starbucks, Walmart, Microsoft, etc.

70. **ANSWER:** A

    WHY: money market mutual funds charge management fees and 12b-1 fees, which are operating expenses. They don't impose sales charges, since the returns are already so low that investors would be guaranteed to lose money after paying, say, a 5% upfront load.

71. **ANSWER:** C

    WHY: the management fees would be the same. The difference is that the A-shares charge a front-end load, while the B-shares charge a back-end load. The 12b-1 fees would also be much higher on the B-shares.

72. **ANSWER:** C

    WHY: the death benefit IS included in the value of the estate, as is the value of an annuity.

73. **ANSWER:** C

    WHY: long-term = high/long duration. I am confident that the test would not go any deeper than that, unless it did.

74. **ANSWER:** A

    WHY: growth is the most aggressive objective, and the smaller the "cap," the higher the risk.

75. **ANSWER:** C

    WHY: open up a mutual fund prospectus and you'll quickly see the bold-letter warning that your investment is not a bank product backed up by FDIC insurance. It is an investment that could—theoretically—become totally worthless, which is, of course, what makes investing so much fun in the first place.

76. **ANSWER:** C

    WHY: if you take a loan against the value of your insurance policy, guess what happens to the value of your insurance policy?

77. **ANSWER:** C

    WHY: read carefully—there is a minimum death benefit, but not a minimum cash value on a variable life policy. What if the individual wants a minimum guaranteed cash value? Sell him some whole life and call it a day.

78. **ANSWER:** C

    WHY: accumulation units are just like mutual fund shares—their number and value fluctuate. While the VALUE of an annuity unit varies, the number is fixed.

79. **ANSWER:** D

    WHY: the mortality guarantee means that you'll get a check as long as you're alive. The expense guarantee means they'll keep their expenses level. But, like most things offered by an insurance company, these things come with little fees attached.

    They're a business; they like fees.

80. **ANSWER:** A

WHY: mutual funds often close off purchases to new investors. Eventually, they end up with too much money and not enough good places to put it.

81. **ANSWER:** C

WHY: mutual funds offer no tax advantages, really, so just eliminate the two choices talking about tax advantages.

82. **ANSWER:** B

WHY: let's see, Dale made a single payment and immediately started receiving annuity payments. What in the world do they call those annuities that pay out immediately after the investor makes a single payment?

83. **ANSWER:** D

WHY: a fixed annuity is not a "security." It's just a contract with an insurance company backed by their general account.

84. **ANSWER:** C

WHY: if the investment goes into the separate account, that means, by definition, it's not guaranteed by the insurance company's general account.

85. **ANSWER:** C

WHY: no matter how cool it is to allocate net premiums to various sub-accounts (growth, growth & income, value, etc.) the main reason to buy a life insurance policy is for the death benefit.

86. **ANSWER:** B

WHY: as long as he is a mortal, he'll receive a monthly check. A mortality guarantee. Who knew?

87. **ANSWER:** A

WHY: creditors could attach the assets of the GENERAL account, because those are the insurance company's assets. The separate account is separate from the general account. These assets belong to customers.

88. **ANSWER:** D

WHY: Deferred annuities are not good if the client ends up surrendering the contract early on in the surrender period, as Heather is about to find out.

89. **ANSWER:** B

WHY: Reg T establishes how much credit the broker-dealer can extend to a margin customer; Reg U tells a bank how much collateral the broker-dealer needs to pledge to borrow the money they then re-lend to the customer in the margin account. Reg T is set by the Federal Reserve Board, and has been 50% of the stock's market value for quite some time.

90. **ANSWER:** C

WHY: if you don't play by the Arbitration Code, FINRA would be happy to give you a little seminar on the painful process called Code of Procedure.

91. **ANSWER:** C

WHY: which order allows the rep to make a big decision—the one that leaves the particular stock up to the rep, right?

92. **ANSWER:** D

WHY: take a quick visit to www.sipc.org and you'll know what SIPC is all about. It protects investors from broker-dealers holding their assets who then go bankrupt. It does not protect against market loss, only broker-dealer bankruptcy/failure.

93. **ANSWER:** C

WHY: actually, if the child—God forbid—dies, the assets go to the child's estate, not the parents.

94. **ANSWER:** C

WHY: transactions of cash > 10K are reported on CTRs (Currency Transaction Reports).

95. **ANSWER:** B

WHY: it's not necessarily suspicious for a client to make cash deposits, but if the client deposits more than $10,000 cash, a Currency Transaction Report must be filed.

96. **ANSWER:** C

WHY: an estate is usually open for 6 months, maybe 2 years. Recommend money market securities, including T-bills, and maybe a 2-year T-note.

97. **ANSWER:** B

WHY: might seem surprising that the account can be opened, but it can. The customer may eventually provide that darned tax identification/social security number here, because he may get really tired of not being able to withdraw all the dividends or bond interest paid into the account. The broker-dealer will be forced to withhold some of the income in the account for the IRS if the customer won't provide a tax identification number.

98. **ANSWER:** D

   WHY: a deposit of over $10,000 cash-money has to be reported on a Currency Transaction Report. This report does not imply that somebody is doing something wrong; just that the U.S. Treasury might want to know about it.

99. **ANSWER:** D

   WHY: a fidelity bond protects customers of a broker-dealer much like a "bond" protects a carpet cleaner or electrician who might accidentally do some damage after entering your home. If your assets are missing due to fraud, loss, misplacement, etc., that is covered by the broker-dealer's fidelity bond.

100. **ANSWER:** B

   WHY: surprisingly, while you can't help people trade the shares of a closed-end fund on the secondary market, with your Series 6 you could be part of the offering/creation of the fund. Always notify your employer of any work done for compensation. And, don't offer financial planning advice unless registered as a financial planner—and with your broker-dealer's knowledge.

Practice Exam 2

1. **Which TWO of the following represent accurate statements concerning fiscal policy?**

    I.   is enacted by Congress and the President

    II. cutting government spending is inflationary

    III. increasing government spending is inflationary

    IV. it involves three tools: the discount rate, the reserve requirement, and open market operations

    A. I, III

    B. I, IV

    C. II, III

    D. II, IV

2. **Which of the following represents an accurate statement concerning hedge funds?**

    A. they are generally illiquid

    B. non-accredited investors may generally not invest directly in hedge funds

    C. non-accredited investors may invest indirectly through "funds of hedge funds," given certain requirements

    D. all choices listed

3. **A bond analyst for Moody's Investor Services or S&P would determine the credit-worthiness of an Industrial Development Revenue Bond by focusing on the financial strength of:**

    A. the issuer

    B. the corporation

    C. the managing underwriter

    D. all choices listed

4. **The ABC Corporation is about to issue three series of bonds. Each offer is of the same size and term to maturity. ABC will issue mortgage bonds, a series of debentures, and a series of subordinated debentures. Which of the following is a true statement?**

A. the subordinated debentures would offer the highest yield to investors

B. the mortgage bonds would offer the highest yield to investors

C. ABC is reducing the leverage component of its capital structure

D. the debentures would offer the highest yield to investors

5. **Which of the following represents a false statement of the primary market?**

A. transactions are for the benefit of an issuer of securities

B. most corporate issuers register with the SEC under the Securities Act of 1933

C. most corporate issuers who register with the SEC under the Securities Act of 1933 are also required to file quarterly and annual reports to the SEC under the Securities Exchange Act of 1934

D. underwriters are compensated with a spread plus a reasonable commission

6. **Which of the following facts should raise suitability concerns for a registered principal when reviewing a purchase transaction involving a deferred variable annuity?**

A. the client is under the age of 55

B. the client is performing a 1035 contract exchange 2 years after performing a similar exchange

C. the client is uncomfortable investing in guaranteed-rate fixed-income products

D. the client's primary investment objective is capital appreciation

7. **A registered representative has several friends and family on her "book of business." If one of her customers happens to be her brother, what is true of any borrowing or lending practices between the two?**

A. they are subject to the firm's supervisory procedures

B. they are outside the purview of principals and members of FINRA staff

C. the registered representative may use her own discretion in making or receiving any such loans

D. the registered representative may borrow or lend with such account holders only if the member is not affiliated with a retail banking institution

8. **Use the following four dates to answer the question below:**
    Friday, January 10 Declaration Date
    Tuesday March 18 Ex-Dividend Date
    Thursday March 20 Record Date
    Tuesday, April 1 Payable Date

    In order for an investor to receive the dividend declared, she must purchase common stock in a regular-way settlement no later than:

    A. Tuesday, March 18

    B. Monday, March 17

    C. Thursday, March 20

    D. Tuesday, April 1

9. **Your client turned 70 on May 15, 2012. On November 1, 2014, she discovers that she has forgotten to withdraw funds from her Roth IRA. What are the consequences?**

    A. 50% insufficient distribution penalty

    B. 50% insufficient distribution penalty, plus ordinary income tax

    C. 10% excess contribution penalty

    D. no consequences at this time

10. **Your client bought a deferred non-qualified annuity with a deposit of $50,000. At retirement, the separate account is worth $80,000. If your client withdraws $20,000, how much will be taxed?**

    A. $10,000

    B. $20,000

    C. $30,000

    D. none

11. **A small business with 15 employees has just established a SIMPLE IRA. Therefore, participants will be fully vested:**

    A. after three work years

    B. after three calendar years

    C. after working 1,000 hours

    D. immediately

12. **An investor, age 53, would like to withdraw money from her Traditional IRA without incurring penalties. She has already purchased her first home and has no medical emergency. Therefore, she would like to take advantage of IRS Rule 72(t). Which of the following represents an accurate statement concerning this withdrawal method?**

   A.   the investor must take a series of substantially equal periodic payments for 5 years or until age 59½, whichever occurs last

   B.   ordinary income taxes will be due but not a 10% penalty tax

   C.   there are several methods used to calculate the amount of the substantially equal periodic payments

   D.   all choices listed

13. **An investor who sells common stock at a loss must wait how long before repurchasing the security in order to use the loss under wash sale rules?**

   A.   15 days

   B.   60 days

   C.   30 days

   D.   45 days

14. **XYZ Equity Income Fund reports net income of $1,000,000 and must distribute how much of this amount to be deemed a Regulated Investment Company under Internal Revenue Code Subchapter M?**

   A. $980,000

   B. $20,000

   C. $1,000,000

   D. $900,000

15. **Which of the following represents a method of tax-free withdrawals from an IRA even if the account owner is younger than 59½?**

   A.   first-time home purchase of a primary residence to $10,000

   B.   death

   C.   series of substantially equal periodic payments under IRS Rule 72(t)

   D.   none of the choices listed

16. In which of the following retirement plans is the employee immediately vested?

    A.   defined benefit

    B.   SEP-IRA

    C.   401(k)

    D.   403(b)

17. Which of the following represents a security?

    A.   whole life insurance

    B.   universal life insurance policy

    C. $70,000 bank certificate of deposit

    D.   investment contract

18. All of the following represent criteria from the so-called "three-pronged approach" provided by SEC Release IA-1092 EXCEPT:

    A.   does the professional provide investment advice?

    B.   is the person compensated for providing investment advice?

    C.   is the person in the business of providing investment advice with some regularity?

    D.   is the person registered as an investment adviser?

19. Which of the following represents an accurate statement concerning securities?

    A.   only non-exempt securities are subject to anti-fraud regulations

    B.   fraud is a violation under federal, not state, law

    C.   if the investment fits the definition of a "security," it is subject to anti-fraud regulations and is subject to registration requirements

    D.   both fixed and variable annuities are defined as securities

20. Under the Securities Exchange Act of 1934, which of the following must register with the SEC?

    A.   national securities associations, such as FINRA

    B.   broker-dealer member firms of FINRA

    C.   both choices listed

    D.   neither choice listed

21. Which of the following represents an inaccurate statement concerning 529 Savings Plans?

    A.   a gift can be made for the current gift tax exclusion times five years without triggering gift taxes

    B.   distributions may be taxable at the state level

    C.   distributions used for education expenses are exempt from federal taxation

    D.   at the age of majority, the beneficiary assumes control of the account assets

22. Which of the following retirement plans are available to a sole proprietor?

    A.   Traditional IRA

    B.   Roth IRA

    C.   401(k)

    D.   all choices listed

23. Which of the following reflects an accurate statement concerning rollovers and transfers in connection with Individual Retirement Arrangements?

    A.   if the check is payable to the account owner, the account owner must complete the rollover in 60 days

    B.   the balance from a 401(k) plan may be transferred to an existing IRA only

    C.   the balance from a 401(k) plan may be transferred to a Traditional IRA provided the amount does not exceed the current maximum contribution limit for the IRA

    D.   the balance from a 401(k) plan may be transferred to a Roth IRA without tax implications

24. Which of the following represents a true statement concerning Traditional and Roth Individual Retirement Arrangements?

    A.   an individual receiving alimony may contribute based on that "earned income"

    B.   a Roth IRA may be converted to a Traditional IRA if taxes are paid on the entire amount going into the Traditional IRA

    C.   the owner of a Roth IRA may always take distributions tax-free after maintaining the account 5 years

    D.   rollovers must be completed within 120 days to avoid taxes and penalties

25. **Under the "conduit theory," which of the following would be taxable to the mutual fund?**

    I. Unrealized capital gains

    II. Un-distributed net income

    III. Net income distributed to shareholders representing 90% + of net income

    A. I

    B. II

    C. I, III

    D. III

26. **Which of the following retirement plans leaves the employer with the least flexibility?**

    A. 401(k)

    B. SIMPLE IRA

    C. SEP-IRA

    D. money purchase

27. **Which of the following may be purchased within a Traditional IRA?**

    I. U.S. minted gold coins

    II. Collectible items, e.g., rare oil paintings

    III. Corporate bonds rated below BB–

    IV. Aggressive growth mutual funds

    A. III

    B. IV

    C. I, II, III

    D. I, III, IV

28. **A schoolteacher participated in her school district's tax-sheltered annuity for 20 years. During her employment the school district contributed $30,000 into the plan. At retirement the teacher takes a lump-sum distribution of $50,000. What is the tax treatment of the distribution?**

    A. $20,000 taxed as ordinary income

    B. $50,000 taxed as ordinary income

    C. $20,000 taxed at short-term capital gains rates

    D. $50,000 taxed at long-term capital gains rates

29. Which of the following is funded with tax-deductible contributions?

    A.   non-qualified variable annuity

    B.   Roth IRA

    C.   SEP-IRA

    D.   529 Plans

30. A Series 6 licensee may accept orders for which of the following?

    A.   closed-end fund in the primary market

    B.   corporate bonds

    C.   preferred stock

    D.   REITs

31. Corporate bond interest received by an individual is taxable as:

    A.   ordinary income

    B.   ordinary income plus penalties

    C.   short-term capital gain

    D.   long-term capital gain

32. Which of the following information is NOT found in the prospectus for a mutual fund?

    A.   total return

    B.   dividend and capital gains distribution policy

    C.   investment adviser's total compensation

    D.   investment restrictions/policies

33. Which of the following statements concerning FINRA Rules on communications of a broker-dealer member firm is NOT correct?

    A.   a seminar text is defined as a retail communication if delivered to more than 25 retail investors

    B.   a letter to fewer than 25 prospects is considered correspondence

    C.   a registered representative explaining variable annuities to a local teachers' organization is considered a public appearance, not subject to prior principal approval

    D.   invitations, but not computer slide-show printouts, for investment seminars are subject to principal review and approval

34. Which of the following is a "retail communication" under FINRA rules?

- A. form letter delivered to 50 large pension funds
- B. form letter delivered to 104 prospective retail investing customers
- C. seminar handout for 20 retail investors, some of them existing customers
- D. email to an existing retail customer concerning a withdrawal of funds from the account

35. Which of the following would be found in a mutual fund's Statement of Additional Information but NOT in the prospectus?

- A. income statement for the fund
- B. name of the investment adviser
- C. list of the individual portfolio counselors of the investment adviser
- D. fees and expenses involved with investing in the fund

36. What is true of a mutual fund's responsibilities when reporting total return figures?

- A. all returns shown must be net of all expenses and fees
- B. all returns shown must be after-tax
- C. the fund may exclude any one of five years when reporting 10-year total return figures
- D. the fund must be clear regarding whether figures shown include expenses and fees

37. Which of the following represent(s) accurate statement(s) concerning mutual funds?

- I. If an investor owns shares of a fund in both an IRA and a taxable account, the holdings may not be combined for purposes of reaching a breakpoint
- II. If an investor fails to satisfy a letter of intent, the mutual fund may charge him the difference between what he intended to invest and what he actually invested
- III. Professional portfolio management and diversification are major advantages of mutual fund investing
- IV. A mutual fund may not have both a contingent deferred sales charge and a 12b-1 fee

- A. I
- B. II, IV
- C. III
- D. I, II, III, IV

38. **A mutual fund sponsor places a full-page color ad in** *Forbes* **promoting the ABC Family of Funds without mentioning any of the specific funds by name. This is known as:**

  A. sales literature

  B. generic advertising

  C. a public appearance

  D. institutional sales literature

39. **An advertisement for a conservative equity income fund shows performance figures for 1-, 5-, and 10-year periods, comparing the total return to the S&P 500 for the same time period. The advertisement contains a caveat that investors should request and read the prospectus before investing in the fund and should understand that people can and do lose money by investing in mutual funds. This advertisement is known as:**

  A. an omitting prospectus

  B. sales literature

  C. a public appearance

  D. correspondence

40. **Joshua is an associate of a FINRA member firm. Joshua's family owns a local hardware store, and Joshua occasionally works weekends at the store. What is true of this situation?**

  A. because it is a family business, Joshua's work does not need to be disclosed to his employer

  B. as long as Joshua worked at the store before taking a job with the member firm, no disclosure of his outside activities is required

  C. in order to continue supervising Joshua's work at the store, his mother must take and pass the Series 26 exam

  D. Joshua must disclose his outside activity to his employer

41. **Michelle recently completed a U4 application with a member firm. In the section on employment history, Michelle wrote that she had worked full-time at a local deli in order to avoid revealing that she was actually unemployed for a period of 11 months. Listing the telephone number of her sister's deli, Michelle instructed her sister to state that Michelle, had, in fact, worked at the deli during the time period indicated when the firm called to check employment references. Which of the following best addresses this situation?**

  A. Michelle is a liar liar pants on fire

  B. filing a misleading application with the FINRA is a violation

  C. because the work history was not securities related, no violation has occurred

  D. because the deli is a family business, no violation has occurred

42. **Which of the following is an INACCURATE statement concerning mutual funds whose names imply a focus on industries, geographic regions, or tax-exempt securities?**

    A. an industry/sector fund must adopt a policy to invest, under normal circumstances, at least 80% of its assets in the industry/sector incorporated in its name

    B. a "China Fund" would have to adopt a policy to invest, under normal circumstances, at least 80% of its assets in investments tied economically to China

    C. the "Maryland Tax-Exempt Fund" would have to adopt a policy to invest, under normal circumstances, at least 80% of its assets in investments whose income is exempt from both federal and Maryland state taxes

    D. a tax-exempt fund could contain only tax-exempt securities

43. **Investment company sales literature could be deemed to be misleading if:**

    I.   Statements about past performance imply that future gain or income may be inferred or predicted

    II. Exaggerated or unsubstantiated claims about management skill or techniques are used

    III. Necessary explanations, qualifications, and limitations are omitted

    IV. Fewer than 67% of investors in the fund have gained significantly from their investment

    A. II

    B. IV

    C. I, II, III

    D. I, II, III, IV

44. **The ABC Mutual Fund Family has launched a U.S. Treasury fund. The investment policies stipulate that 100% of fund assets are invested in securities guaranteed by the U.S. Treasury. Therefore, this fund may be described in sales literature in which of the following ways?**

    A. your investment in the fund is guaranteed by the United States Treasury

    B. your investment is guaranteed against significant loss

    C. your investment is insured by the Federal Deposit Insurance Corporation up to $100,000

    D. your investment in the fund is not a direct obligation of the United States Treasury

45. Which of the following statements is NOT accurate concerning sales literature for money market mutual funds?

A.   may describe the fund as "stable value"

B.   must disclose that maintaining the NAV at $1 is not guaranteed

C.   must disclose that it is possible to lose money by investing in the fund

D.   must disclose projected yield and total return for a period of not less than 1 year

46. Mutual fund advertising must contain a statement that:

I.   Advises an investor to consider the investment objectives, risks, charges and expenses of the investment company carefully before investing

II.   Explains that the prospectus contains this and other information about the investment company

III.   Identifies a source from which an investor may obtain a prospectus

IV.   Encourages investors to consider an equal amount of life insurance protection for every dollar invested in the fund

A.   I, II

B.   II, III

C.   I, II, III

D.   I, II, III, IV

47. Which of the following statements concerning mutual fund promotional materials is NOT true?

A.   an advertisement for a particular fund must contain a statement that investors should carefully consider the risks and objectives, fees and expenses of the fund before investing

B.   advertising can be used with a profile or abbreviated prospectus provided that the material advises the investor to carefully consider the risks and objectives, fees and expenses of the fund before investing and indicates the availability of the prospectus

C.   advertising that contains performance data must contain a legend disclosing that the data concerns past performance, which is not predictive of future performance

D.   advertising that publishes performance data must also indicate the probability that returns will match or exceed past performance

48. Which of the following statements concerning mutual fund advertising containing performance data is NOT correct?

    A.   if the fund imposes a sales charge, the maximum charge must be disclosed

    B.   if figures are shown without the sales charge factored in, a statement must be made that the sales load is not reflected and that actual results would be lower if it were

    C.   if the fund imposes a sales charge, the average sales charge (based on net assets) may be disclosed

    D.   the required legend must contain a toll-free number or a website address where investors may obtain more current data

49. Under FINRA conduct rules, which of the following could be deemed to represent conduct that is consistent with just and equitable principles of trade?

    A.   refusal to pay an arbitration award of under $25,000

    B.   filing misleading information on a Form U4

    C.   selling mutual funds just below a breakpoint

    D.   opening a customer account identified only by number

50. Which of the following mutual funds is probably least susceptible to currency exchange risk?

    A.   global

    B.   international

    C.   domestic equity

    D.   emerging market

51. Which of the following mutual funds is probably most susceptible to business risk?

    A.   small cap growth

    B.   mid-cap value

    C.   large cap growth

    D.   large cap value

52. Which of the following types of fixed income mutual funds is probably least susceptible to interest-rate risk?

    A.   intermediate-term tax-exempt fund

    B.   intermediate-term high-yield fund

    C.   long-term U.S. Treasury fund

    D.   short-term investment-grade fund

53. Which of the following types of mutual funds is probably least susceptible to purchasing power risk?

  A. intermediate-term U.S. Treasury
  B. long-term high-yield
  C. small cap growth
  D. money market

54. Which of the following types of mutual funds is most aggressive?

  A. high-yield bond
  B. small cap growth
  C. money market
  D. mid-cap value

55. Reinvestment risk would harm a fixed-income investor most in which of the following environments?

  A. stable interest rates
  B. falling interest rates
  C. rising interest rates
  D. the risk would be equal in all environments if the bonds were related below investment grade

56. Jason is a 26-year-old graduate student earning a modest stipend teaching comparative literature courses. Jason would like to invest $5,000 today in order to have the $10,000 he needs to attend a year of school in Paris two years from now. Which of the following should you discuss first with Jason?

  A. currency exchange risk
  B. reinvestment risk
  C. time horizon
  D. business risk

57. Which of the following mutual fund portfolios would likely be the most aggressive?

  A. long-term bond fund
  B. intermediate-term high-yield bond fund
  C. emerging market equity fund
  D. large cap value fund

58. **Ethan is a registered representative whose client, Calvin, is investing for the purpose of college-related expenses for his now 15-year-old daughter. In a low-interest-rate environment, Ethan does not feel that the fixed income market can provide the yield Calvin needs. Calvin is skeptical of the stock market and tells Ethan that he would be more comfortable investing in Treasury notes or something similar. Ethan convinces Calvin that small cap stocks are ripe for a rally over the next two or three years, and so Calvin allocates 80% of his capital to a small cap growth fund and 20% to a high-yield bond fund. Calvin's investments perform well and therefore Ethan:**

    A. exercised good judgment in recommending a superior investment plan

    B. exercised the implied discretionary authority he would have over such an account

    C. violated FINRA Rules on recommendations to customers by recommending equities

    D. violated FINRA Rules on recommendations to customers by recommending securities inappropriate given the client's time horizon and risk tolerance

59. **All of the following represent violations of FINRA conduct rules EXCEPT:**

    A. instructing a client to write a check in the name of the sales agent

    B. recommending low-priced, speculative securities to income investors with short time horizons

    C. splitting commissions with another agent at the firm

    D. recommending the purchase of C-shares to an investor with a long time horizon and $300,000 to invest

60. **Mary Ellen plans to invest for her remaining three years of college in order to buy her first home upon graduation. She and her registered representative have allocated her capital as follows: 40% intermediate-term fixed income, 40% short-term fixed income, 20% growth & income. The mutual fund family to which the three funds belong offers A-, B-, and C-class shares. In general, Mary Ellen, with $12,000 to invest, should:**

    A. purchase the A-shares because the maximum sales charge is only 5.5%

    B. purchase the B-shares, because the contingent deferred sales charge drops to 4% during the third year

    C. purchase the C-shares, which are suitable for a short-term mutual fund investment

    D. purchase the B-shares because of the relatively low 12b-1 fees typically charged

61. **An equity indexed annuity has a minimum guaranteed rate of 2%, a participation rate of 70%, and an annual cap of 8%. Therefore, what happens to the contract value if the underlying index advances 17%?**

    A.   the value is increased by 2%

    B.   the value is increased by 8%

    C.   the value is increased by 11.9%

    D.   as a fixed annuity, the contract value remains the same

62. **FINRA rules on fair dealing with customers declare that which of the following should be used in determining the fairness of a member firm's sales activities?**

    A.   whether they can be reasonably said to represent fair treatment of customers

    B.   whether they result in profits to customers

    C.   both choices listed

    D.   neither choice listed

63. **Which of the following is/are deducted from the premium paid (purchase payment) into a variable contract?**

    A.   sales charges

    B.   premium tax

    C.   administrative fee

    D.   all choices listed

64. **Certain fees are deducted from the premium when an investor purchases a variable annuity. Which of the following is/are deducted from the sub-account values after being allocated to the separate account?**

    A.   mortality risk fee

    B.   expense risk fee

    C.   both choices listed

    D.   neither choice listed

65. **If a variable annuity has an AIR of 4% and the separate account grows at an annualized rate of return equal to 5%, this appreciation:**

    A.   is taxable only to the separate account

    B.   is taxable as ordinary income to an annuitant in the accumulation phase

    C.   will increase the amount received by annuitants in the pay-out phase

    D.   is taxable as a long-term capital gain to an annuitant in the accumulation phase

66. **A mutual fund and a variable annuity separate account are similar in all the following ways EXCEPT:**

    A. professional management of the portfolio

    B. registered under Investment Company Act of 1940

    C. investor assumes investment risk

    D. tax deferral

67. **AIR is a factor in determining value for:**

    I.   Death benefit in a variable life policy

    II.   Cash value in a variable life policy

    III. An accumulation unit

    IV.   An annuity unit

    A. I, II, III, IV

    B. II, IV

    C. III, IV

    D. I, IV

68. **If a client prefers fixed/scheduled payment of premium, she should purchase:**

    I.   Variable Life Insurance

    II.   Variable Universal Life Insurance

    III. Whole Life Insurance

    IV.   Universal Life Insurance

    A. II, III

    B. II, IV

    C. I, IV

    D. I, III

69. **All of the following statements concerning Variable Life Insurance are true EXCEPT:**

    A. variable life insurance has a death benefit that may fluctuate

    B. variable life insurance has a cash value that may fluctuate

    C. variable life insurance is primarily an insurance vehicle

    D. variable life insurance is primarily an investment vehicle

70. All of the following may be deducted from the proceeds of a mutual fund redemption EXCEPT:

    A.   contingent deferred sales charge

    B.   redemption fee

    C.   backup withholding tax

    D.   management fee

71. An investor seeking to minimize volatility would LEAST likely purchase:

    A.   growth funds

    B.   equity income funds

    C.   balanced funds

    D.   short-term corporate bond funds

72. An investor seeking to minimize price volatility would most likely purchase:

    A.   balanced funds

    B.   equity income funds

    C.   intermediate-term government bond funds

    D.   short-term government bond funds

73. All of the following statements concerning contingent deferred sales charges are correct EXCEPT:

    A.   associated with B shares

    B.   charges decline gradually and typically are eliminated within 6–8 years

    C.   such charges are synonymous with redemption fees that revert to the fund's portfolio

    D.   a confirmation for a fund that assesses a contingent deferred sales charge must disclose that a charge may be assessed upon redemption, even if the same disclosure is made in the prospectus

74. Which of the following investments would be expected to have the lowest volatility?

    A.   small cap growth fund

    B.   mid-cap value fund

    C.   government bond fund

    D.   money market fund

75. Which of the following statements regarding open-end mutual funds is NOT true?

    A.   may not close off purchases to new investors

    B.   do not have to maintain diversified portfolios

    C.   must register with the SEC

    D.   do not trade on the secondary market

76. You could accurately inform an investing customer that sales charge percentages are expressed in which of the following ways?

    A.   upon customer demand

    B.   as a percentage of the net amount invested

    C.   as a percentage of the gross amount invested

    D.   as a percentage of the fund's total return

77. If an investor were reading a prospectus profiling all of the mutual funds offered within a mutual fund complex, she would expect to see which of the following categorized as having the lowest price volatility?

    A.   growth

    B.   equity income

    C.   balanced

    D.   growth & income

78. A short seller would only be interested in which of the following?

    A.   growth & income fund

    B.   tax-exempt bond fund

    C.   exchange-traded fund

    D.   equity income fund

79. The Johnson Aggressive Growth Fund had a NAV of $10 at the beginning of the year, ending the year at $9. The fund distributed $.50 in dividends and $1.00 in capital gains. Therefore, the total return was:

    A.   −25%

    B.   5%

    C.   25%

    D.   −10%

80. All of the following represent the functions of a mutual fund's investment adviser EXCEPT:

    A.   deciding which securities to purchase

    B.   deciding when to purchase particular securities

    C.   establishing investment policy

    D.   performing economic/portfolio analysis

81. Which of the following is NOT a function of a mutual fund's board of directors?

    A.   overseeing the investment adviser

    B.   managing the portfolio

    C.   overseeing the custodian and transfer agent

    D.   establishing investment policy

82. Which of the following statements concerning systematic withdrawal plans from mutual funds is NOT correct?

    A.   investors should not make further investments into the fund when a systematic withdrawal plan is in place

    B.   a fixed percentage withdrawal plan involves liquidating varying numbers of shares

    C.   a fixed share withdrawal plan pays out a varying amount of money to the investor

    D.   investors may expect to earn a minimum rate of return during the withdrawal period

83. Which of the following terms describes the fact that an investor in a mutual fund owns a percentage of all securities held in the portfolio?

    A.   duration

    B.   beta

    C.   undivided interest

    D.   fractional shares

84. Which of the following correctly describe accumulation units and annuity units?

    I.   the number of accumulation units varies

    II.   the value of accumulation units is fixed

    III.   the number of annuity units is fixed

    IV.   the value of annuity units varies

    A.   I, III

    B.   II, IV

    C.   III, IV

    D.   I, III, IV

85. **FINRA rules require registered representatives to consider suitability when making recommendations to customers. If a registered representative recommends the purchase of a security that is suitable on its face but becomes unsuitable given the size or frequency of trading recommended, FINRA rules cover this concern under which of the following?**

    A. customer-specific suitability

    B. quantitative suitability

    C. reasonable-basis suitability

    D. insider trading rules

86. **If a customer wants to bet against the price of a common stock and take on the least amount of risk, he should perform which of the following options transactions?**

    A. buy a put

    B. sell a call

    C. buy a call

    D. sell a put

87. **Which of the following payout options typically offers the smallest monthly payment to the annuitant?**

    A. life with 10-year period certain

    B. straight life

    C. joint with last survivor

    D. life with 5-year period certain

88. **Which TWO of the following statements concerning taxation of insurance policies are true?**

    I. Death benefits are not taxable to the beneficiary

    II. Death benefits are taxable to the beneficiary

    III. Death benefits are included in the insured's estate

    IV. Death benefits are not included in the insured's estate

    A. I, III

    B. I, IV

    C. II, III

    D. II, IV

89. **Under FINRA rules member firms may purchase open-end investment company shares:**

   I.   in order to fill existing customer orders

   II.   for the firm's proprietary account

   III. in order to fill anticipated orders

   A.   I

   B.   II

   C.   I, II

   D.   I, II, III

90. **A suspicious activity report (SAR-SF) should be filed:**

   A.   only if the broker-dealer has actual knowledge of criminal activity

   B.   only if the broker-dealer has obtained a proper search warrant

   C.   only if the parties are on the OFAC list

   D.   for most types of suspicious activity, depending on the facts/circumstances

91. **A registered rep working for Broker-Dealer Blue wants to start an investment account with Broker-Dealer Red. If both firms are FINRA members, which of the following correctly describes the steps that need to be taken?**

   A.   the account may not be opened

   B.   the account may be opened upon court order

   C.   Red must receive written permission from Blue

   D.   Red must notify Blue in writing and send duplicate trade confirmations upon request

92. **Which of the following would protect an investor against missing assets due to the failure of her broker-dealer firm?**

   A.   FDIC

   B.   SIPC

   C.   SEC

   D.   FRB

93. A broker-dealer delivers a trade confirmation to a customer. The trade confirmation indicates that the firm acted in an "agency" capacity. Therefore, the firm acted as a:

A. fiduciary

B. dealer

C. broker

D. market maker

94. Which of the following customer requests would be considered a discretionary order requiring written authorization from the client before being executed?

A. buy 1,000 shares of IBM this afternoon.

B. sell 1,000 shares of ORCL this afternoon

C. purchase 1,000 shares of a bank holding company today

D. buy 1,000 shares of IBM at the best price you think we can obtain today

95. A member of an underwriting syndicate claims that the managing underwriter owes the firm $300,000. If the syndicate member submits the claim to FINRA Arbitration and loses, the firm may immediately appeal the ruling to:

A. DOE

B. NAC

C. SEC

D. none of the choices listed

96. Which of the following represents an accurate statement concerning variable annuities?

A. an investor younger than 59½ may take a series of substantially equally periodic payments for 5 years or until age 59½ (whichever occurs last) tax-free

B. an investor younger than 59½ may take a series of substantially equally periodic payments for 5 years or until age 59½ (whichever occurs last) without incurring a 10% penalty tax

C. when a beneficiary receives the proceeds of the death benefit, the proceeds are taxed at long-term capital gains rates

D. when a beneficiary receives the proceeds of the death benefit, the excess over cost basis is tax-free

97. **Melvin invested $25,000 into a single-payment deferred annuity (SPDA) three years ago, at age 58. If the account is now worth $40,000 and Melvin takes a random withdrawal of $20,000, what are the tax implications?**

    A.   no taxes are due because Melvin is 61 years old

    B.   because he is 61 years old, the withdrawal will be considered a long-term capital gain

    C.   the entire $20,000 is taxable as ordinary income

    D. $15,000 is taxable as ordinary income

98. **A registered representative has a client who is looking to invest for retirement, but also wants a current tax deduction. The RR would suggest a:**

    A.   Roth IRA

    B.   401(k)

    C.   Coverdell IRA

    D.   529 Savings Plan

99. **Which of the following statements is NOT accurate concerning Roth IRAs?**

    A.   the investor may remove the amount contributed without tax implications after 5 years

    B.   contributions are not deducted from the individual's taxable income

    C.   distributions are tax-free, subject to some restrictions

    D.   mutual funds and annuities are the only investment options currently allowed

100. **If an investor wants to cover his granddaughter's college expenses, including room and board, and has a substantial amount to invest, you would most likely recommend a:**

    A.   Coverdell account

    B.   529 Prepaid Tuition plan

    C.   529 Savings Plan

    D.   Roth IRA

Answers to Practice Exam 2

1. **ANSWER:** A

   WHY: Congress & The President enact fiscal policy through taxing and spending policies. The less they tax, and the more they spend, the better for the economy.

2. **ANSWER:** D

   WHY: three things to know about hedge funds, a topic that could show up on the exam (or not). These alternative investments are open to sophisticated investors due to the aggressive trading strategies and the inability to turn them into cash when the investor wants to.

3. **ANSWER:** B

   WHY: the issuer uses the bond proceeds to build a facility that is leased to a corporation. Those lease payments back up the bond interest and principal, so the bonds are as solid as the corporation leasing the facility.

4. **ANSWER:** A

   WHY: the mortgage bonds are backed up by real estate, while the debentures are backed by a promise to pay you. The mortgage bonds offer the lowest yield, the debentures higher than that, and the subordinated debentures still higher.

5. **ANSWER:** D

   WHY: remember that all compensation to the underwriters and selling group is built into the price paid by an investor in a primary market transaction. The spread is built into the public offering price, in other words; the firm cannot also tack on a commission here.

6. **ANSWER:** B

   WHY: frequent annuity switches are a red flag.

7. **ANSWER:** A

   WHY: Agents must consult the firm's written supervisory procedures before borrowing or lending with any customer of the firm.

8. **ANSWER:** B

   WHY: on the ex-date, it's too late to get the dividend. The investor needs to purchase no later than the day before the ex-date if she wants the upcoming dividend. And, the registered rep had better not be pushing her to do it—remember that she could just skip the upcoming dividend, buy the stock cheaper on the ex-date and avoid paying tax on the dividend. If the RR tries to push it, he/she is "selling dividends," a violation of FINRA Rules.

9. **ANSWER:** D

   WHY: did you catch the word "Roth"? Since distributions from a Roth are tax-free, the IRS could sort of care less if you take them. In fact, if you have earned income, you can even keep contributing to a Roth IRA.

10. **ANSWER:** B

    WHY: if there are $30,000 of earnings, the first money coming out represents part of that. The entire $20,000—and the next $10,000—will be considered the earnings or "excess over cost basis," taxable as ordinary income.

11. **ANSWER:** D

    WHY: in any IRA, the individual is immediately vested. That means the employer can't control things as much. If the employee wants to pay the penalties and taxes in order to buy a Harley, there's nothing you can do to stop him. If you want to discourage that sort of nonsense, set up a 401(k) and make them wait 5 years until all the money you've contributed for them rightfully belongs to them.

12. **ANSWER:** D

    WHY: three things to know about 72(t) programs that allow people to take money out of retirement plans early without paying a penalty. The money is still taxed, but avoiding a 10% penalty is always nice.

13. **ANSWER:** C

    WHY: wait 30 days, buy it back on the 31st day. Otherwise, you can't use the loss you took.

14. **ANSWER:** D

    WHY: to qualify for the conduit/pipeline treatment under "IRC Subchapter M," the fund needs to send at least 90% or $900,000 in this example to get special tax treatment.

15. **ANSWER:** D

    WHY: remember that avoiding the 10% penalty is not the same thing as avoiding the ordinary income tax rates due on the early distribution, but these are three ways of avoiding the penalty.

16. **ANSWER:** B

    WHY: in any IRA, the participant is immediately vested. They might be smart enough not to take early distributions; then again, they might not be. Either way, it's their money as soon as the employer makes the contribution on their behalf in a SEP or SIMPLE IRA.

17. **ANSWER:** D

WHY: and, as you may recall, the Howey case/decision further clarifies what an "investment contract" is. Basically, if you invest money into something where you'll benefit solely through the efforts of others, it's an investment contract, which is a security. The other choices are investments, but not "securities." They are either insurance products or bank products.

18. **ANSWER:** D

WHY: the three-pronged approach is trying to pull people into the fold and make them register. If one of the criteria for deciding if you had to register were whether you were registered, then, that would mean that as long as you aren't registered, you don't have to be registered.

19. **ANSWER:** C

WHY: fraud takes place when ANY person in connection with the offer, sale, or purchase of ANY security misleads or uses deception. So, whether the thing has to register or not is irrelevant. If it is a "security," it is subject to anti-fraud rules.

20. **ANSWER:** C

WHY: because of the Securities Exchange Act of 1934, the SEC is at the top of the ladder, the regulator of the regulators, you might say. Securities offerings, stock exchanges, securities associations, and broker-dealers all have to register with the SEC under this federal securities law.

21. **ANSWER:** D

WHY: some states let residents deduct their contributions from state income taxes, so it's important to consider the account owner's state of residence when selling 529 plans. Unlike with a Coverdell, in a 529 Plan, the account owner always maintains control of the assets.

22. **ANSWER:** D

WHY: even though we normally think of 401(k) plans as being available to larger companies, a sole proprietor can actually set one up to take advantage of the higher contribution limits versus the Roth and the Traditional IRA.

23. **ANSWER:** A

WHY: if you take your 401(k) balance and roll it into an IRA, that doesn't count as a current-year contribution. If you want to move a pre-tax plan balance into a Roth, you'd have to pay taxes on everything, because the only money that goes into a Roth IRA is after-tax money.

24. **ANSWER:** A

WHY: alimony is earned income, but the point of the question was not to teach you that—it was to force you to eliminate the other three wrong answers. A Traditional IRA could be converted to a Roth IRA after taxes are paid on the money coming out of the Traditional—not the other way around. In order to take tax-free distributions from a Roth IRA, the individual has to be both 59½ years old and the account has to be five years old. For a true "rollover," where the custodian cuts a check in your name, you must complete that process in 60, not 120, days.

25. **ANSWER:** B

WHY: nobody gets taxed on unrealized capital gains. If you're up $40,000 on an investment, good for you. There is no capital gain until you pull the trigger and sell the investment. Under the conduit tax treatment, if the fund distributes 90% +, the fund is taxed only on the part they did not distribute to shareholders.

26. **ANSWER:** D

WHY: in a money purchase plan the employer has to make contributions whether the business is profitable or not.

27. **ANSWER:** D

WHY: no collectible items in the IRA, but U.S. Gold/Silver coins are okay. There are really no securities that can't be purchased for an IRA; however, municipal bonds would make no sense, since the money coming out of a pre-tax IRA is taxable when distributed. A municipal bond pays interest that is tax-free, so it belongs in a taxable account.

28. **ANSWER:** B

WHY: real simple—the TSA/403(b) plan is funded with pre-tax dollars, so the IRS taxes all the dollars on the way out. There is no cost basis—as with a Traditional IRA, it's all taxable when distributed at retirement. And, remember, we don't pay capital gains rates on retirement plan money. Many people wish they could do that, but that's another story.

29. **ANSWER:** C

WHY: the SEP and the SIMPLE IRAs are funded with pre-tax/tax-deductible dollars.

30. **ANSWER:** A

WHY: a Series 6 license holder can be part of the IPO (primary offering) for a closed-end fund. The other securities cannot be sold individually by a Series 6 licensee. They have to be purchased as a packaged set inside a mutual fund, annuity, or variable life policy. Also, once the closed-end fund has been sold to investors on the primary market, a Series 6 license holder may not execute trades on it, since it is now trading as an individual share of stock, just like GE, MSFT, SBUX, etc.

31. **ANSWER:** A

WHY: when bond interest is taxable, it's taxable as ordinary income.

32. **ANSWER:** C

WHY: try to read through a prospectus and an SAI for at least one mutual fund before taking the Series 6. For now, know that the total compensation paid to the adviser—as well as the income statement and balance sheet for the fund—would be found in the more detailed SAI or shareholder report. The other information is in both the prospectus and the summary prospectus.

33. **ANSWER:** D

WHY: Seminar invitations and computer slideshows are both considered "communications," so if they're delivered to > 25 retail investors, they are deemed "retail communications" subject to prior principal approval and filing.

34. **ANSWER:** B

WHY: Written communications to > 25 retail investors are retail communications. The e-mail is correspondence, and the communication to institutional investors = an institutional communication.

35. **ANSWER:** A

WHY: the SAI shows the exact securities in the portfolio, as well as how much dividend and interest income the portfolio generated over the year, minus the operating expenses (income statement). The prospectus, on the other hand, would show usually just the industry sectors and the top 10 holdings.

36. **ANSWER:** D

WHY: the prospectus must be clear whether results shown reflect expenses or not. If not, they must indicate that returns would be lower if expenses had been included. Same thing for the effect of taxation. When they show "after-tax" returns, they use the highest tax bracket, which means investors in lower brackets actually enjoyed higher returns, and those holding the fund in a retirement plan would not find the after-tax return relevant.

37. **ANSWER:** C

WHY: in almost all cases, the fund family lets you combine purchases of the fund across all your accounts. Your Traditional IRA, Roth IRA, UGMA account for your daughter, joint account with your husband or wife…even when we call the fund a "sub-account" within your variable annuity…all of those purchases are generally combined for purposes of a breakpoint. If an investor fails to satisfy a letter of intent, he doesn't get all the shares he intended to get—the shares held in escrow are redeemed to cover the higher sales charge that now applies, but the fund does NOT get to send a bill for the difference between the $100,000 he intended to invest and the $69,000 he actually invested. A mutual fund with a CDSC (B-shares) would also have a 12b-1 fee, and that 12b-1 fee would be higher than it would be on the A-shares.

38. **ANSWER:** B

   WHY: an advertisement promoting a fund family (not a particular growth, income, value, etc., fund) is considered generic advertising.

39. **ANSWER:** A

   WHY: an omitting prospectus promotes a particular fund within the family. So, if it's a print ad for T Rowe Price, that's generic advertising. If it's a print ad for the T Rowe Price Equity Income Fund, that's an omitting prospectus. It promotes the fund but—obviously—omits many, many details contained in the prospectus, which is why it has to have a warning that investors should read the prospectus before investing.

40. **ANSWER:** D

   WHY: keep it simple and tell the firm about any work you do for compensation.

41. **ANSWER:** B

   WHY: be a good test-taker—there is only one tempting answer here. Well, two tempting answers, but only one that the exam will accept.

42. **ANSWER:** D

   WHY: mutual fund names are never exactly what they imply, but under normal circumstances 80% of the portfolio must comply with what the name suggests.

43. **ANSWER:** C

   WHY: remember that no one is assured of having gains when investing in securities. There are a few income-producing securities that are guaranteed to pay income, but you won't see the phrase "guaranteed profits" or "guaranteed results" when it comes to investing. In fact, if you do see phrases like that, the person using them is probably going to end up hearing from the regulators eventually if not sooner.

44. **ANSWER:** D

   WHY: the mutual fund owns U.S. Treasury Securities. Your chance of losing a bunch of money is very, very slim. Then again, you might be the impatient sort, or the type of investor who can't stick to a plan. You promised you'd invest for at least 10 years, but—turns out—you want your money back 18 months after purchasing the fund, when interest rates have skyrocketed. You would sell at a NAV much lower than you paid to get in. Therefore, your investment is not insured against loss or foolishness. NOT FDIC INSURED, MAY LOSE VALUE, NO BANK GUARANTEE.

45. **ANSWER:** D

WHY: no projections of mutual fund performance are allowed, ever. Money market mutual funds have to be clear that nothing is guaranteed—these are mutual funds, not bank deposits. They will always keep the shares priced at $1, unless the shares drop below $1. Most of these funds are in the "stable value" category. If so, they have to make these disclosures, that even though they'll most likely keep the share price stable at $1, if interest rates get ridiculously low, or if the credit markets seize up as they did in 2008, it's going to be tough to cover expenses and keep the shares priced at $1. When the credit markets "seized up" in 2008, money market funds were only able to maintain the share price at 97 cents. Maybe I've been buying stocks too long, but if this counts as a "catastrophe," I think I'll survive.

46. **ANSWER:** C

WHY: there is no requirement to talk investors into buying life insurance, but the other three statements must be contained in mutual fund advertising.

47. **ANSWER:** D

WHY: no projections of future performance are allowed for mutual fund promotional materials or sales efforts by registered representatives.

48. **ANSWER:** C

WHY: a company such as American Funds, with front-end loads, would use the highest sales charge imposed, not some average paid by all investors investing at various breakpoints.

49. **ANSWER:** D

WHY: numbered accounts are okay, provided the broker-dealer has the customer's statement of ownership on file.

50. **ANSWER:** C

WHY: if the fund focuses on U.S. companies (domestic), there shouldn't be a huge amount of currency exchange risk.

51. **ANSWER:** A

WHY: small cap growth stocks don't pay dividends, generally, so how strong can the businesses really be, especially when the value of their outstanding shares is small?

52. **ANSWER:** D

WHY: long-term bonds pay higher yields but leave the investor with more interest-rate risk. Rates up/price way down. If you want to reduce interest-rate risk, you buy short-term bonds, but the tradeoff is that they pay lower yields. There is no free lunch.

53. **ANSWER:** C

   WHY: buy stock to protect against loss of purchasing power (inflation) over the long-term. But factor in "loss of sleep" as you hold a more volatile investment than bonds or money market securities.

54. **ANSWER:** B

   WHY: high-yield bond funds are aggressive…for bond funds. But investing in stocks is a much rougher sport. Now, the lower the "cap," the more aggressive the portfolio. Small cap growth is the most aggressive, with large cap value being the least aggressive on the equity style box.

55. **ANSWER:** B

   WHY: you've seen many questions that focus on rates up—price down. That's interest rate risk. When rates are falling, the reinvested interest payments buy bonds with lower and lower yields. That's reinvestment risk. And, yes, you get hit coming or going when you own bonds. Luckily, your principal value is MUCH more stable than it would be in a stock fund.

56. **ANSWER:** C

   WHY: if somebody wants to double his money in two years, he needs a 36% return both years. This, by the way, is the so-called "rule of 72." Take the rate and divide it into 72— that's how many years it takes to double your money. Or, the other side of the coin is this—take the number of years you can wait for your money to double and divide that into 72—that's the rate of return you would need to get. Jason, buddy, let's talk about time horizon first. Then, perhaps, we can discuss vocational choices and the importance of getting a job when and if your college days finally end.

57. **ANSWER:** C

   WHY: emerging markets—lots of potential, but also very volatile.

58. **ANSWER:** D

   WHY: not only is the customer uncomfortable with stocks, but also his time horizon is too short to be messing around with equities. Check out the bar charts for most small cap funds. You will find plenty of three-year periods where $100,000 invested would end up being worth about $50,000 when the investor sells. Can you imagine facing this client after you talked him out of something safe and ended up halving his money for him?

59. **ANSWER:** C

   WHY: you can split commissions with other registered agents at your firm. You would discuss this with your principal/supervisor, of course. Remember that C-shares are for short-term investors, especially with smaller amounts of money to invest.

60. **ANSWER:** C

    WHY: if she had a longer time horizon and more money to invest, the A-shares would have been better. A large amount of money could knock down the sales charge, and spreading that upfront load over several years makes it more palatable. But, she won't reach the first breakpoint, and she'll be jumping out pretty soon, so the C-shares make sense. She'll avoid a front- and back-end load, and even though she'll pay a higher 12b-1 fee, it will only be for 3 years.

61. **ANSWER:** B

    WHY: The participation rate is the percentage of the index's increase credited to the account, but that amount is capped, so the cap rate is applied here.

62. **ANSWER:** A

    WHY: hey, as long as the customer made money, what's the big deal? Wrong.

63. **ANSWER:** D

    WHY: use "S-A-S" to remember this, which stands for Sales charge, Administrative fee, State premium tax.

64. **ANSWER:** C

    WHY: mortality guarantees and expense guarantees are only possible because the insurance company charges ongoing mortality and expense risk fees.

65. **ANSWER:** C

    WHY: when the account does better than AIR, the annuitant's check gets bigger. If you chose "B," you might have been reading too quickly—you don't pay taxes during the accumulation phase, during which the investment grows tax-deferred.

66. **ANSWER:** D

    WHY: the main difference between the variable annuity and the mutual fund is that the annuity offers tax deferral. It also offers a death benefit, assuring that your beneficiary will receive at least as much as you put in.

67. **ANSWER:** D

    WHY: on the way in there is no AIR. You're just hoping the investments grow. On the way out (annuity payment, death benefit), they take actual returns versus AIR, just to keep everything nice and simple.

68. **ANSWER:** D

    WHY: the word "universal" means "flexible premium." In these policies, clients are forever changing the value of the contract and how much they pay in. Maybe they cannibalize the contract and let the cash value pay the premium for them.

69. **ANSWER:** D

WHY: if you market variable life insurance primarily as an investment vehicle, the regulators will get mighty ticked. Even though it has investment features, it should be marketed primarily as an insurance policy with a death benefit.

70. **ANSWER:** D

WHY: management fees are a separate line item in the expenses of the fund. The fund cannot bury them—they disclose the separate management fee, along with the 12b-1 fee, and other fees charged by the fund.

71. **ANSWER:** A

WHY: it is accepted in this industry that growth funds in particular, and stock funds in general, are pretty freaking volatile. Now, when you start buying things that provide regular income, you reduce the volatility of the fund. So, a growth fund is the most volatile. An equity income fund would buy stocks with high dividend yields, so there would be less volatility. A balanced fund, with a big chunk of assets in the bond market, would be less volatile than either.

72. **ANSWER:** D

WHY: you can rule out the equity fund first, then the balanced fund, which devotes a big chunk to equity securities. Now, which of the two fixed-income funds is most susceptible to interest rates? The longer-term fund. Go with the short-term fund and call it a day.

73. **ANSWER:** C

WHY: the contingent deferred sales charge (back-end load) goes to the distributors of the fund. A redemption fee is a little penalty that stays in the portfolio to cover the pain-in-the-neck process of redeeming shares for impatient investors.

74. **ANSWER:** D

WHY: most money market mutual funds are called "stable value," so that should be a pretty good clue. Why would a Treasury fund have volatility? Rates up/price down.

75. **ANSWER:** A

WHY: mutual funds often realize they have more money than they know what to do with. When that happens, they close off the fund to new investors. And, no, that doesn't make them closed-end funds—they don't suddenly start trading among investors on the secondary market.

76. **ANSWER:** C

WHY: the sales charge percentage is the percentage of the gross amount invested that goes to sales charges. If the NAV is $10.00 and the POP is $10.50, the sales charge is 50 cents divided by $10.50, which is less than 5%.

77. **ANSWER:** C

WHY: since equity securities are inherently more volatile than fixed-income, you can answer the question by deciding which fund has the highest concentration in bonds/lowest concentration in equities.

78. **ANSWER:** C

WHY: an ETF trades like any other share of stock, so it can be sold short and purchased on margin.

79. **ANSWER:** B

WHY: the NAV went down $1, but the fund also paid out $1.50, so the investor would be up 50 cents outa' $10, or up 5% in total.

80. **ANSWER:** C

WHY: the adviser would follow the investment policies established by the board of directors.

81. **ANSWER:** B

WHY: the board has a contract with an investment adviser, who manages the portfolio. How do they cover the cost of the investment adviser? By charging investors management fees.

82. **ANSWER:** D

WHY: you will not find a minimum rate of return coming from a mutual fund.

83. **ANSWER:** C

WHY: if you chose "beta" or "duration" please drop and give us 25 push-ups and stop being so darned lazy. It wasn't going to be "beta" or "duration" and you knew it.

84. **ANSWER:** D

WHY: this is a very likely question. The only thing to associate with "fixed" in this question is the number of annuity units. Everything else varies.

85. **ANSWER:** B

WHY: The quantity of trade recommendations is considered under the quantitative suitability standard. A recommendation that makes sense by itself can become unsuitable if it's over-used, for example.

86. **ANSWER:** A

WHY: to bet against a stock, investors can buy a put or sell a call. Buying options is always safer than selling them. A put buyer can only lose the premium paid, while a call seller faces unlimited risk.

87. **ANSWER:** C

WHY: if you want to cover your life plus the life of your 21-year-old daughter, the annuity company would be using a really long life expectancy to determine the rather meager monthly payment. Then again, does it really matter how large the monthly payment is—if they pay your daughter starting at age 48 and keep on paying until she's 83, that's going to represent a whole lot of income, no matter how slowly it was paid to her.

88. **ANSWER:** A

WHY: please memorize these two important points about the tax implications of insurance.

89. **ANSWER:** C

WHY: the main point is that they don't place orders unless they have a customer order or they're buying for the firm's account.

90. **ANSWER:** D

WHY: the broker-dealer is not a law enforcement agency applying for warrants—their requirement is simply to file an SAR-SF when they see suspicious activity.

91. **ANSWER:** D

WHY: the other member firm has to notify the employing member firm, and they will send duplicate trade confirmations if the employing broker-dealer requests it.

92. **ANSWER:** B

WHY: mutual fund shares are typically held by a transfer agent, but other securities and cash held by broker-dealers are protected against their failure, up to $500,000 total per account.

93. **ANSWER:** C

WHY: the word "broker-dealer" is hyphenated and should remind us that the firm can either act as a broker (agency capacity) or a dealer (principal capacity) on any trade.

94. **ANSWER:** C

WHY: which bank holding company will the investor end up owning? All depends on the agent's discretion, right?

95. **ANSWER:** D

WHY: no appeals to arbitration. Don't confuse arbitration with Code of Procedure. Code of Procedure, which handles rule violations and doles out harsh punishments to wayward firms and agents, has an appeal process for those who can handle the hefty legal bills.

96. **ANSWER:** B

   WHY: you can't avoid paying ordinary income tax on the excess over cost basis, but it is nice to be able to touch the money earlier than expected without paying the 10% penalty tax. Keep it simple—we don't get to pay capital gains rates on retirement money. If it's taxable, it's taxable as ordinary income. And, in an annuity the excess over cost basis is what is taxable, not tax-free.

97. **ANSWER:** D

   WHY: he has $15,000 in earnings, and he's taking all of that out plus another $5,000 of his cost basis.

98. **ANSWER:** B

   WHY: only the 401(k) in this question offers tax-deductible contributions.

99. **ANSWER:** D

   WHY: since the money you put in went in after-tax, the IRS could sort of care less if you want to be all restless and take that money out. However, if you think you're getting any amount above what you put in back tax-free, you'll have to wait at least 5 years AND be at least 59½. The investment options would be the same between a Roth or a Traditional IRA held by the same custodian.

100. **ANSWER:** C

   WHY: the Coverdell is great for folks with a limited amount to invest. The prepaid tuition plans are generally only used for—get this—tuition. The 529 money can be used for just about any legitimate college expense other than quarter beer nights and bad late-night pizzas.

Glossary

1035 Contract Exchange: a tax-free exchange of one annuity contract for another, one life insurance policy for another, or one life insurance policy for an annuity. The contracts do not have to be issued by the same company.

12b-1 Fee: annual fee deducted quarterly from a mutual fund's assets to cover distribution costs, e.g., selling, mailing, printing, advertising. An operating expense, unlike the sales charge that is deducted from the investor's check.

401(k) Plan: qualified defined contribution plan offering employer-matched contributions.

403(b): qualified plan for tax-exempt, nonprofit organizations.

529 Plans: education savings plans offering tax-deferred growth and tax-free distributions at the federal level for qualified educational expenses. Prepaid tuition plans allow clients to purchase a certain number of tuition credits at today's prices to be used at a school within a particular state. 529 Savings Plans allow clients to contribute up to the current gift tax exclusion without paying gift taxes. Earnings grow tax-deferred and may be used for qualified education expenses (more than just tuition) later without federal taxation. States can tax the plans—so know the customer's situation!

72(t): a neat trick under IRS tax code allowing people to take money from retirement plans including annuities without paying penalties, even though they aren't 59½ yet.

75-5-10 Rule: diversification formula for a fund advertising itself as "diversified." 75% of the portfolio must have no more than 5% of assets invested in any one security, and no more than 10% of a company's outstanding shares may be owned.

A

A-shares: mutual fund shares sold with a front-end sales load/charge. Lower annual expenses than B- and C-shares.

Account Executive (AE): another name for a registered representative or agent.

Acceptance, Waiver, and Consent (AWC): method of resolving a disciplinary matter in which the respondent does not dispute the charges and waives his right to appeal the decision of the hearing panel.

Accredited Investors: large institutional investors, and individuals meeting certain income or net worth requirements allowing them to participate in, for example, a private placement under Reg D of the Securities Act of 1933, or hedge funds.

Accrued Interest: the interest that the buyer of a debt security owes the seller. Bond interest is payable only twice a year, and the buyer will receive the next full interest payment. Therefore, the buyer owes the sellers for every day of interest since the last payment up to the day before the transaction settles.

Accumulation Phase/Period: the period during which contributions are made to an annuity, at which time the investor holds "accumulation units."

Accumulation Units: what the purchaser of an annuity buys during the pay-in or accumulation phase, an accounting measure representing a proportional share of the separate account during the accumulation/deposit stage.

Active Management: a style of investing where the investor actively selects certain securities over other alternatives. Based on the premise that information is not immediately acted upon and that markets are not perfectly efficient.

Adjustable Rate Preferred Stock: preferred stock whose dividend is tied to another rate, often the rate paid on T-bills.

Adjusted Gross Income (AGI): earned income plus passive income, portfolio income, and capital gains. The amount upon which we pay income tax.

Administrator: (1) the securities regulator of a particular state, (2) a person or entity authorized by the courts to liquidate an estate.

ADR/ADS: American Depository Receipt/Share. A foreign stock on a domestic market. Toyota and Nokia are two examples of foreign companies whose ADRs trade on American stock markets denominated in dollars. Carry all the risks of owning stocks, plus "currency exchange risk."

Advertising: communications by a member firm directed at a general, uncontrolled audience, e.g., billboard, radio/TV/newspaper ads, website.

Affiliated Person: anyone in a position to influence decisions at a public corporation, including board members (directors), officers (CEO, CFO), and large shareholders (Warren Buffett at Coca-Cola or Wells Fargo).

After-tax Yield: the amount of interest income remaining after the investor pays taxes on it. For example, the after-tax yield on a 10% bond is 7% if the investor is in the 30% tax bracket.

Agency Issue (Agency Bond): a debt security issued by an agency authorized by the federal government but not directly backed by the federal government.

Agency Transaction: a securities transaction in which the broker-dealer acts as an agent for the buyer or seller, completing the transaction between the customer and another party.

Agent: an individual representing a broker-dealer or issuer in effecting/completing transactions in securities for compensation. What you will be after passing your exams and obtaining your securities license.

Agreement Among Underwriters: a document used by an underwriting syndicate bringing an issue of securities to the primary market. This document sets forth the terms under which each member of the syndicate will participate and details the duties and responsibilities of the syndicate manager.

AIR: Assumed Interest Rate. Determined by an actuary, representing his best estimate of the monthly annualized rate of return from the separate account. Used to determine value of annuity units for annuities and death benefit for variable life contracts.

All or None: a type of underwriting in which the syndicate will cancel the offering if a sufficient dollar amount is not raised as opposed to being responsible for the unsold shares (as in a "firm commitment").

Alternative Minimum Tax: See AMT.

American Stock Exchange (AMEX): a private, not-for-profit corporation that handles roughly 20% of all securities trades in the U.S. One of the big secondary markets, along with NYSE, and the various NASDAQ markets.

AMT (Alternative Minimum Tax): tax computation that adds certain "tax preference items" back into adjusted gross income. Some municipal bond interest is treated as a "tax preference item" that can raise the investor's tax liability through the AMT.

Annual Compliance Review: a broker-dealer's annual compliance meeting that is mandatory for principals and registered representatives.

Annual Gift Tax Exclusion: annual amount that an individual may give to another person without having to pay gift taxes.

Annual Report: a formal statement issued by a corporation to the SEC and shareholders discussing the company's results of operations, challenges/risks facing the company, any lawsuits against the company, etc. Required by the Securities Exchange Act of 1934.

Annuitant: the person who receives an annuity contract's distribution.

Annuitize: the process of changing the annuity contract from the "pay-in" or accumulation phase to the "pay-out" or distribution phase. Defined benefit pension plans, such as the ones that have done so much good for GM and Ford, generally offer their pensioners either a lump sum payment or the chance to annuitize. Hint to GM pensioners—take the LUMP SUM AND RUN!

Annuity: a contract between an individual and an insurance company that generally guarantees income for the rest of the individual's life in return for a lump-sum or periodic payment to the insurance company.

Annuity Units: what the annuitant holds during the pay-out phase. Value tied to AIR.

Anti-fraud Statute: legislation in federal and state securities law outlawing deception and manipulation in the offer or sale of securities. Violators subject to administrative penalties, civil action, and criminal prosecution.

Appreciation: the increase in an asset's value that is not subject to tax until realized.

Arbitrage: a word that has no business being mentioned on the Series 6. Arbitrage involves taking advantage of the disparity of two things. If you think GE will buy a small company, you can make a bet that GE's stock will temporarily drop and the small company's stock will skyrocket. Then, when you make your fantastic and fortuitous gain, you can explain to the SEC how you happened to make that bet.

Arbitration: settling a dispute without going to an actual court of law.

Arbitration Award: the decision rendered through FINRA Arbitration.

Ask, Asked: the higher price in a quote representing what the customer would have to pay/what the dealer is asking the customer to pay. Customers buy at the ASK because dealers sell to customers at the ASK price. Ask/asked is also called "offer/offered."

Asset Allocation: maintaining a percentage mix of equity, debt, and money market investments, based either on the investor's age (strategic) or market expectations (tactical).

Asset Allocation Fund: a mutual fund that focuses on a mix of equity, bond, and money market exposure, e.g., 50% equity, 45% bonds, 5% money market.

Asset-to-Debt: the ratio of assets to debts (3-to-1) that an open-end mutual fund must maintain when borrowing money.

Assets: something that a corporation or individual owns, e.g., cash, investments, accounts receivable, inventory, etc.

Associated Person: a registered representative or principal of a FINRA member firm.

Assumed Interest Rate: see AIR.

Auction Market: the NYSE, for example, where buyers and sellers simultaneously enter competitive prices. Sometimes called a "double auction" market because buying and selling occur at the same time, as opposed to Sotheby's, where only buyers are competing.

Authorized Stock: number of shares a company is authorized to issue by its corporate charter. Can be changed by a majority vote of the outstanding shares.

Automatic Reinvestment: a feature offered by mutual funds allowing investors to automatically reinvest dividend and capital gains distributions into more shares of the fund, without paying a sales charge.

Average Cost Basis: a method of figuring cost basis on securities for purposes of reporting capital gains and/or losses. The investor averages the cost for all purchases made in the stock, as opposed to identifying particular shares to the IRS when selling.

Award: The written determination of the arbitrator(s).

B

B-shares: mutual fund shares charging a load only when the investor redeems/sells the shares. Associated with "contingent deferred sales charges." B-shares have higher operating expenses than A-shares by way of a higher 12b-1 fee. Although the back-end load or "contingent deferred sales charges" decline over time, the higher 12b-1 fee usually makes B-shares appropriate only for investors who lack the ability to reach the first or second breakpoint offered on A-shares.

Back-end Load: a commission/sales fee charged when mutual fund or variable contracts are redeemed. The back-end load declines gradually, as described in the prospectus. Associated with B-shares and, occasionally C-shares.

Backdating: pre-dating a letter of intent for a mutual fund in order to include a prior purchase in the total amount stated in the letter of intent. LOIs may be backdated up to 90 calendar days.

Backing Away: a violation in which a market maker fails to honor a published firm quote to buy or sell a security at a stated price.

Balance Sheet: a financial statement of a corporation or individual showing financial condition (assets vs. liabilities) at a particular moment in time.

Balance Sheet Equation: Assets – Liabilities = Shareholders' Equity, or Assets = Liabilities + Shareholders' Equity.

Balanced Fund: a fund that maintains a mix of stocks and bonds at all times. Asset allocation funds are a type of balanced fund (or so darned close that they should be).

Bank Secrecy Act (BSA): legislation that prevents financial institutions from being used as tools by criminals to hide or launder money earned through illegal activities. Financial institutions such as banks and broker-dealers must report currency transactions over $10,000 and must report suspicious activity to the Department of Treasury's Financial Crimes Enforcement Network (FinCEN).

Banker's Acceptance (BA): money-market security that facilitates importing/exporting. Issued at a discount from face-value. A secured loan.

Bar: the most severe sanction that FINRA can impose on an individual, effectively ending his/her career

Basis Points: a way of measuring bond yields or other percentages in the financial industry. Each basis point is 1% of 1%. Example: 2% = .0200 = 200 basis points. 20 basis points = .2% or 2/10ths of 1%.

Basis Quote: the price at which a debt security can be bought or sold, based on the yield. A bond purchased at a "5.50 basis" is trading at a price that makes the yield 5.5%.

Bear, Bearish: an investor who takes a position based on the belief that the market or a particular security will fall. Short sellers and buyers of puts are "bearish." They profit when stocks go down. Seriously.

Bear Market: a market for stock or bonds in which prices are falling and/or expected to fall.

Bearer Bond: an unregistered bond that pays principal to the bearer at maturity. Bonds have not been issued in this way for over two decades, but they still exist on the secondary market.

Beneficiary: the one who benefits. An insurance policy pays a benefit to the named beneficiary. IRAs and other retirement plans, including annuities, allow the owner to name a beneficiary who will receive the account value when the owner dies. A 529 plan names a beneficiary, who will use the money for educational expenses someday.

Best Efforts: a type of underwriting leaving the syndicate at no risk for unsold shares, and allowing them to keep the proceeds on the shares that were sold/subscribed to. Underwriters act as "agents," not principals, in a best efforts underwriting.

Beta: a way of measuring the volatility of a security or portfolio compared to the volatility of the overall market. A beta of more than 1 is associated with an investment or portfolio that is more volatile than the overall market. A beta of less than 1 is associated with an investment or portfolio that is less volatile than the overall market.

Beta Coefficient: another way of referring to "beta."

Bid: what a dealer is willing to pay to a customer who wants to sell. Customers sell at the bid, buy at the ask.

Blend Fund: a fund that can't decide if it wants to be a growth fund or a value fund.

Blue Chip: stock in a well-established company with proven ability to pay dividends in good economic times and bad. Lower risk/reward ratio than other common stock.

Blue Sky: state securities law, tested on the Series 63 exam.

Board of Directors: the group elected by shareholders to run a mutual fund or a public company and establish corporate management policies.

Bond: a debt security issued by a corporation or governmental entity that promises to repay principal and pay interest either regularly or at maturity.

Bond Anticipation Note (BAN): a short-term municipal debt security backed by the proceeds of an upcoming bond issue. Often found in tax-exempt money market funds.

Bond Fund: a mutual fund with an objective of providing income while minimizing capital risk through a portfolio of—get this—bonds.

Bond Point: 1% of a bond's par value. 1 bond point = $10.

Bond Rating: an evaluation of a bond issue's chance of default published by companies such as Moody's, S&P, and Fitch.

Bonus Annuities: annuities with various features/enhancements added to the contract.

Book Entry: a security maintained as a computer record rather than a physical certificate. All U.S. Treasuries and many mutual funds are issued in this manner.

Branch Office: any location identified by any means to the public or customers as a location at which the member conducts an investment banking or securities business. The small Charles Schwab or E-Trade office at the nearby mall or office complex is a "branch office."

Breakpoint: a discounted sales charge or "volume discount" on mutual fund purchases offered on A-shares at various levels of investment.

Breakpoint Selling: preventing an investor from achieving a breakpoint. A violation.

Broad-based Index: an index such as the S&P 500 or the Value Line Composite Index that represents companies from many industries.

Broker: an individual or firm that charges a commission to execute securities buy and sell orders submitted by another individual or firm.

Broker Call Loan Rate: interest rate that broker-dealers pay when borrowing on behalf of margin customers.

BrokerCheck: service offered by FINRA in which information in the CRD system is made available to the public, allowing investors to verify the registration of firms and their agents as well as view arbitration awards and disciplinary actions against the individual or the broker-dealer.

Broker-Dealer: a person or firm in the business of completing transactions in securities for the accounts of others (broker) or its own account (dealer).

Brokered CD: A CD purchased from a broker rather than directly from a bank. These promise higher yields but involve fees and possibly less liquidity than envisioned; investors can lose principal.

Bull, Bullish: an investor who takes a position based on the belief that the market or a particular security will rise. Buyers of stock and call options are bullish.

Bull Market: a market for stocks or bonds in which prices are rising and/or expected to rise.

Bulletin Board: OTC stocks too volatile and low-priced for NASDAQ.

Business Cycle: a progression of expansions, peaks, contractions, troughs, and recoveries for the overall (macro) economy.

Business Risk: the risk that the company whose stock or bond you own will not be successful as a business. Competition, poor management, obsolete products/services are all examples of business risk.

C

C-shares: often called "level load" because of the high 12b-1 fee. Usually involve no front-end load, sometimes have a contingent deferred sales charge for 1 or 1.5 years. Appropriate for shorter-term investing only.

Call: (n.) a contract that gives the holder the right to buy something at a stated exercise price.

Call: (v.) to buy.

Call Premium: the price paid and received on a call option. Or, the amount above the par value paid by the issuer to call/retire a bond.

Call Protection: the period during which a security may not be called or bought by the issuer, usually lasting five years or more.

Call Provision: agreement between the issuer and the bondholders or preferred stockholders that gives the issuer the ability to repurchase the bonds or preferred stock on a specified date or dates before maturity.

Call Risk: the risk that interest rates will drop, forcing investors to sell their bonds back early to the issuer.

Callable: a security that may be purchased/called by the issuer as of a certain date, e.g., callable preferred, callable bonds. Generally pays a higher rate of return than non-callable securities, as it gives the issuer flexibility in financing.

Capital: a fancy word for "money." When a corporation raises cash by offering stocks/bonds to investors on the primary market, we dignify the cash by calling it "capital."

Capital Appreciation: the rise in an asset's market price. The objective of a "growth stock investor."

Capital Gain: the amount by which the proceeds on the sale of a stock or bond exceed your cost basis. If you sell a stock for $22 and have a cost basis of $10, the capital gain or profit is $12.

Capital Gains Distribution: distribution from fund to investor based on net capital gains realized by the fund portfolio. Holding period determined by the fund and assumed to be long-term.

Capital Loss: loss incurred when selling an asset for less than the purchase price. Capital losses offset an investor's capital gains and can offset ordinary income to a certain amount.

Capital Preservation: investment objective that allows for no risk of capital loss and, secondarily, income that is consistent with the main goal of not losing money.

Capital Structure: the make-up of a corporation's financing through equity (stock) and debt (bonds) securities.

Cash Account: an investment account in which the investor must pay for all purchases no later than 2 business days following regular way settlement. Not a margin account.

Cash Dividend: money paid to shareholders from a corporation's current earnings or accumulated profits.

Cash Equivalent: a security that can readily be converted to cash, e.g., T-bills, CDs, and money market funds.

Cash Settlement: same-day settlement of a trade requiring prior broker-dealer approval. Not the "regular way" of doing things.

Cash Value: the value of an insurance policy that may be "tapped" by the policyholder through a loan or a surrender.

CDSC: See Contingent Deferred Sales Charge.

Central Registration Depository or CRD: a computerized system in which FINRA maintains the employment, qualification, and disciplinary histories of more then 600,000 securities industry professionals who deal with the public.

CEO: chief executive officer. Individual ultimately responsible for a corporation's results.

CFO: chief financial officer. Individual in charge of a corporation's financial activities.

Check-writing Privileges: a privilege offered by mutual funds, especially money market funds, by which investors can automatically redeem shares by writing checks.

Chinese Wall: the separation that is supposed to exist between the investment banking department and the traders and registered representatives in order to prevent insider trading violations.

Churning: excessive trading in terms of frequency and size of transactions designed to generate commissions without regard for the customer.

Closed-end Fund: an investment company that offers a fixed number of shares that are not redeemable. Shares are traded on the secondary market at a price that could be higher or lower than NAV (or even the same as NAV).

CMO: Collateralized Mortgage Obligation. A complicated debt security that few people actually understand. Based on a pool of mortgages or a pool of mortgage-backed securities. Pays interest monthly but returns principal to one tranche at a time.

Code of Arbitration: FINRA method of resolving disputes (usually money) in the securities business. All decisions are final and binding on all parties.

Code of Procedure: FINRA system for enforcing member conduct rules.

Collateral Trust Certificate: a bond secured by a pledge of securities as collateral.

Combination Annuities: variable annuities in which some part of the payment is guaranteed by deposits in the general account.

Combination Privilege: allows investors to combine purchases of many funds within the mutual fund family to reach a breakpoint/reduced sales charge.

Commercial Paper: a short-term unsecured loan to a corporation. Issued at a discount from the face value. See "money market."

Commissions: why you're still reading this book, a service charge an agent earns for arranging a security purchase or sale.

Common Stock: the most "junior security," because it ranks last in line at liquidation. An equity or ownership position that usually allows the owner to vote on major corporate issues such as stock splits, mergers, acquisitions, authorizing more shares, etc.

Compliance Department: the principals and supervisors of a broker-dealer responsible for making sure the firm adheres to SEC, exchange, and SRO rules.

Conduct Rules: an SRO's rules for member conduct that, if violated, may lead to sanctions and fines.

Conduit Theory (Tax Treatment): a favorable tax treatment achieved if a company (REIT, mutual fund) distributes 90%+ of net income to the shareholders.

Confirmation: document stating the trade date, settlement date, and money due/owed for a securities purchase or sale. Delivered on or before the settlement date.

Constant Dollar Plan: a defensive investment strategy in which an investor tries to maintain a constant dollar amount in the account, meaning that securities are sold if the account value rises and purchased if it goes down.

Constructive Receipt: the date that the IRS considers an investor to have put his grubby little hands on a dividend, interest payment, retirement plan distribution, etc. For example, IRA funds are not taxable until "constructive receipt," which usually starts somewhere between age 59½ and 70½.

Consumer: for purposes of Regulation S-P, a prospect, someone interested in establishing some type of account.

Consumer Price Index (CPI): a measure of inflation/deflation for basic consumer goods and services. A rising CPI represents the greatest risk to most fixed-income investors.

Contingent Deferred Sales Charge (CDSC): associated with B-shares, the sales charge is deducted from the investor's check when she redeems/sells her shares. The charge is deferred until she sells and is contingent upon when she sells—the sales charges decline over time, eventually disappearing after 7 years, at which point the B-shares become A-shares, in order to keep everything nice and simple.

Continuing Commissions: the practice of paying retired registered representatives and principals commissions on business written while still employed with the firm, e.g., 12b-1 fees on mutual funds and annuities.

Contraction: phase of the business cycle associated with general economic decline, recession, or depression.

Contractual Plan: a plan allowing the participant to gradually accumulate mutual fund shares by paying regular installments to a "plan company." Not legal in all states due to complexity of rules and high sales loads.

Contribution: the money you put into a retirement plan subject to the limits imposed by the plan.

Conversion/Exchange Privilege: a feature offered by many mutual funds whereby the investor may sell shares of one fund in the family and use the proceeds to buy another fund in the family at the NAV (avoiding the sales load). All gains/losses are recognized on the date of sale/conversion for tax purposes.

Conversion Ratio: the number of shares of common stock that the holder of a convertible bond or preferred stock would receive upon conversion. A bond "convertible at $50" has a conversion ratio of 20 (20 shares of stock per $1,000 par value).

Convertible: a preferred stock or corporate bond allowing the investor to use the par value to "buy" shares of the company's common stock at a set price.

Cooling Off Period: a minimum 20-day period that starts after the registration statement is filed. No sales or advertising allowed during this period, which lasts until the effective or release date.

Corporation: the most common form of business organization, in which the business's total value is divided among shares of stock, each representing an ownership interest or share of profits.

Correspondence: under FINRA rules = any written (including electronic) communication that is distributed or made available to 25 or fewer retail investors within any 30 calendar-day period.

Cost Basis: the amount that has gone into an investment and has been taxed already. For stock, includes the price paid plus commissions. For a variable annuity, equals the after-tax contributions into the account. Investors pay tax only on amounts above their cost basis, and only when they sell or take "constructive receipt."

Coupon Rate: a.k.a. "nominal yield." The interest rate stated on a bond representing the percentage of the par value received by the investor each year. For example, a bond with a 5% "coupon rate" or "nominal yield" pays $50 per bond to the holder per year. Period.

Coverdell Plan: tax-deferred educational savings account funded with after-tax dollars and giving legal control of the assets to the minor child when he/she reaches adulthood.

Covered Call: a position in which an investor generates premium income by selling the right to buy stock the investor already owns, and at a set price.

CPI: Consumer Price Index, a measure of inflation/deflation for basic consumer goods and services. A rising CPI represents the greatest risk to most fixed-income investors.

Credit Risk: a.k.a. "default" or "financial" risk. The risk that the issuer's credit rating will be downgraded, or that the issuer will default on a debt security.

Cumulative Preferred Stock: preferred stock where missed dividends go into arrears and must be paid before the issuer may pay dividends to other preferred stock and/or common stock.

Cumulative Voting: method of voting whereby the shareholder may take the total votes and split them up any way he chooses. Said to benefit minority over majority shareholders. Total votes are found by multiplying the number of shares owned by the number of seats up for election to the Board of Directors.

Currency Exchange Risk: the risk that the value of the U.S. dollar versus another currency will have a negative impact on businesses and investors.

Currency Transaction Report (CTR): a report that broker-dealers must file with the U.S. Treasury whenever customers deposit more than $10,000 cash-money on the same day.

Current Income: investment objective in which the investor seeks a regular, dependable stream of income, usually to pay regular expenses.

Current Yield: annual interest divided by market price of the bond. For example, an 8% bond purchased at $800 has a CY of 10%. $80/$800 = 10%.

CUSIP number: an identification number/code for a security.

Custodial Account: an investment account in which a custodian enters trades on behalf of the beneficial owner, who is usually a minor child.

Custodian: maintains custody of a mutual fund's securities and cash. Performs payable/receivable functions for portfolio purchases and sales. In an UGMA, the custodian is the adult named on the account who is responsible for the investment decisions and tax reporting.

Customer: for purposes of Regulation S-P, someone who has now opened a financial relationship with the firm.

Customer Identification Program: regulations requiring broker-dealers to verify customers through photo IDs, passports (for non-citizens), and a check against the OFAC list of suspected terrorists.

Cyclical Industry: a term of fundamental analysis for an industry that is sensitive to the business cycle. Includes: steel, automobiles, mining and construction equipment.

D

Dealer: a person who buys or sells securities for his/its own account, taking the other side of the trade. A dealer buys securities from and sells securities directly to a customer, while a broker merely arranges a trade between a customer and another party.

Death Benefit: the amount payable to the beneficiary of a life insurance (or annuity) contract, minus any outstanding loans and/or unpaid premiums.

Debenture: an unsecured corporate bond backed by the issuer's ability (or inability) to pay. No collateral.

Debt Security: a security representing a loan from an investor to an issuer. Offers a particular interest rate in return for the loan, not an ownership position.

Debt Service: the schedule for repayment of interest and principal on a debt security.

Declaration Date: the date the Board declares a dividend.

Default: when the issuer of the bond stiffs you.

Default Risk: the risk that the issuer of the bond will stiff you. Measured by S&P and Moody's, with their fancy little lettering system (AAA, Aaa and on down the scale).

Defensive Industry: a company that can perform well even during rough economic times. For example, food and basic clothing represent two products purchased through both good and bad economic times; therefore, stocks of food and basic clothing companies would be "defensive" investments.

Deferred Annuity: an annuity that delays payments of income, installments, or a lump sum until the investor elects to receive it. Usually subject to surrender charges during this period.

Deferred Compensation Plan: a non-qualified business plan that defers some of the employee's compensation until retirement.

Deficiency Letter: SEC notification of additions or corrections that an issuer must make to a registration statement before the offering can be cleared for distribution.

Defined Benefit Plan: a qualified corporate pension plan that, literally, defines the benefit payable to the retiree.

Defined Contribution Plan: a qualified corporate plan that defines the contribution made on behalf of the employee, e.g., profit sharing, 401(k).

Deflation: a general drop in the level of prices across the economy, usually connected to an economic slump.

Delivery: the change in ownership of a security that takes place when the transaction settles. The seller delivers the securities purchased to the buyer.

Department of Enforcement: FINRA enforcers of the member conduct rules, a group you never want to hear from, especially by certified mail.

Depression: six quarters (18 months) or longer of economic decline.

Designated Examining Authority: another name for an SRO or Self-Regulatory Organization, e.g., CBOE or FINRA

Dilution: a reduction in the earnings per share of common stock, often due to convertible bonds or preferred stock being converted to common stock.

Direct Transfer: moving assets of one plan directly to the custodian of another plan.

Discount: the difference between the (lower) market price for a bond and the par value.

Discount Bond: any bond traded below the par value, e.g., @97.

Discount Rate: interest rate charged by the 12 Federal Reserve Banks to member banks who borrow from the FRB.

Discretion: authority given to someone other than the account owner to make trading decisions for the account.

Discretionary Account: a brokerage account in which the firm/registered representative may choose the asset/amount/activity without first speaking to the client.

Discretionary Authorization Form: form that grants discretion to the broker-dealer, allowing the firm/registered representative to enter trades without first discussing them with the client.

Distribution: the money you take out of a retirement plan.

Distribution Expenses: the cost of distributing/marketing a mutual fund, including selling, printing prospectuses and sales literature, advertising, and mailing prospectuses to new/potential clients. Covered by sales charges/12b-1fees.

Distribution Stage: the period during which an individual receives payments from an annuity.

Distributor: a.k.a. "sponsor," "underwriter," "wholesaler." A FINRA member firm that bears distribution costs of a fund upfront, profiting from the sales charges paid by the investors.

Diversification: purchasing securities from many different issuers, or industries or geographic regions to reduce "nonsystematic risk."

Diversified Mutual Fund: complies with an SEC rule so that no more than 5% of assets are invested in a particular stock or bond and so that the fund does not own more than 10% of any issuer's outstanding stock. Often called the "75-5-10 rule," where the 75 means that only 75% of the assets have to be diversified this way just to keep things nice and simple.

Dividend: money paid from profits to holders of common and preferred stock whenever the Board of Directors is feeling especially generous.

Dividend Payout Ratio: the amount of dividends paid divided by the earnings per share. Stocks with high dividend payout ratios are typically found in "equity income" funds.

Dividend Yield: annual dividends divided by market price of the stock. Equivalent to current yield for a debt security.

Dividend/Income Distributions: distributions from a fund to the investors made from net investment income. Typically, may be reinvested at the NAV to avoid sales charge.

Dodd-Frank: The Dodd-Frank Wall Street Reform and Consumer Protection Act, passed in 2010, which includes financial reforms intended to prevent risky practices such as those that led to the 2008 economic collapse.

Dollar Cost Averaging: investing fixed dollar amounts regularly, regardless of share price. Usually results in a lower average cost compared to average of share prices, as investors' dollars buy majority of shares at lower prices.

Donor: a person who makes a gift of money or securities to another.

Dow Jones Industrial Average (DJIA): an index comprised of 30 large companies.

Dual-Purpose Fund: a closed-end fund with two classes of stock: income shares and capital shares. The income shares receive dividends and interest, while the capital shares receive capital gains distributions.

Due Diligence: meeting between issuer and underwriters with the purpose of verifying information contained in a registration statement/prospectus

E

Earned Income: income derived from active participation in a business, including wages, salary, tips, commissions, and bonuses. Alimony received is also considered earned income. Earned income can be used toward an IRA contribution.

Earnings Per Share (EPS): the amount of earnings or "net income" available for each share of common stock. A major driver of the stock's price on the secondary market.

Education IRA: another name for the Coverdell Education Savings Account in which after-tax contributions may be made to pay qualified education expenses for the beneficiary.

Effective Date: a.k.a. "release date," date established by SEC as to when the underwriters may sell new securities to investors.

Electronic Communications Networks (ECNs): electronic systems allowing for direct trading of securities in the so-called "fourth market."

Eligibility: a section of ERISA that outlines who is/is not eligible to participate in a qualified plan. Those 21 years old who have worked "full time" for one year (1,000 hours or more) are eligible to participate in the plan.

Emerging Market: the financial markets of a developing country. Generally, a small market with a short operating history, not as efficient or stable as developed markets. For example, Brazil, China, India.

Equipment Trust Certificate: a corporate bond secured by a pledge of equipment, e.g., airplanes, railroad cars.

Equity: ownership, e.g., common and preferred stock in a public company.

Equity Fund: a mutual fund investing primarily in equity securities.

Equity Income Fund: a mutual fund that purchases common stocks whose issuers pay consistent and, perhaps, increasing dividends. The fund has less volatility than an equity fund with "growth" as an objective.

Equity Indexed Annuity (EIA): fixed annuity with a minimum guaranteed return plus participation in some of the upward movement of a particular index, usually the S&P 500.

ERISA: the Employee Retirement Income Security Act of 1974 that governs the operation of most corporate pension and benefit plans.

Estate: a legal entity/person that represents all assets held by a deceased person before he, you know, died.

Estate Tax: an annoying tax on estates over a certain amount, often called the "death tax" by those who don't like it.

ETF: "Exchange Traded Fund," a fund that trades on an exchange, typically an index fund tracking the S&P 500, the Dow Jones Industrial Average, etc. Unlike an open-end index fund, the ETF allows investors to sell short, trade throughout the day, and even purchase shares on margin.

Ex-Date: two days before the Record Date for corporate stock. The date upon which the buyer is not entitled to the upcoming dividend. Note that for mutual funds, this date is established by the board of directors, usually the day after the Record Date.

Excess Over Cost Basis: any amount received on a non-qualified variable annuity above the after-tax contribution into the account; the part that is taxable upon constructive receipt at ordinary income rates.

Exchange-listed Security: a security that has met listing requirements to trade on a particular exchange such as NYSE, AMEX, or NASDAQ.

Exchange Traded Fund: see ETF.

Exchanges: any electronic or physical marketplace where investors can buy and sell securities. For example, NASDAQ, NYSE, AMEX.

Exclusion Ratio: method of determining which part of an annuity payment is taxable, and which part represents the tax-free return of the annuitant's after-tax cost basis.

Executor: person named in the will charged with distributing assets to the beneficiaries of the estate.

Exempt Security: a security not required to be registered under the Securities Act of 1933. Still subject to anti-fraud rules; not subject to registration requirements, e.g., municipal bonds and bank stock.

Exempt Transaction: a transactional exemption from registration requirements based on the manner in which the security is offered and sold, e.g., private placements under Reg D.

Expansion: phase of the business cycle associated with increased activity.

Expense Ratio: a fund's expenses divided by/compared to average net assets. Represents operating efficiency of a mutual fund, where the lower the number the more efficient the fund.

Expenses: ongoing charges against the mutual fund portfolio to cover operational costs.

F

Face Amount Certificate Company: a debt security bought at a lower price than the face-amount. An investment company.

Farm Credit System: organization of privately owned banks providing credit to farmers and mortgages on farm property.

FDIC (Federal Deposit Insurance Corporation): federal government agency that provides deposit insurance for member banks and prevents bank and "thrift" failures. Bank deposits are currently insured up to $250,000, a number that could have changed by the time you read this definition. A trip to your local bank will give you the updated number.

Federal Covered: a security or an investment adviser whose registration is handled exclusively by the federal government (SEC).

Federal Open Market Committee (FOMC): council of Federal Reserve officials that sets monetary policy based on economic data. The money supply is tightened to fight inflation, loosened to provide stimulus to a faltering economy.

Federal Reserve Board: a seven-member board directing the operations of the Federal Reserve System.

Federal Reserve System: the central bank system of the United States, with a primary responsibility to manage the flow of money and credit in this country.

Fed Funds Rate: interest rate charged on bank-to-bank loans. Subject to daily fluctuation.

Fees and Expenses: ongoing charges against the mutual fund portfolio including the management fee, 12b-1 fees, custodial and transfer agent fees, etc.

FHLMC: a.k.a. "Freddie Mac." Like big sister Fannie Mae, a quasi-agency, public company that purchases mortgages from lenders and sells mortgage-backed securities to investors. Stock is listed on NYSE.

Fiduciary: someone responsible for the financial affairs of someone else, e.g., custodian, trustee, or registered rep in a discretionary account.

Filing Date: the date that an issuer files a registration statement with the SEC for a new issue of securities.

Final Prospectus: document delivered with final confirmation of a new issue of securities detailing the price, delivery date, and underwriting spread.

FINRA (Financial Industry Regulatory Authority): the SRO formed when the NASD and the NYSE regulators merged.

Financial Risk: another name for "credit risk," or the risk that the issuer of a bond could default.

FinCEN: U.S. Treasury's "Financial Crimes Enforcement Network." Suspicious Activity Reports must be provided to FinCEN if a broker-dealer notices activity in accounts that appears suspicious or possibly related to fraud or money laundering activities.

Firm Commitment: an underwriting in which the underwriters agree to purchase all securities from an issuer, even the ones they failed to sell to investors. Involves acting in a "principal" capacity, unlike in "best efforts," "all or none," and "mini-max" offerings.

Firm Element: annual training program that member firms require of their registered representatives to satisfy FINRA rules for continuing education.

First-In-First-Out (FIFO): an accounting method used to value a company's inventory or to determine capital gains/losses on an investor's securities transactions.

First Market: the exchange market, e.g., NYSE or New York Stock Exchange.

Fiscal Policy: Congress and President. Tax and Spend.

Fixed-amount Settlement Option: payment option on an insurance contract in which a fixed amount is received over time until the account is depleted.

Fixed Annuity: an insurance product (not a security) in which the annuitant receives fixed dollar payments, usually for the rest of his or her life.

Fixed-income Security: a security promising a fixed rate of interest or dividends.

Fixed-period Settlement Option: payment option on an insurance contract in which the account is depleted over a fixed period of time, e.g., 5 years.

Flexible Premium: a premium that is flexible. Characteristic of "universal" insurance. Allows the policyholder to adjust the premiums and death benefit according to changing needs.

FNMA: a.k.a. "Fannie Mae." Like little brother Freddie Mac, Fannie buys mortgages from lenders and sells mortgage-backed securities to investors. A quasi-agency, a public company listed for trading on the NYSE.

FOMC: the Federal Reserve Board's Federal Open Market Committee. Sets short-term interest rates by setting discount rate, reserve requirement and buying/selling T-bills to/from primary dealers.

Form 1099-DIV: tax filing form showing dividends and capital gains distributed to an investor.

Form U4: registration form for agents and principals submitted to the CRD system.

Form U5: termination form for agents and principals submitted to the CRD system.

Forward Pricing: the method of valuing mutual fund shares, whereby a purchase or redemption order is executed at the next calculated price. Mutual fund shares are bought and sold at the next computed price, not yesterday's stale prices.

Fourth Market, INSTINET: an ECN (electronic communications network) used by institutional investors, bypassing the services of a traditional broker. Institutional = INSTINET.

Fractional Share: a portion of a whole share of stock. Mutual fund shares typically are issued as whole and fractional shares, e.g., 101.45 shares.

Fraud: using deceit to wrongfully take money/property from someone under false pretenses.

Free Credit Balance: the cash in a customer account that can be withdrawn.

Free-Look: period during which a contract- or policyholder may cancel and receive all sales charges paid. Not a popular phrase among seasoned insurance agents.

Freeriding and Withholding: a violation in which underwriters fail to distribute all shares allocated in an offering of a "hot issue."

Front-end Load: a mutual fund commission or sales fee charged when shares are purchased (A-shares). The amount of the load is added to the NAV to determine the public offering price (POP).

Frozen Account: an account in which purchase orders will be accepted only if the cash is in the account due to the customer's failure to comply with Reg T.

Fund of Funds: a mutual fund holding shares of other mutual funds.

Funds of Hedge Funds: a mutual fund holding shares of hedge funds.

Funding: an ERISA guideline that stipulates, among other things, that retirement plan assets must be segregated from other corporate assets.

Fungible: interchangeable, e.g., $20 bills or shares of stock, where one is just as good as another.

Fully Registered Bonds: bonds that are fully registered. A physical certificate with the owner's name, and interest payable automatically by the paying agent (no coupons).

G

GDP: Gross Domestic Product, the sum total of all goods and services being produced by the economy. A positive GDP number is evidence of economic expansion.

General Account: where an insurance company invests net premiums in order to fund guaranteed, fixed payouts.

General Obligation Bond: a municipal bond that is backed by the issuer's full faith and credit or full taxing authority.

General Securities Representative: an agent who passed the Series 7 and may sell virtually any security, unlike a Series 6 holder, who sells mutual funds and variable contracts only.

Generic Advertising: communications with the public that promote securities as investments but not particular securities.

Gift: transferring property to someone else and expecting nothing in return, or selling something to someone for far less than its fair market value.

Gift Splitting: method of claiming that a gift over the annual gift tax exclusion is partly from the husband and partly from the wife. For example, a gift of $25,000 can be deemed a gift of $12,500 from Grandma and $12,500 from Grandpa to avoid gift taxes.

Gift Tax: a tax paid when a gift exceeds the current exclusion limit. For tax year 2009, the excess of a gift over $13,000 is taxable at gift tax rates.

Global Fund: a mutual fund investing in companies located and doing business all across the globe, including the U.S.

GNMA: a.k.a. "Ginnie Mae," nickname for Government National Mortgage Association. A government agency (not a public company) that buys insured mortgages from lenders, selling pass-through certificates to investors. Monthly payments to investors pay interest and also pass through principal from a pool of mortgages. Recall that bonds pay interest and return principal only at maturity, while "pass throughs" pass through principal monthly. Thus, the clever name "pass through."

Grantor: the party who transfers assets into a trust.

Growth: investment objective that seeks "capital appreciation." Achieved through common stock, primarily.

Growth & Income: a fund that purchases stocks for growth potential and also for dividend income. Less volatile than pure growth funds due to the income that calms investors down when the ride becomes turbulent.

Growth Fund: mutual fund seeking stocks in companies expected to grow faster than the overall market and/or competitors.

Guaranteed Bond: bond that is issued with a promise by a party other than the issuer to maintain payments of interest and principal if the issuer cannot.

Guardian: a fiduciary who manages the financial affairs of a minor or a person declared mentally incompetent by a court of law.

Guardian Account: account set up through a court order designating an adult as custodian for the affairs of a minor child or a mentally incompetent adult.

H

Hedge: to bet the other way. If you own stock, you can hedge by purchasing puts, which profit when the stock goes down.

Hedge Fund: a private investment partnership open to accredited investors only. Illiquid investments that generally must be held one or two years before selling. Typically charge a management fee plus the first 20% of capital gains in most cases.

High-yield: an investment whose income stream is very high relative to its low market price. A high-yield bond is either issued by a shaky company or municipal government forced to offer high nominal yields, or it begins to trade at lower and lower prices on the secondary market as the credit quality or perceived credit strength of the issuer deteriorates.

High-yield Corporate Bond Fund: mutual fund investing in lower-rated corporate bonds.

High-yield Tax-exempt Fund: mutual fund investing in lower-rated municipal bonds.

Howey Decision: a U.S. Supreme Court decision that defined an "investment contract" as "an investment of money in a common enterprise where the investor will profit solely through the efforts of others."

Holding Company: a company organized to invest in other corporations, e.g., Berkshire-Hathaway, which holds large stakes in other companies such as Coca-Cola, See's Candy, Dairy Queen, and Wells Fargo.

Holding Period: the period during which a security was held for purposes of determining whether a capital gain or loss is long- or short-term.

HR-10: a reference to a Keogh plan.

Hypothecate: to pledge securities purchased in a margin account as collateral to secure the loan.

I

IDR: or "Industrial Development Revenue Bond," a revenue bond that builds a facility that the issuing municipality then leases to a corporation. The lease payments from the corporation back the interest and principal payments on the bonds.

Immediate Annuity: an insurance contract purchased with a single premium that starts to pay the annuitant immediately. Purchased by individuals who are afraid of outliving their retirement savings.

Income: investment objective that seeks current income, found by investing in fixed income, e.g., bonds, money market, preferred stock. An equity income fund buys stocks that pay dividends; less volatile than a growth & income fund or a pure growth fund.

Income Bond: a bond that will pay interest only if the issuer earns sufficient income and the board of directors declares the payment.

Income Statement: a financial statement showing a corporation's results of operations over the quarter or year. Shows revenue, all expenses/costs, and the profit or loss the company showed over the period. Found in the annual shareholder report among other places.

Index: a theoretical grouping of stocks, bonds, etc., that aids analysts who want to track something. The Consumer Price Index is a theoretical grouping or "basket" of things that consumers buy, used to track inflation. The Dow Jones Industrial Average is a theoretical grouping of 30 large-company stocks that analysts use to track the stock market. The NASDAQ 100 is an index or grouping of the 100 most important stocks trading on NASDAQ.

Index Fund: a passively managed mutual fund that mirrors a particular index, e.g., S&P 500.

Indication of Interest: an investor's expression of interest in purchasing a new issue of securities after reading the preliminary prospectus; not a commitment to buy.

Individual Retirement Account (IRA): also called an "individual retirement arrangement" to make sure it has at least two names. A tax-deferred account that generally allows any individual with earned income to contribute 100% of earned income up to the current maximum contribution allowed on a pre-tax basis that reduces the current tax liability and allows investment returns to compound.

Inflation: rising prices, as measured by the Consumer Price Index (CPI). Major risk to fixed-income investors (loss of purchasing power).

Inflation Risk: also called "constant dollar risk" or "purchasing power risk," it is the risk that inflation will erode the value of a fixed-income stream from a bond or preferred stock.

Initial Public Offering (IPO): a corporation's first sale of stock to public investors. By definition, a primary market transaction in which the issuer receives the proceeds.

Inside Information: material information about a corporation that has not yet been released to the public and would likely affect the price of the corporation's stock and/or bonds. Inside information may not be "disseminated" or acted upon.

Insider: for purpose of insider trading rules, an "insider" is anyone who has or has access to material non-public information. Officers (CEO, CFO), members of the board of directors, and investors owning > 10% of the company's outstanding shares are assumed to possess and have access to inside information. As fiduciaries to the shareholders, insiders may not use inside information to their benefit.

Insider Trading and Securities Fraud Enforcement Act (ITSFEA) of 1988: an Act of Congress that addresses insider trading and lists the penalties for violations of the Act. Insider traders may be penalized up to three times the amount of their profit or their loss avoided by using inside information.

Insurance: protection against loss of income due to death, disability, long-term care needs, etc.

Institutional Investor: not an individual. An institution is, for example, a pension fund, insurance company, or mutual fund. The large institutions are "accredited investors" who get to do things that retail (individual) investors often do not get to do.

Integration: stage of money laundering when the funds are invested in legitimate enterprises or investment vehicles.

Interest Only Settlement Option: a settlement option in which the insurance company keeps the proceeds from the policy and invests it, promising the beneficiary a guaranteed minimum rate of interest.

Interest Rate Risk: the risk that interest rates will rise, pushing the market value of a fixed-income security down. Long-term bonds most susceptible.

Interest Rates: the cost of a commodity called money. In order to borrow money, borrowers pay a rate called an interest rate on top of the principal they will return at the end of the term. A one-year loan of $1,000 at 5% interest would have the borrower pay $50 on top of the $1,000 that will be returned at the end of the year.

Internal Revenue Code (IRC): tax laws for the U.S. that define, for example, maximum IRA contributions, or the "conduit tax theory" that mutual funds use when distributing 90% of net income to shareholders, etc.

Internal Revenue Service (IRS): an agency for the federal government that no one seems to like very much. Responsible for collecting federal taxes for the U.S. Treasury and for administering tax rules and regulations.

International Fund: a mutual fund investing in companies established outside the U.S.

Interstate Offering: an offering of securities in several states, requiring registration with the SEC.

Intrastate Offering: an offering of securities completed in the issuer's home state with investors who reside in that state, and, therefore, eligible for the Rule 147 Exemption to registration with the SEC. Intrastate offerings generally register with the state Administrator.

Inverse Relationship: when one goes up, the other goes down, and vice versa. Interest Rates and Yields are inversely related to Bond Prices. Your rate of speed is inversely related to your travel time to and from the office.

Investment Adviser: a business or professional that is compensated for advising others as to the value of or advisability of investing in securities. The entity that manages mutual funds/separate accounts for an asset-based fee. Financial planners are also advisers.

Investment Adviser Representative: a representative of an investment advisory firm receiving compensation for managing accounts or selling the services of the firm.

Investment Banker: see "underwriter." A firm that raises capital for issuers on the primary market.

Investment Banking: the business of helping companies with mergers and acquisitions, performing IPOs and additional offerings. In other words, investment bankers raise capital for issuers not by loaning money (like a traditional bank) but by finding investors willing to contribute to the cause.

Investment Company: a company engaged in the business of pooling investors' money and trading in securities on their behalf. Examples include unit investment trusts (UITs), face-amount certificate companies, and management companies.

Investment Company Act of 1940: classified Investment Companies and set rules for registration and operation.

Investment Contract: a security, defined through Howey Decision, as "an investment of money whereby the investor profits solely through the efforts of others."

Investment Grade: a bond rated at least BBB by S&P or Baa by Moody's. The bond does not have severe default risk, so it is said to be appropriate for investors, as opposed to the speculators who buy non–investment grade bonds.

Investment Objective: any goal that an investor has including current income, capital appreciation (growth), capital preservation (safety), or speculation.

Investment Style: an approach to investing, such as active, passive, or buy-and-hold.

IRA: Individual Retirement Account. A retirement account/arrangement for any individual with earned income. The Traditional IRA offers pre-tax contributions while the Roth IRA is funded with after-tax contributions.

Irrevocable Trust: a trust that may not be altered or revoked/canceled by the grantor. Because the trust is irrevocable, the grantor is no longer responsible for paying taxes on the income generated by the trust, and the assets do not count as part of the grantor's estate when he, you know, dies.

Issued Shares: the number of shares that have been issued by a corporation.

Issued Stock: the shares that have been issued to investors by the corporation at this time. Often a lower number than the number of shares authorized.

Issuer: any individual or entity who issues or proposes to issue any security. For example, the issuer of Google common stock is Google.

Issuing Securities: raising capital by offering securities to investors on the primary market.

J

Joint Account: investment account owned by more than one individual. Account owners sign a joint account agreement that stipulates which percentage of the assets is owned by each individual. Joint accounts are either "tenants in common" or "tenants with rights of survivorship." See "JTIC" and "JTWROS."

Joint with Last Survivor: a settlement/payout option on an annuity that requires the insurance company to make payments to the annuitants as long as they are alive.

JTIC (Joint Tenants in Common): account where the assets of the deceased party pass to the deceased's estate, not the other account owner(s).

JTWROS (Joint Tenants With Rights Of Survivorship): account where the assets of the deceased party pass to the other account owner(s).

Junk Bond: a bond backed by a shaky issuer. It was either issued by an entity with shaky credit, or is now trading at a frightfully low price on the secondary market because the issuer's credit has suddenly or recently been downgraded. Since the price is low, given the low quality of the debt, the yield is high. High-yield and junk are synonymous.

K

K-1: a tax form required of people who own direct participation interests (limited partnership, S-corp).

Keogh: qualified retirement plan available to sole proprietorships.

Keynesian Economics: economic school of thought that advocates government intervention through fiscal policy as a way to stimulate demand for goods and services.

L

Large Cap: a stock where the total value of the outstanding shares is large, generally greater than $10 billion. For example, GE, MSFT, IBM.

Last-In-First-Out: LIFO, an accounting method used for random withdrawals from an annuity. The IRS assumes that all withdrawals represent part of the taxable "excess over cost basis" first.

Layering: stage of money laundering when a confusing set of transactions is conducted to make it unclear where these funds originated.

Legislative Risk: the risk to an investor that laws will change and have a negative impact on an investment. For example, if municipal bonds lose their tax-exempt interest, their value would plummet.

Letter of Intent: LOI, a feature of many mutual funds whereby an investor may submit a letter or form expressing the intent to invest enough money over 13 months to achieve a breakpoint.

Level Load: an ongoing asset-based sales charge (12b-1 fee) associated with mutual fund C-shares. Appropriate for short-term investments only.

Leverage: using borrowed money to increase returns. Debt securities and margin accounts are associated with "leverage."

Liabilities: what an individual or corporation owes, e.g., credit card debt, bonds, mortgage balance, accounts payable.

Life-income Settlement Option: payment stream from an insurance contract in which the insurance company provides the beneficiary with a guaranteed income for the rest of his or her life by annuitizing the death benefit.

Life Only/Life Annuity: a payout option whereby the insurance/annuity company promises to make payments only for the rest of the annuitant's life.

Life With Joint and Last Survivor: a payout option whereby the insurance/annuity company promises to make payments to the annuitant for the rest of his life, then to the survivor for the rest of her life.

Life With Period Certain: a payout option whereby the insurance/annuity company promises to make payments to the annuitant for the rest of his life or a certain period of time, whichever is greater.

Life With Unit Refund: a payout option whereby the insurance/annuity company promises to make at least a certain number of payments to the annuitant or beneficiary.

Lifetime Gift Tax Credit: the maximum amount of gifts an individual may make over her lifetime before having to pay gift taxes. Deductible against the lifetime estate credit.

Limited Liability: an investor's ability to limit losses to no more than the amount invested. Holders of common stock and limited partnership interests enjoy "limited liability," which means they can only lose 100% of what they invest.

Limited Representative: what you'll be after passing the Series 6 and getting registered to represent your broker-dealer. You would be a "general securities representative" if you were crazy or bold enough to sit for the 6-hour, 250-question Series 7 exam.

Limited Trading Authorization: an authorization for someone other than the account owner to enter purchase and sale orders but make no withdrawals of cash or securities.

Liquid Net Worth: easily liquidated assets minus all liabilities.

Liquidation Priority: the priority of claims on a bankrupt entity's assets that places creditors (bondholders) ahead of stockholders and preferred stockholders ahead of common stockholders.

Liquidity: ability to quickly convert an investment to cash and get a fair price. A home is not a liquid investment—100 shares of GE are extremely liquid. Mutual funds are very liquid, since the issuer has to pay the NAV promptly. The most liquid investment imaginable is the money market mutual fund—just write checks and the fund redeems enough shares to cover it.

Liquidity Risk: the risk of not being able to quickly convert an asset to cash at a fair price.

Long: to buy or own.

Long-term Capital Gain: a profit realized when selling stock held for at least 12 months plus 1 day. Subject to lower capital gains tax rates than short-term gains.

Long-term Capital Loss: a loss realized when selling stock held for at least 12 months plus 1 day. Used to offset long-term capital gains.

Lump Sum Payment: a settlement/payout option for annuities or insurance where the annuitant or beneficiary receives a lump sum payment. Go figure.

M

Maloney Act: An amendment to the Securities Exchange Act of 1934 creating the NASD as the self-regulatory organization (SRO) for the over-the-counter market (OTC).

Management Company: one of the three types of Investment Companies, including both open-end and closed-end funds.

Management Fee: the percentage of assets charged to the mutual fund portfolio to cover the cost of portfolio management.

Manager's Fee: typically the smallest piece of the spread, paid to the managing underwriter for every share sold by the syndicate.

Margin: amount of equity contributed by a customer as a percentage of the current market value of the securities held in a margin account.

Marginal Tax Bracket: tax on the next dollar of income earned.

Markdown: the difference between the highest bid price for a security and the price that a particular dealer pays an investor for her security.

Market Letter: a publication of a broker-dealer sent to clients or the public and discussing investing, financial markets, economic conditions, etc. Can be considered correspondence if sent to a limited number of clients; otherwise, considered retail communication and subject to pre-approval.

Market Maker: a dealer in the OTC market maintaining an inventory of a particular security and a firm Bid and Ask price good for a minimum of 100 shares. Acts as a "principal" on transactions, buying and selling for its/their own account.

Market Order: an order to buy or sell a security at the best available market price.

Market Risk: also called "systematic risk," the risk inherent to the entire market rather than a specific security. The risk that the stock market may suffer violent upheavals due to unpredictable events including natural disaster, war, disease, famine, credit crises, etc. Market risk can only be reduced by hedging with options or ETFs.

Marketability: the ease or difficulty an investor has when trying to sell a security for cash without losing his shirt. Thinly traded securities have poor marketability.

Markup: the difference between the lowest ask/offer price for a security and the price that a particular dealer charges.

Material Information: any fact that could reasonably affect an investor's decision to buy, sell, or hold a security. For example, profits and losses at the company, product liability lawsuits, the loss of key clients, etc.

Maturity Date: the date that a bond pays out the principal and interest payments cease. Also called "redemption."

Mediation: an alternative to FINRA arbitration proceedings.

Member Firm: a broker-dealer and/or underwriting firm that belongs to FINRA or another securities association (MSRB, CBOE).

Mini-Max: a type of best efforts underwriting where the syndicate must sell a minimum amount and may sell up to a higher, maximum amount.

Minimum Death Benefit: the minimum death benefit payable to the insured, regardless of how lousy the separate account returns are in a variable policy.

Monetary Policy: what the FRB implements through the discount rate, reserve requirement, and FOMC open market operations. Monetary policy tightens or loosens credit in order to affect short-term interest rates and, therefore, the economy.

Money Laundering: process of turning "dirty" money "clean." Hiding ill-gotten profits by disguising them as legitimate funds through a series of complex transactions.

Money Market: the short-term (1 year or less) debt security market. Examples include commercial paper, banker's acceptance, T-bills.

Money Market Mutual Fund: a highly liquid holding place for cash. Sometimes called "stable value" funds, as the share price is generally maintained at $1. The mutual funds invest in—surprisingly—money market securities.

Money Purchase: a retirement plan in which the employer must contribute a set percentage of the employee's salary, regardless of profitability.

Moody's Investors Service: one of the top three credit rating agencies for corporate and municipal bonds as well as stocks.

Mortality and Expense Risk Fee: expenses on variable contracts allowing the insurance company to offer death benefits and keep their expenses reasonable.

Mortality Guarantee: a promise from an insurance company to pay an annuitant no matter how long he lives, or to pay an insurance policyholder no matter how soon he dies.

Mortality Risk: the risk to the insurance company that the insured will die too soon or the annuitant will live too long.

Mortality Risk Fee: fee charged on a variable annuity allowing the insurance company to offer a death benefit and promise an income stream for life.

Mortgage-backed Security: a fixed-income security created with a pool of mortgages, e.g., GNMA.

Mortgage Bond: a corporate bond secured by a pledge of real estate as collateral.

Municipal Bond: a bond issued by a state, county, city, school district, etc., in order to build roads, schools, hospitals, etc., or simply to keep the government running long enough to hold another election.

Municipal Bond Fund: a mutual fund that invests in municipal bonds with an objective to maximize federally tax-exempt income.

Municipal Note: a short-term obligation of a city, state, school district, etc., backed by the anticipation of funds from revenues, taxes, or upcoming bond issues.

MSRB (Municipal Securities Rulemaking Board): the self-regulatory organization overseeing municipal securities dealers.

Mutual Fund: an investment company offering equity stakes in a portfolio that is usually managed actively and that always charges management fees and other expenses.

N

NASD (National Association of Securities Dealers): former name of the SRO empowered with the passage of the Maloney Act of 1938. Regulates its own members and enforces SEC rules and regulations. Now called FINRA after a merger with the regulators from the NYSE.

NASDAQ: National Association of Securities Dealers Automated Quotation system. The main component of the OTC market. Stocks that meet certain criteria are quoted throughout the day on NASDAQ, e.g., MSFT, ORCL, and INTC.

National Adjudicatory Council: NAC, the first level of appeal for a party sanctioned by the Department of Enforcement (DOE) under FINRA's Code of Procedure.

NAV: the net asset value of a mutual fund share. (Assets – Liabilities)/Outstanding Shares.

Negotiable: the characteristic of a security that allows an investor to sell or transfer ownership to another party. For example, savings bonds are not negotiable, while Treasury Bills are negotiable (able to be traded).

Negotiable CDs: large-denominated certificates of deposit that may be traded (negotiable) on a secondary market.

Negotiated Market: not an auction market, a market in which dealers/market makers negotiate prices on large blocks of securities.

Net Investment Income: the source of an investment company's dividend distributions to shareholders. It is calculated by taking the fund's dividends and interest collected on portfolio securities, minus the operating expenses. Funds using the "conduit tax theory" distribute at least 90% of net investment income to avoid paying taxes on the amount distributed to shareholders.

Net Worth: the difference between assets and liabilities. For example, the difference between the market value of a home and the mortgage balance still owed would represent the total net worth for many Americans. Other components would be checking, savings, and retirement accounts minus credit card debt. Add the pluses, subtract the minuses, and you have the individual's financial net worth.

New Account Form: the form that must be filled out for each new account opened with a broker-dealer. The form specifies, at a minimum, the name of the account owner, trading authorization, method of payment, and the type of investment securities that are appropriate for this particular account.

New Issue Market: the primary market, where securities are issued to investors with the proceeds going to the issuer of the securities. Initial public offerings (IPOs), for example, take place on the "new issue market."

NYSE: New York Stock Exchange, an auction market where buyers and sellers shout out competitive bid and asked/offered prices throughout the day.

No-load Fund: a mutual fund sold without a sales charge, but one which may charge an ongoing 12b-1 fee or "asset-based sales charge" up to .25% of net assets.

Nominal Yield: the interest rate paid by a bond or preferred stock. The investor receives this percentage of the par value each year, regardless of what the bond or preferred stock is trading for on the secondary market.

Non-accredited Investor: an investor who does not meet various SEC net worth and/or income requirements. For a Reg D private placement, accredited investors may participate, but only a limited number of non-accredited investors may purchase the issue.

Non-cumulative Preferred Stock: a type of preferred stock that does not have to pay missed dividends (dividends in arrears).

Non-diversified Fund: a fund that doesn't care to meet the 75-5-10 rule, preferring to concentrate more heavily in certain issues.

Non-NASDAQ OTC: securities trading on the over-the-counter market that do not meet NASDAQ requirements. For example, the Pink Sheets.

Non-systematic Risk: the risk of holding any one particular stock or bond. Diversification spreads this risk among different issuers and different industries in order to minimize the impact of a bankruptcy or unexpected collapse of any one issuer.

Note: a short-term debt security.

Nolo Contendere: a phrase you hope you've never uttered in open court when it comes time to complete the U4. Curious? Look it up under item 14 on Form U4. Latin for "no contest," which means, "Yeah, I done it—now what?"

O

Odd Lot: an order for fewer than 100 shares of common stock or 5 bonds.

Offer: another name for "ask," or the price an investor must pay if he wants to buy a security from a dealer/market maker.

Offer of Settlement: a respondent's offer to the disciplinary committee of FINRA to settle his or her recent rule violations.

Office of Foreign Asset Control (OFAC): office of the federal government that maintains a list of individuals and organizations viewed as a threat to the U.S.

Omitting Prospectus: an advertisement for a mutual fund that typically shows performance figures without providing (omitting) the full disclosure in the prospectus. Therefore, it must present caveats and encourage readers to read the prospectus and consider all the risks before investing in the fund.

Open-end Fund: an investment company that sells an unlimited number of shares to an unlimited number of investors on a continuous basis. Shares are redeemed by the company rather than traded OTC or on the exchanges.

Operating Expenses: expenses that a mutual fund deducts from the assets of the fund, including board of director salaries, custodial and transfer agent services, management fees, 12b-1 fees, etc.

Option: a derivative giving the holder the right to buy or sell something for a stated price up to expiration of the contract. Puts and calls.

OSJ: office of supervisory jurisdiction, a centralized office responsible for overseeing branch offices of a member firm.

OTC/Over-the-Counter: called a "negotiated market." Securities traded among dealers rather than on exchanges. Includes NASDAQ and also Bulletin Board and Pink Sheets stocks, plus government, corporate, and municipal bonds.

Outstanding Shares: the number of shares a corporation has outstanding. Found by taking Issued shares minus Treasury stock.

P

Par, Principal: the face amount of a bond payable at maturity. Also, the face amount of a preferred stock. Preferred = $100, Bond = $1,000.

Par Value: the face amount that a debt security will pay at maturity, e.g., $1,000. For preferred stock, the amount against which the dividend percentage is calculated, e.g., $100 par value.

Partial Surrender: life insurance policyholder cashes in part of the cash value. Excess over premiums is taxable.

Participating Preferred Stock: preferred stock whose dividend is often raised above the stated rate.

Participation: provision of ERISA requiring that all employees in a qualified retirement plan be covered within a reasonable length of time after being hired.

Pass-through Certificate: a mortgage-backed security (usually GNMA) that takes a pool of mortgages and passes through interest and principal monthly to an investor.

Passive Income: as opposed to "earned income," the income derived from rental properties, limited partnerships, or other enterprises in which the individual is not actively involved.

Passive Management: style of portfolio management using indexes based on a belief that markets are efficient and active management provides no value.

Payable (or Payment) Date: the date that the dividend check is paid to investors.

Payroll Deduction: non-qualified retirement plan offered by some businesses.

P/E or Price-to-Earnings Ratio: the market price of a stock compared to the earnings per share. Stocks trading at high P/E ratios are "growth stocks," while those trading at low P/E ratios are "value stocks."

Peak: the phase of the business cycle between expansion (good times) and contraction (bad times).

Penny Stock Cold Calling Rules: rules to protect consumers receiving telemarketing pitches to buy risky stocks trading below $5 a share. Rules require special disclosure and investor signatures when selling penny stocks.

Pension Plan: a contract between an individual and an employer that provides for the distribution of benefits at retirement.

Performance Figures: total return for a mutual fund over 1, 5, and 10 years, and/or "life of fund." Only past performance may be indicated, and there must be a caveat that past performance does not guarantee future results.

Periodic Deferred Annuity: method of purchasing an annuity whereby the contract holder makes periodic payments into the contract. The pay-out phase must be deferred for all periodic payment plans.

Periodic-payment Annuity: annuity in which the annuitant makes contributions periodically, as he/she is able.

Permanent Insurance: life insurance other then "term."

Pink Sheets: a virtually unregulated part of the OTC market where thinly traded, volatile stocks change hands.

Placement: the stage of money laundering when funds are moved into the system.

Political Risk: the risk that a country's government will radically change policies or that the political climate will become hostile or counterproductive to business and financial markets.

POP: public offering price. For an IPO, this includes the spread to the underwriters. For a mutual fund, this includes any sales loads that go to the underwriter/distributor.

Portfolio: a batch of stocks, bonds, money market securities, or any combination thereof that an investor owns.

Power of Attorney: having the authority to make decisions on behalf of someone else, e.g., financial and health care decisions for someone ruled mentally incompetent.

Power of Substitution: a document that when signed by the security owner authorizes transfer of the certificate to another party.

Pre-emptive Right: the right of common stockholders to maintain their proportional ownership if the company offers more shares of stock.

Precious Metals Fund: a mutual fund focusing on mining companies.

Preferred Stock: a fixed-income equity security whose stated dividends must be paid before common stock can receive any dividend payment. Also gets preference ahead of common stock in a liquidation (but behind all bonds and general creditors).

Preliminary Prospectus: a.k.a. "red herring." A prospectus that lacks the POP and the effective date. Used to solicit indications of interest.

Premium: the amount above the par value in a bond's market price. For example, a bond trading for $1,100 is trading at a $100 premium.

Premium Bond: a bond purchased for more than the par value, usually due to a drop in interest rates.

Prepayment Risk: the risk that the mortgages underlying a mortgage-backed security/pass-through will be paid off sooner than expected due to a drop in interest rates. Investors reinvest the principal at a lower rate going forward.

Preservation of Capital: an investment objective that places the emphasis on making sure the principal is not lost. Also called "safety."

Price-to-Earnings (P/E) Ratio: the market price of a stock compared to the earnings per share. Stocks trading at high P/E ratios are "growth stocks," while those trading at low P/E ratios are "value stocks."

Primary Market: where securities are issued to raise capital for the issuer.

Primary Offering: offering of securities in which the proceeds go to the issuer.

Prime Rate: interest rate charged to corporations with high credit ratings for unsecured loans.

Principal: (1) the face amount of a debt security, (2) a supervisor at a broker-dealer, (3) capital at risk in a transaction.

Principal-protected Fund: a mutual fund for people who want their principal protected. Involves holding the investment for several years, at which point the fund guarantees that the value of the investment will be equal to at least what the investor put in.

Private Placement: an exempt transaction under Reg D (Rule 506) of the Securities Act of 1933, allowing issuers to sell securities without registration to accredited investors, who agree to hold them fully paid 1 year before then selling them through Rule 144.

Private Securities Transaction: offering an investment opportunity not sponsored by the firm. Requires permission from the firm and any disclosure demanded; otherwise, a violation called "selling away."

Profit Sharing: a defined contribution plan whereby the company shares any profits with employees in the form of contributions to a retirement account.

Progressive Tax: a tax that increases as a percentage as the thing being taxed increases, including gift, estate, and income taxes. Not a flat tax.

Prospectus: a disclosure document that details a company's plans, history, officers, and risks of investment. It's the red herring plus the POP and the effective date.

Proxy: a form granting the power to vote according to a shareholder's instructions when the shareholder will not attend the meeting.

Public Appearance: addressing an audience on topics related to securities. Before speaking at a local Chamber of Commerce function, for example, registered representatives need prior principal approval.

Public Offering: the sale of an issue of common stock, either an IPO or an additional offer of shares.

Public Offering Price (POP): the price an investor pays for a mutual fund or an initial public offering. For a mutual fund = NAV + the sales charge.

Purchaser Representative: someone independent of the issuer in a private placement who can represent the needs of a non-accredited investor.

Purchasing Power Risk: also called "constant dollar" or "inflation" risk, the risk that a fixed payment will not be sufficient to keep up with rising inflation (as measured through the CPI).

Put (n.): a contract giving the owner the right to sell something at a stated exercise price.

Put (v.): to sell.

Q

Qualified Dividend: a dividend that qualifies for a lower tax rate vs. ordinary income. An idea that generally finds more favor among Republicans than Democrats.

Qualified Plan: a retirement plan that qualifies for deductible contributions on behalf of employers and/or employees and covered by ERISA. For example, 401(k), defined benefit, Keogh. Must meet IRS approval, unlike more informal "non-qualified plans."

Quote, Quotation: a price that a dealer is willing to pay or accept for a security. A two-sided quote has both a bid and an asked/offer price.

R

Random Withdrawals: a settlement option in an annuity whereby the investor takes the value of the sub-accounts in two or more withdrawals, rather than one lump sum.

Rating Service: e.g., S&P and Moody's; a company that assigns credit ratings to corporate and municipal bonds.

Real Estate Investment Trust (REIT): a corporation or trust that uses the pooled capital of investors to invest in ownership of either income property or mortgage loans. 90% of net income is paid out to shareholders.

Real Rate of Return: the rate of return minus the rate of inflation.

Realized Gain: the amount of the "profit" an investor earns when selling a security.

Recession: two quarters (6 months) or more of economic decline. Associated with rising unemployment, falling interest rates, and falling gross domestic product.

Record Date: the date determined by the Board of Directors upon which the investor must be the holder "of record" in order to receive the upcoming dividend. Settlement of a trade must occur by the record date for the buyer to receive the dividend.

Red Herring: a.k.a. "preliminary prospectus." Contains essentially the same information that the final prospectus will contain, minus the POP and effective date.

Redeemable Security: a security that may be redeemed or presented to the issuer for payment

Redemption: for mutual funds, redemption involves the sale of mutual fund shares back to the fund at the NAV (less any redemption fees, back-end loads). For bonds, the date that principal is returned to the investor, along with the final interest payment.

Redemption Fee: a charge to a mutual fund investor who sells her shares back to the fund much sooner than the fund would prefer.

Reg A: a laid-back and predictable form of island music. Also, an exempt transaction under the Securities Act of 1933 for small offerings of securities ($5 million issued in a 12-month period).

Reg D: an exempt transaction under the Securities Act of 1933 for private placements.

Reg T: established by the FRB as the amount of credit a broker-dealer may extend to a customer pledging a security as collateral for a margin loan. In a margin account, customers must put down ½ of the security's value, or at least $2,000.

Reg U: established by the FRB as the amount of credit a bank may extend to a broker-dealer or public customer pledging a security as collateral.

Registered As to Principal Only: a bond with only the principal registered. Interest coupons must be presented for payment.

Registered Principals: individuals who supervise registered representatives and perform compliance activities for member broker-dealers.

Registered Representative: an associated person of an investment banker or broker-dealer who effects transactions in securities for compensation.

Registrar: audits the transfer agent to make sure number of authorized shares is never exceeded.

Registration Statement: the legal document disclosing material information concerning an offering of a security and its issuer. Submitted to SEC under Securities Act of 1933.

Regressive Tax: a flat tax, e.g., gasoline, sales, excise taxes.

Regular Way Settlement: T + 3, trade date plus three business days. T + 1 for Treasury securities.

Regulated Investment Company: an investment company using the conduit tax theory by distributing 90% or more of net investment income to shareholders.

Regulation S-P: federal legislation designed to fight identity theft and to protect consumers and customers from having too much of their information shared with people they've never met.

Regulatory Element: a FINRA continuing education requirement that must be completed on your second registration anniversary and every third year thereafter.

Regulatory Risk: a.k.a. "legislative risk," the risk that a regulatory/legislative decision could have an adverse impact on an investment. For example, if tax rates are cut, municipal bonds lose their attractiveness.

Reinstatement Privilege: a feature of some mutual funds allowing investors to make withdrawals and then reinstate the money without paying another sales charge.

Reinvestment Risk: the risk that a fixed-income investor will not be able to reinvest interest payments or the par value at attractive interest rates. Happens when rates are falling.

REIT (Real Estate Investment Trust): a corporation or trust that uses the pooled capital of investors to invest in ownership of either income property or mortgage loans. 90% of net income is paid out to shareholders.

Release Date: a.k.a. "effective date," date established by the SEC as to when the underwriters may sell new securities to the buyers.

REMIC: real estate mortgage investment conduit. A type of mortgage-backed security.

Reporting: section of ERISA requiring that participants receive regular reports on their accounts (at least quarterly).

Repurchase Agreement: an agreement in which one party sells something to the other and agrees to repurchase it for a higher price over the short-term.

Required Minimum Distribution (RMD): the required minimum distribution that must be taken from a retirement plan to avoid IRS penalties. Usually April 1 of the year following the individual's 70½th birthday.

Reserve Requirement: amount of money a bank must lock up in reserve, established by the FRB.

Residual Claim: the right of common stockholders to claim assets after the claims of all creditors and preferred stockholders have been satisfied.

Revenue: the proceeds a company receives when selling products and services.

Revenue Bond: a municipal bond whose interest and principal payments are backed by the revenues generated from the project being built by the proceeds of the bonds. Toll roads, for example, are usually built with revenue bonds backed by the tolls collected.

Revocable Trust: a trust that can be altered or terminated by the grantor and, therefore, subjects the grantor to taxation on income while the grantor is alive and also counts as part of the estate upon death.

Rights: short-term equity securities that allow the holder to buy new shares below the current market price.

Rights of Accumulation: feature of many mutual funds whereby a rise in account value is counted the same as new money for purposes of achieving a breakpoint.

Rights Offering: additional offer of stock accompanied by the opportunity for each shareholder to maintain his/her proportionate ownership in the company.

Risk Tolerance: the ability to withstand wide fluctuations in investment values and even principal loss both financially and psychologically.

Rollover: moving retirement funds from a 401(k) to an IRA, or from one IRA to another. In a "60-day rollover," the check is cut to the individual, who must then send a check to the new custodian within 60 days to avoid early distribution penalties.

Roth IRA: individual retirement account funded with non-deductible (after-tax) contributions. All distributions are tax-free provided the individual is 59½ and has had the account at least five years.

Round Lot: the usual or normal unit of trading. 100 shares for common stock.

Rule 147: exemption under the Securities Act of 1933 for intra-state offerings of securities.

S

Safety: an investment objective that seeks to avoid loss of principal first and foremost. Bank CDs, Treasury securities, and fixed annuities are generally suitable.

Sales Charge, Sales Load: a deduction from an investor's check that goes to the distributors/sellers of the fund. Deducted from investor's check, either when she buys (A-shares) or sells (B-shares).

Sales Literature: communications of a member broker-dealer delivered to a targeted, controlled audience, e.g., brochures, research reports, cold calling scripts.

Savings Bond: a U.S. Government debt security that is not "negotiable," meaning it can't be traded or pledged as collateral for a loan. Includes EE and HH series bonds.

Scheduled Premium: life insurance with established, scheduled premium payments, e.g., whole life, variable life. As opposed to "universal" insurance, which is "flexible premium."

Second Market: a "negotiated market" including NASDAQ and non-NASDAQ securities trading.

Secondary Offering/Distribution: a distribution of securities owned by major stockholders—not the issuer of the securities.

Secondary Market: where investors trade securities among themselves and proceeds do not go to the issuer.

Section 457 Plan: retirement plan for state and local government workers funded with pre-tax contributions, with similar rules as 403(b) and 401(k) plans.

Sector Fund: a.k.a. "specialized." A fund that concentrates heavily in a particular industry or geographic area, e.g., "The Japan Fund," or the "Technology Fund." Higher risk/reward than funds invested in many industries.

Secured Bond: a corporate bond secured by collateral, e.g., mortgage bond, collateral trust certificate, equipment trust certificate.

Securities Act of 1933: a.k.a. "Paper Act," regulates the new-issue or primary market, requiring non-exempt issuers to register securities and provide full disclosure.

Securities and Exchange Commission: SEC, empowered by passage of Securities Exchange Act of 1934. A government body, the ultimate securities regulator.

Securities Exchange Act of 1934: prevents fraud in the securities markets. No security and no person exempt from anti-fraud regulations. Created/empowered the SEC. Requires broker-dealers, exchanges and securities associations to register with SEC. Requires public companies to report quarterly and annually to SEC.

Security: an investment of money subject to fluctuation in value and negotiable/marketable to other investors. Other than an insurance policy or fixed annuity, a security is any piece of securitized "paper" that can be traded for value.

Self-Regulatory Organization: SRO, e.g., FINRA. An organization given the power to regulate its members. Not government bodies like the SEC, which oversees the SROs.

Selling Away: a violation that occurs when a registered representative offers investment opportunities not sponsored by the firm.

Selling Concession: typically, the largest piece of the underwriting spread going to the firm credited with making the sale.

Selling Dividends: a violation where an investor is deceived into thinking that she needs to purchase a stock in order to receive an upcoming dividend.

Selling Group: certain broker-dealers with an agreement to act as selling agents for the syndicate (underwriters) with no capital at risk.

Semi-annual: twice per year, or "at the half year," literally. Note that "bi-annually" means "every two years." Bond interest is paid semi-annually. Mutual funds report to their shareholders semi-annually and annually. Nothing happens "bi-annually" as a general rule of thumb.

Senior Security: a security that grants the holder a higher claim on the issuer's assets in the event of a liquidation/bankruptcy.

SEP-IRA: pre-tax retirement plan available to small businesses. Favors high-income employees (compared to SIMPLE). Only employ-er contributes.

Separate Account: an account maintained by an insurance/annuity company that is separate from the company's general account. Used to invest clients' money for variable annuities and variable insurance contracts. Registered as an investment company under Investment Company Act of 1940.

Series EE bond: a nonmarketable, interest-bearing U.S. Government savings bond issued at a discount from the par value. Interest is exempt from state and local taxation.

Series HH bond: a nonmarketable, interest-bearing U.S. Government savings bond issued at par and purchased only by trading in Series EE bonds at maturity. Interest is exempt from state and local taxation.

Series I Bond: a savings bond issued by the U.S. Treasury that protects investors from inflation or purchasing power risk.

Settlement: final completion of a securities transaction wherein payment has been made by the buyer and delivery has been made by the seller.

Settlement Options: payout options on annuities and life insurance including life-only, life with period certain, and joint and last survivorship.

Share Identification: a method of calculating capital gains and losses by which the investor identifies which shares were sold, as opposed to using FIFO or average cost.

Short Sale: method of attempting to profit from a security whose price is expected to fall. Trader borrows certificates through a broker-dealer and sells them, with the obligation to replace them at a later date, hopefully at a lower price. Bearish position.

Short-term Capital Gain: a profit realized on a security held for 12 months or less.

Short-term Capital Loss: a loss realized on a security held for 12 months or less, deductible against Short-Term Capital Gains.

SIMPLE IRA: a retirement plan for businesses with no more than 100 employees that have no other retirement plan in place. Pre-tax contributions, fully taxable distributions. Both employer and employees may contribute.

Simple Trust: a trust that accumulates income and distributes it to the beneficiaries annually.

Simplified Arbitration: a method of resolving disputes involving a small amount of money (currently $25,000).

Single-payment Deferred Annuity: annuity purchased with a single payment wherein the individual defers the payout or "annuity" phase of the contract.

Single-payment Immediate Annuity: annuity purchased with a single payment wherein the individual goes immediately into the payout or "annuity" phase of the contract.

Sinking Fund: an account established by an issuing corporation or municipality to provide funds required to redeem a bond issue.

SIPC: Securities Investor Protection Corporation, a nonprofit, non-government, industry-funded insurance corporation protecting investors against broker-dealer failure.

Small Cap: a stock where the total value of all outstanding shares is considered "small," typically between $50 million and $2 billion.

Sole Proprietor: business ownership structure that provides no separate legal entity between the business and the owner him- or herself. Leaves the business owner liable for lawsuits against the company and debts of the company.

Solvency: the ability of a corporation or municipality to meet its obligations as they come due.

Specialist: NYSE member that maintains a fair and orderly market in a particular exchange-listed security.

Specialized Fund: another name for a sector fund, e.g., "Telecommunications Fund," or "Financial Services Fund" focusing on a particular industry sector.

Speculation: the highest-risk investment objective, in which the speculator makes a bold bet that an asset's value will rise.

Spousal Account: an IRA established for a non-working spouse.

Spread: generally, the difference between a dealer's purchase price and selling price, both for new offerings (underwriting spread) and secondary market quotes. For underwritings the spread is the difference between the proceeds to the issuer and the POP.

Spread Load: sales charges for a mutual fund contractual plan that permits a maximum charge of 20% in any one year and 9% over the life of the plan.

Stabilizing/Stabilization: the surprising practice by which an underwriting syndicate bids up the price of an IPO whose price is dropping in the secondary market.

Standby Offering: a firm commitment in a rights offering in which an underwriter will use any rights not subscribed to.

Standby Underwriting: a commitment by an underwriter to purchase any shares that are not subscribed to in a rights offering.

Statement of Additional Information, or SAI: a document with more detailed information than what's contained in the mutual fund prospectus.

Statute of Limitations: a time limit that, once reached, prevents criminal or civil action from being filed.

Statutory Disqualification: prohibiting a person from associating with an SRO due to disciplinary or criminal actions within the past 10 years, or due to filing a false or misleading application or report with a regulator.

Statutory Voting: method of voting whereby the shareholder may cast no more than the number of shares owned per candidate/item.

Stock: an ownership or equity position in a public company whose value is tied to the company's profits (if any) and dividend payouts (if any).

Stock Dividend: payment of a dividend in the form of more shares of stock; not a taxable event.

Stock Split: a change in the number of outstanding shares designed to change the price-per-share; not a taxable event.

Straight Life Annuity: a settlement option in which the annuity company pays the annuitant only as long as he or she is alive. Also called "straight life" or "life only."

Straight Preferred: a.k.a. "non-cumulative preferred," a preferred stock whose missed dividends do not go into arrears.

STRIPS: Separate Trading of Registered Interest and Principal of Securities. A zero-coupon bond issued by the U.S. Treasury in which all interest income is received at maturity in the form of a higher (accreted) principal value. Avoids "reinvestment risk."

Subaccount: investment options available within the separate account for variable contract holders. Basically, these are mutual funds that grow tax-deferred.

Subchapter M: section of the Internal Revenue Code providing the "conduit tax treatment" used by REITs and mutual funds distributing 90% or more of net income to shareholders. A mutual fund using this method is technically a Regulated Investment Company under IRC Subchapter M.

Subordinated Debenture: corporate bond with a claim that is subordinated or "junior" to a debenture and/or general creditor.

Subscription Right(s): the securities used in additional offerings of stock to purchase available shares, usually at a slight discount.

Suitability: a determination by a registered representative that a security matches a customer's stated objectives and financial situation.

Supervision: a system implemented by a broker-dealer to ensure that its employees and associated persons comply with federal and state securities law, and the rules and regulations of the SEC, exchanges, and SROs.

Surrender: to cash out an annuity or life insurance policy for its surrender value.

Suspicious Activity Report (SAR-SF): a report that broker-dealers must file with the Treasury department whenever they suspect that a customer or other party may be using investment accounts to further criminal activities.

Syndicate: a group of underwriters bringing a new issue to the primary market.

Systematic Risk: another name for "market risk," or the risk that an investment's value could plummet due to an overall market panic or collapse.

Systematic Withdrawal Plans: method of taking money out of a mutual fund investment gradually.

T

T + 3: regular way settlement, trade date plus three business days.

T-bills: direct obligation of U.S. Government. Sold at discount, mature at face amount. Maximum maturity is 1 year.

T-bonds: direct obligation of U.S. Government. Pay semiannual interest. Quoted as % of par value plus 32nds. 10–30-year maturities.

T-notes: direct obligation of U.S. Government. Pay semiannual interested. Quoted as % of par value plus 32nds. 2–10-year maturities.

Tax Anticipation Notes (TANs): short-term loans issued by municipalities and backed up by tax revenues.

Tax Credit: an amount that can be subtracted from the amount of taxes owed.

Tax-deferred: an account where all earnings remain untaxed until "constructive receipt."

Tax-equivalent Yield: the rate of return that a taxable bond must offer to equal the tax-exempt yield on a municipal bond. To calculate, take the municipal yield and divide that by (100% − investor's tax bracket).

Tax-exempt Bond Fund: mutual fund investing in municipal bonds.

Tax-exempt Bonds: municipal bonds whose interest is not subject to taxation by the federal government.

Tax-exempt Money Market Fund: mutual fund investing in short-term debt obligations of municipalities.

Tax Preference Item: certain items that must be added back to an investor's income for purposes of AMT, including interest on certain municipal bonds.

Tax-Sheltered Annuity (TSA): an annuity funded with pre-tax (tax-deductible) contributions. Available to employees of nonprofit organizations such as schools, hospitals, and church organizations.

Telemarketing: to market by telephone. Assuming you can get past the caller ID.

Telephone Consumer Protection Act of 1991: federal legislation restricting the activities of telemarketers, who generally may only call prospects between 8 a.m. and 9 p.m. in the prospect's time zone and must maintain a do-not-call list, also checking the national registry.

Tenants in Common: see Joint Tenants in Common, a joint account wherein the interest of the deceased owner reverts to his/her estate.

Tender Offer: an offer by the issuer of securities to repurchase the securities if the investors care to "tender" their securities for payment.

Term Life Insurance: form of temporary insurance that builds no cash value and must be renewed at a higher premium at the end of the term. Renting rather than buying insurance.

Third Market: exchange-listed stock traded OTC primarily by institutional investors.

Third-Party Account: account managed on behalf of a third party, e.g., trust or UGMA.

Timing Risk: the risk of purchasing an investment at a peak price not likely to be sustained or seen again. Timing risk can be reduced through dollar cost averaging, rather than investing in a stock with one purchase.

Tippee: the guy who listened

Tipper: the guy who told the other guy the insider information

Tombstone: an advertisement allowed during the cooling off period to announce an offer of securities, listing the issuer, the type of security, the underwriters, and directions for obtaining a prospectus.

Total Net Worth: assets minus liabilities.

Total Return: measuring growth in share price plus dividend and capital gains distributions.

Trade Confirmation: a printed document containing details of a securities transaction, e.g., price of the security, commissions, stock symbol, number of shares, registered rep code, trade date and settlement date, etc.

Trade Date: the date that a trade is executed.

Trading Authorization: a form granting another individual the authority to trade on behalf of the account owner. Either "limited" (buy/sell orders only) or "full" (buy/sell orders plus requests for checks/securities) authorization may be granted. Sometimes referred to as "power of attorney."

Tranche: a class of CMO. Principal is returned to one tranche at a time in a CMO.

Transfer Agent: issues and redeems certificates. Handles name changes, validates mutilated certificates. Distributes dividends, gains, and shareholder reports to mutual fund investors.

Transfer and Hold in Safekeeping: a buy order for securities in which securities are bought and transferred to the customer's name, but held by the broker-dealer.

Transfer and Ship: a buy order for securities in which securities are purchased and transferred to the customer's name, with the certificates sent to the customer.

Transfer on Death: individual account with a named beneficiary—assets transferred directly to the named beneficiary upon death of the account holder.

Treasury Bill: see T-bill.

Treasury Bond: see T-bond.

Treasury Fund: a mutual fund investing in U.S. Treasury securities.

Treasury Note: see T-note.

Treasury Receipts: zero-coupon bonds created by broker-dealers backed by Treasury securities held in escrow. Not a direct obligation of U.S. Government.

Treasury Securities: securities guaranteed by U.S. Treasury, including T-bills, T-notes, T-bonds, and STRIPS.

Treasury Stock: shares that have been issued and repurchased by the corporation. Has nothing to do with the U.S. Treasury.

Treasury STRIPS: see STRIPS.

Trough: phase of the business cycle representing the "bottoming out" of a contraction, just before the next expansion/recovery.

Trust: a legal entity holding title to various assets.

Trust Account: a brokerage account opened in the name of a trustee.

Trust Indenture: a written agreement between an issuer and creditors wherein the terms of a debt security issue are set forth, e.g., interest rate, means of payment, maturity date, name of the trustee, etc.

Trust Indenture Act of 1939: corporate bond issues in excess of $5 million with maturities greater than 1 year must be issued with an indenture.

Trustee: a person legally appointed to act on a beneficiary's behalf.

TSA: Tax-Sheltered Annuity. A retirement vehicle for 403(b) and 501c3 organizations.

Turnover Rate: expresses the frequency of trading that a mutual fund portfolio engages in.

U

(Form) U4: registration form for agents and principals submitted to the CRD system.

(Form) U5: termination form for agents and principals submitted to the CRD system.

UGMA: Uniform Gifts to Minors Act. An account set up for the benefit of a minor, managed by a custodian.

UIT: Unit Investment Trust. A type of investment company where investments are selected, not traded/managed. No management fee is charged. Shares are redeemable.

Unauthorized Transaction: a violation in which an agent enters a transaction without actually talking to the customer about it.

Underwriter: see "investment banker." Just kidding. An underwriter or "investment banker" is a broker-dealer that distributes shares on the primary market.

Underwriting Spread: the profit to the syndicate. The difference between the proceeds to the issuer and the POP.

Unearned Income: income derived from investments and other sources not related to employment, e.g., savings account interest, dividends from stock, capital gains, and rental income.

Uniform Practice Code: how the FINRA promotes "cooperative effort," standardizing settlement dates, ex-dates, accrued interest calculations, etc.

Uniform Securities Act: a model act that state securities laws are based on. Designed to prevent fraud and maintain faith in capital markets through registration of securities, agents, broker-dealers, and investment advisers. Main purpose is to provide necessary protection to investors.

Unit of Beneficial Interest: what an investor in a Unit Investment Trust (UIT) owns.

Universal Life Insurance: a form of permanent insurance that offers flexibility in death benefit and both the amount of, and method of paying, premiums.

Unrealized Gain: the increase in the value of a security that has not yet been sold. Unrealized gains are not taxable.

Unsecured Bond: a debenture, or bond issued without specific collateral.

Unsolicited Order: an order placed after a customer tells the agent what he/she wants to buy or sell, not a recommended/solicited trade.

USA Patriot Act: federal government legislation requiring broker-dealers and other financial institutions to help the government monitor suspicious activity that could be tied to money laundering.

User Fees or User Charges: the revenues used to support municipal revenue bonds, e.g., tolls or parking charges.

UTMA: A custodial account for the benefit of a minor child.

V

Value: as in "value investing" or a "value fund," the practice of purchasing stock in companies whose share price is currently depressed. The value investor feels that the stock is trading below its "estimated intrinsic value" and, therefore, sees an opportunity to buy a good company for less than it's really worth. Like a "fixer-upper" house in need of a little "TLC." With a few quick improvements, this property is going to be worth a lot more than people realize.

Variable Annuity: an annuity whose payment varies. Investments allocated to separate account as instructed by annuitant. Similar to investing in mutual funds, except that annuities offer tax deferral. No taxation until excess over cost basis is withdrawn.

Variable Contract: an annuity or insurance policy whose values are tied to the fluctuating stock and bond markets.

Variable Life Insurance: form of insurance where death benefit and cash value fluctuate according to fluctuations of the separate account.

Variable Universal Life Insurance: flexible-premium insurance with cash value and death benefit tied to the performance of the separate account.

Vesting: a schedule for determining at what point the employer's contributions become the property of the employee.

Viatical Settlement: the purchase of a life insurance policy wherein the investor buys the death benefit at a discount and profits as soon as the insured dies.

Volatility: the up and down movements of an investment that make investors dizzy and occasionally nauseated.

Voluntary Accumulation Plan: a mutual fund account into which the investor commits to depositing amounts of money on a regular basis.

W

Warrants: long-term equity securities giving the owner the right to purchase stock at a set price. Often attached as a "sweetener" that makes the other security more attractive.

Wash Sale: selling a security at a loss but then messing up by repurchasing it within 30 days and, therefore, not being able to use it to offset capital gains for that year.

Whole Life Insurance: form of permanent insurance with a guaranteed death benefit and minimum guaranteed cash value.

Withdrawal Plan: a feature of most mutual funds that allows investors to liquidate their accounts over a fixed time period, or using a fixed-share or fixed-dollar amount.

Written Complaints: complaints against an agent or broker-dealer that are written in any form whatsoever.

Y

Yield: the income a security produces to the holder just for holding it.

Yield to Maturity: calculation of all interest payments plus/minus gain/loss on a bond if held to maturity.

Z

Zero-Coupon Bond: a bond sold at a deep discount to its gradually increasing par value.

Index

T